Developing Web Applications in PHP and AJAX

Developing Web Applications in PHP and AJAX

B. M. Harwani
Microchip Computer Education,
Ajmer

Tata McGraw Hill Education Private Limited
NEW DELHI

McGraw-Hill Offices

New Delhi New York St Louis San Francisco Auckland Bogotá Caracas
Kuala Lumpur Lisbon London Madrid Mexico City Milan Montreal
San Juan Santiago Singapore Sydney Tokyo Toronto

Tata McGraw Hill

Published by Tata McGraw Hill Education Private Limited,
7 West Patel Nagar, New Delhi 110 008.

ISBN (13): 978-0-07-070710-8
ISBN (10): 0-07-070710-3

Managing Director: *Ajay Shukla*
Head—Professional and Healthcare: *Roystan La'Porte*
Executive Publisher—Professional: *R Chandra Sekhar*
Asst. Sponsoring Editor—Computing: *Ritesh Ranjan*
Manager—Production: *Sohan Gaur*
Manager—Sales and Marketing: *S Girish*
Deputy Marketing Manager—Science, Technology and Computing: *Rekha Dhyani*
General Manager—Production: *Rajender P Ghansela*
Asst. General Manager—Production: *B L Dogra*

Typeset at Text-o-Graphics, B1/56 Arawali Apartment, Sector 34, Noida 201 301 and
printed at S.P. Printers, 30-A, Patpar Ganj Village, Delhi 110 091

Cover Printer: S.P. Printers

Cover Design: Kapil Gupta, New Delhi

RCZLCDLZRYDRD

The McGraw·Hill Companies

To

My mother Nita Harwani,

My mother who is next to God for me and whose moral values made me what I am today

and

Bill Gates,

Chairman of Microsoft, who inspired me with his admirable program writing skills that he developed during his school days and that later helped him in establishing his own computer software company, and with his dedication with which he personally reviewed every line of code that his company shipped—a quality that made him the best known entrepreneurs of the personal computer revolution

Preface

There is no doubt that the flexibility, scalability, reliability and simplicity of AMP—Apache, MySQL and PHP—have attracted the attention of a large number of web developers around the world. From my long teaching experience of over 15 years at the Computer Education Centre MCE (Microchip Computer Education) Ajmer, I have realised the dire need for a systematic approach in understanding AMP and using it for making a fully functional web application.

That's why this book begins with simple statements, loops and conditional statements for making easy-to-follow PHP scripts to familiarise the reader with the features of PHP. Then it goes on to discuss the application of PHP functions in accessing, inserting, and updating MySQL database tables. I have tried to keep the treatment of topics simple and have explained every statement used in the manipulation of database tables via PHP scripts. Once the reader has a firm grasp of the technique of updating database tables, s/he can easily understand the steps involved in developing a Shopping Cart project.

In view of the growing demand of AJAX for making highly responsive websites, I have explained AJAX and its different functions that help in sending messages to the server asynchronously. To make the concept clearer, I have written and explained separate programs for each element, i.e., how the options selected from combobox, listbox, checkbox, radio button, etc., are sent to the server asynchronously. Again, to make the reader understand the core of AJAX, the steps of developing a fully functional AJAX-based Shopping Cart have been explained.

Moreover, I have explained the use of NuSOAP toolkit in developing server- and client-side web services and the steps to consume publicly available web services. The WSDL document generated is also explained statement wise. Figures accompany the explanation of critical concepts to add further charity.

Chapter 1 introduces PHP and its features and also provides step-by-step instructions for the installation of Apache Server, PHP and MySQL server respectively.

Chapter 2 explains how to invoke MySQL, change root password, and apply the basic SQL commands for maintaining databases that include Create database, Show databases, Use database, Show tables, Drop database, Create table, Describe table name, Alter table, Drop table, Insert into table, Select from table, Update table, and Delete from table.

Chapter 3 introduces small PHP scripts and explains different loops and conditional statements with their syntax and examples. It further elucidates arrays, associative array, multi-dimensional arrays, for each statement, forms, $_GET array, $_POST array, $_REQUEST, etc., which are required in passing information from one web page to another

Chapter 4 explains how PHP scripts are connected with the back-end database and how database contents are maintained through PHP. It further explains several programs such as creating a table in PHP, getting information from the user, inserting records in the table, retrieving all records from the table, searching records from the table (retrieving only the desired records) and deleting records from the table.

Chapter 5 introduces AJAX, XML and JSON and explains the use of XmlHttpRequest object in implementing AJAX, and the steps for installing AJAX.

Chapter 6 is in the form of a workbook containing several running examples of how to: access form elements in JavaScript, use POST method, use Styles, send data from combo box to server asynchronously, send data from listbox to server asynchronously, and send data selected from checkbox and radio to server asynchronously.

Chapter 7 explains how different validation checks are implemented and how email id is validated in three different ways. Validation checks include checking if any field is left blank; checking if any field has less than the required data; validating user id, i.e., checking if it already exists; and validating the form and storing the record in the table (if data is valid).

Chapter 8 explains what is JSON, how it is installed, and how data is received in JSON format. It also elucidates the process of receiving XML response, displaying contents of selected children and nodes; the process of converting data entered by user into JSON format; and finally how the data from the database is accessed and displayed in the JSON format.

Chapter 9 explains web services and their connection with WSDL, UDDI, XML and SOAP; different methods of producing and consuming web services; and the characteristics of XML-RPC, REST and SOAP.

Chapter 10 introduces the most popular SOAP tool: NuSOAP and its installation steps together with several running examples of: how server-side and client-side web services are created, how complex type is used in NuSOAP, and how database driven web services are made.

Chapter 11 explains how to register web services in public UDDI like xmethods.net and how to write web service clients for the publicly available web services like Google Search and Google Maps, etc.

Chapter 12 explains different PHP frameworks and how to work with them. It further introduces XAMPP (from Apache Friends), a PHP Framework; phpMyAdmin, a software used for creating and maintaining MySQL databases; and CodeIgniter, a PHP framework. It also lays down the steps to run PHP programs using these frameworks.

Any suggestion for improving the book will be highly appreciated and can be mailed to bmharwani@yahoo.com.

B. M. Harwani

Companion Web Supplement

A companion web supplement has been designed and made available to the readers of this book. It contains two Shopping Cart projects in PHP and AJAX.

INSTRUCTIONS TO EXECUTE THE SHOPPING CART PROJECTS

Assuming that all the three softwares: Apache HTTP Server, PHP and MySQL are properly installed and configured on your computer. The inscriptions given below are to be followed:

- Download the ShoppingCartProjects.zip file from the URL: http://highered.mcgraw-hill.com/sites/0070144524.
- Set the password of the "root" of the MySQL server to "mce". In both the projects, we assume that the password of the "root" is "mce".
- Execute the SQL script shoptables.sql in MySQL to create all the tables required for the project.
- Copy the 'images' folder in the 'htdocs' folder of the server.
- Unzip the Shopping Cart project and copy its unzipped files into the 'htdocs' folder of the server (only one project will execute at a time).
- Start the HTTP server.
- Open the browser and point it at the address:http://localhost/index.php to execute the project.

B. M. HARWANI

Acknowledgements

I am grateful to Mr. Ajay Shukla, Managing Director, Tata McGraw Hill Education and Mr. Roystan La'Porte, Head, Professional & Healthcare, for giving me the opportunity of publishing the book with Tata McGraw Hill. I thank Mr. R. Chandra Sekhar, Executive Publisher, Professional, and Mr. Ritesh Ranjan, Assistant Sponsoring Editor, Computing, for their constant support during the preparation of this book.

I am very thankful to the entire management, editorial and production teams of Tata McGraw Hill Education, for their invaluable efforts in bringing out this book in record time.

I also thank my family and my wife Anu and my sons Chirag and Naman for allowing me to work on the book.

B. M. Harwani

Contents

1

Introduction to PHP

Every organisation today needs a dynamic website for advertising its products and services. A dynamic website not only gives a global presence to an organisation but is also a great medium to be in touch with its customers. Feedback from globally distributed customers and their problems can be easily received via a website hence increasing customer satisfaction. Three important pillars required for making and hosting a dynamic website are:

- Web server
- Scripting language
- Database

The web server is software that is loaded and runs on the server computer. The server computer is the computer where our web applications (websites) are uploaded (hosted). The most popular web server softwares are: IIS (Internet Information Server) of Microsoft and Apache HTTP Server of Apache Server Foundation. A web application is accessed by the client using a web browser. The web browser requests the server for the web application. The web applications that we want to be accessible to the clients are uploaded on the server. The main role of the web server is to receive the requests from the clients, execute the relevant scripts to process the information passed or to retrieve the required information from the back-end databases and send the response back to the client in the form of a HTML document. This whole process from sending the request till receiving response is also known as the web request life cycle (Figure 1.1).

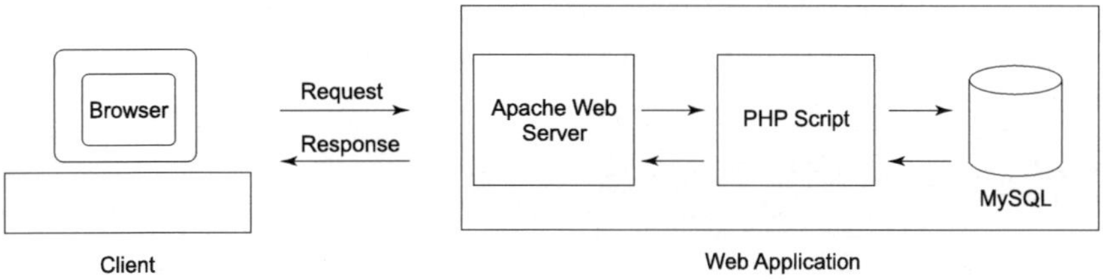

Figure 1.1 ***Web Request Life Cycle***

In terms of Apache, PHP and MySQL, we may set out the above web request life cycle as under:

1. The client places the request to the Apache web server in terms of HTTP GET or POST message.
2. The Apache web server parses the request, and depending on the request locates the desired PHP script and executes it.
3. The PHP script depending on the user's request either fetches the desired information from the MySQL database or updates its contents.
4. The MySQL database returns the desired information and the status of the database to the PHP script.
5. The PHP script combines the database information with an HTML template and sends it to the Apache web server program.
6. Apache sends an HTTP response in the form of the HTML document to the user's browser.

So, let's start with the installation and configuration of these softwares. In this chapter, we are going to see:

- What is PHP and its features
- Installation of Apache server
- Installation of PHP
- Installation of MySQL

1.1 WHAT IS PHP?

PHP stands for Hypertext Preprocessor and is a very popular web scripting engine. It is the first choice of web developers to make dynamic web pages for the simple reason that it is very flexible and very easy to learn. Being a server-side scripting language, all PHP scripts are executed on the server and the output is sent to the client as plain HTML. As a result, if anybody tries to view the source code of our website, he will be able to view only the HTML code generated by the execution of the PHP script and not the PHP script itself, hence making it more secure.

1.1.1 Features of PHP

PHP is a widely used scripting language used in developing websites. It is a fully featured programming language that makes it possible to develop complex web applications with least effort. A few of its features are as under:

- PHP supports many databases (MySQL, Informix, Oracle, Sybase, Solid, PostgreSQL, Generic ODBC, etc.). So data can be stored or retrieved from the back-end database.
- PHP is open source software (OSS) i.e. freely available on the web resulting in reduced software development cost. Open source also ensures faster bug fixing and quick integration of new and enhanced features.

- PHP can be easily embedded with HTML tags and scripts
- PHP runs on different platforms (Windows, Linux, Unix, etc.)
- PHP is compatible with almost all servers used today (Apache, IIS, etc.)

Note: There are several scripting languages in existence today which can be embedded in HTML. One of them is JavaScript, but the difference between JavaScript and PHP is that JavaScript is interpreted by the web browser, i.e., on the client machine, whereas PHP being server-side scripting language, is interpreted by the web server and the result in the form of HTML code is sent to the browser hence reducing the load on the client.

For PHP to work, we need three things: the PHP parser, a web server and a web browser. We need to run the web server with a connected PHP installation. Also, we may need a database to store and retrieve information. So, before working with PHP, we need to install the following:

- An Apache server
- PHP
- MySQL

1.2 APACHE SERVER INSTALLATION

Apache is a fully featured web server that is compatible with PHP and is freely available on the net. Recall that a web server is software on which websites are hosted (uploaded) and that serves the requests of the clients. We can download Apache server from the site: http://httpd.apache.org/. I have downloaded the latest version that is available at the time of this writing: Apache server version 2.2.8. After downloading it in any directory, just double click on its installer file to install it. On double clicking the installer file, Apache server installation wizard opens and displays the initial welcome screen somewhat as shown in Figure 1.2.

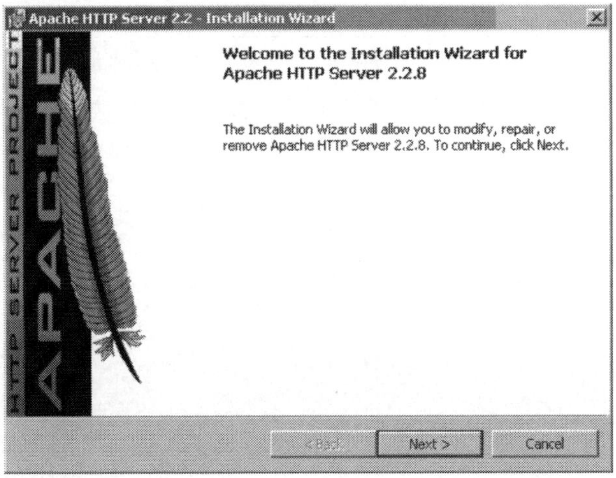

Figure 1.2 ***Welcome Screen of Apache Server***

The welcome screen informs us that we can modify, repair and even remove Apache server through this installation wizard. So, let us move ahead and select the `Next` button. A screen showing the License Agreement and terms and conditions for using, reproducing and distributing the software is displayed (Figure 1.3).

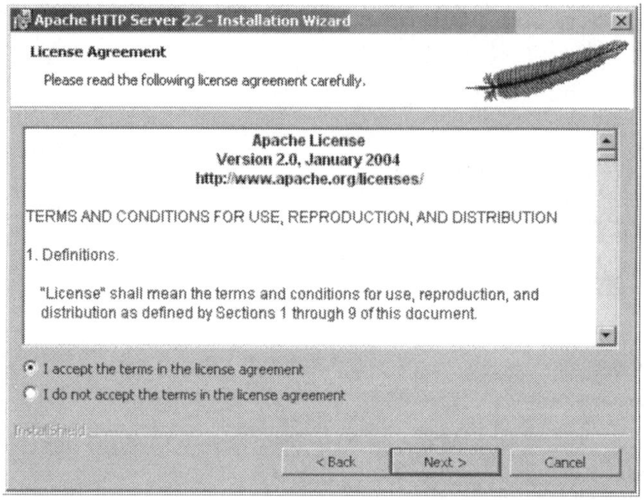

Figure 1.3 ***License Agreement***

After reading the License Agreement, we can accept the terms and conditions specified in it by selecting the option: "`I accept the terms in the license agreement`" and clicking the `Next` button. The following screen asks us to enter server information (Figure 1.4). The server information includes the domain name, server name and the email address of the administrator.

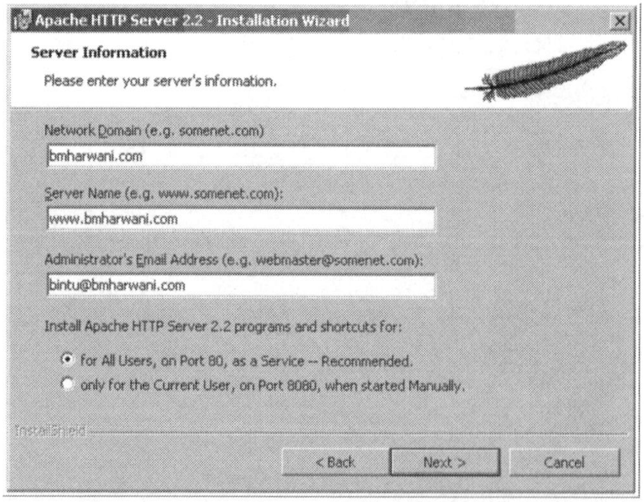

Figure 1.4 ***Specification of Apache Server Information***

We specify the server information as:

Network Domain: `bmharwani.com` (any)

Server Name: `www.bmharwani.com` (any)

Administrator's Email Address: `bintu@bmharwani.com` (any)

Select the option: "for All Users, on Port 80, as a Service – Recommended" for all users to access the server from port 80.

At the moment, the information provided is not very important as we are doing a local installation. But if the server is installed on a remote machine, then the client will be able to access the server only via the information provided in this dialog box. In other words, in a local installation, we will be accessing the server as "`localhost`" i.e., the PHP script will be invoked by writing the following URL in the browser:

```
http://localhost/php_script
```

But if the server is installed on a remote server and the server name specified is say: www.bmharwani.com (as in Figure 1.4), then we need to access the PHP script by pointing the browser at the following URL:

```
http://www.bmharwani.com/php_script
```

Note: The administrator's email address is used to report transactions done on the server, bandwidth used etc. (only when installation is done on a remote machine).

On clicking the `Next` button, we get a screen asking to select the type of setup (Figure 1.5). The two options available are: `Typical` and `Custom`. If the option Typical is selected, it will not ask the user any question but will install the server with all necessary programming features. If the option "`Custom`" is selected, it will prompt certain questions such as what programming features are to be installed and what are to be skipped.

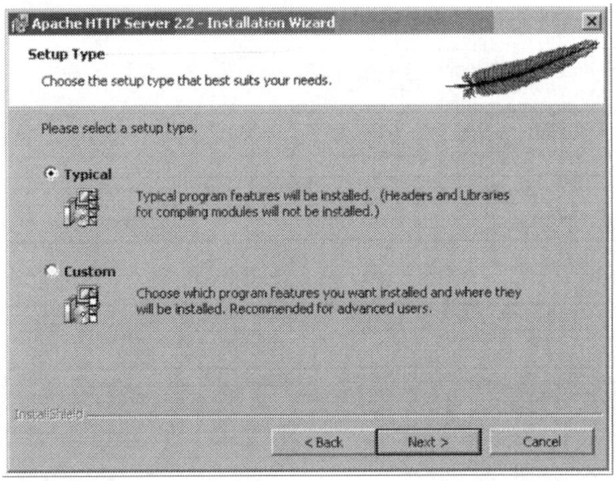

Figure 1.5 ***Selecting the Type of Installation***

Let us select the "`Typical`" type of installation to install the minimum and only necessary programming features automatically and click the `Next` button. We are prompted to specify the drive and folder to install the Apache server (Figure 1.6). We select the "`Change`" button to specify a location on our local computer.

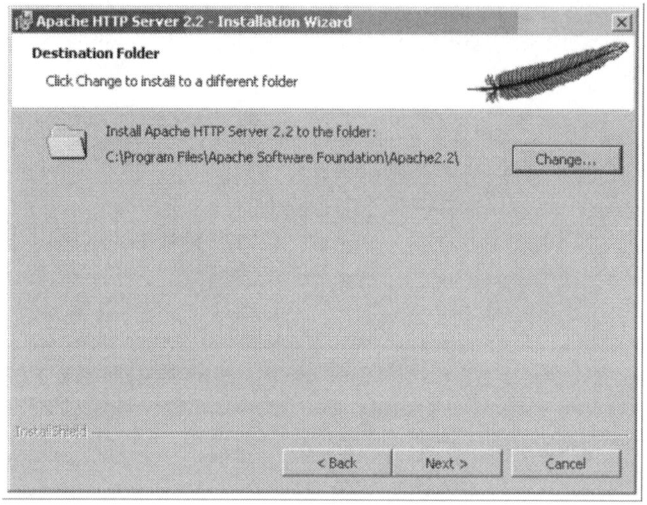

Figure 1.6 ***Destination Folder***

Let us specify D:\apache folder to install the Apache server (any drive or directory), assuming that a folder named apache already exists in D: drive. On selecting the `Change` button, we get a dialog box to select the disk drive. We select Drive D: and from the list of folders, select the folder "`apache`" and finally click the `OK` button (Figure 1.7).

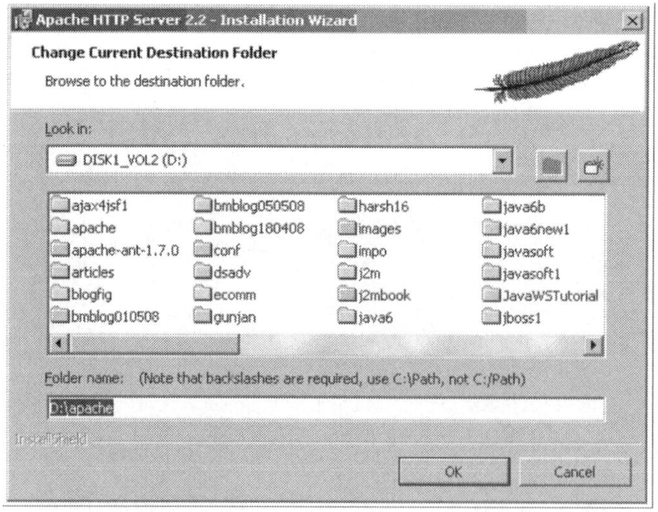

Figure 1.7 ***Specifying the Disk Drive and Folder Name***

On clicking the `OK` button, all the apache server files will be copied into this apache folder along with a "`htdocs`" subfolder. The `htdocs` folder is a very important folder to run PHP scripts. When the server is asked to execute a PHP script, it searches for the script file in "`htdocs`" folder by default. That is, in order to run any PHP script using the Apache server, that script must exist in this `htdocs` subfolder (for the server to recognise it). Once all the server files are copied onto our local disk drive, we get a dialog box reporting the successful installation of Apache HTTP Server (Figure 1.8). Click the `Finish` button to complete server installation.

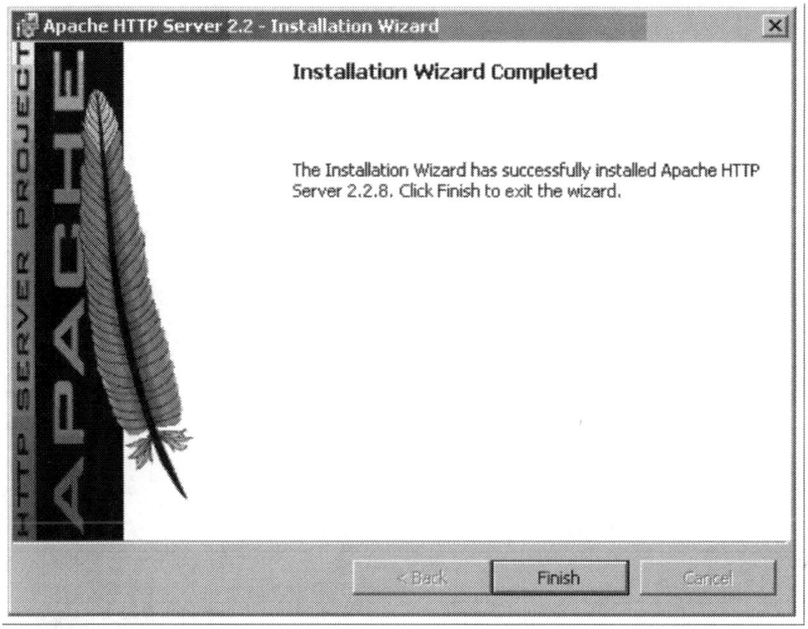

Figure 1.8 ***Installation Wizard Completed***

After the installation of the Apache server, it is time to install PHP. Remember that PHP is a server side scripting language that makes a website dynamic i.e., its contents change as per the user's response.

1.3 INSTALLING PHP

PHP is available for all the operating systems: Windows, Linux and Mac OS X. Let us download the latest version from `http://www.php.net/downloads.php` for free. I have downloaded the Windows version and the most recent release at the time of publication is version 5.2.5. Its installer is: `php-5.2.5-win32-installer.exe`. Let us double click on it to invoke the PHP setup wizard. The first screen the PHP setup wizard displays is a welcome screen (Figure 1.9).

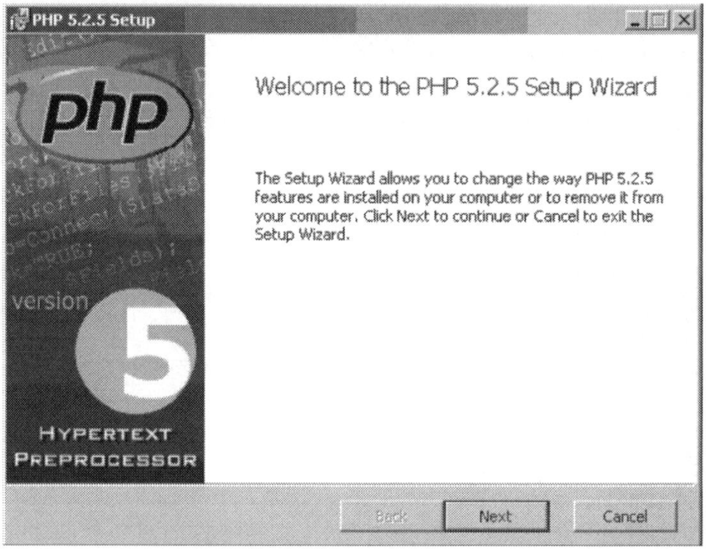

Figure 1.9 ***PHP 5.2.5 Setup Wizard***

The welcome screen tells us that with this setup wizard, we can change PHP features and also can remove them from our computer. Let us select the `Next` button to move ahead. We get a dialog box displaying the License Agreement (Figure 1.10).

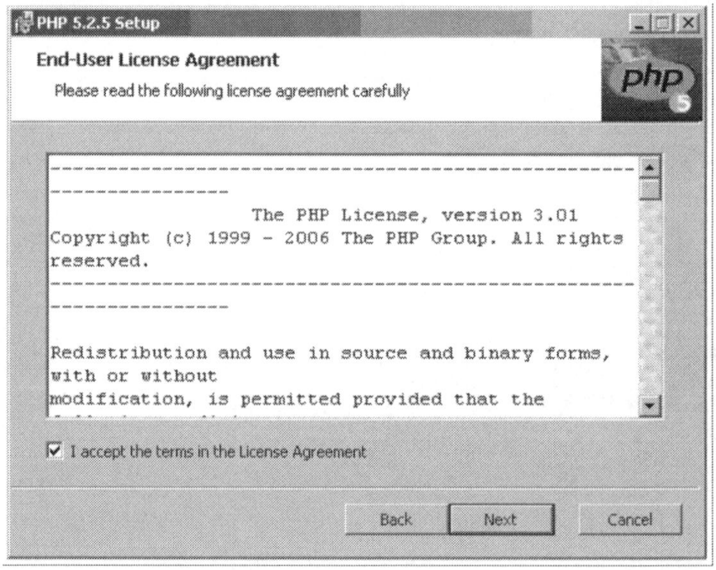

Figure 1.10 ***End-User License Agreement***

Let us read the license agreement carefully and select the checkbox: "`I accept the terms in the License Agreement`" to move to the next step. On clicking the `Next` button, we get a dialog box that prompts us to choose the web server to work with. Let us select Apache 2.2.x Module as we have already installed Apache 2.2.8 server in the preceding section (Figure 1.11).

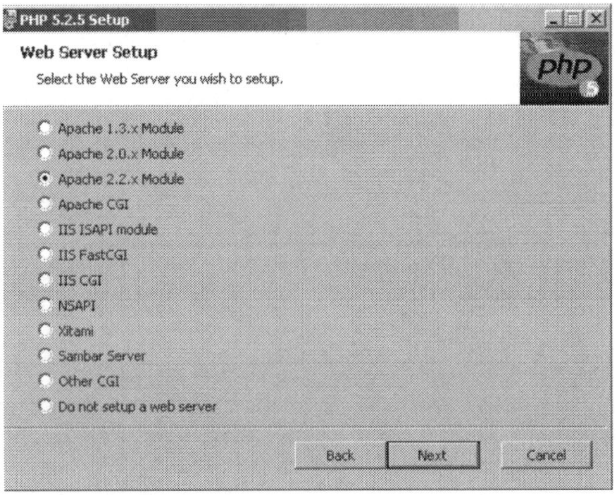

Figure 1.11 ***Selection of Web Server for the Setup***

After selecting the web server, click the `Next` button. The next dialog box will ask us to provide the directory name where Apache configuration files (httpd.conf and others) are installed. The apache configuration files are stored in the conf sub folder of the apache directory. Recall that we have installed Apache server in D:\apache folder. This means the Apache Configuration Directory is at location: `D:\apache\conf`. Let us select the `conf` sub folder of apache directory in D: drive and click the `OK` button (Figure 1.12).

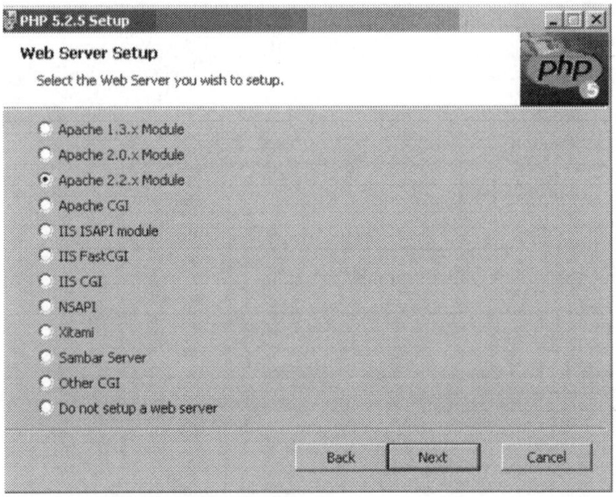

Figure 1.12 ***Selection of Apache Configuration Directory***

We get a dialog box that asks you to select different items (programming features) to install. While installing PHP, don't forget to install "`Script Executables`" and a few extensions, especially `GD2` and `MySQL`. Script executables are meant for executing PHP scripts through the Apache server. GD2 is responsible for displaying different graphic images properly and the MySQL extension is required for establishing the connection between PHP and MySQL. Let us select the "`Script Executables`" dropdown box to open it and from the list of available options, select "`Will be installed on local hard drive`" (Figure 1.13).

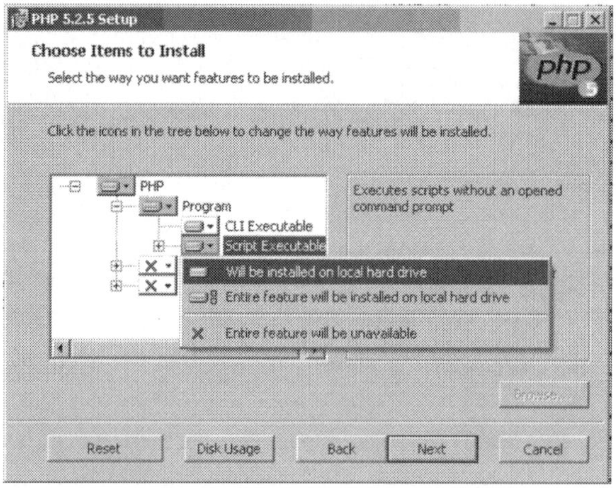

Figure 1.13 ***Selection of Items to be Installed***

To install GD2 and MySQL extensions, we take the help of Extensions node as shown in Figure 1.14. We can see that there are three nodes: `Program, Extensions and Extras`. Let us expand the Extensions node (by selecting the + sign on its left) and search for GD2 and MySQL nodes.

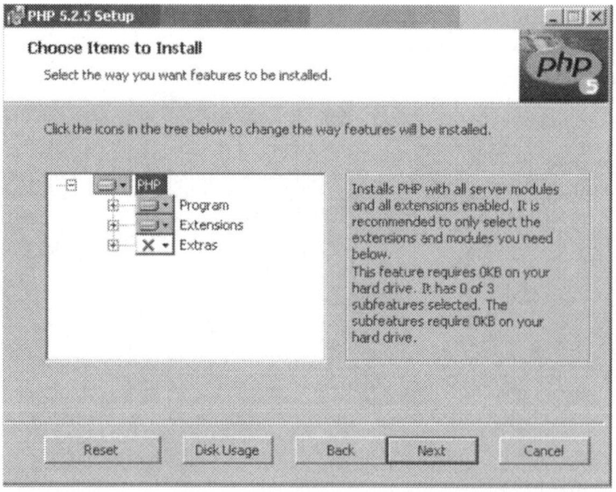

Figure 1.14 ***Expansion of Node of Extensions***

Among several extensions, we find a node of `GD2` extension. Let us select the extension GD2 (by selecting its dropdown arrow) to see all the options that it provides. We will select the option "`Will be installed on local hard drive`" to install this extension (Figure 1.15).

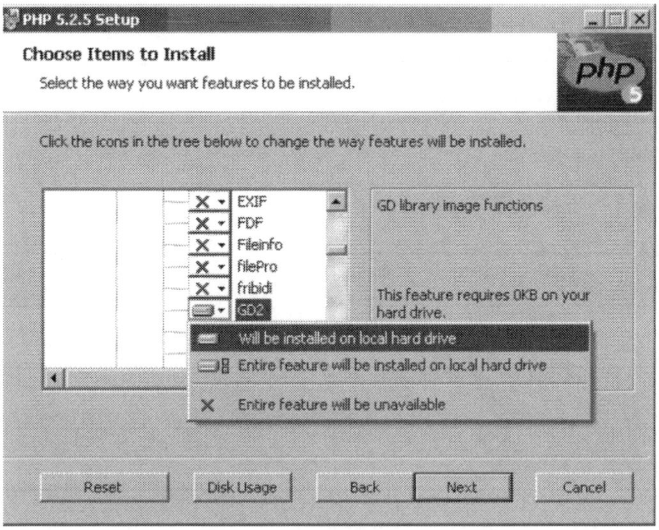

Figure 1.15 ***GD2 Extension Selected***

Similarly, we will select and expand the `MySQL` node. From its available options, we choose "`Will be installed on local hard drive`" to install it (Figure 1.16).

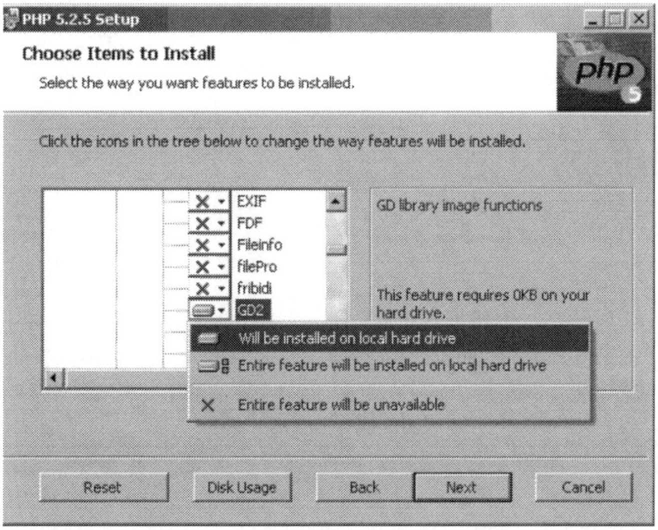

Figure 1.16 ***Installation of Extension Module of MySQL***

After installation of GD2 and MySQL extensions let us move on by clicking the `Next` button. We get a dialog box displaying the message that PHP Setup Wizard is complete. Click `Finish` button to exit the Setup Wizard (Figure 1.17).

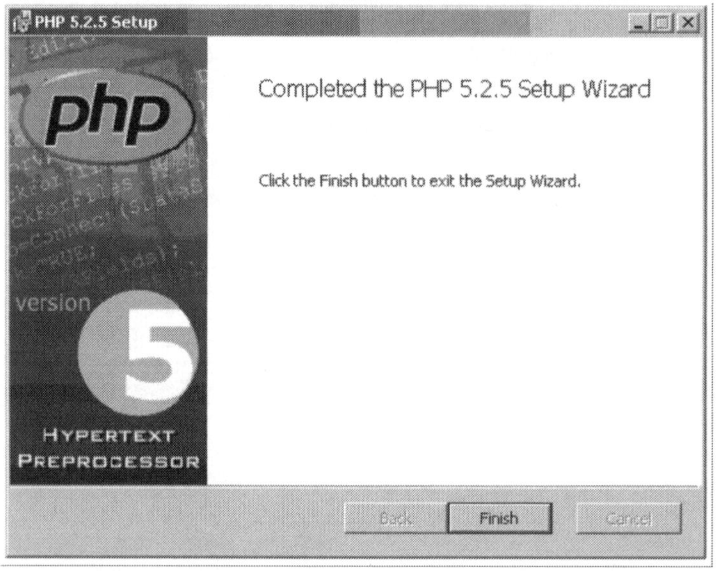

Figure 1.17 ***Completion of Setup Wizard***

We have installed the Apache Server for hosting and uploading our PHP website and a PHP parser to enable the server to execute PHP scripts. The last step left is the installation of a DBMS from where information will be retrieved, stored and updated via PHP scripts. The DBMS that we will be using for our website is MySQL. So, let us go ahead and install it.

1.4 INSTALLING MYSQL

MySQL is a relational database management system released under the GNU General Public License (GPL), and is thus free for most uses on all of the platforms it supports. Simply download the latest software from `http://dev.mysql.com/downloads/`. The latest version available at the time of this publication is version `5.0`. I have downloaded the file `mysql-essential-5.0.45-win32.msi` from the Internet. Double click the file to install MySQL. The MySQL setup wizard opens to display a welcome screen (Figure 1.18).

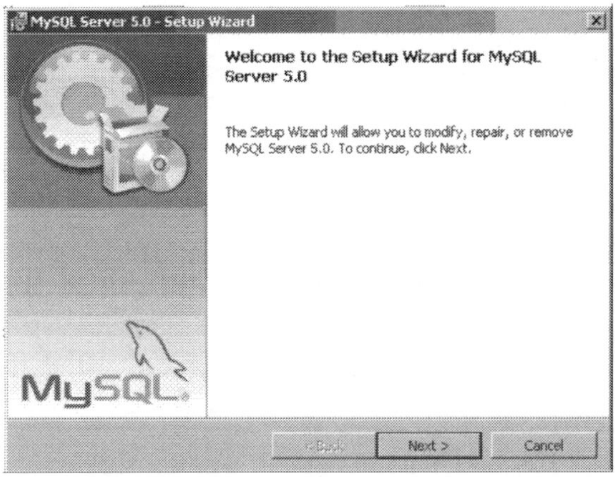

Figure 1.18 ***Setup Wizard for MySQL Server***

The welcome screen displays all the things that we can do via this setup wizard such as modify, repair and even remove MySQL server. Let us move on to the following dialog box by selecting the `Next` button. The next dialog box helps us in choosing the type of setup. The available options are: `Typical`, `Complete` and `Custom` (Figure 1.19).

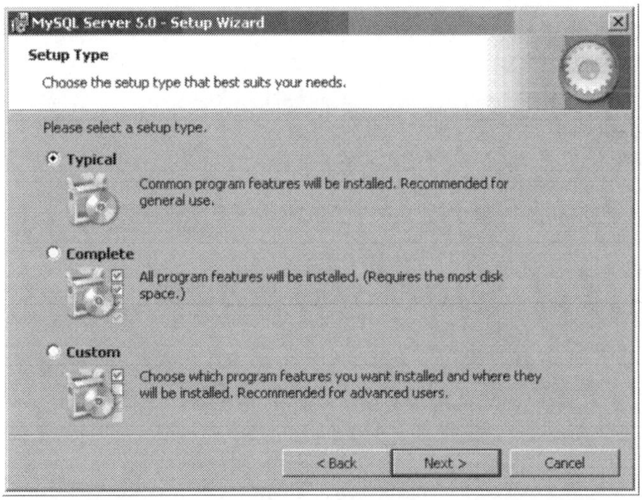

Figure 1.19 ***Selection of Type of Installation***

Usually a "`Typical`" setup is chosen as it installs the most common program features and consumes minimum hard disk space. The `Complete` type of setup will install all the program features and hence consumes the maximum hard disk space of all setup types. The `Custom` type of setup allows us to choose the program features that we want. That is, only the chosen program features will be installed. Let us select the "`Typical`" type of setup type and click the `Next` button. We get a "`Wizard Completed`" dialog box (Figure 1.20).

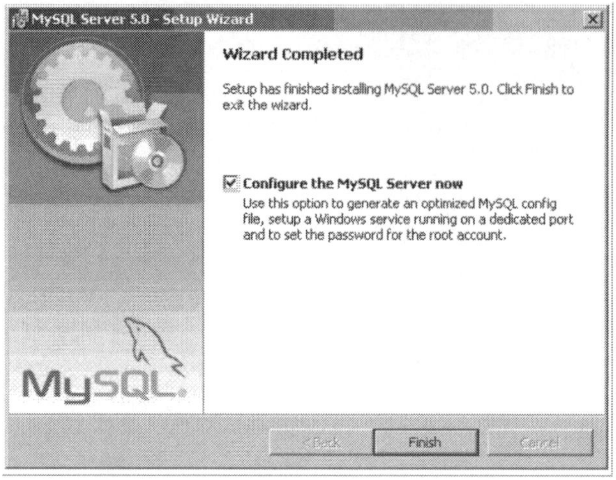

Figure 1.20 ***Completion of the Wizard***

The dialog box confirms that MySQL server is installed on our machine and only its configuration is left. Therefore we click the "`Finish`" button to exit from the MySQL setup wizard and move on to its configuration. After MySQL installation, MySQL Server Instance Configuration Wizard is automatically activated to configure MySQL server (Figure 1.21). The first screen of this Configuration Wizard is the welcome screen.

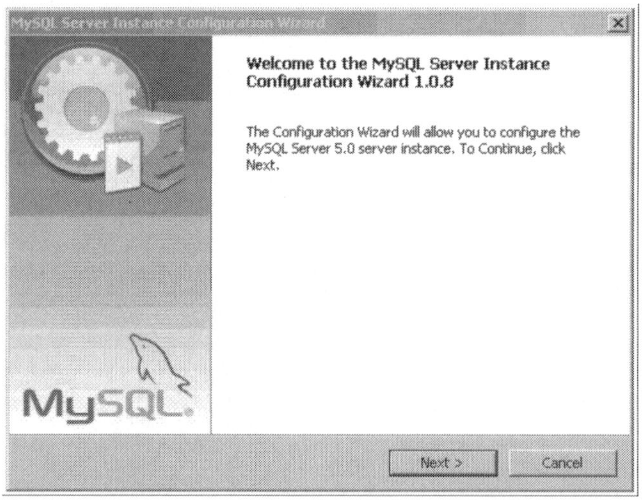

Figure 1.21 ***Welcome Screen of MySQL Server Instance Configuration Wizard***

The welcome screen displays a confirming message that we can use this wizard to configure the MySQL Server instance. Click the `Next` button. The next dialog box allows us to select the type of configuration we want (Figure 1.22). The available options are: `Detailed Configuration` and `Standard Configuration`.

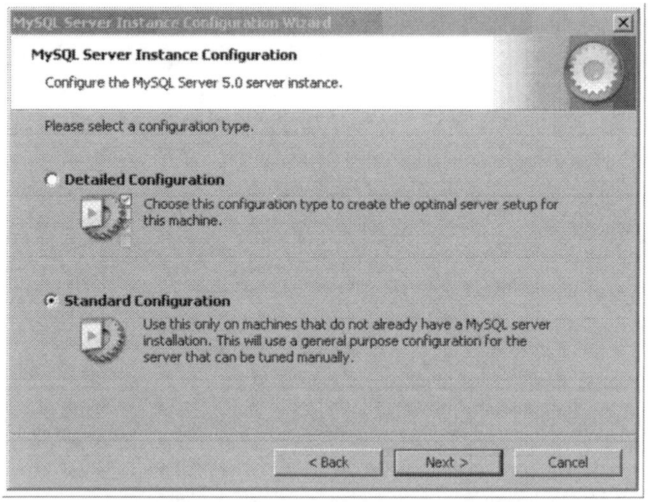

Figure 1.22 ***Selection of Type of Configuration***

The `Detailed Configuration` option is for creating the optimal server setup. It prompts the user to select different configurations settings and accordingly configures the MySQL server whereas the standard configuration option sets the general purpose configuration that we can manually tune later. Let us select the `Standard Configuration` option and select the `Next` button. The next dialog box gives us two options to choose from: `Install As Windows Service` and `Include Bin Directory in Windows PATH` (Figure 1.23).

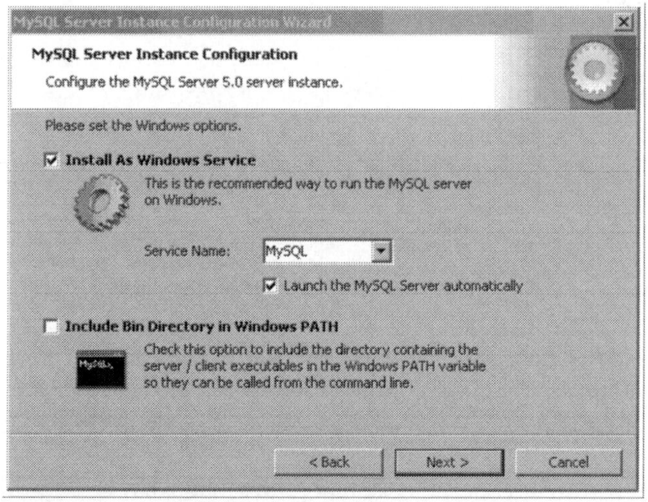

Figure 1.23 ***Setting the Window Options***

Select the checkbox "`Install As Windows Service`" if you want to run the MySQL server on Windows. This option also lets the MySQL server automatically start up on booting. We select the checkbox "`Include Bin Directory in Windows PATH`" to include the folder consisting of executables of the server as well as those of the client in the Windows PATH variable. By checking this option, we will be able to invoke the MySQL server from the command line too. Let us select the first checkbox "`Install As Windows Service`" and select the `Next` button. We get a dialog box that prompts us to specify the root password (Figure 1.24).

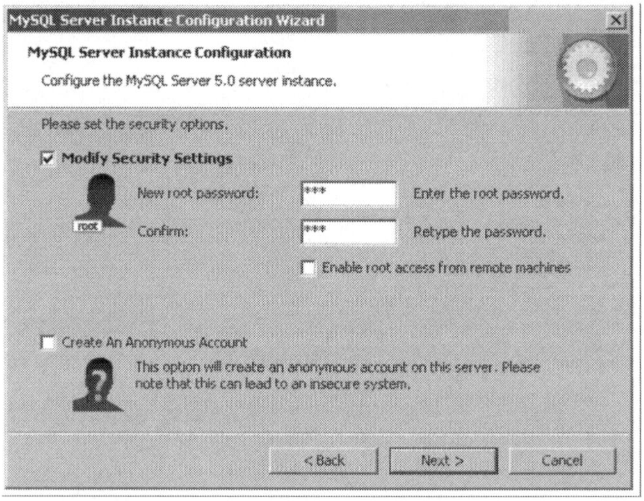

Figure 1.24 ***Specification of the Password***

The passwords entered in `New root password` field and in `Confirm` field must be exactly the same. The dialog box also provides a checkbox "`Create An Anonymous Account`". If we want anyone to access MySQL server without any authentication, we can select this checkbox but it will include a security risk. Therefore this checkbox is usually left unchecked. Click the `Next` button and we get a message that MySQL server is installed and configured on our machine.

SUMMARY

This chapter provided a small introduction to PHP and the steps in installing the three major components of developing dynamic web applications: PHP, MySQL and Apache server are explained. In the next chapter we will see different SQL commands used to create and manipulate MySQL databases and tables. It is always a good idea to understand the working of different SQL commands by executing them from the command line before executing them from PHP scripts. Therefore the main emphasis in the next chapter will be on understanding different SQL commands required in modifying rows, inserting rows, viewing rows and deleting undesired rows from MySQL tables.

2

MySQL Commands

Every organisation maintains all of the information related to its products, customers, orders, services etc. in databases. The benefit of keeping information in databases is that fetching data is faster than from traditional file systems as the databases use indexing, hashing and several schemes to isolate the desired data quickly. At the same time databases have auto backup and restore facility, encryption for higher security, integrity constraints etc. that make them the first choice as storage and retrieval media. Among the databases, we have chosen MySQL for our website as it is one of the most popular open source software of today. MySQL is fast, reliable and very easy to learn.

In this chapter, we will see different MySQL commands used in manipulation of databases and their tables. We are going to learn simple MySQL statements via the following topics:

- Logging on to MySQL
- Creating tables in MySQL
- Modifying table structure
- Inserting rows in a table
- Viewing data stored in table
- Modifying table contents
- Deleting undesired rows from table

Since all the web applications require a back-end database in order to store the information of the visitors, products sold, feedback from the clients etc., we need to understand some basic commands of MySQL. In this chapter we will see the usage of each MySQL command by executing it from the command line. Once we understand the utility of each MySQL command, we will use it in retrieving information from tables and to update contents of tables through PHP scripts in Chapter 4.

Before we execute any of the MySQL commands, we have to first login to the MySQL server. So let us see how this is done.

2.1 LOGGING ON TO MYSQL

For working with MySQL databases, we have to first connect to the MySQL server software. To connect to the server, we require a MySQL client program. In Windows, the MySQL client program is called `mysql.exe` and is located by default in the `C:\Program Files\MySQL\MySQL Server 5.0\bin` folder. It is executed by giving a command with the following syntax:

```
mysql -h hostname -u username -p
```

- hostname is the name or IP address of the computer on which the MySQL server is running. If the client program is running on the same computer as the server, we will use: `-h localhost` or `-h 127.0.0.1`.
- –u argument is followed by the user name
- –p argument tells the program to prompt for the password before it tries to connect to MySQL server.

If the username and password entered are correct, the MySQL client program will introduce itself and display the MySQL command prompt. It is at the MySQL command prompt that we type and execute different MySQL commands.

Let us connect to MySQL server with the following command:

```
C:\Program Files\MySQL\MySQL Server 5.0\bin>mysql -u root -p
Enter password:
```

On entering the root password (the password that we specified while installing MySQL server – refer Figure 1.24), we get the MySQL command prompt (`mysql>`).

The `-u root` argument informs the server that we want to be identified as the MySQL user called `root`.

2.2 CHANGING ROOT PASSWORD

Suppose we want to change the password of the root that we specified during the MySQL server installation, we can do so with the help of the following two commands:

```
mysql>UPDATE mysql.user SET Password=PASSWORD("new password") WHERE
User="root";
mysql>FLUSH PRIVILEGES;
```

Query OK, 0 rows affected (0.24 sec)

The message: Query OK means the command is successfully executed. In the above command, the term `new password` will be replaced by the password that we want to apply. For example, the following two commands will change the root password to "gold2009":

```
mysql>UPDATE mysql.user SET Password=PASSWORD("gold2009") WHERE
User="root";
mysql>FLUSH PRIVILEGES;
```

2.3 UNDERSTANDING MYSQL COMMANDS

The SQL commands are basically of two main categories: DDL and DML.

- `DDL` stands for Data Definition Language and consists of SQL commands that help in defining the structure of tables and the relationship among them. SQL commands like create table, create database, drop table, drop database, alter table etc. belong to the DDL category.
- `DML` stands for Data Manipulation Language and consists of the SQL commands that are used to add, delete, update records from tables, doing queries, joining tables etc. SQL commands like select, delete, update, insert, etc. belong to the DML category.

The MySQL commands we will be dealing with are:

1. Create database
2. Show databases
3. Use database
4. Show tables
5. Drop database
6. Create table
7. Describe table name
8. Alter table
9. Drop table
10. Insert into table
11. Select from table
12. Update table
13. Delete from table

2.3.1 Create Database

It creates a database. A database is an entity that stores tables, their indexes, foreign key constraints, primary key constraints etc. That is, complete information to be stored at the back-end of a web application is maintained in one place: the database. We need to backup only a database instead of individually backing up tables, their indexes, constraints etc.

Syntax:

```
create database database_name;
```

Example:

```
mysql> create database shopping_development;
```

It creates a database named shopping_development. In place of shopping_development, we can give any name for the database we want to create

Note: ; (semi colon) is essential after every SQL statement in MySQL

MySQL is not case sensitive i.e. commands can be given in any case we want.

2.3.2 Show Databases

It shows all the databases created thus far and currently existing on the MySQL server.

Syntax:

```
show databases;
```

Example:

```
mysql> show databases;
```

2.3.3 Use Database

This command is used for loading the specified database in memory to look at all the tables and indexes made in it. At any time, only one database can be in use (i.e. active in memory). When we use another database, the previous database is automatically unloaded from memory (closed).

Syntax:

```
use database_name;
```

Example:

```
use shopping_development;
```

By giving the above command, the database file shopping_development is loaded in memory. We can now view, edit or insert information in the tables present in this database. We can also create new constraints, indexes etc. in the currently active database. We get a confirmation message: "`Database changed`" on loading a database (Figure 2.1).

```
Mysql> use shopping_development;
Database changed
mysql>_
```

Figure 2.1 ***Loading Shopping_development Database in Memory***

2.3.4 Show Tables

It displays all the tables that exist in the currently opened database (i.e. the database that is currently in use).

Syntax:

```
show tables
```

If our database is empty i.e. if it has no tables, we get a message "`Empty set`" otherwise the list of tables will be displayed in the following format (Figure 2.2).

```
Mysql> show tables;
+-------------------------------+
| Tables_in_shopping_development|
+-------------------------------+
| product                       |
+-------------------------------+
1 row in set (0.00 sec)
```

Figure 2.2 ***List of Tables in Currently Active Database***

2.3.5 Drop Database

This command is for deleting the specified database.

Syntax:

```
drop database_name
```

Example:

```
mysql>DROP DATABASE shopping_development;
```

It deletes the shopping_development database and all the tables, indexes, constraints etc. will be deleted with it.

2.3.6 Create Tables

The first thing to do in a database is to create a table. A table is a section of the database for storing information about a person, item entity or object. It consists of several fields (columns). For example, in a table `products` (meant for storing information about a product), the fields (columns) that it may contain are: item_code, item_name, description, price etc. These fields are defined of a particular data type (depending on what kind of data: numerical, character, date etc. the field is supposed to store). The data type of a field also decides how much width can be assigned to a field.

The field (column) in a MySQL table can be defined of any of the following data types:

Data Type	What it can store
SMALLINT, MEDIUMINT, INT, BIGINT	Integer values
FLOAT	Single precision floating point values
DOUBLE	Double precision floating point values

CHAR	Fixed length strings up to 255 characters
VARCHAR	Variable length strings up to 255 characters
TINYBLOB, BLOB, MEDIUMBLOB, LONGBLOB	Large blocks of binary data
TINYTEXT, TEXT, MEDIUMTEXT, LONGTEXT	Longer blocks of text data
DATE	Date values
TIME	Time values or durations
DATETIME	Combined date and time values

The syntax for creating a table is:

```
mysql>CREATE TABLE table_name (
-> column1 data_type1,
-> column2 data_type2,
-> ...
->);
```

Example:

```
mysql> create table product<
    -> id int<6> not null auto_increment,
    -> name varchar<50> not null,
    -> price float,
    -> primary key <id>>;
Query OK, 0 rows affected <0.20 sec>
mysql> _
```

Figure 2.3 ***Creating a Table Named Product***

- The first line says that we want to create a new table named `product`.
- The second line says that we want a column called `id` that will contain an integer (`int`), that is, a whole number and may not be left blank (`not null`). Next, if we don't specify any value for this field while adding a new row in the table, then MySQL will pick a value that is one more than the highest value in the table so far (this is what `auto_increment` means). Finally, this column is to act as a unique identifier for the entries in the table, therefore all values in this column must be unique (`primary key`).
- The third line defines a column called `name` that will contain character data and its contents may not be left blank.
- The fourth line defines a column called `price` that will contain `float` value (value with decimals).
- The fifth line confirms that the column `id` specified on the second line is a primary key (so it may not contain null or similar values).

Note: We can type SQL commands in upper or lowercase. If MySQL server is running on a UNIX based system then take care while giving database and table names, as they are case sensitive because these correspond to directories and files in the MySQL data directory.

As we can see in the above example, if the command is given correctly, MySQL creates a table and responds with a message: "`Query OK`". But if we make a typing mistake, MySQL will inform us that there is a problem with the query typed.

2.3.7 Describe Table Name

This command is for listing the fields (columns) of a table along with their data types. It also explains whether a field can store NULL value or not. It even specifies any default value that can be assigned to any field and also which field is set as a primary key.

Syntax:

```
describe table_name
```

Example:

```
mysql>DESCRIBE products;
```

where `products` is the name of the table. The output displays the complete structure of the products table (Figure 2.4).

```
mysql> describe product;
+--------------+--------------+------+-----+---------+----------------+
| Field        | Type         | Null | Key | Default | Extra          |
+--------------+--------------+------+-----+---------+----------------+
| id           | int<6>       | NO   | PRI | NULL    | auto_increment |
| name         | varchar<50>  | NO   |     |         |                |
| price        | float        | YES  |     | NULL    |                |
+--------------+--------------+------+-----+---------+----------------+
3 rows in set <0.13 sec>
```

Figure 2.4 ***Example of Describe Command***

We can see in the figure that the product table contains three columns: `id`, `name` and `price` out of which `id` is a primary key i.e. it can neither have null value nor it can store duplicate value (i.e. no two rows can have the same `id`). The `name` column can store a name of at most 50 characters and the `price` column can store a value in decimals (because it is declared as float data type).

2.3.8 Modifying Table Structure

The command for modifying table structure is: `alter table` and as the name suggests, it is used to alter the structure of any table i.e. to add a field, or drop any existing field or change its data type or its width etc.

The command to add a new column by name, say, `category_id` of `int` data type to the `product` is as shown below:

```
alter table product add category_id int (6);
```

The value 6 in parentheses represents the width of the column. The execution of this command and its impact on the product table can be seen in Figure 2.5.

```
mysql> alter table product add category_in int<6>;
Query OK, 0 rows affected <0.33 sec>
Records: 0 Duplicates: 0 Warnings: 0

mysql> describe product;
+-------------+-------------+------+-----+---------+----------------+
| Field       | Type        | Null | Key | Default | Extra          |
+-------------+-------------+------+-----+---------+----------------+
| id          | int<6>      | NO   | PRI | NULL    | auto_increment |
| name        | varchar<50> | NO   |     |         |                |
| price       | float       | YES  |     | NULL    |                |
| category_id | int<6>      | YES  |     | NULL    |                |
+-------------+-------------+------+-----+---------+----------------+
4 rows in set <0.05 sec>
```

Figure 2.5 ***Modifying Table Structure—Adding a Column***

We can see in Figure 2.5 that the new column name must be followed by the data type and width. To change the name of the column from `price` to `rate` (keeping the data type same: `float`), we have to give the following command:

```
alter table product change price rate float;
```

where `price` is the column name to be changed, `rate` is the new name that we want to assign and `float` is the data type to be assigned to the renamed column. The execution of the command can be seen in Figure 2.6.

```
mysql> alter table product
    -> change price rate float;
Query OK, 0 rows affected <0.09 sec>
Records: 0 Duplicates: 0 Warnings: 0

mysql> describe product;
+-------------+-------------+------+-----+---------+----------------+
| Field       | Type        | Null | Key | Default | Extra          |
+-------------+-------------+------+-----+---------+----------------+
| id          | int<6>      | NO   | PRI | NULL    | auto_increment |
| name        | varchar<50> | NO   |     |         |                |
| rate        | float       | YES  |     | NULL    |                |
| category_id | int<6>      | YES  |     | NULL    |                |
+-------------+-------------+------+-----+---------+----------------+
4 rows in set <0.02 sec>
```

Figure 2.6 ***Modifying Table Structure—Changing Column (field) Name***

To drop (delete) a column by name, say, `rate` from the product table, we have to give the command:

```
alter table product drop rate;
```

All the information stored in column `rate` will be lost. The execution of this command and its effect on the structure of the `product` table can be seen in Figure 2.7.

```
mysql> alter table product
    -> drop rate;
Query OK, 0 rows affected <0.28 sec>
Records: 0 Duplicates: 0 Warnings: 0

mysql> describe product;
+--------------+-------------+------+-----+---------+----------------+
| Field        | Type        | Null | Key | Default | Extra          |
+--------------+-------------+------+-----+---------+----------------+
| id           | int<6>      | NO   | PRI | NULL    | auto_increment |
| name         | varchar<50> | NO   |     |         |                |
| category_id  | int<6>      | YES  |     | NULL    |                |
+--------------+-------------+------+-----+---------+----------------+
3 rows in set <0.00 sec>
```

Figure 2.7 ***Modifying Table Structure—Deleting a Column***

To convert the data type of column: `rate` from `float` to `integer`, we use the same command that we used for changing the name of the column but this time we assign the same name to old column name and new column name. The command may appear as shown:

```
alter table product change rate rate int(6);
```

where the first word `rate` is the column name whose data type we want to change, and the second word `rate` is to confirm that we want the new column name as rate itself (i.e. we don't want to change the name of the column but data type) and `int(6)` defines that the new data type of `rate` column must be an integer that can store at most 6 digits. The execution of the command and its effect on the product table can be seen in Figure 2.8.

```
mysql> alter table product
    -> change rate rate int<6>;
Query OK, 0 rows affected <0.30 sec>
Records: 0 Duplicates: 0 Warnings: 0

mysql> describe product;
+--------------+-------------+------+-----+---------+----------------+
| Field        | Type        | Null | Key | Default | Extra          |
+--------------+-------------+------+-----+---------+----------------+
| id           | int<6>      | NO   | PRI | NULL    | auto_increment |
| name         | varchar<50> | NO   |     |         |                |
| category_id  | int<6>      | YES  |     | NULL    |                |
| rate         | int<6>      | YES  |     | NULL    |                |
+--------------+-------------+------+-----+---------+----------------+
4 rows in set <0.01 sec>
```

Figure 2.8 ***Modifying Table Structure—Changing Data Type of the Column***

If we forget to create a primary key in our table, we can add it subsequently. It is a two-step process: First we add a column, say, `id` which is of not null nature and then declare that `id` column as primary key (Figure 2.9).

```
mysql> alter table product add id int<6> not null;
Query OK, 0 rows affected <0.08 sec>
Records: 0 Duplicates: 0 Warnings: 0

mysql> alter table product add primary key <id>;
Query OK, 0 rows affected <0.09 sec>
Records: 0 Duplicates: 0 Warnings: 0

mysql> describe product;
+--------------+-------------+------+-----+---------+-------+
| Field        | Type        | Null | Key | Default | Extra |
+--------------+-------------+------+-----+---------+-------+
| name         | varchar<50> | NO   |     |         |       |
| category_id  | int<6>      | YES  |     | NULL    |       |
| rate         | int<6>      | YES  |     | NULL    |       |
| id           | int<6>      | NO   | PRI |         |       |
+--------------+-------------+------+-----+---------+-------+
4 rows in set <0.05 sec>
mysql>
```

Figure 2.9 ***Modifying Table Structure—Adding a New Column and Making it a Primary Key***

We can see in Figure 2.9 that a column `id` is added to `product` table of type `int` (that can store at most 6 digits) and that cannot have null value. In the second statement, the `id` column is added as a primary key to the product table.

Although we should not try it, if we still want to drop the primary key column, it is again a two-step process. First we remove the primary key constraint from that column (we do it by drop primary key command) and then drop that column. The command to remove the primary key constraint is as shown in Figure 2.10.

In the first half of the Figure 2.10, we can see that with column `id`, `PRI` (in `Key` column) is attached which designates that it has a primary key constraint attached to it. On execution of following command:

```
alter table product drop primary key;
```

We see that the PRI (from `Key` column) is removed which shows that the primary key constraint is removed from the column `id` as shown in second half of the figure.

After removing the primary key constraint, the second step is to drop that column. So, we give the command:

```
alter table product drop id;
```

to drop the column `id`. The effect of the command can be seen in Figure 2.11.

```
mysql> describe product;
+---------------+--------------+------+-----+---------+-------+
| Field         | Type         | Null | Key | Default | Extra |
+---------------+--------------+------+-----+---------+-------+
| name          | varchar<50>  | NO   |     |         |       |
| category_id   | int<6>       | YES  |     | NULL    |       |
| rate          | int<6>       | YES  |     | NULL    |       |
| id            | int<6>       | NO   | PRI |         |       |
+---------------+--------------+------+-----+---------+-------+
4 rows in set <0.05 sec>
mysql>

mysql> alter table product drop primary key;
Query OK, 0 rows affected <0.08 sec>
Records: 0 Duplicates: 0 Warnings: 0

mysql> describe product;
+---------------+--------------+------+-----+---------+-------+
| Field         | Type         | Null | Key | Default | Extra |
+---------------+--------------+------+-----+---------+-------+
| name          | varchar<50>  | NO   |     |         |       |
| category_id   | int<6>       | YES  |     | NULL    |       |
| rate          | int<6>       | YES  |     | NULL    |       |
| id            | int<6>       | NO   | PRI |         |       |
+---------------+--------------+------+-----+---------+-------+
4 rows in set <0.02 sec>
mysql> -
```

Figure 2.10 ***Removal of Primary Key Constraint***

```
mysql> alter table product drop id;
Query OK, 0 rows affected <0.28 sec>
Records: 0 Duplicates: 0 Warnings: 0

mysql> describe product;
+---------------+--------------+------+-----+---------+-------+
| Field         | Type         | Null | Key | Default | Extra |
+---------------+--------------+------+-----+---------+-------+
| name          | varchar<50>  | NO   |     |         |       |
| category_id   | int<6>       | YES  |     | NULL    |       |
| rate          | int<6>       | YES  |     | NULL    |       |
+---------------+--------------+------+-----+---------+-------+
3 rows in set <0.02 sec>
mysql> -
```

Figure 2.11 ***Deletion of Column: Id***

2.3.9 Drop Table

This command is for deleting any table in the currently opened database. All rows, along with the structure of the table, will be erased permanently.

Syntax is:

```
mysql>DROP TABLE tablename;
```

Example

```
mysql>drop table product;
```

By above command, the product table will be removed from the currently active database.

2.3.10 Inserting Rows in a Table

There are two methods of adding rows (records) in a table. The syntax of both methods is shown:

```
1) mysql>INSERT INTO table name SET
-> column1 = value1,
-> column2 = value2,
-> ...
->;
2) mysql>INSERT INTO table name
-> (column, column2, ...)
-> VALUES (value1, value2, ...);
```

Note that in the second form of the INSERT command, the order in which we list the columns must match the order in which we list the values. That is, if the sequence of columns in the column list is: `name, category_id, rate`..., then the values in the value list should also be in the same sequence i.e. the first value in the value list must be `name`, second value must be the `category id` and so on, else the wrong values will be placed in wrong columns. The example of commands to insert rows in product table is shown in Figure 2.12.

```
mysql> insert into product<Name, category_id, rate> values<'camera',1,3200>;
Query OK, 1 row affected <0.03 sec>

mysql> insert into product<Name, rate> values<'mobile',4500>;
Query OK, 1 row affected <0.00 sec>

mysql> select * from product;
+--------------+-------------+------+
| name         | category_id | rate |
+--------------+-------------+------+
| camera       |           1 | 3200 |
| mobile       |        NULL | 4500 |
+--------------+-------------+------+
2 rows in set <0.00 sec>
```

Figure 2.12 ***Insertion of Rows in a Table***

In the first example, we have specified values for all the three columns of the product table. But in the second example, we have not specified a value for the column `category_id`. The columns for which data is not passed are set to `NULL`.

2.3.11 Viewing Data Stored in Table

In order to retrieve the desired rows from the given table, we use `select` SQL command. The SQL command select has following syntax:

```
select * [field1, field2…] from table_name [where field1 = expression1
[and/or field2=expression2 …..]]
```

- If * is used instead of field names then all the fields of the table are displayed.
- With the help of `where` clause, we can specify a condition and only the rows which satisfy the given condition will only be displayed. If `where` clause is omitted then all the rows with specified fields will be displayed.
- If we want to specify more than one condition then they can be connected with the logical operators: `and, or`

Examples:

1. `select * from product;`

   Show all the rows with all the columns of the table `product`.

2. `select * from product where category_id=1;`

   Show all the rows with all the columns of the table `product` whose category_id=1.

3. `select * from product where name like 'camera';`

   Show all the rows with all the columns of the table `product` whose product name is camera.

4. `select * from product where name like 'mob%';`

   Show all the rows with all the columns of the table `product` whose product name begins with word `mob`. The symbol: `%` stands for "anything" i.e. the first three characters of the product name must be `mob`, followed by any character(s) or digit(s).

5. `select * from product where rate >=5000;`

   Show all the rows with all the columns of the table `product` whose `rate` is greater than or equal to 5000.

6. `select * from product where rate >=5000 and rate <=10000;`

   Show all the rows with all the columns of the table `product` whose `rate` is between `5000` and `10000`.

7. `select * from product where rate between 5000 and 10000;`

   Show all the rows with all the columns of the table product whose rate is between 5000 and 10000.

8. `select * from product order by name asc;`

   Show all the rows with all the columns of the table `product` sorted in alphabetical order of product name. The keyword `asc` means ascending or alphabetical order.

9. `select * from product order by category_id desc;`

   Show all the rows with all the columns of the table `product` sorted in descending order of category_id. The keyword `desc` stands for descending or reverse alphabetical order.

10. `select distinct category_id from product;`

    Show the distinct category_id from the table product. Distinct means even if category_id is repeated in one or more rows (i.e. if there are more than one product of a given category_id), it will be displayed only once.

11. `select count(*) from product;`

    Show the number of rows in the table product. Output may be as shown in Figure 2.13.

```
mysql> select count<*> from product;
+--------------+
|   count<*>   |
+--------------+
|            2 |
+--------------+
1 row in set <0.03 sec>
```

Figure 2.13 ***Displays the Number of Rows in the Table***

The value 2 designates that the product table has two rows in it.

12. `select * from product group by category_id;`

    Show all the rows with all the columns of the table `product` grouped on the basis of category_id. Let us assume there are five rows in product table divided among two categories (Figure 2.14).

```
mysql> select * from product;
+--------------+--------------+-------+
| name         | category_id  | rate  |
+--------------+--------------+-------+
| C1001        |            1 |  3200 |
| C1002        |            1 |  4500 |
| M1001        |            2 |  8000 |
| M1002        |            2 |  7450 |
| M1003        |            2 | 10500 |
+--------------+--------------+-------+
5 rows in set <0.00 sec>
```

Figure 2.14 ***Rows in the Product Table Divided in Two Categories***

Although there are five rows in the product table, they are divided among two categories with category_id: 1 and 2. So, if we give the command to see the rows of the product table grouped on category_id, we will get two rows (Figure 2.15).

```
mysql> select * from product group by category_id;
+-------------+--------------+-------+
| name        | category_id  | rate  |
+-------------+--------------+-------+
| C1001       |            1 | 3200  |
| M1001       |            2 | 8000  |
+-------------+--------------+-------+
2 rows in set <0.03 sec>
```

Figure 2.15 ***Rows of the Product Table Grouped on Category_id***

13. `select category_id, count(category_id) from product group by category_id;`

    This command shows category_id, number of rows in that category_id from the table `product`. Since the number of rows belonging to category_id=1 is two and the number of rows belonging to category_id=2 is three, we may get the output as shown in Figure 2.17.

```
mysql> select category_id, count<category_id>
from product group by category_id;
+-------------+--------------------+
| category_id | count<category_id> |
+-------------+--------------------+
|           1 |                  2 |
|           2 |                  3 |
+-------------+--------------------+
2 rows in set <0.06 sec>
```

Figure 2.16 ***Display of Category_id and the Count of Rows that Belong to it***

14. `select category_id, count(category_id) from product group by category_id having count(category_id) >=3;`

    Shows category_id, number of rows in that category_id from the table `product` whose number of records in a particular category are more than or equal to three. We know that the number of rows of category_id =2 is three, so only that category_id along with the count of its rows will be displayed (Figure 2.17).

```
mysql> select category_id, count<category_id>
from product group by category_id;
+-------------+--------------------+
| category_id | count<category_id> |
+-------------+--------------------+
|           1 |                  2 |
|           2 |                  3 |
+-------------+--------------------+
2 rows in set <0.06 sec>
```

Figure 2.17 ***Display of Category_id and the Count of its Rows When the Count >=3***

2.3.12 Modifying Table Contents

To modify the contents of the given table, the SQL statement used is called `update`. In this statement, we specify the new value of the column(s) followed by the condition that decides the range of updating i.e. whether the updating has to performed on a single row, a range of rows or on all rows of the table.

Syntax:

```
mysql>UPDATE table_name SET
-> column = new_value, ...
->WHERE conditions;
```

Example:

```
update product
set rate=3700 where name like 'camera';
```

By the above command, the value of the `rate` column of all rows in the `product` table that contains the name as `'Camera'` will be updated to `3700`.

Note: If the condition specified by the where command is omitted, then changes will take place in all the rows.

2.3.13 Deleting Undesired Rows from Table

To delete any row from the given table, the SQL statement used is `delete`.

Syntax:

```
mysql>DELETE FROM table_name WHERE conditions;
```

Examples:

1. `delete from product;`

   Deletes all the rows (records) from the `product` table.
2. `delete from product where name like 'camera';`

   Deletes all the rows (records) from the `product` table whose product `name` is `camera`.
3. `delete from product where category_id=1;`

   Deletes all the rows (records) from the `product` table whose category_id=1.

To come out of MySQL, type quit at the MySQL prompt followed by pressing Enter key:

```
mysql>quit.
```

MySQL will reply with the message: `Bye` and exit.

SUMMARY

This chapter provided a sound start of how to work with MySQL. That is, how to create a database, tables and also how the records (rows) in the table can be inserted and modified. All these commands are demonstrated at the mysql> prompt. The knowledge of these commands will be very helpful when we'll be executing these commands via PHP scripts in later chapters. Remember that in a web application the back-end MySQL database is accessed and updated through PHP scripts. In the next chapter, we will look at all the essential concepts of PHP programming. That is, we will learn the basic syntax and commands of PHP that are used for making small programs. We will also learn how to use conditional statements, loops, arrays, and multi-dimensional arrays in PHP scripts. Finally, we will also see the role of forms in accepting user data and how GET and POST methods are used for passing information from one form to another.

3

Starting with PHP Programming

PHP is an open source server side scripting language with no license fees. Moreover, it is flexible and very easy to learn, which makes it very popular among web developers. In the previous chapters we saw the process of installation and configuration of AMP (Apache, MySQL and PHP) as all three combine to make an environment for developing dynamic websites. We have also seen MySQL commands for creating and deleting databases and tables, defining and altering the structure of tables and maintaining the contents of a table. This chapter covers all the essential concepts of PHP programming which a user "must know" before beginning with the practical examples of "PHP and MySQL programming", i.e. before learning how the MySQL database can be manipulated via PHP scripts. The chapter provides information on the following:

- Basic syntax and commands of PHP
- Echo command
- Variables in PHP
- Comments in PHP
- PHP operators
- Conditional statements
- Looping
- Arrays
- Associative array
- Multi-dimensional arrays for each statement
- Forms
- $_GET Array
- $_POST Array

- $_REQUEST
- Functions
- Passing parameters to functions
- Returning a value
- Global variables

3.1 STARTING WITH PHP PROGRAMMING

A PHP file normally contains HTML tags, and some embedded PHP scripting code. It certainly reveals one more advantage of PHP that it can be embedded in HTML pages. To enable the PHP interpreter to distinguish PHP codes from HTML tags, the PHP commands are enclosed within special start and end tags: `<?php` and `?>`. Let's see the first example:

```
<html>
    <body>
        <?php echo "Believe in God"; ?>
    </body>
</html>
```

We can see in this simple script that PHP commands can be easily embedded with HTML with the help of special start and end tags:

```
<?php
PHP commands
?>
```

```
<?php tag means open the PHP mode and
?> tag means close the PHP mode.
```

There are two basic statements to output text with PHP: `echo` and `print`. In the example above we have used the `echo` statement to output the text "Believe in God".

Let us see how to execute this PHP script.

3.1.1 Steps to Run PHP Script

To run the above PHP script, the steps are as under:

- Type the above program using any editor and save it by name, say, `prog1.php` (file extension must be php) in the `htdocs` subfolder of apache directory. Recall from Chapter 1 that on installation, the Apache web server creates an `apache` directory with one of its subfolders named: "`htdocs`". In order for the Apache web server to recognise PHP scripts, they have to be placed in the `htdocs` sub folder.

- Make sure that the Apache web server is running. To confirm it, we need to open the Apache Service Monitor dialog box. To open the Apache Service Monitor dialog box, right click on Apache server icon in the taskbar and select the "`Open Apache Monitor`" option (Figure 3.1).

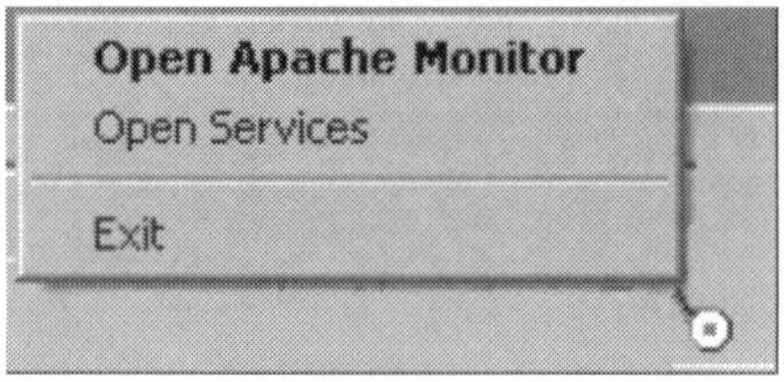

Figure 3.1 ***Apache Icon in Taskbar***

The Apache Service Monitor dialog box shows the status of the Apache server i.e., whether it is in running mode or is in stopped mode (Figure 3.2). Not only can we view the status of the Apache server from this dialog box but also control its status.

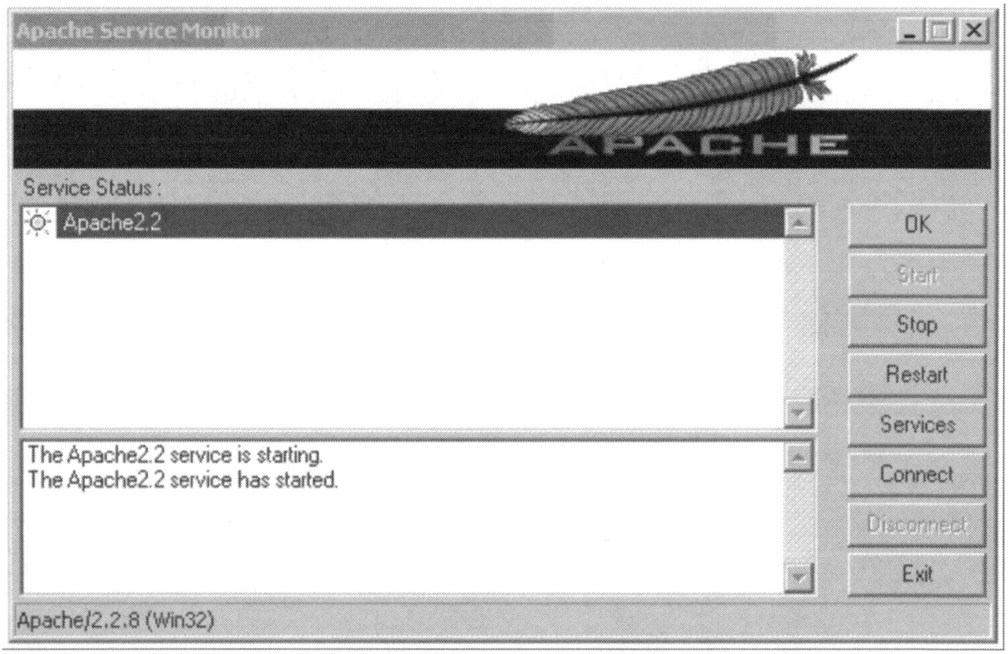

Figure 3.2 ***Apache Service Monitor Window Showing Status of Apache Server***

Figure 3.2 confirms that the PHP server is running. If we find it in Stop mode, we can run it by clicking the `Start` button.

- We can now execute our PHP script by opening the browser and pointing it to the following address: `http://localhost/prog1.php`. The PHP script displays the output in the form of a text message: "Believe in God" (Figure 3.3).

Figure 3.3 ***Output of prog1.php Script***

Note: The term `"localhost"` used in the URL: "http://localhost/prog1.php" signifies that our PHP script is located on the local web server. It is replaced by the domain name when the PHP script is hosted on the remote server. For example: http://bmharwani.com/prog1.php (assuming that the script is uploaded on server: bmharwani.com).

In the above example, when we request our local Apache web server for PHP script prog1.php, it assigns the script to the PHP interpreter. PHP parses the script and executes the code between the special start and end tags (`<?php` and `?>`), generates the output and sends it back to the web server. The web server transmits the output in the form of HTML code to our browser screen (client's browser).

3.2 BASIC SYNTAX AND COMMANDS

PHP code is written between the special start and end tags: `<?php` and `?>` tags.

- <?php means "begin PHP code" and
- ?> means "end PHP code".

The PHP interpreter reads and interprets only the statements between these tags and the statements before and after these tags are simply ignored, assumed to be HTML code. The PHP scripting block can be placed anywhere in the HTML document. Each code line in PHP must end with a semicolon. The semicolon is a separator and is used to distinguish one set of instructions from another.

Example:

```
<html>
    <head>
    </head>
    <body>
        This is HTML code
    ..................
    ..................
```

```
        <?php
            PHP statement must be terminated with semi colon;
            PHP statement;
            PHP statement;
        ?>
    </body>
</html>
```

The best part of using PHP is that not only can it be easily embedded in HTML but we can also switch between PHP and HTML and vice versa easily. Let's see this with the following example:

```
<html>
    <head>
    </head>
    <body>
        <h1>Welcome to PHP</h1>
        <?php
            echo '<b>Believe in God</b>';
        ?>
    </body>
</html>
```

Note: The `echo` statement is used to send output to the browser.

As we can see the above program appears as a simple HTML document with an open HTML tag, head, body tag, etc. `<?php` tag marks the beginning of PHP code and **?>** tag designates that PHP coding is over. The PHP code in between <?php and ?> is converted into HTML code.

The point to remember is that not PHP code but the output of the PHP code (in the form of HTML) is actually sent to the client. The output that may be sent to the client for the example above is as follows:

```
<html>
    <head>
    </head>
    <body>
        <h1>Welcome to PHP</h1>
        <b>Believe in God</b>
    </body>
</html>
```

If a user views the source of a PHP page in a text editor they will not see the PHP code; all they will see is the output of that code. Again, this is another advantage of using PHP; nobody can see the actual PHP script used in our web application but only the generated HTML code, making it more secure.

3.2.1 Variables in PHP

While making web applications, we need to store the information entered by the user temporarily. We also need to store intermediate results (of processing) for final outcome. To serve this requirement of temporary storage, variables are used. Variables may be used not only for storing the data entered by the user but also for storing constant numerical values or text. The value to the variable is assigned with the help of the assignment operator **(=)**. All variables in PHP start with a **$** sign symbol followed by either a letter or underscore. After the $ sign, the variable should not begin with a numerical or any other symbol other than underscore.

Example:

```
<html>
    <body>
        <?php
            $name="John";
            echo $name;
            $a=10;
            $b=20;
            echo $a+$b;
        ?>
    </body>
</html>
```

In this PHP script, the string: "John" (strings have to be enclosed in double quotes) is assigned to variable `$name` and two numericals, 10 and 20, are assigned to variables `$a` and `$b` respectively. The contents of `$name` variable and the sum of variables $a and $b are displayed using the `echo` statement.

When we run the above PHP script, the output we get is:

```
John 30
```

3.2.2 Echo

An `echo` statement is used for displaying the output on the browser screen. There are two basic statements to output text with PHP: `echo` and `print`.

Example:

```
<?php
    echo 'Believe in God';
    echo '<b>Be Polite in your approach <b>';
?>
```

`<?php` tag switches on the PHP mode. The first `echo` statement displays the string "Believe in God" and the second `echo` statement displays the string "Be Polite in your approach" in bold on the screen.

Note: The string is enclosed in single quotes.

An `echo` statement can be used with single quotes, double quotes or no quotes. Let's see when to use what.

Single quotes

We use single quotes when we want to print a message without any variables.

```
<?php
    echo 'Believe in God';
?>
```

No quotes

If we are just printing a variable, there is no need to use quotes at all.

```
<?php
    $msg = 'Believe in God';
    echo $msg;
?>
```

In the above example, we simply display the contents of the variable `$msg` without any accompanying text message.

Double quotes

These are used when we want to print contents of the variable along with a text message.

```
<?php
    $msg = 'Believe in God';
    echo "The slogan of the day is: $msg";
?>
```

In above example, the variable `$msg` is enclosed in double quotes along with the text: `"The slogan of the day is:"`. The output on the browser screen will be:

```
The slogan of the day is: Believe in God
```

3.2.3 String Concatenation

String concatenation deals with addition of two or more text messages, addition of two or more string variables or addition of text messages with string variables. For string concatenation, `dot (.)` operator is used:

```
<html>
    <body>
        <?php
            $a="Thanks";
            $b="Good Bye";
            echo "The two strings are " . $a . " and " . $b ;
        ?>
    </body>
</html>
```

The output of the script above will be:

```
The two strings are Thanks and Good Bye
```

3.2.4 Comments in PHP

Comments are an important part of program documentation. They are helpful in explaining the working of an application as well as for specifying the reason for using a particular function or code. Sometimes comments are used in debugging too, i.e., the part of the code giving erroneous results can be isolated by commenting out the rest of the code. In PHP, we use // to make a single-line comment. For comments extending over more than a line, enclose them between a pair of /* and *.

Example:

```
<html>
    <body>
        <?php
            //This is a comment
            /*
                This is
```

```
            a comment
            block
        */
    ?>
  </body>
</html>
```

3.3 PHP OPERATORS

Operators are used for performing certain operations. In PHP, we have the following types of operators:

Arithmetic Operators

Operator	Description
+	Addition
–	Subtraction
*	Multiplication
/	Division
%	Modulus (division remainder)
++	Increment
– –	Decrement

Assignment Operators

Operator	Example	Meaning
=	x=y	x=y
+=	x+=y	x=x+y
–=	x–=y	x=x–y
*=	x*=y	x=x*y
/=	x/=y	x=x/y
%=	x%=y	x=x%y

Comparison Operators

Operator	Description
==	is equal to
!=	is not equal
>	is greater than

<	is less than
>=	is greater than or equal to
<=	is less than or equal to

Logical Operators

Operator	**Description**
&&	and
||	or
!	not

The usage of these operators we will soon see in the examples that follow.

3.4 CONDITIONAL STATEMENTS

Conditional statements are used for choosing a set of statements out of two or more sets depending on the validity of the logical expression included. In PHP, we have two conditional statements:

- if (...else) statement
- switch statement

3.4.1 If Statement

An `if` statement consists of a logical expression which may result in `true` or `false`. If the result of the logical expression is true then the set of statements defined in the `if` block will be executed otherwise the set of statements in the `else` block will be executed.

Syntax:

```
if (logical expression)
        code to be executed if condition is true;
else
        code to be executed if condition is false;
```

Example:

```
<?php
    $a=20;
    $b=40;
    if($a > $b)
    {
        echo $a. " is larger ";
```

```
    }
    else
    {
        echo $b. " is larger ";
    }
?>
```

Output:

The statement defined in the `else` block will be executed and the output will be: "`40 is larger`" (Figure 3.4) because the logical expression: "`20 > 40`" is false

Figure 3.4 ***Output of Ifcommand.php Script***

3.4.2 Switch Statement

If we have to choose one statement out of several statements depending on the value of an expression, then instead of using several `if else` statements, a `switch` statement is preferred. That is, the `switch` statement is a better alternative when there are several conditions to deal with.

Syntax:

```
switch (expression)
{
    case value1:
            code to be executed if expression = value1;
            break;
    case value2:
            code to be executed if expression = value2;
            break;
```

```
    :       :       :       :
    :       :       :       :
    :       :       :       :
    default:
            code to be executed if none of condition is met
}
```

The value of the expression is compared with the values for each `case` in the structure. If there is a match, the block of code associated with that case is executed. The `break` statement is used for coming out of the `switch` statement. If `break` is not used, it will execute the code of the next **case** automatically. The `default` statement is executed if the expression does not match any value specified in cases.

Example:

```
<?php
    $k=2;
    switch($k)
    {
        case 1:    echo "One";
                   break;
        case 2:    echo "Two";
                   break;
        case 3:    echo "Three";
                   break;
        case 4:    echo "Four";
                   break;
        default:
                echo "Sorry the value is not between 1 and 4 ";
    }
?>
```

The output of above script will be:

```
Two
```

Since the value of `$k` is `2,` it will execute the statement defined in `case 2` i.e., it will print the string: `Two`

3.5 LOOPING STATEMENTS

Looping statements in PHP are used to execute the same block of code a specified number of times. In PHP we have the following looping statements:

- while — loops through a block of code for the time the specified condition is true
- do...while — loops through a block of code once, and then repeats the loop as long as a special condition is true. Here the validity condition is checked at the end of the loop
- for — loops through a block of code for a specified number of times. This loop is usually used when we know beforehand how many times a loop is supposed to be executed
- foreach — loops through a block of code for each element in an array

3.5.1 While Loop

The `while` statement executes a block of code for the time the specified condition is true.

Syntax:

```
while (condition)
{
code to be executed;
..........................
..........................
}
```

Example:

```
<?php
    $i=1;
    while($i<=5)
    {
        echo $i . "<br>";
        $i++;
    }
?>
```

Output

We can see that the `while` loop in the above PHP script executes until value of `$i` crosses the value 5, hence displaying the sequence numbers from 1 to 5 (Figure 3.5).

Figure 3.5 ***Output of Whileloop.php Script***

3.5.2 Do. . . While Loop

In this loop too, a block of statements is executed for the time the given condition is true. But since here the validity condition is specified at the end of the loop, this loop executes at least once.

Syntax:

```
do
{
code to be executed;
…………………..
…………………..
}while (condition);
```

Example:

```
<?php
    $i=1;
    do
    {
        echo $i . "<br>";
        $i++;
    }while($i<=5);
?>
```

The above script also prints the sequence numbers from 1 to 5. The only difference is that here the validity check of the expression is done at the end of the loop as a result whatever may be the initial value of variable `$i`, the loop will execute at least once.

3.5.3 For Loop

This loop is used for repeating a set of statements a specified number of times. This loop is generally used when we already know how many times a statement(s) has to be executed.

Syntax:

```
for (initialization; condition; increment)
{
    code to be executed;
}
```

Note: A `for` statement has three parameters. The first parameter is for initialising variables, the second parameter holds the validity condition, and the third parameter contains any increment/decrement operator.

Example:

```
<?php
    for ($i=1; $i<=5; $i++)
    {
        echo $i . "<br>";
    }
?>
```

Note: Since foreach loop can work with arrays only, it is explained after the description of arrays.

3.6 ARRAYS

An array is a special kind of variable consisting of a collection of several memory locations in order to store multiple values. An array in PHP is created using the built-in array function: array()

The syntax of using array() is:

```
arrayname= array ( [element1, element2 ...] )
```

Example:

```
$p = array(10, 15, 22);
```

The above example creates an array by name `$p` which stores three values: 10, 15 and 22. The values are stored in the array at different memory locations referred to by different indices/subscripts. An index begins with 0. So 10 is stored at `$p[0]` index, 15 is stored at `$p[1]` index and 22 is stored at `$p[2]` index (Figure 3.6).

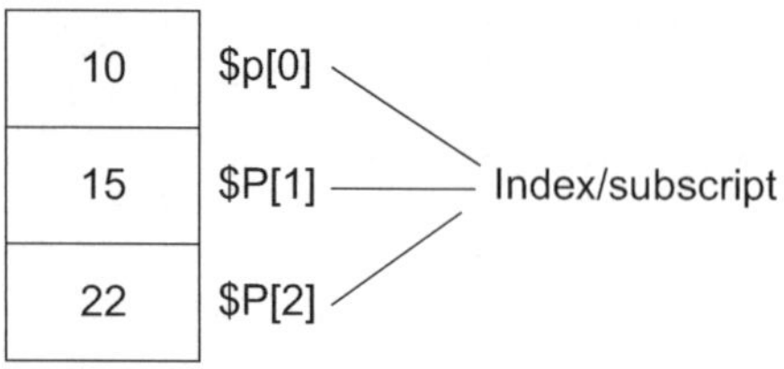

Figure 3.6 ***Array p and its Contents***

These indices/subscripts i.e. 0, 1, 2... are used to update and retrieve the values stored in an array.

Example:

```
echo $p[0];
```

This will display value 10 on the screen (as 10 is stored at index `p[0]`).

An index can also be used to update or assign a new value to an array.

Example:

```
$p[1]=50;
```

It will update the value at `p[1]` index i.e. the value 15 will be removed and 50 will be stored at that index location.

```
$p[3] = 40;
```

'john'	$k[0]
'charles'	$k[1]
'peter'	$k[2]
'robert'	$k[3]
'jack'	$k[4]

Figure 3.7 ***Contents of Array k***

It will add a new value to the array.

We can also create an array of strings:

```
$k = array('john', 'charles', 'peter', 'robert', 'jack');
```

Every string will be stored at its respective index, i.e., 'john' will be stored at `$k[0]` index, 'charles' will be stored at `$k[1]` index and so on (Figure 3.7).

3.6.1 Foreach Statement

This statement loops over the array. On each loop, the value of the current element is assigned to a variable and the array pointer is advanced by one.

Syntax:

```
foreach (array as value)
{
```

```
    code to be executed;
}
```

Example:

The following example demonstrates a loop that will print the values of the given array:

```
<?php
    $p=array("apple", "bat", "cat");
    echo "Data in array are: <br />";
    foreach ($p as $k)
    {
        echo "$k <br>";
    }
?>
```

In the above program, an array `$p` is defined with three strings: "apple", "bat", and "cat" which will be stored at locations: `$p[0]`, `$p[1]`, `$p[2]` respectively. In a `foreach` loop, `$k` is the variable which will be assigned one element of the array `$p` at a time. That is, the first element of the array `$p` is assigned to `$k` (`"apple"` is assigned to `$k`) and the loop is executed. In the next iteration, the next element of the array (`"bat"`) is assigned to variable `$k` and again the loop is executed and so on.

Output of the above program:

```
Data in array are:
apple
bat
cat
```

3.6.2 Associative Array

This is an array which stores an element (value) bound to a key. That is, every element in this array is in terms of pairs: `key-value` pair

```
$student["roll"]=101;
$student["name"]="John";
$student["marks"]=85;
```

By the above examples of associative array, we can conclude that array indices can be strings too. This type of array is called associative because it associates values with meaningful indices.

We can also create an associative array by using the array() function.

```
$student=array("roll" => 101, "name" =>"John", "marks" => 85);
```

As with any array, to retrieve the values stored in an associative array, indices are used.

Example :

```
echo $student["name"];
```

This statement will print "John" on the screen.

Arrays can be single dimensional (as explained above) or multidimensional.

3.6.3 Multidimensional Arrays

These arrays are also known as array of arrays. These arrays therefore use two or more indices/ subscripts. For a two-dimensional array, there are two index/subscript – one represents row and the other represents column.

Example:

```
$p[3][3];
```

This example defines an array of 3 rows and 3 columns. Since the indices/subscripts begin with 0, the first location of this two dimensional array is represented by `p[0][0]` (for 0th row and 0th column).

Let us assign the values to the two dimensional array as:

```
$p[0][0]=10;
$p[0][1]=20;
$p[1][0]=30;
$p[1][1]=40;
```

This array can be represented as shown in Figure 3.8.

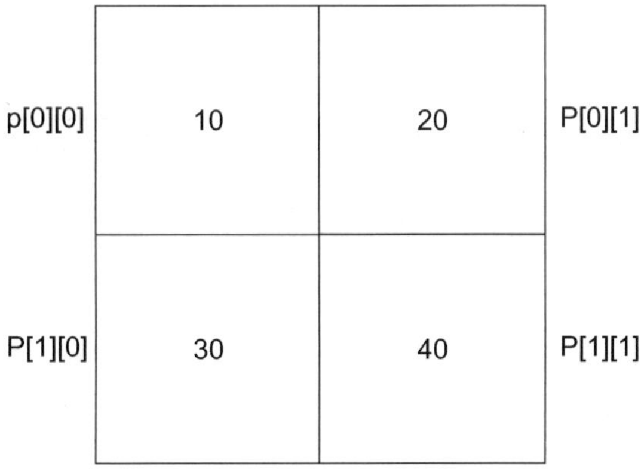

Figure 3.8 ***Contents of a Two-dimensional Array: p***

Note: An index/subscript can be in form of strings too.

Example:

```
p['tea']=100;
```

Syntax of creating a multidimensional array:

```
$array = array(
        'key1' => 'value1',
        'key2' => 'value2',
        'key3' => array(
                'key1' => 'othervalue1',
                'key2' => 'othervalue2',
                'key3' => 'othervalue3'
                )
);
```

Example:

```
$student = array (
    '1' => array (
        'roll' => 101,
        'name' => 'John',
        'marks' => 85),
    '2' => array (
        'roll' => 102,
        'name' => 'Charles',
        'marks' => 72)
);
```

This example creates two rows with indices: `1` and `2` respectively and each row has three columns with indices: `roll`, `name` and `marks`. To display `'roll'` of the first row, we write the following command:

```
echo $student['1']['roll'];
```

This command will display value: 101

Similarly, to display `'name'` of the second row, we write the following command:

```
echo $student['2']['name'];
```

This command will display Charles.

3.7 FORMS

When we want some feedback from the user on some topic or want some information to be supplied by the user, we take the help of forms. A form consists of certain tags to accept user data and this data is then passed on to a specified PHP script for processing on the click of the submit button.

```
<form action="display.php" method="get">
    Name: <input type="text" name="name" />
    Age: <input type="text" name="age" />
    <input type="submit" />
</form>
```

This form has two input boxes named "name" and "age". The form "action" points to a PHP file: "display.php" and the "method" is "get". The contents of the form will be submitted to the PHP script: "display.php" using the HTTP request-method GET for further processing.

The information is passed from one PHP script to another using any of the following HTTP request methods:

- GET
- POST

GET

In this method the information passed is less secure as it is displayed in the browser's address bar and moreover, there is a limit on the amount of information passed (it can be of a maximum 100 characters).

POST

In this method, the information passed is more secure as it is not displayed in the browser's address bar.

3.7.1 $_GET Array

The $_GET array is an array where data from the previous form sent using HTTP GET method are stored. The data from the previous form are sent in the form of pairs: `variable name(s)` and its `value(s)`.

Recall that information sent from a form with the GET method is less secure as it is displayed in the browser's address bar and the size of the information passed is limited.

When the user clicks the "Submit" button, the URL sent will look something like this:

```
http://localhost/display.php?name=john&age=22
```

We can see that when we use the GET method, all the information passed is attached in the browser address bar after the ? mark.

The target file: "display.php" file can now extract the data from $_GET array using following statements:

```
Welcome <?php echo $_GET["name"]; ?>.<br>
Your age is <?php echo $_GET["age"]; ?>
```

The name and age sent from the source PHP script is accessed from $_GET array and displayed.

3.7.2 $_POST Array

The $_POST array is an array which collects the values sent from a form using HTTP POST method.

Example:

```
<form action="display.php" method="post">
   Enter your name: <input type="text" name="name" />
   Enter your age: <input type="text" name="age" />
   <input type="submit" />
</form>
```

When the user clicks the "Submit" button, the $_POST["name"] and $_POST["age"] variables will be automatically set by PHP. The $_POST array contains all POST data and the URL will not display any form data (so it is more secure).

The destination PHP script: "display.php" file can now use the $_POST array to retrieve the form data with the help of the following code:

```
Welcome <?php echo $_POST["name"]; ?>.<br>
Your age is <?php echo $_POST["age"]; ?>
```

Note: Information sent from a form with the POST method is invisible to others and there is no limit to the amount of information sent.

To conclude: HTTP POST method is a better way of transmitting data because:

- Variables sent with HTTP POST are not shown in the URL
- Variables have no length limit

3.7.3 $_REQUEST Array

$_REQUEST array contains the contents of both $_GET and $_POST. That is, it is used to collect the information from a form which is sending data by either method: GET or POST method.

So, if we are not aware of the HTTP method used by the source PHP script, it is wise to access the information using a $_REQUEST array. The target file: display.php made in the earlier examples can be rewritten as:

Example:

```
Welcome <?php echo $_REQUEST["name"]; ?>.<br />
Your age is <?php echo $_REQUEST["age"]; ?>
```

This will access the information sent from the source PHP file sent by any method: `GET` or `POST`.

3.8 FUNCTIONS

Functions are small modules or sub programs which are written once and can be invoked several times hence avoiding repetition of statements. Functions are usually made to manipulate and process data. Functions are of two types: `built-in` and `user defined`. PHP has hundreds of built-in functions each meant for a particular purpose. These built-in functions can be directly used in PHP scripts. User defined functions are made by the programmer and are also known as `custom functions`.

Example:

```
function disp_welcome() {
    echo 'Welcome to our Shopping Mall <br>';
    echo "You will find different varieties of items at lowest price';
}
```

We can see that a function is defined by writing function followed by the function name, followed by two brackets. We then open a curly bracket to start the function statements. It ends with a closing curly bracket. This function is invoked by just writing its name as shown:

```
<?php
    disp_welcome();
?>
```

The above function call will result in execution of statements defined inside the `disp_welcome()` function.

3.8.1 Passing Parameters to Functions

A function can be made more useful by asking it to work on the given data. We can then process different data by the same function by sending different values to it as `parameters`.

```
function disp_welcome($st1, $st2) {
```

```
    echo $st1 . '<br>';
    echo $st2;
}
```

This function is made to accept two parameters. So, while invoking this function, we have to send two parameters as shown:

```
<?php
disp_welcome('Welcome to our Shopping Mall', 'You will find different varieties of items at lowest price');
?>
```

As we can see the two strings are passed while invoking the function which will be assigned to two arguments: `$st1` and `$st2`. These arguments: `$st1` and `$st2` are then displayed.

3.8.2 Returning a Value

A function can also return processed information. To return something to the caller program, a `return` statement is used.

```
function average($a, $b, $c) {
    $av=($a+$b+$c)/3;
    return $av;
}
```

This function calculates the average of three variables and returns the computed result to the caller.

3.9 GLOBAL VARIABLES

When any variable is defined within a function, it becomes its local variable and if we want that variable to be used in another function, we have to send it to another function as an argument. But if we define a variable as global, then it can be accessed by any of the functions and the effect of processing done by one function on that variable will be visible to another function.

To make a variable global, just define it at the top, that is, above the body of any function as shown:

```
<?php
    $l=50;
    $b=10;
    $a=0;
function area() {
```

```
    $a=$l*$b;
}
echo "Area of rectangle is " . $a;
?>
```

We can see in the above program that we have made three global variables, `$l`, `$b` and `$a`. Variables `$l` and `$b` are initialised to values 50 and 10 respectively and being global variables (declared before the function), they can be directly accessed in the `area()` function. Moreover, the area of rectangle computed by `area()` function in `$a` variable can be accessed outside the body of the function.

3.10 DISPLAYING INFORMATION ABOUT PHP

The phpinfo() function is used to output PHP information and is very useful for troubleshooting. The phpinfo() function options are:

Name	Description
INFO_GENERAL	The configuration line, php.ini location, build date, web server, system etc.
INFO_CREDITS	PHP 5 credits
INFO_CONFIGURATION	Local and master values for PHP directives
INFO_MODULES	Loaded modules
INFO_ENVIRONMENT	Environment variable information
INFO_VARIABLES	All predefined variables from EGPCS (Environment, GET, POST, Cookie, Server)
INFO_LICENSE	PHP license information
INFO_ALL	Shows all of the above. This is the default value

Example:

```
<html>
    <body>
        <?php
            // Show all PHP information
            phpinfo();
        ?>
        <?php
            // Show only the general information
```

```
            phpinfo(INFO_GENERAL);
        ?>
    </body>
</html>
```

Output:

All the information of PHP will be displayed (Figure 3.9).

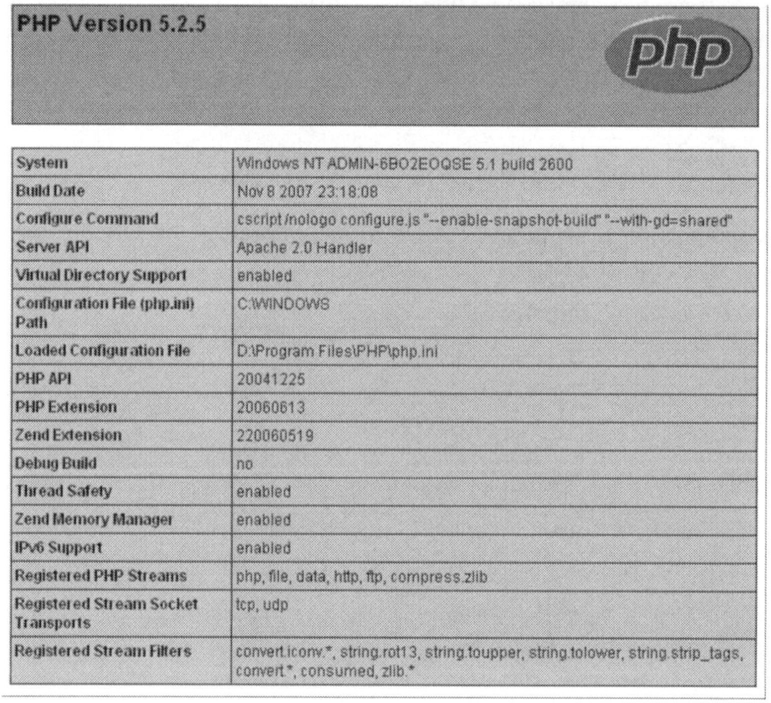

System	Windows NT ADMIN-6B02EOQSE 5.1 build 2600
Build Date	Nov 8 2007 23:18:08
Configure Command	cscript /nologo configure.js "--enable-snapshot-build" "--with-gd=shared"
Server API	Apache 2.0 Handler
Virtual Directory Support	enabled
Configuration File (php.ini) Path	C:\WINDOWS
Loaded Configuration File	D:\Program Files\PHP\php.ini
PHP API	20041225
PHP Extension	20060613
Zend Extension	220060519
Debug Build	no
Thread Safety	enabled
Zend Memory Manager	enabled
IPv6 Support	enabled
Registered PHP Streams	php, file, data, http, ftp, compress.zlib
Registered Stream Socket Transports	tcp, udp
Registered Stream Filters	convert.iconv.*, string.rot13, string.toupper, string.tolower, string.strip_tags, convert.*, consumed, zlib.*

Figure 3.9 ***Output of Phpinfo() Function***

SUMMARY

The outline of the topics that we covered in this chapter is:

- how to make and run small PHP programs
- how HTML and PHP scripts are embedded
- how variables are initialised in PHP scripts
- Usage of conditional statements: if else and switch statements
- how different loops work: while, do..while, for, foreach etc.

- how arrays are used: single dimensional, associative and multidimensional arrays
- how to get feedback from users with the help of forms
- role of $_GET, $_POST and $_REQUEST array in passing information from one form to another
- what are functions and how parameters are passed to them
- what are global variables

In the next chapter, we will concentrate on the creation of a database and tables via PHP scripts. That is, we will learn how to maintain the information in the data tables through PHP programs. We will see how to get information from the user and how that information can be stored in the back-end tables. We will also see how to retrieve desired information from the tables through the PHP interface and finally how to delete the undesired records from the table.

4

PHP and MySQL Programming

This chapter covers how to create databases and tables in MySQL via PHP scripts. Instead of maintaining the information in the data tables through the MySQL prompt, we will learn doing it through PHP programming. Maintenance of database tables through the MySQL prompt is cumbersome and also requires the user to be well versed with SQL commands. To make it easier for visitors to our website, we will provide them an easy-to-use GUI form (made in PHP) and the information entered in the form will be automatically stored in the database tables. Similarly, to fetch some information from the tables, the visitor will be asked to fill an enquiry form and the desired information will be retrieved from the database and displayed. The information of the database name, table name and different MySQL commands used to extract information from the database will not be visible to the visitor, making the web application more secure. In this chapter we will make and understand small PHP modules that perform the following tasks:

- Creating a table in PHP
- Getting information from the user
- Inserting records in the table
- Retrieving all records from the table
- Searching records from the table (retrieving only the desired records, not all)
- Deleting records from the table

Before we begin with these tasks, let us first look at all the statements and functions that we will require for accessing MySQL from PHP.

4.1 FUNCTIONS ACCESSING MYSQL FROM PHP

The following are the functions that we will be using for selecting databases, accessing tables, executing SQL statements and fetching results. Let us look at them one by one:

4.1.1 MySQL_Connect()

This function is used for establishing the connection to the MySQL database. It returns `true` if the connection is established else `false` is returned. This function takes three parameters; the first one is hostname, then user-id and then password.

Syntax:

```
mysql_connect ("$servername","$dbuser","$dbpassword");
```

Example:

```
$connect = mysql_connect("localhost", "root", "mce");
if(!$connect) { die("Please, check your server connection."); }
```

`Die` is the command to exit. If the `mysql_connect()` returns false then we exit from the PHP scripts using `die` command after displaying the message: "Please, check your server connection".

This example can also be written as:

```
$connect = mysql_connect("localhost", "root", "mce") or die("Please, check your
server connection.");
```

When two statements are connected with `or` operator, then the second statement is only executed if the first statement returns `false`.

4.1.2 Mysql_Select_db()

This function is used for selecting a MySQL database to be operated on.

Syntax:

```
bool mysql_select_db (string $database_name [, resource $link_identifier])
```

This selects the active database on the server with which connection is established by using a link identifier. If the link identifier is not specified, the last link opened by `mysql_connect()` is assumed. If no such link is found, it will create one by executing the MySQL with no arguments. An error is displayed if a connection is not established. It returns `true` if the database is found in the MySQL server else `false` is returned.

Examples:

- `mysql_select_db("shopping",$connect);`
- `mysql_select_db("shopping");`

4.1.3 Mysql_Query()

This function sends the query to the currently active database on the server and the records fetched are stored in an array.

Syntax:

```
resource mysql_query (string $query [, resource $link_identifier])
```

where `link_identifier` identifies the connection established with MySQL. If the link identifier is not specified, the last link opened by `mysql_connect()` is assumed. If no such link is found, it tries to create one by executing `mysql_connect()` with no arguments. An error is displayed if a connection is not established.

The returned result resource may be passed to `mysql_fetch_array()`, to display fetched records one by one.

Example:

```
$result = mysql_query($query) or die(mysql_error());
```

The `$result` returned by `mysql_query()` contains all the records fetched from the table on the basis of the specified query and by passing this array of records `$result` to `mysql_fetch_array()`, we can extract one record at a time from it.

4.1.4 $_POST()

The `$_POST` array is an array which collects the values sent from a form using HTTP POST method. When the user clicks the `"Submit"` button, the value of the `$_POST["variable_name"]` will be automatically set by PHP where `variable_name` is the id of the input HTML tag used on the form. The destination PHP script can use the `$_POST` array to retrieve the form data with the help of the following code:

```
local_variable=$_POST["variable_name"];
```

Hence `local_variable` will contain the information passed by another web form.

4.1.5 mysql_fetch_array()

This function is used for fetching one record at a time from the array of records (produced as a result of a query). It gets one row from the recordset and returns `true`, and `false` when there are no more rows left in the recordset. It returns a row from a recordset as an associative array or a numeric array.

Syntax:

```
row=mysql_fetch_array(data,array_type)
```

where the data pointer is the result from the `mysql_query()` function and array_type is optional that specifies what kind of array to return. Its value can be:

MYSQL_ASSOC -	Associative array
MYSQL_NUM -	Numeric array
MYSQL_BOTH -	Default. Both associative and numeric array

Note: After the data is retrieved, this function moves to the next row in the recordset. Each subsequent call to `mysql_fetch_array()` returns the next row in the recordset.

Example:

```
$row = mysql_fetch_array($results)
```

One record is extracted from the recordset `$results` and is stored in variable: `$row`

4.1.6 Extract()

This function is used for extracting all the variables stored in the specified array (or record).

Syntax:

```
extract(array name)
```

Example:

```
extract($row);
```

If `$row` contains a record (row) of a table, say `customers`, with two fields say `userid` and `address`, then by the above `extract()` function, two variables `$userid` and `$address` will be generated that will contain the information of `userid` and `address` in that particular row (record).

4.1.7 mysql_close()

This is a very important command as it closes the connection to the database server. It is a better idea to close the connection with the server when all the operations are performed on the database or else it may diminish the efficiency of the web host.

4.1.8 mysql_numrows()

To know how many rows there are in the resultset, we use this function. Recall that we get the rows extracted from the table and stored in the form of resultset when an SQL query consisting of `"select"` clause is executed. Thus this function counts how many rows there are in the given resultset.

Syntax:

```
mysql_numrows(resultset name);
```

Example:

```
$num=mysql_numrows($result);
```

This will set the value of `$num` to be the number of rows stored in `$result` (the array where the records retrieved from the table are stored on execution of the SQL statement with select clause).

4.2 CREATING A TABLE IN PHP

Creating a table in a MySQL database from PHP script requires the following steps:

1. Establishing connection with MySQL server
2. Creating a database (if it does not exist). If database already exists then skip this step
3. Selecting the database (in which table is to be created)
4. Writing the SQL statement for creating a table
5. Executing the SQL statement

To understand the above steps let us look at the following program that creates a table named `products` in the `shopping` database. The products table that we are going to create will have five fields (columns): `id`, `item_code`, `item_name`, `quantity` and `price`. The fields `id`, `item_code` and `quantity` are considered to be of `int` (integer) data type, `item_name` of `character` data type and `price` of `float` data type.

createtable_products.php

```
<?php
$user="username";
$password="password";
$connect = mysql_connect("localhost", $user, $password) or die ("Please
check your server connection.");

//create the database if it doesn't already exist
$create = mysql_query("CREATE DATABASE IF NOT EXISTS shopping") or
die(mysql_error());
mysql_select_db("shopping");

$sql = "CREATE TABLE products(
    id int(6) NOT NULL auto_increment,
    item_code int(4),
    item_name varchar(50),
```

```
        quantity int(4),
        price float)";
        $res = mysql_query($sql) or die (mysql_error());
    echo "products table successfully created!";
?>
```

The above program has all the five steps of creating a table. In the first two lines, two variables `$user` and `$password` are initialised to the username and password of the MySQL server respectively. From the third line onwards, we see that the five steps for creating a table are executed. Let us see look at each statement step by step:

1. Establishing connection with MySQL server

Before proceeding with the creation of a database or a table, first we need to connect to the MySQL server. The connection is established with the help of a valid user name and password.

```
$connect = mysql_connect("localhost", $user, $password) or die ("Please check
your server connection.");
```

In the above command `localhost` signifies that the MySQL server is installed on the local machine. The string `localhost` will be replaced by the IP address of the server or server name (Example: sqlserver.com or 216.237.120.79) if we try to connect to the remote server. The `$user` and `$password` variables contain the valid userid and password supplied by the administrator. The keyword `die` is for displaying error messages if any information supplied is wrong.

2. Creating a database

After we are connected to the MySQL server, we must then create the database (if it does not exist) followed by selecting it i.e. making it active in memory. The command for creating database is:

```
$create = mysql_query("CREATE DATABASE IF NOT EXISTS shopping") or
die(mysql_error());
```

The above statement creates a database named `"shopping"` if it doesn't already exist. If the database is already there, this command won't do anything.

3. Selecting the database

Selecting the database means loading the database in memory (i.e. making it active). The command for selecting a given database is:

```
mysql_select_db("shopping");
```

The above command selects the database `shopping`. Now all SQL statements that are executed will be applied to the tables belonging to this (`shopping`) active database.

4. Writing the SQL statement for creating the table

The SQL statement given below creates a table named `products` that has five fields out of which `id` field is set to `auto_increment` i.e. its value will automatically increase by 1 with every record inserted.

```
$sql = "CREATE TABLE products(
id int(6) NOT NULL auto_increment,
item_code int(4),
item_name varchar(50),
quantity int(4),
price float)";
```

The rest of the fields (columns) in the table are `item_code` that will store an integer values of up to four digits, `item_name` field will store the name of the item of up to 50 characters long and `quantity` field can store an integer value of up to four digits and `price` field can store a fractional value (value with decimal points).

5. Executing the SQL statement

The statement given below executes the above SQL statement of creating the products table

```
$res = mysql_query($sql) or die (mysql_error());
```

The `$res` variable is for storing the result of the execution of the SQL statement.

4.3 GETTING INFORMATION FROM THE USER

In every website, getting information from the visitor is an essential requirement. Either in the form of a Sign Up form, Order form or a Feedback form, we gather information from the visitor. Getting information from the visitor requires the following steps:

1. Providing the text boxes, radio buttons, checkboxes etc. to the visitor to enter information
2. Submitting the information for some action. The action may be either storing the information in the tables, fetching information from the tables or updating information in the tables

Consider the following program, where we provide two textboxes to the visitor to fill in `userid` and `address`. After filling up the information, the visitor is supposed to select `submit` button to proceed with necessary action.

enterinfo.php

```
<html>
    <head>
```

```
    </head>
    <body>
        <form action="insertrec.php" method="post">
            <table border="0" cellspacing="1" cellpadding="3">
                <tr><td>Userid: </td><td> <input size="20" type="text"
                    name="userid"></td></tr>
                <tr><td>Address: </td><td> <input size="80" type="text"
                    name="add"></td></tr>
                <tr><td><input type="submit" name="submit" value="Submit">
                    </td><td><input type="reset" value="Cancel"></td></tr>
            </table>
        </form>
    </body>
</html>
```

Explanation

```
<form action="insertrec.php" method="post">
```

The above statement means that when the `Submit` button is pressed, we will be navigated to the file: `insertrec.php` and the HTTP Request method that is used for passing the information entered in the current file is `Post` method.

In other words, when the user clicks the "Submit" button, the `$_POST["userid"]` and `$_POST["add"]` variables will be automatically initialised to the data entered by the user. The information in these variables can be retrieved in the `insertrec.php` file to physically store it in the table.

```
<table border="0" cellspacing="1" cellpadding="3">
```

This statement defines a table with the specified cell spacing and cell padding. Tables are usually used for the purpose of aligning labels and textboxes on the web form.

```
<tr><td>Userid: </td><td> <input size="20" type="text"
            name="userid"></td></tr>
<tr><td>Address: </td><td> <input size="80" type="text"
              name="add"></td></tr>
```

The user is provided with two textboxes to enter the information (we can use other controls like checkboxes, radio buttons, drop down lists etc. to get information from the user). The information entered by the user will be automatically stored in `$_POST["userid"]` and `$_POST["add"]` variables.

```
<tr><td><input type="submit" name="submit" value="Submit">
```

This will navigate us to another PHP web form: `insertrec.php` file.

The conclusion is that the information filled up by the user is stored in `$_POST["userid"]` and `$_POST["add"]` variables and is sent to `insertrec.php` file for further action.

4.4 INSERTING RECORDS IN THE TABLE

The information sent by the user via enterinfo.php program: userid and add (for address) is passed to insertrec.php program (as declared by the statement: <form action="insertrec.php" method="post">). In the insertrec.php program we will be storing the received information in a table. Insertion of records in a table through PHP program requires the following steps:

1. Establishing connection with the MySQL server
2. Selecting the database containing the table in which record is supposed to be inserted
3. Collecting information to be stored in the table
4. Writing the SQL statement for inserting the record
5. Executing the SQL statement

Let us observe the following PHP program where a step-by-step approach is taken for inserting the information (`userid` and `add`) passed from the previous PHP program (`enterinfo.php`) into a table named `customers`. The program is as shown below:

insertrec.php

```
<?php
    connect = mysql_connect("localhost", "root", "mce") or die ("Please,
        check the server connection.");
    mysql_select_db("shopping");
    userid = $_POST['userid'];
    add = $_POST['add'];

    $sql = "INSERT INTO customers (userid, address) VALUES ('$userid',
    '$add')";
    $result = mysql_query($sql) or die(mysql_error());
    echo "Record is saved";
?>
```

Explanation

The five steps of inserting records can be seen:

1. Establishing connection with MySQL server

```
connect = mysql_connect("localhost", "root", "mce") or die ("Please,
    check the server connection.");
```

The above statement establishes the connection with the local MySQL server with the `userid` as `"root"` and the `password` of the root is assumed to be `"mce"` (any text).

2. Selecting the database

```
mysql_select_db("shopping");
```

This statement selects the database "`shopping`" (i.e. loads it in memory) so that we can insert record in its `"customers"` table (We assume that a `customers` table exists in the shopping table and the table has two fields (columns): `userid` and `address`).

3. Collecting information to be stored in the table

```
userid = $_POST['userid'];
add = $_POST['add'];
```

These two statements are for collecting information from the `$_POST` array (containing the information – `userid` and `add` passed by the `enterinfo.php` program).

4. Writing SQL statement for inserting the record

```
$sql = "INSERT INTO customers (userid, address) VALUES ('$userid', '$add')";
```

This is the SQL statement for inserting the record into `customers` table of `shopping` database. It is a simple SQL statement where `$userid` and `$add` represent the information entered by the visitor and are enclosed in single quotes as both contain text matter.

5. Executing the SQL statement

```
$result = mysql_query($sql) or die(mysql_error());
```

This statement executes the SQL statement stored in `$sql` variable and the result of the execution (whether record insertion was successful or failure) is stored in `$result` variable.

Note: Inserting records in a table requires two PHP programs; one gathers information from the visitor and passes it to the other program, while the second program processes the information received from the earlier program. Processing here means any task such as inserting the information into the table, searching information from the table, deleting information from the table etc.

It also means that the process of searching records from the table (Section 4.6) and deleting records from the table (in Section 4.7) will also be requiring two programs, one for gathering information and the other for processing information.

4.5 RETRIEVING ALL RECORDS FROM THE TABLE

The information stored in the back-end database tables is often required to be retrieved for displaying it to visitors to our website. Good examples of records retrieval include the list of the products for sale on a website, display of facilities provided on different plans (PostPaid or Prepaid) on a telecommunication website or display of examination results on a university website etc.

Retrieving all records from the table requires following five steps:

1. Establishing a connection with the MySQL server
2. Selecting the database containing the table whose records have to be retrieved
3. Writing the SQL statement for selecting the desired fields from the table
4. Executing the SQL statement and storing the fetched records in a resultset
5. Fetching one row at a time from the result set and displaying it one by one

Let us look at the following program that fetches all the records from the `customers` table of `shopping` database and displays them on the screen in tabular format. All the steps followed in retrieval of records can be clearly seen in the program below:

customers_list.php

```
<?php
   $connect = mysql_connect("localhost", "root", "mce")
      or die("Please, check your server connection.");
   mysql_select_db("shopping");
   $query = "SELECT userid, address from customers ";
   $results = mysql_query($query) or die(mysql_error());
   echo "<table border=\"1\">\n";
  echo "<th>Userid</th><th>Address</th>\n";
  while ($row = mysql_fetch_array($results)) {
   extract($row);
   echo  "<tr>";
   echo  "<td>";
   echo  $userid;
   echo  "</td>";
   echo  "<td>";
   echo  $address;
   echo  "</td>";
   echo  "</tr>\n";
   }
```

```
    echo "</table>\n";
?>
```

Explanation

The five steps of retrieving all records from the table are clearly visible:

1. Establishing a connection with the MySQL server

```
$connect = mysql_connect("localhost", "root", "mce")
or die("Please, check your server connection.");
```

This statement establishes the connection with the local MySQL server with the userid as "`root`" and the password of the root is assumed to be "`mce`" (any text).

2. Selecting the database

```
mysql_select_db("shopping");
```

This statement selects the database "`shopping`" so that we can retrieve records from its `customers` table. (We assume that a customers table exists in the shopping database and it consists of two fields (columns): `userid` and `address`).

3. Writing the SQL statement for selecting the desired fields

```
$query = "SELECT userid, address from customers ";
```

This is the SQL statement that will retrieve `userid` and `address` fields (columns) from the `customers` table.

4. Executing the SQL statement

```
$results = mysql_query($query) or die(mysql_error());
```

This statement executes the SQL statement, and all the fetched records (rows) from the `customers` table are stored temporarily in the resultset: `$results`. The resultset is a sort of array where rows of the tables are fetched and temporarily stored.

5. Fetching one row at a time from the result set

```
while ($row = mysql_fetch_array($results)) {
```

The `mysql_fetch_array()` is a function used for extracting one record (row) at a time from the array of records - `$results` (resultset). In the above statement, we are using a `while` loop for extracting one row at a time from the resultset and storing it in a variable `$row`. When all rows from the resultset are extracted (i.e. when there are no rows left in the $results array), `mysql_fetch_array()` function will return `false`, hence will come out of the `while` loop. The row returned by the `mysql_fetch_array()` from the resultset will be in a form of an associative array or a numeric array. In other words, the `$row` that will contain one row (record) at a time is an associative array or a numeric array.

In the `while` loop, we use extract function to extract the fields (columns) from array `$row` that is assumed to contain one row at a time of the table:

```
extract($row);
```

The extract function extracts all the fields (columns) stored in the specified array. After getting all the fields extracted from `$row` array, they are displayed one by one with the help of the following statements:

```
echo "<tr>";
echo "<td>";
echo $userid;
echo "</td>";
echo "<td>";
echo $address;
echo "</td>";
echo "</tr>\n";
```

The `$userid` and `$address` are the variables or fields that are extracted from `$row` array (by using `extract()` function) which contain the information of the userid and address.

4.6 SEARCHING RECORDS FROM THE TABLE

Searching is the most popular and frequent activity among visitors to a website. Visitors enter certain keywords (text) related to the product, service etc. which they are interested in and submit it. That keyword is searched for in the database tables and the matching rows (records) are displayed on the screen. A search engine is the most common example of searching records as here we specify the keyword related to the object whose information we want to look at. On submission of keyword, we get the desired information.

Let us make a searching program where a visitor enters the `userid` of the user whose information (address) he wants to access. The specified userid will be then searched in the `customers` table of `shopping` database and the information (address) of the matching record is displayed on the screen.

As said earlier, the tasks of insertion, searching, deletion etc. in the database require two PHP programs, one gathers information from the visitor and passes on to the next program which subsequently takes the necessary action.

Let us name the first PHP program which will prompt the visitor to enter `userid` (whose information has to be searched) as `search.php` and its code may appear as shown below:

search.php

```
<html>
    <head>
    </head>
    <body>
        <form action="searchcustomer.php" method="post">
            <table border="0" cellspacing="1" cellpadding="3">
                <tr><td>Userid: </td><td> <input size="20" type="text"
                    name="userid"></td></tr>
                <tr><td><input type="submit" name="submit" value="Submit">
                    </td><td><input type="reset" value="Cancel"></td></tr>
            </table>
        </form>
    </body>
</html>
```

We can see that in the above program, the `userid` entered by the visitor will be passed to the PHP program named: `searchcustomer.php` that will search the information of the user from the tables whose userid is passed. Searching records from the table requires the following steps:

1. Establishing a connection with the MySQL server
2. Selecting the database containing the table in which the desired record is supposed to be searched
3. Getting the criteria i.e. the condition to retrieve the record
4. Writing the SQL statement for searching the record
5. Executing the SQL statement and retrieving the desired record in the resultset
6. Fetching one row at a time from the result set and displaying it one by one

Let us study the following `searchcustomer.php` program that fetches the `userid` sent by `search.php` program and searches the `customers` table of `shopping` database and retrieves the desired information (address) of the `userid` supplied and displays it on the screen.

searchcustomer.php

```
<?php
    $connect = mysql_connect("localhost", "root", "mce")
```

```
    or die("Please, check your server connection.");
    mysql_select_db("shopping");
    $uid=$_POST['userid'];
    $query = "SELECT userid, address from customers where userid like
    '$uid'";
    $results = mysql_query($query) or die(mysql_error());
    echo "<table border=\"1\">\n";
    echo "<th>Userid</th><th>Address</th>\n";
    while ($row = mysql_fetch_array($results)) {
        extract($row);
        echo "<tr>";
        echo "<td>";
        echo $userid;
        echo "</td>";
        echo "<td>";
        echo $address;
        echo "</td>";
        echo "</tr>\n";
    }
    echo "</table>\n";
?>
```

Explanation

The six steps of searching the desired record from the table can be easily seen in the above program:

1. Establishing a connection with the MySQL server

```
$connect = mysql_connect("localhost", "root", "mce")
    or die("Please, check your server connection.");
```

This statement establishes the connection with the local MySQL server with the `userid` as `"root"` and the password as `"mce"`.

2. Selecting the database containing the table to be searched

```
mysql_select_db("shopping");
```

This statement selects the database "shopping" so that we can retrieve the desired record from its customers table.

3. Getting the criteria i.e. the condition to retrieve the record

```
$uid=$_POST['userid'];
```

As we know the current program is invoked by the earlier program search.php where the visitor was prompted to enter the userid of the person whose information is required. In search.php program, after entering the userid of the person, when Submit button is clicked, the current PHP program: searchuser.php will be invoked and here, we retrieve that userid (entered in the search.php program) through $_POST array and store it in a local variable: $uid.

4. Writing the SQL statement for searching the record

```
$query = "SELECT userid, address from customers where userid like '$uid'";
```

This is the SQL statement that retrieves the userid and address fields from the customers table whose userid is supplied from search.php file.

5. Executing the SQL statement and retrieving the desired record in the resultset

```
$results = mysql_query($query) or die(mysql_error());
```

Executing the SQL statement and storing the fetched records from the table in the resultset: $results

6. Fetching one row at a time from the result set and displaying it one by one

```
while ($row = mysql_fetch_array($results)) {
    extract($row);
    echo "<tr>";
    echo "<td>";
    echo $userid;
    echo "</td>";
    echo "<td>";
    echo $address;
    echo "</td>";
    echo "</tr>\n";
}
```

The mysql_fetch_array() is a function used for fetching one record at a time from the array of records ($results). It gets one row from the resultset and stores it in the variable $row.

The `extract()` function is used for extracting all the variables i.e. fields or columns stored in the `$row` array. The `$row` is an array that contains one record of the customer and the elements of this array are the fields (columns) of the record. The extracted variables `$userid` and `$address` (from `$row`) are displayed one by one with the help of `while` loop.

4.7 DELETING RECORDS FROM THE TABLE

In the task of deleting a record from the database table, again we will require two PHP programs; one of them will prompt the visitor to enter the `userid` of the user to be deleted. After entering the `userid`, when the visitor clicks the Submit button, that `userid` will be passed to another PHP program which then deletes the record from the `customers` table that contains the supplied `userid`. There is no need of making the first PHP program (that asks the visitor to enter `userid`) from scratch as we can use the same one that we used in searching program (Section 4.6), i.e. `search.php`. The only change we need to do in that program is that we replace the following statement:

```
<form action="searchcustomer.php" method="post">
```

with the below statement:

```
<form action="deletecustomer.php" method="post">
```

because this time, we want the `userid` to be passed to `deletecustomer.php` program instead of `searchcustomer.php` program.

The task of deleting records from the table requires the following steps:

1. Establishing a connection with the MySQL server
2. Selecting the database containing the table from where we want to delete the record(s)
3. Getting the criteria i.e. the condition to delete the record
4. Writing the SQL statement for deleting the record(s)
5. Executing the SQL statement to physically delete the record(s) from the table

Let us study the following `deleteuser.php` program that fetches the `userid` sent by `search.php` program and deletes the record with the matching `userid` from the `customers` table of `shopping` database and displays a message: "Record successfully deleted" on successful deletion of record.

deleteuser.php

```
<?php
   $connect = mysql_connect("localhost", "root", "mce")
      or die("Please, check your server connection.");
   mysql_select_db("shopping");
   $uid=$_POST['userid'];
```

```
    $sql = "DELETE from customers where userid like '$uid'";
    $res = mysql_query($sql) or die (mysql_error());
    echo "Record successfully deleted";
?>
```

Explanation

The five steps of deleting the desired record(s) from the table can be seen:

1. *Establishing a connection with the MySQL server*

```
$connect = mysql_connect("localhost", "root", "mce")
or die("Please, check your server connection.");
```

This statement establishes the connection with the local MySQL server with the `userid` as `"root"` and the password as "`mce`".

2. *Selecting the database containing the table*

```
mysql_select_db("shopping");
```

This statement selects the database `"shopping"` so that we can delete the desired record from its `customers` table.

3. *Getting the criteria i.e. the condition to delete the record*

```
$uid=$_POST['userid'];
```

We know that the current program `deleteuser.php` is invoked by an earlier program named `search.php` where the user was asked to enter the `userid` of the person whose information has to be erased. The `userid` entered in that program is passed to the current program and here, we retrieve it through `$_POST` array and store it in a local variable: `$uid.`

4. *Writing the SQL statement for deleting the record(s)*

```
$sql = "DELETE from customers where userid like '$uid'";
```

This is the SQL statement that deletes the record from the `customers` table whose `userid` is supplied from `search.php` file.

5. *Executing the SQL statement to delete the record(s)*

```
$res = mysql_query($sql) or die (mysql_error());
```

Executing the SQL statement that physically deletes the record from the `customers` table of the `shopping` database.

SUMMARY

In this chapter, we have seen different functions that are used for accessing MySQL tables from PHP programs. Then using these functions we have seen all the modules that are essential in making a complete website. We also saw the statements used in these modules along with their meanings. The modules that we saw in this chapter were: Creation of table, Getting information from the user, Inserting records in the table, Retrieving all records from the table, Searching desired records from the table and Deleting records from the table.

In the next chapter, we will see the sample output of our Shopping Cart Project. We will see step-by-step the different outputs that will appear on selecting different links and buttons on our website. Also we will see how different items can be selected in the Shopping Cart, how Shopping Cart is updated and finally how an order is placed on our website.

5
AJAX

In this chapter we will look at:

- AJAX basics
- Limitations of traditional web applications
- Items for implementing AJAX

5.1 AJAX BASICS

Ajax stands for Asynchronous JavaScript and XML. Usually in a traditional web application, when we want to access certain data from the database on the server, an HTTP request from the client is made to the server either by GET or POST method. After receiving the data from the server, the web page needs to be *reloaded* to show the fetched data. In AJAX technology we can request and receive the data from the server in the background and can display it on the page without a reload.

With AJAX, JavaScript communicates directly with the server, through the JavaScript XMLHttpRequest object (XML over HTTP) and it is with the help of this object that a web page can make a request to, and get a response from a web server without reloading the page.

A traditional web page takes a longer time to get the desired results because of the *round trip*: all the information entered by the user on the form is sent from the client to the web server. The web server processes the data and the desired information is sent back to the client. Even if small changes are made in the form, all the data on the form is sent to the web server and the entire page is refreshed. In a traditional web application, we don't have a facility to refresh only a small portion of the web page; instead the complete page is refreshed, which is very time consuming

In Figure 5.1, we can clearly see the three steps of communication performed in the traditional web application model:

The client makes an HTTP request to the web server.

The web server searches for the desired data from the database and

The fetched data (from the database) is sent back (postback) to the client (the whole page is reloaded with the new information).

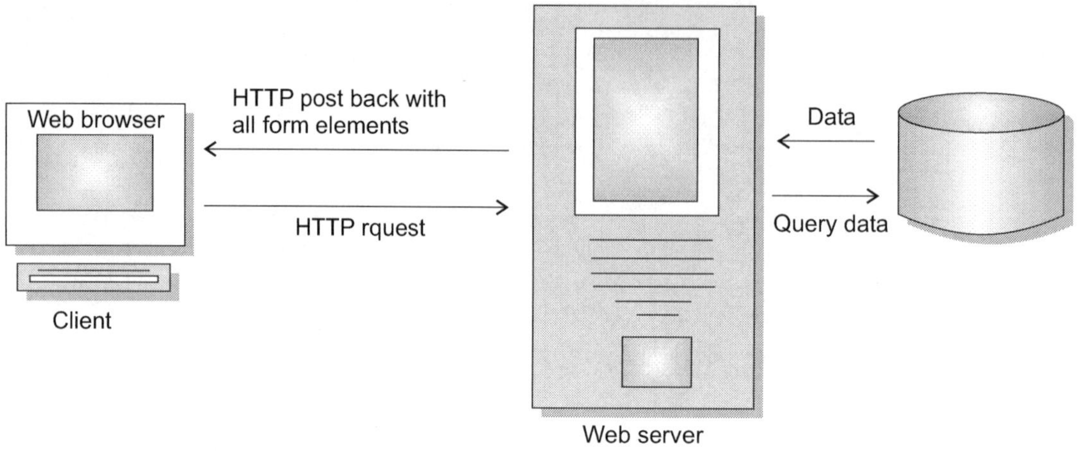

Figure 5.1 ***Traditional Web Application Model***

We face the following limitations in a conventional web application.

5.2 LIMITATIONS OF TRADITIONAL WEB APPLICATIONS

- All the data of the form is sent to the web server—even if small changes are made
- Results in network congestion because of large amount of data transferred during a postback
- Until and unless the user clicks a button or another control that posts data back to the server, no result will be displayed

In AJAX, A stands for *Asynchronous* and it means getting server response without refreshing the whole page. We can even update a portion of a web page with this technology. Let's try for a deeper understanding of what AJAX consists of.

With AJAX all the above limitations of traditional web applications are removed as it consists of following items:

- XmlHttpRequest
- JavaScript
- DOM (Document Object Model)
- CSS (Cascading Style Sheets)

5.3 ITEMS FOR IMPLEMENTING AJAX

5.3.1 XmlHttpRequest

It is this object that is used to talk to the server asynchronously, meaning it allows the browser to talk to the server without requiring a postback of the entire web page. The way this capability is provided varies from browser to browser. For example, in Internet Explorer, this capability is provided by the MSXML ActiveX component. With Mozilla Firefox and other web browsers, this capability is provided by the object called XmlHttpRequest.

5.3.2 JavaScript

Ajax applications use JavaScript code for the following reasons:

- It is a scripting language which is interpreted
- The syntax of commands is easier to learn
- It can automate several tasks like validation of userid, email id etc.

Note: JavaScript is the client side scripting language which is supported by all major browsers.

5.3.3 DOM (Document Object Model)

It provides a tree-like structure to a web page as a set of programmable objects which can be manipulated using JavaScript code. It allows dynamic updating of a part of a web page.

5.3.4 CSS (Cascading Style Sheets)

It is a centralised way of defining all the styles to be applied to different elements of a web page at one place. It makes web applications appear more consistent and attractive. CSS styles are implemented by defining style rules in a separate document which is then referred to by the web page where styles have to be applied.

In Figure 5.2, we can clearly see that XMLHttpRequest plays a major role in performing asynchronous request in the Ajax web application model:

- The client makes an XMLHTTP Request object to communicate with the web server (fetching data from server without postback). The client may use:
- JavaScript to automate validation or navigation tasks
- CSS for applying styles uniformly
- DOM to update a part of the web page
- The Web Server searches for the desired data from the database and

- The fetched data (it may constitute a part of the whole page) is sent back to the client so as to update a portion of the web page without delay.

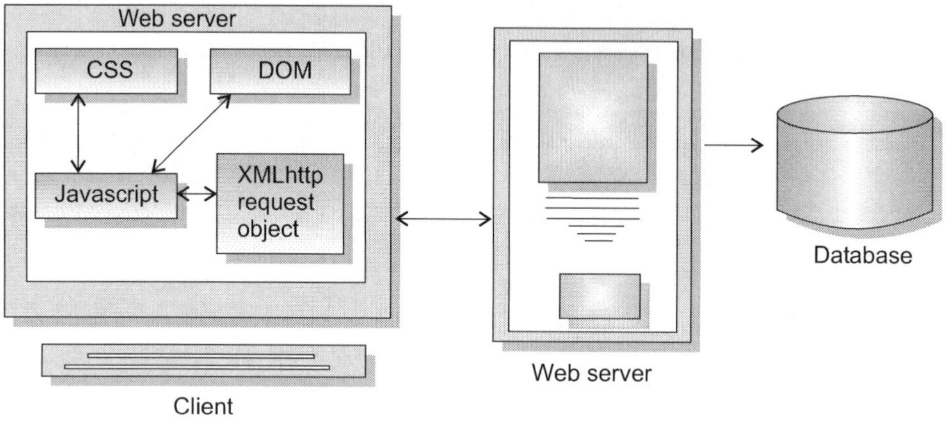

Figure 5.2 ***Ajax Web Application Model***

So, it is clear that Ajax applications make use of XmlHttpRequest object for talking to the server asynchronously and to retrieve only the data that is needed (while the user is working). And on the client side, JavaScript plays a major role as it processes the server's response and modifies the document contents by manipulating its DOM to specify that action is completed. The job of CSS is to provide a consistent look and feel to the web application.

Note: The data are mostly communicated to the web server in XML format but it may also be in JSON (JavaScript Object Notation) format (we will see it in Chapter 8).

SUMMARY

In this chapter we learnt that the main components that make up AJAX are Asynchronous JavaScript and XML and it is a technique which makes a web page highly responsive. It makes use of a XMLHttpRequest object with the help of which a web page can make a request to, and get a response from a web server without reloading the page. Also in this technique, even a small portion of a web page can be refreshed instead of the entire page. We also saw the limitation of the traditional web page in this chapter. Finally we had an introduction to all the four items used in implementing AJAX: XmlHttpRequest, JavaScript, DOM and CSS.

In the next chapter, we will see the practical demonstration of AJAX with the help of running examples. We will learn the basics of JavaScript, role of DOM in accessing form elements, the way in which an asynchronous request is placed to the server, handling of Key Events, using JavaScript in accessing form elements, performing XMLHttp Post Requests, separating JavaScript code from the PHP program, specifying our own function in JavaScript file, using CSS (cascading style sheets), sending data selected from the combo box, items selected from a list box, items selected from radio and checkboxes to the server asynchronously. Finally, we will also see how AJAX, PHP and MySQL all combine for accessing a database.

6

Web Forms–Get Wet in AJAX

In this chapter we will look at:

- JavaScript basics
- Understanding DOM
- How to place asynchronous requests to the server
- How to handle Key Events
- How form elements can be accessed through JavaScript
- Performing XMLHttp Post Requests
- How to separate JavaScript code from the web page
- How to specify our own function in .js file
- How to use CSS (cascading style sheets)
- Sending data from combobox to server asynchronously
- Sending items selected from listbox to server asynchronously
- Sending items selected from radio and checkboxes to server asynchronously
- AJAX, PHP and MySQL combined for accessing database
- Accessing database in AJAX

6.1 JAVASCRIPT BASICS

JavaScript is a lightweight, fully interpreted language which is supported by all major web browsers like Internet Explorer, Opera, Safari, Firefox etc. JavaScript code can be embedded in an HTML program by writing its statements in `<script>` element or can also be written in a separate file with extension .js and then including that JavaScript code file in <script> element. The later method is usually preferred to avoid clutter. Statements in JavaScript are terminated by a semi colon.

The following are the characteristics of JavaScript:

- It is a scripting language which is interpreted
- The syntax of commands is easier to learn
- Can automate several tasks like validation of userid, email id etc.

In the following example we create a JavaScript file named prog1.js in `htdocs` subfolder of the directory where Apache is installed and then this JavaScript file is referenced in HTML file in order to invoke the methods defined in it. The contents of both files are as under:

prog1.html

```
1. <html>
2. <head>
3. <script type="text/JavaScript" src="prog1.js"></script>
4. </head>
5. <body onload="showdata()">
6. Welcome to our Shopping Mall <br>
7. <div id="info" />
8. </body>
9. </html>
```

prog1.js

```
1. function showdata()
2. {
3. var msg;
4. msg = "We provide wide variety of items at reasonable price";
5. document.getElementById("info").innerHTML = msg;
6. }
```

Explanation of prog1.html program

```
3. <script type="text/JavaScript" src="prog1.js"></script>
```

The above instruction imports the JavaScript file: prog1.js in the current web page.

There are two ways to include JavaScript in our web page:

1. Place JavaScript in the <head> element
2. Place JavaScript in a separate file, save it with extension .js and use <script> element to include the code file (by including the JavaScript file, its codes will be merged in the HTML at that location). This approach is preferred as it keeps HTML code clean and all the JavaScript code at one place

<script> element is usually included within the <head> section to include JavaScript code file. The type of this tag is set to "text/JavaScript" to specify the type of script to be included in the <script> tag. The `src` specifies the JavaScript file name along with the path.

For example src="/javascript/prog1.js" means to look for the prog1.js script file in JavaScript folder and import it into the current web page.

```
5. <body onload="showdata()">
```

`onload()` function used in the body tag is an event handler which means that when the page is all rendered, the browser looks for the code specified in the `onload()` event and executes it. That is, the code specified in `showdata()` method (present in prog1.js script file) will be executed.

```
7. <div id="info" />
```

<div> element is a block element used for specifying the location for displaying the results. Since it takes up all the available width of the browser, larger information including tables can also be displayed with this element. We can have several <div> elements in a web page, so they are assigned separate ids.

Note: Beside <div> element, we can also use <span> element for showing results.

Why we use <div> or <span> element?

<div> and <span> element have a property called innerHTML, the contents of which can be changed dynamically. The idea is that we set up a <div> element on a page and with that page still showing, the browser sends the asynchronous request to the server and gets the result which is then placed in the innerHTML property of the <div> element.

Explanation of prog1.js

```
5. document.getElementById("info").innerHTML = msg;
```

`document.getElementById()` method is used for searching a web page for an object with the specified id. The object placed anywhere on the page with the given id is searched for by this method. The above instruction is searching for an element on the web page with id `info` (our <div> element) and sets the contents of its innerHTML property equal to that of string `msg` in order to display string contents at the location of the <div> element.

The output of the program prog1.html may appear as shown in Figure 6.1.

Output:

Figure 6.1 ***Output of the Program Prog1.html***

6.2 UNDERSTANDING DOM

Document Object Model is an object by which all the elements in an HTML document can be accessed by a JavaScript engine. When a HTML page is loaded and rendered by a browser, a document tree is constructed that represents the displayed document. This document tree is composed of elements or nodes which may contain child nodes within them that can be manipulated and updated programmatically using JavaScript code.

The root node of the web page is accessed by the global variable `document` and is considered as the starting point of all DOM manipulations. Every node in the DOM is a child of `document`. Since DOM nodes are arranged in the form of a tree structure, every DOM node has a parent and one or more children which can be accessed by `parentNode` and `childNodes` properties respectively. `parentNode` returns a DOM node object and `childNodes` returns a JavaScript array of nodes.

6.2.1 CreateElement()

This is the method to create new nodes to be added to the document. We can create any HTML element by this method.

Syntax:

```
document.createElement(tag type)
```

`tag type` is the argument sent to it

Example:

```
obld=document.createElement("b");
```

It creates a bold element by name obld

6.2.2 CreateTextNode()

This creates a DOM node representing the supplied text. This text is then nested inside the given tag. Text nodes are different from elements in the sense that no styles can be applied to them directly and hence they consume less memory. Styles are applied to the text node with the help of DOM elements containing it.

Syntax:

```
document.createTextNode (text message)
```

Example:

```
omsg=document.createTextNode("We provide wide variety of items at reasonable
price");
```

A DOM node named `omsg` is created with the above text.

6.2.3 AppendChild()

This method is for attaching the given node to the document. A node never appears in the browser window until and unless it is attached to the document using `appendChild` method. The child node can be attached to any element.

Syntax:

```
appendChild (child node)
```

Example:

```
obld.appendChild(omsg);
```

The text node `omsg` made in the above example is attached to the `obld` element made earlier. Now the text matter of the `omsg` node will appear in bold (because the `obld` element has the bold tag applied to it).

So we see that a new structure can be added to a document using these three methods: `createElement()`, `createTextNode()` and `appendChild()`.

6.2.4 <div>

In AJAX usually we use `<div>` element for displaying or modifying dynamic contents. In order to identify a `<div>` element uniquely, we tag it with a unique id. An id can be assigned to any DOM node which can then be used to refer that element later.

6.2.5 GetElementById()

This is a method to get the programmatic reference to the node with the specified id.

Syntax:

```
document.getElementById(ID);
```

This method refers to the element whose ID is supplied as argument.

Now let's understand the above DOM methods with an example. In the following example we create a JavaScript file named prog2.js in `htdocs` subfolder of the `apache` directory and then the JavaScript code is invoked by the HTML program prog2.html. The contents of both files are as under:

prog2.html

```
<html>
<head>
<script type="text/JavaScript" src="prog2.js"></script>
</head>
```

```
<body onload="showdata()">
Welcome to our Shopping Mall <br>
<div id="info" />
</body>
</html>
```

What this Program is Doing

This program is first importing the JavaScript file prog2.js in the current web page so that the functions defined in that file can be invoked from the current web page. The `onload()` event is fired when the page is all rendered, invoking the `showdata()` method specified in the JavaScript file. Also, a message "Welcome to our Shopping Mall" followed by a line break appears on the browser screen. A `<div>` element is tagged with an id `info` so that it can be referred by `getElementById()` method in the `showdata()` method of JavaScript file to display contents dynamically.

prog2.js

```
function showdata()
{
obld=document.createElement("b");
omsg=document.createTextNode("We provide wide variety of items at reasonable price");
obld.appendChild(omsg);
getdiv= document.getElementById("info");
getdiv.appendChild(obld);
}
```

What this Program is Doing

This JavaScript file contains a single function `showdata()` which when invoked creates an element named `obld` with <b> (bold) tag applied to it. Thereafter, a text node named `omsg` is created with a message: "We provide wide variety of items at reasonable price". This text node is appended to the `obld` element (so that text appears in bold when displayed). In short, the `obld` element is made containing a text message in bold. To make this text appear on the browser screen, we first find the element in the document with id `info` (It is for this reason that we have created a div element in the web page with id `info`). To make the text message in bold appear on the browser screen, the `obld` element is appended to the div element with id `info`.

The output of the program prog2.html may appear as shown in Figure 6.2.

Output:

Figure 6.2 ***Output of the Program Prog2.html***

6.3 STEPS TO PLACE ASYNCHRONOUS REQUESTS TO THE SERVER

We know that the XMLHttpRequest object is used for making asynchronous calls to the web server. So before we start with its examples, let's see the outline of the methods and properties of the XMLHttpRequest object.

Table 6.1 ***Methods of the XMLHttpRequest Object***

Method	Description
abort	Cancels the current request.
getAllResponseHeaders( )	Returns the complete set of HTTP headers as a string.
getResponseHeader("headername")	Returns the value of the specified HTTP header.
open("method","URL","boolean","uname", "pswd")	Specifies the method, URL, and other attributes of a request. The method can be of GET, POST, or PUT type. The boolean parameter specifies whether the request should be handled asynchronously or not. `True` means the request is asynchronous and `false` means the request is a synchronous one.
send(content)	Sends the request.
SetRequestHeader("label", "value")	Adds a label/value pair to the HTTP header to be sent.

Table 6.2 *Properties of the XMLHttpRequest Object*

Property	Description
onreadystatechange	An event handler that fires at every state change.
readystate	Returns the state of the object:(read-only). It may return any of the following values: 0 = uninitialised 1 = loading 2 = loaded 3 = interactive 4 = complete
responseText	Returns the response as a string (read-only)
responseXML	Returns the response as XML.
status	Returns the status as a number (like 404 for "Not Found" or 200 for "OK", 500 for "Server Error").
statusText	Returns the status as a string: "Not Found" or "OK".

In all there are five steps involved in facilitating asynchronous requests (to perform server side processing without a postback):

1. Create an XMLHttpRequest object.
2. Using this object, request data from the server.
3. Monitor for the changing of state of the request.
4. If the response is successful, retrieve data from the response stream
5. Use the response in the web page.

These steps can be better explained with the help of a running example. The following program asks the user to enter his name. As the user begins typing his name, a welcome message appears on the screen. The JavaScript code is embedded in this program (but we can always make a separate file for keeping JavaScript code). Let's make two files named ajaxform1.php and ajaxdata1.php with the contents as below in the `htdocs` subfolder of the `apache` directory.

ajaxform1.php

```
<head>
<script language="JavaScript" type="text/JavaScript">
function makeRequestObject(){
var xmlhttp=false;
try {
xmlhttp = new ActiveXObject('Msxml2.XMLHTTP');
```

```
} catch (e) {
try {
xmlhttp = new
ActiveXObject(‘Microsoft.XMLHTTP’);
} catch (E) {
xmlhttp = false;
}
}
if (!xmlhttp && typeof XMLHttpRequest!=’undefined’) {
xmlhttp = new XMLHttpRequest();
}
return xmlhttp;
}

function showdata(user)
{
var xmlhttp=makeRequestObject();
var file = ‘ajaxdata1.php?usernme=’;
xmlhttp.open(‘GET’, file + user, true);
xmlhttp.onreadystatechange=function() {
if (xmlhttp.readyState==4 && xmlhttp.status == 200) {
var content = xmlhttp.responseText;
if( content ){
document.getElementById(‘info’).innerHTML = content;
}
}
}
xmlhttp.send(null)
}
</script>
</head>

<body>
```

```
Enter your Name: <input type="text" onkeyup="showdata(this.value)"/>
<div id="info"></div>

</body>
</html>
```

ajaxdata1.php

```
<?php
echo "Welcome " . $_GET['usernme'] . " to our Shopping Mall" ;
?>
```

Explanation of the ajaxform1.php program

First of all the <body> section of any web page is executed. In the body section the code is:

```
Enter your Name: <input type="text" onkeyup="showdata(this.value)"/>
```

This code asks the user to enter his/her name and as any key is released (while typing the name), the matter typed so far is passed to the `showdata()` method as argument. Before we go further let's quickly understand different key events.

6.3.1 Handling Key Events

There are three events which deal with keys:

- keydown
- keypress
- keyup

Event	**Description**
keydown event	fires when a user presses a key on the keyboard but before any changes occur to the textbox
keypress event	fires only when a character key is pressed
keyup event	fires after changes are made to the textbox

In the `showdata()` method a XMLHttpRequest object is made. Let's recall the steps involved in performing asynchronous request to the server:

1. Create an XMLHttpRequest object.
2. Using this object, request data from the server.
3. Monitor for the changing of state of the request.
4. If the response is successful, retrieve data from the response stream
5. Use the response in the web page.

Step 1. Create an XMLHttpRequest object

XMLHttpRequest object is the object which enables JavaScript code to make asynchronous HTTP server requests. It is using this object that we can make HTTP requests, receive responses and update a region of the page completely in the background.

XMLHttpRequest object was implemented by Microsoft as an ActiveX object in Internet Explorer and is supported by all its versions except IE6.

Since in some browsers XMLHttpRequest is a native object whereas in Internet Explorer XMLHttpRequest is implemented as an ActiveX control, the method of making its instance is different for each browser.

```
var xmlhttp=makeRequestObject();
```

We are creating an XMLHttpRequest object named xmlhttp.

In order to make an HTTP request to the server using JavaScript, we need an instance of a class that provides this functionality. Such a class was originally introduced in Internet Explorer as an ActiveX object, called XMLHTTP. Then Mozilla, Safari and other browsers followed, implementing an XMLHttpRequest class that supports the methods and properties of Microsoft's original ActiveX object.

JavaScript has a built-in XMLHttpRequest() function which we can use for browsers like Firefox, Safari, and Opera. For Internet Explorer, we use the ActiveXObject; there is also a difference between IE 5.0 and IE 6.0+ in how to create the object. The following code creates an XMLHttpRequest for all browsers:

```
var xmlhttp;
if(window.XMLHttpRequest){
//For Firefox, Safari, Opera
xmlhttp = new XMLHttpRequest();
}
else if(window.ActiveXObject){
//For IE 5
xmlhttp = new ActiveXObject("Microsoft.XMLHTTP");
} else if(window.ActiveXObject){
//For IE 6+
xmlhttp = new ActiveXObject("Msxml2.XMLHTTP");
}
else{
//Error for an old browser
alert('Your browser is not IE 5 or higher, or Firefox or Safari or Opera');
   }
```

Here, first we are using the built-in JavaScript function XMLHttpRequest() for creating an XMLHttpRequest object for Firefox, Safari and Opera. If the browser does support window. Active XObject, then it is Internet Explorer. For IE versions 5.0+, use new ActiveXObject ("Microsoft. XMLHTTP") and for IE 6.0+ use new ActiveXObject("Msxml2.XMLHTTP"). If the browser does not support the built-in JavaScript function XMLHttpRequest() or ActiveXObject, then it does not support AJAX. We can also use JavaScript try-catch blocks for creating XMLHttpRequest object as used in above program:

```
var xmlhttp=false;
try {
xmlhttp = new ActiveXObject('Msxml2.XMLHTTP');
} catch (e) {
try {
xmlhttp = new
ActiveXObject('Microsoft.XMLHTTP');
} catch (E) {
xmlhttp = false;
}
}
if (!xmlhttp && typeof XMLHttpRequest!='undefined') {
xmlhttp = new XMLHttpRequest();
}
```

Here first we are trying to create a XMLHttpRequest object using Active XObject ("Msxml2.XMLHTTP") assuming that the browser is IE6+, and if it fails we try ActiveXObject("Microsoft.XMLHTTP") assuming the browser is IE5.0. If all these fail, the built-in function XMLHttpRequest() is used to create the XMLHttpRequest object.

Step 2. Using this object, request data from the server

After creating the XMLHttpRequest object, we now need to send the web request to get data from the server. The request is made using the open method.

Syntax:

```
XMLHttpRequest object.open(HTTP request method, filename to execute, boolean)
```

Where

HTTP request method:	This may be GET, POST or any other method that is supported by our server. Note: These methods are always written in upper case.
filename:	It is the URL of the file residing on the server that we are requesting. This file when executed retrieves the desired information.

boolean: It is an optional parameter to specify whether the request is asynchronous or not. If it is set to `true`, it means the request is asynchronous, that is the execution of the JavaScript function will continue without waiting for the server response (in that case, we must use an event handler to watch for the response to the request). If this parameter is set to `false`, the request is set synchronously which means JavaScript waits for a response from the server before continuing execution of code.

Example:

```
xmlhttp.open("GET","filename.php", true);
```

Here, xmlhttp is the XMLHttpRequest object. It requests the server to execute filename.php file using GET method.

Let's understand the following instruction used in the program above:

```
23. var file = 'ajaxdata1.php?usernme=';
24. xmlhttp.open('GET', file + user, true);
```

In the instruction above, we are making a request to the server with GET method and passing the file name ajaxdata1.php to be executed (residing on the server). A variable `usernme` set to the name entered by the user is also sent.

```
33. xmlhttp.send(null)
```

This is the instruction which actually sends the request to the server. The argument in it is a string for the requested file. If the request file doesn't require anything, the argument passed to this method is null. In other words, if there is no query string to be sent to the file being invoked, ajaxdata1.php, we write null in the `send()` method otherwise the query string is sent instead of null. (Query string is used while using POST method explained later).

Note: GET request doesn't require any query string to be sent to the requested file.

But things will be different in the case of the POST method.

Step 3. Monitor for the changing of state of the request

```
25. xmlhttp.onreadystatechange=function() {
26. if (xmlhttp.readyState==4 && xmlhttp.status == 200) {
27. var content = xmlhttp.responseText;
```

As said earlier when an asynchronous request is made to the server, we need to watch for the state of the request and the response to the request. For doing so, we assign a function to xmlhttp.onreadystatechange which continuously checks the status of the request:

```
xmlhttp.onreadystatechange=function()
{
if(xmlhttp.readyState==4 && xmlhttp.status == 200)
```

```
{
var resp = xmlhttp.responseText;
}
}
```

Or like this,

```
xmlhttp.onreadystatechange = functionname;


function functionname (){
if(xmlhttp.readyState == 4 && xmlhttp.status == 200){
var response = xmlhttp.responseText;
}
}
```

The readyState property holds the status of the server's response. Each time the readyState changes, the onreadystatechange function will be executed. Here are the possible values for the readyState property:

State	Description
0	The request is not initialised
1	The request has been set up
2	The request has been sent
3	The request is in process
4	The request is complete

And status is the status of the HTTP Request, like 500 for Internal Server Error, 400 for Bad Request, 401 for Unauthorized, 403 for Forbidden, 404 for Not Found, 200 means no error etc.

The onreadystatechange function checks for the state of the request. If the state has a value of 4, that means that the full server response is received. If the status has a value of 200, that means the response is OK and without any error and we can continue processing it.

Step 4. If the response is successful, retrieve data from the response stream

```
if (xmlhttp.readyState==4 && xmlhttp.status == 200) {
var content = xmlhttp.responseText;
```

Since the response is successful, we need to retrieve and process the response data. To retrieve data from the response stream, we can use the following properties:

xmlhttp.responseText will return the server response as a string of text

xmlhttp.responseXML will return the response as an XMLDocument object which we can traverse using the JavaScript DOM functions

In the above instructions, we are retrieving the server response in the form of text and assigning it to the variable `content`.

Step 5. Use the response in the web page

In this step, the response retrieved from the server is displayed on the web page.

```
if( content ){
document.getElementById('info').innerHTML = content;
}
```

In the instructions above, the object with id `info` is searched for in the document (web page). Recall that <div> element(s) are placed in the web page tagged with unique ids. These <div> elements are searched for with the help of `getElementById()` methods and their contents can be modified dynamically. In the instructions above, the element with id `info` is searched for in the web page and its innerHTML property (property used to display results) is assigned the server response stored in variable `content`. So, the response retrieved from the server is displayed at the place of element <div> of id: `info`.

Note the response generated by the server is based on the execution of the file ajaxdata1.php (placed on the server). Let's analyse what it returns.

Explanation of the ajaxdata1.php program

`ajaxdata1.php`

```
<?php
echo "Welcome " . $_GET['usernme'] . " to our Shopping Mall" ;
?>
```

This program returns the text "Welcome `name` of the user to our Shopping Mall" to the client. The `name` of the user is retrieved from `$_GET` array (explained in Chapter 4).

The output of the program ajaxform1.php may appear as shown in Figure 6.3.

Output:

As we can see in the figure, the screen displays a textbox for the user to enter his name.

Figure 6.3 ***Screen Displaying a Textbox to Enter Name***

The moment the user presses a key, a welcome message is displayed along with the matter typed by him (Figure 6.4).

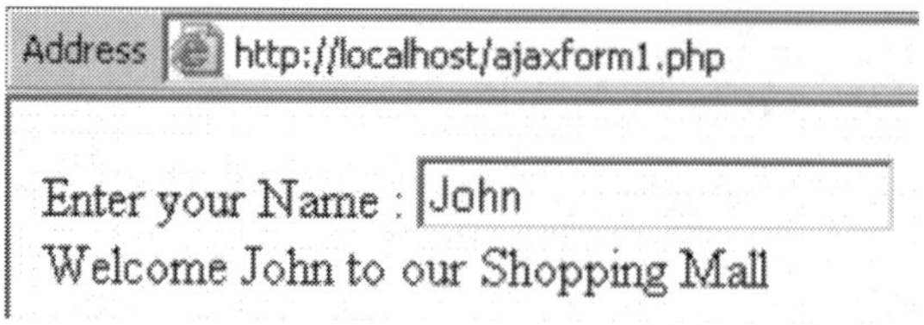

Figure 6.4 ***As Soon as the User Finishes Typing, a Message is Displayed on the Screen***

That is, with every character typed, we get the output displayed on the screen.

6.3.2 Using onblur() Event

While running the program above, we find that it doesn't wait for feeding the complete name, instead every character typed is displayed on the screen. If we want the name to be displayed when the user has finished, then the statement in <body> element is changed as follows:

```
Enter your Name: <input type="text" onblur="showdata(this.value)"/>
```

onblur event on a control results when a user press tab key (after feeding data) or clicks elsewhere on the web page, meaning when the focus on that control is lost.

6.4 ACCESSING FORM ELEMENTS

We know that `getElementById()` method is used for searching any element in the form with the given ID. Let's see the following example which demonstrates how this method can be used to access the data stored in different form elements.

This program asks the user to enter his name and email id which are then displayed on screen when the submit button is pressed. Let's make two files named ajaxaccess.php and ajaxaccessdata1.php with the contents as below in the `htdocs` subfolder of the `apache` directory.

ajaxaccess.php

```
<head>
<script language="JavaScript" type="text/JavaScript">
function makeRequestObject(){
var xmlhttp=false;
try {
xmlhttp = new ActiveXObject('Msxml2.XMLHTTP');
} catch (e) {
```

```
try {
xmlhttp = new
ActiveXObject('Microsoft.XMLHTTP');
} catch (E) {
xmlhttp = false;
}
}
if (!xmlhttp && typeof XMLHttpRequest!='undefined') {
xmlhttp = new XMLHttpRequest();
}
return xmlhttp;
}

function showdata()
{
var xmlhttp=makeRequestObject();
user=document.getElementById('user_name').value;
email=document.getElementById('email_id').value;
var file = 'ajaxaccessdata1.php?usernme=';
xmlhttp.open('GET', file + user+'&emailid='+email, true);
xmlhttp.onreadystatechange=function() {
if (xmlhttp.readyState==4 && xmlhttp.status == 200) {
var content = xmlhttp.responseText;
if( content ){
document.getElementById('info').innerHTML = content;
}
}
}
xmlhttp.send(null)
}
</script>
</head>
```

```
<body>
Enter your Name: <input type="text" name="user_name"><br>
Enter your email id : <input type="text" name="email_id"><br>
<input type="button" onclick="showdata()" value="Submit"><br><br>
<div id="info"></div>
</body>
</html>
```

Explanation of ajaxaccess.php program

First of all the <body> section of any web page is executed. In the body section the code is:

```
Enter your Name: <input type="text" name="user_name"><br>
Enter your email id : <input type="text" name="email_id"><br>
<input type="button" onclick="showdata()" value="Submit"><br><br>
<div id="info"></div>
```

The statements above prompt the user to feed his/her name and email id which are stored in variables named `user_name` and `email_id` respectively. Also it specifies that when submit button is clicked, it will invoke `showdata()` method. Finally, a div element with id `info` is defined for displaying the response sent by the server.

In the `showdata()` method as explained in the earlier program, an XMLHttpRequest object is created.

```
user=document.getElementById('user_name').value;
email=document.getElementById('email_id').value;
```

The values entered in the textboxes named `user_name` and `email_id` in the <body> section are retrieved and stored in variables `user` and `email` respectively.

```
var file = 'ajaxaccessdata1.php?usernme=';
xmlhttp.open('GET', file + user+'&emailid='+email, true);
```

We are making a request to the server with GET method and pass the filename ajaxaccessdata1.php to be executed and also pass the name and email id of the user to this filename. The data is passed to a file in the following format:

```
filename?variable1=value1&variable2=value2.....
```

In the target filename, the values: value1, value2 can be accessed using `$_GET` array

```
Example: echo $_GET['variable1'];
```

Since an asynchronous request is made to the server, we need to watch for the state of the request and the response to the request. For doing so, we take the help of the event handler: *onreadystatechange* which fires at every state change. So, whenever the state of the request changes, the `function()` is executed where value of the *readyState* property is checked (to see if it has become 4 meaning the request is complete i.e. full server response is received) and also the status of the HTTP request is checked to see if its value is 200 which means no error.

The response is then retrieved from the response stream in the form of text (it can be in XML and JSON form also) and is assigned to the variable `content`.

Then, the element with id `info` is searched for in the document (web page) and its innerHTML property (property used to display results) is assigned the server response stored in the variable. So, the response retrieved from the server is displayed at the place of element `info`.

The instruction: `xmlhttp.send(null)` is used to actually send the request to the server. We don't want to pass anything to the requested file, so, the argument passed to this method is null. That is, if there is no query string to be sent to the file being invoked ajaxaccessdata1.php, we write null in the `send()` method otherwise the query string is sent instead of null.

Note the response generated by the server is based on the execution of the file ajaxaccessdata1.php. Let's analyse what it returns.

ajaxaccessdata1.php

```
<?php
echo "Welcome " . $_GET['usernme'] . " to our Shopping Mall <br>" ;
echo "Your email id is " . $_GET['emailid'] ;
?>
```

This returns two lines of text to the client: "Welcome `name` of the user to our Shopping Mall" and "Your email id is ". The name and email id of the user are retrieved from `$_GET` array.

The output of the program ajaxaccess.php will be as shown in Figure 6.5.

Output:

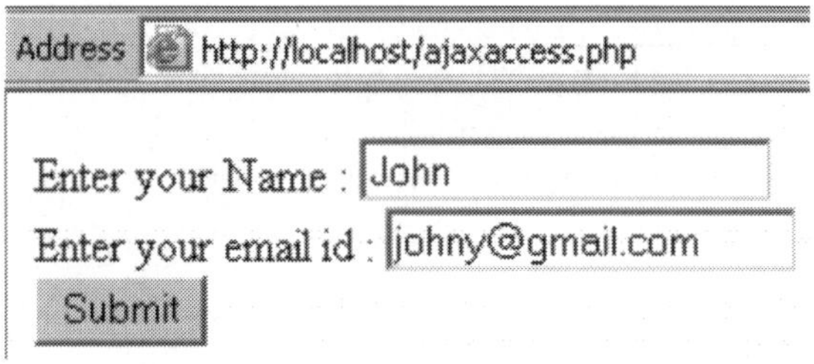

Figure 6.5 ***Screen to Enter Name and Email Id***

After feeding the name and email id, when we press Submit button, both are displayed (Figure 6.6).

Figure 6.6 ***After Pressing Submit Button, Both Messages are Displayed***

6.5 XMLHTTP POST REQUESTS

While using POST requests, we have to pass the information to the requested file in the form of a query string as shown:

```
name=value1&address=value2&….
```

The data is first arranged in this format before being sent to the server. One more thing to remember is that if we want to POST data, we have to change the MIME type of the request using the following line:

```
httpRequest.setRequestHeader('Content-Type', 'application/x-www-form-urlencoded');
```

Otherwise, the server will discard the POSTed data.

The following program asks the user to enter his name and then he is greeted with a welcome message on clicking the submit button. The main attraction of this program is the `setQueryString()` method which just takes the data from the form and converts them in the query string format as shown above. Let's make two files named ajaxpost1.php and ajaxpostdata1.php with the contents given below in the `htdocs` subfolder of the `apache` directory.

ajaxpost1.php

```
<head>
<script language="JavaScript" type="text/JavaScript">
var queryString;
function makeRequestObject(){
var xmlhttp=false;
try {
xmlhttp = new ActiveXObject('Msxml2.XMLHTTP');
} catch (e) {
```

```
try {
xmlhttp = new
ActiveXObject(‘Microsoft.XMLHTTP’);
} catch(E) {
xmlhttp = false;
}
}
if (!xmlhttp && typeof XMLHttpRequest!=’undefined’) {
xmlhttp = new XMLHttpRequest();
}
return xmlhttp;
}

function showdata()
{
var xmlhttp=makeRequestObject();
setQueryString();
var file = ‘ajaxpostdata1.php’;
xmlhttp.open(‘POST’, file, true);
xmlhttp.setRequestHeader(“Content-Type”,
“application/x-www-form-urlencoded; charset=UTF-8”);
xmlhttp.onreadystatechange=function() {
if (xmlhttp.readyState==4 && xmlhttp.status == 200) {
var content = xmlhttp.responseText;
if( content ){
document.getElementById(‘info’).innerHTML = content;
}
}
}
xmlhttp.send(queryString)
}

function setQueryString(){
queryString="";
var frm = document.forms[0];
var numberElements = frm.elements.length;
for(var i = 0; i < numberElements; i++) {
```

```
44. if(i < numberElements-1) {
45. queryString += frm.elements[i].name+"="+
46. encodeURIComponent(frm.elements[i].value)+"&";
47. } else {
48. queryString += frm.elements[i].name+"="+
49. encodeURIComponent(frm.elements[i].value);
50. }
51. }
52. }

53. </script>
54. </head>
55. <body>
56. <form method="post" onsubmit="showdata(); return false">
57. Enter your Name: <input type="text" name="usernme"/><br/>
58. <button type="submit">Submit</button>
59. </form>
60. <div id="info"></div>
61. </body>
62. </html>
```

ajaxpostdata1.php

```
1. <?php
2. echo "Welcome " . $_POST['usernme'] . " to our Shopping Mall" ;
3. ?>
```

Explanation of the ajaxpost1.php program

The program begins its execution from the <body> element onwards.

```
56. <form method="post" onsubmit="showdata(); return false">
```

onsubmit is an event handler which executes when submit type button is pressed. This event handler calls the `showdata()` function. This event handler returns `false` to prevent actual form submission. That is, we don't want the form to be submitted to server instead we just want the control to invoke the `showdata()` function.

In the `showdata()` method, we are first making an object to make an HTTP request to the server.

Since in POST requests, data sent to the server is in the form of a query string, like:

```
name=value1&address=value2&.......
```

So, to convert the data fed by the user in the form into above format, the `setQueryString()` method is invoked.

In the query string, the name and the value of each parameter must be URL-encoded in order to avoid data loss during transmission. `encodeURIComponent()` is a built-in function in JavaScript which is used to perform this encoding.

Note that if you want to use POST request, you have to change the MIME type of the request using the following line:

```
httpRequest.setRequestHeader('Content-Type', 'application/x-www-form-urlencoded');
```

Otherwise, the server will discard the POSTed data.

The output of the program ajaxpost1.php may appear as shown in Figure 6.7.

Output:

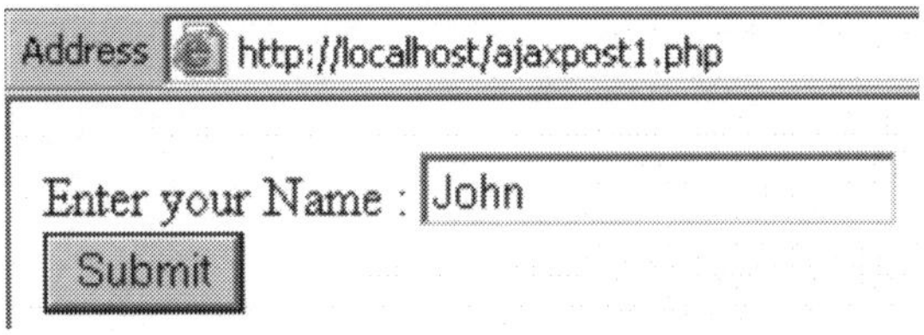

Figure 6.7 ***Enter the Name***

We feed the user name and press Submit button, we get the server response as shown in Figure 6.8.

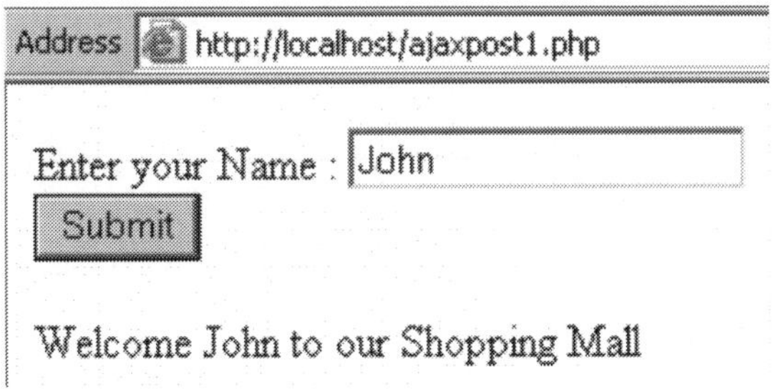

Figure 6.8 ***Server Response is Displayed***

6.6 SEPARATING JAVASCRIPT CODE IN ANOTHER FILE

Instead of writing the JavaScript code in the <script> tag of a HTML file which looks a bit untidy, it is always better to write the JavaScript code in a separate file with .js extension and then refer the JavaScript file in the current web page. This makes the web page appear neat and readable. For example in the following program, we are writing the JavaScript code in a separate file ajaxform2.js which is then referred in the file ajaxform2.php file.

ajaxform2.js

```
function makeRequestObject(){
var xmlhttp=false;
          try {
                xmlhttp = new ActiveXObject('Msxml2.XMLHTTP');
          } catch (e) {
                try {
                         xmlhttp = new
                         ActiveXObject('Microsoft.XMLHTTP');
             } catch (E)  {
                xmlhttp = false;
                         }
             }
             if (!xmlhttp && typeof XMLHttpRequest!='undefined') {
             xmlhttp = new XMLHttpRequest();
             }
return xmlhttp;
}

function showdata()
{
var xmlhttp=makeRequestObject();
user=document.getElementById('user_name').value;
             var file = 'ajaxdata1.php?usernme=';
         xmlhttp.open('GET', file + user, true);
         xmlhttp.onreadystatechange=function() {
             if (xmlhttp.readyState==4 && xmlhttp.status == 200) {
                    var content = xmlhttp.responseText;
                    if( content ){
                       document.getElementById('info').innerHTML = content;
```

```
                    }
            }
            }
            xmlhttp.send(null)
}
```

ajaxform2.php

```
<html>
<head>
<script language="JavaScript" type="text/JavaScript" src="ajaxform2.js"></
script>
</head>
<body>
Enter your Name: <input type="text" name="user_name"><br>
<input type="button" onclick="showdata()" value="Submit"><br>
<div id="info"></div>
</body>
</html>
```

We can see that the above php script file appears neat and tidy as all the JavaScript code is now in a separate file ajaxform2.js.

ajaxdata1.php

```
<?php
echo "Welcome " . $_GET['usernme'] . " to our Shopping Mall" ;
?>
```

This file is reused from earlier examples and is just returning a Welcome message to the client.

The output of the program ajaxform2.php may appear as shown in Figure 6.9.

Output:

There will be no change in the output (on separating the JavaScript code).

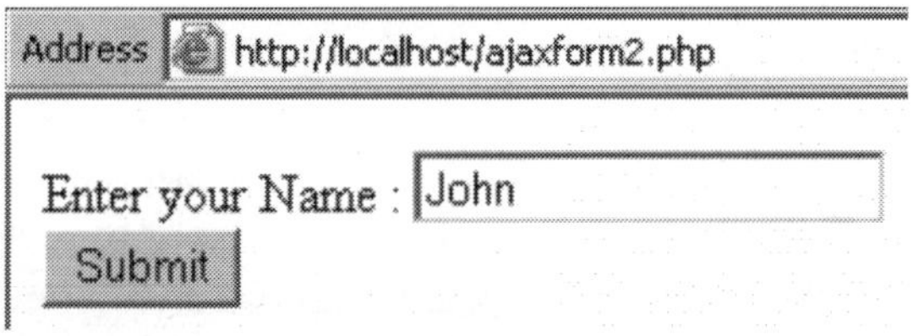

Figure 6.9 ***Enter the User Name***

On entering the user's name and selecting Submit button, a Welcome message appears as shown in Figure 6.10.

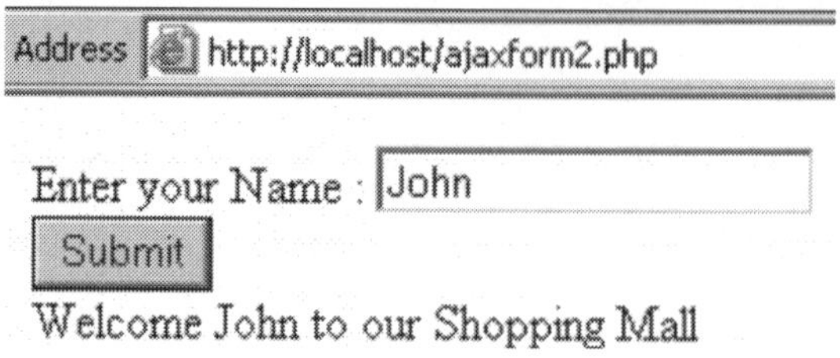

Figure 6.10 ***Server Response is Displayed (no Change in the Output)***

6.7 ACCESSING JAVASCRIPT FUNCTION USING HYPERLINK

The following program asks the user to enter his/her name. After entering the name when the user selects a hyperlink, a JavaScript method is invoked which displays a Welcome message to the user. In other words instead of using any events like onkeyup or onblur etc., in this example, a hyperlink is used for sending a request to the server asynchronously. Let's make two files named ajaxlink.php and ajaxlink.js with the contents below in the `htdocs` subfolder of the `apache` directory. We also need a file ajaxdata1.php created in earlier examples for returning server response.

ajaxlink.php

```
<head>
<script language="JavaScript" type="text/JavaScript" src="ajaxlink.js">
</script>
</head>
<body>
Enter your Name: <input type="text" name="user_name"><br>
<a href="javascript:showdata()"> Enter</a><br>
<div id="info"></div>
</body>
</html>
```

This program asks the user to enter his name in a textbox and that name is assigned to variable "user_name". A hyperlink exists on the page with text: "Enter" on it which when selected invokes the JavaScript method `showdata()` defined in ajaxlink.js file. Also a <div> element with id `info` is defined in the web page that will be used for displaying the server response.

ajaxlink.js

```
function makeRequestObject(){
var xmlhttp=false;
	try {
		xmlhttp = new ActiveXObject('Msxml2.XMLHTTP');
	} catch (e) {
		try {
			xmlhttp = new
			ActiveXObject('Microsoft.XMLHTTP');
	  } catch (E) {
	     xmlhttp = false;
		}
	}
	if (!xmlhttp && typeof XMLHttpRequest!='undefined') {
	     xmlhttp = new XMLHttpRequest();
	}
return xmlhttp;
}

function showdata()
{
var xmlhttp=makeRequestObject();
user=document.getElementById('user_name').value;
	var file = 'ajaxdata1.php?usernme=';
   xmlhttp.open('GET', file + user, true);
   xmlhttp.onreadystatechange=function() {
	if (xmlhttp.readyState==4) {
		var content = xmlhttp.responseText;
		if( content ){
			document.getElementById('info').innerHTML = content;
		}
	}
	}
```

```
        xmlhttp.send(null)
}
```

This program is first making an XMLHttpRequest object and then making a request to the server for the file ajaxdata1.php, sending the user name entered by the user to it. The ajaxdata1.php generates the Welcome message as server response. The div element with id `info` is located in the web page and the server response is pasted at that element by setting its innerHTML property.

ajaxdata1.php

```
<?php
echo "Welcome " . $_GET['usernme'] . " to our Shopping Mall" ;
?>
```

This file is reused from earlier examples and is just returning a Welcome message to the client.

Output:

The user is prompted to enter his name (Figure 6.11).

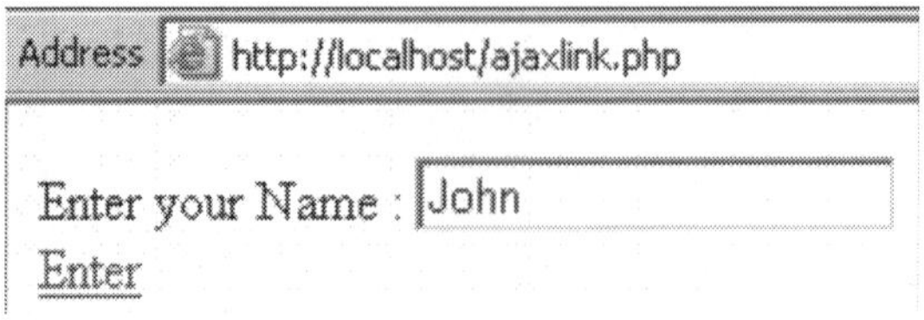

Figure 6.11 ***Enter the User Name***

After entering the name, when user clicks the link: "Enter", a welcome message is displayed (Figure 6.12).

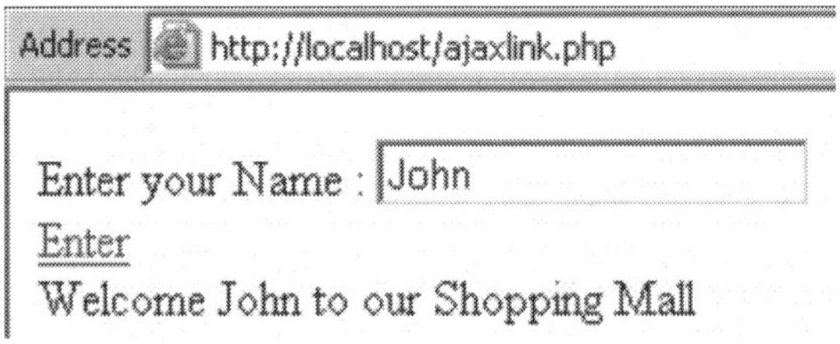

Figure 6.12 ***Welcome Message is Displayed***

6.8 SPECIFYING OUR FUNCTION IN .JS FILE

In the above JavaScript file, though the function is executed when the status of the request changes and the event is handled by onreadystatechange handler, we haven't specified any name for the function. The code is written is as follows:

```
function showdata()
{
var xmlhttp=makeRequestObject();
user=document.getElementById('user_name').value;
        var file = 'ajaxdata1.php?usernme=';
        xmlhttp.open('GET', file + user, true);
        xmlhttp.onreadystatechange=function() {
        if (xmlhttp.readyState==4 && xmlhttp.status == 200) {
                    var content = xmlhttp.responseText;
                    if( content ){
                          document.getElementById('info').innerHTML = content;
                    }
        }
        }
        xmlhttp.send(null)
}
```

We can see in the above code, that the statement:

```
xmlhttp.onreadystatechange=function() {
```

specifies that if any change in the status of the request takes place, execute the following function body `function()`, but the function name is not specified.

In the following sample, we have re-written this code with the difference that we have specified the function to be executed if any change in the status of the request takes place. The function name specified is `getdata()` and it is assigned to the onreadystatechange event handler with the following command:

```
xmlhttp.onreadystatechange=getdata;
```

This instruction executes the `getdata()` method if there is any change in the status of the request. So, our `showdata()` method will be modified as follows:

```
function showdata()
{
xmlhttp=makeRequestObject();
var user=document.getElementById('user_name').value;
        var file = 'ajaxdata1.php?usernme=';
        xmlhttp.open('GET', file + user, true);
   xmlhttp.onreadystatechange=getdata;
```

```
        xmlhttp.send(null)
}

function getdata()
   {
        if (xmlhttp.readyState==4 && xmlhttp.status == 200) {
                var content = xmlhttp.responseText;
                if( content ){
                        document.getElementById('info').innerHTML = content;
                }
        }
}
```

6.9 CONVERTING A STRING INTO UPPERCASE

The example below asks the user to enter a string which is converted into uppercase asynchronously and is displayed to the client. Let's make three files ajaxcaps.php, ajaxcaps.js and convertcaps.php with the following contents in the `htdocs` subfolder of the `apache` directory.

ajaxcaps.php

```
<html>
<head>
<script language="javascript" type="text/javascript" src="ajaxcaps.js">
</script>
</head>
<body>
Enter text: <input type="text" onblur="showdata();" name="inputname"
id="inputname" /> <br>
Text in Capital is: <input type="text" name="outputname" id="outputname" />
</body>
</html>
```

A JavaScript file ajaxcaps.js is imported into the current web page so that the methods defined in it can be accessed from here. The user is prompted to enter a text in one textbox. After feeding the text, as tab key is pressed i.e. the moment focus to the textbox is lost, `showdata()` method is invoked (which will convert the text to upper case and display it in the second textbox).

ajaxcaps.js

```
function makeRequestObject(){
var xmlhttp=false;
          try {
                xmlhttp = new ActiveXObject('Msxml2.XMLHTTP');
          } catch (e) {
                     try {
                           xmlhttp = new
                           ActiveXObject('Microsoft.XMLHTTP');
             } catch (E) {
                xmlhttp = false;
                           }
          }
          if (!xmlhttp && typeof XMLHttpRequest!='undefined') {
                     xmlhttp = new XMLHttpRequest();
          }
return xmlhttp;
}

function showdata()
{
var xmlhttp=makeRequestObject();

xmlhttp.open("GET",
"convertcaps.php?inputname="+document.getElementById('inputname').value, true);
   xmlhttp.onreadystatechange=function() {
   if (xmlhttp.readyState==4) {
document.getElementById('outputname').value = xmlhttp.responseText;
}
}
xmlhttp.send(null);
}
```

This program is first making an XMLHttpRequest object and then making a request to the server for the file convertcaps.php, sending the text entered by the user to it. The text entered by the user is stored in textbox with name "inputname". The requested file convertcaps.php converts the text to uppercase and is the file which generates a server response. The response generated by the server (text in upper case) is retrieved in the form of text and is assigned to the textbox with name:

"outputname" ("outputname" is the second textbox made on the web page to display server response). The statement: `xmlhttp.send(null);` is to actually send the request to the server. Since we don't want to pass any query string to the requested file convertcaps.php, the argument passed to this method is null.

convertcaps.php

```
<?php
if (isset($_GET['inputname']))
echo strtoupper($_GET['inputname']);
?>
```

This program is retrieving the text sent from the client (in the inputname variable) and returning it to the client after converting it into upper case (Figure 6.13).

Output:

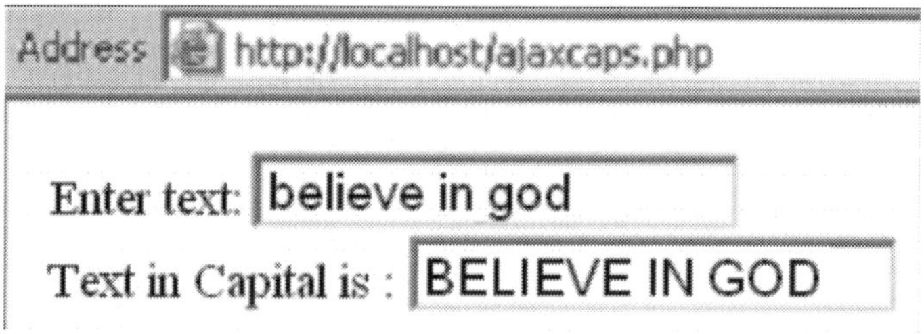

Figure 6.13 *Output of the Program ajaxcaps.php*

6.10 CSS (CASCADING STYLE SHEETS)

Using CSS styles is considered as the consistent method of setting the styles of the elements on a web page. All the font styles and their appearance that we want to apply to different elements on a web page are stored in a separate file with extension .css which is then referenced in the web page. The style sheet contains different selectors each with different font size, colours etc. To apply the characteristics of the CSS selector on any web page element, that element has to specify the particular CSS selector as its class.

Since in CSS method, the information is separated from presentation of the information i.e. all the formatting attributes are at one place, any changes if desired in the format can also be easily applied.

Let's use CSS style sheet in an example. The following example asks the user to enter his name and the moment user presses the tab key or clicks somewhere out of the textbox, a welcome message will be displayed to him (as is done in earlier programs). But here, the welcome message will be applied some characteristics like fonts, colours etc. Let's make three files named styles1.css, phpajaxstyle1.php and phpajaxstyle1.js with the contents below in the `htdocs` subfolder of the `apache` directory. For the server response, we need the file ajaxdata1.php (made earlier).

styles1.css

```
.name
{
    font-family: Verdana;
    font-weight:bold;
    background-color: Cyan;
    font-size: 20pt;
}
```

This code is defining a CSS selector named `name` which contains font Verdana of size 20 points which will appear in bold and its background colour will be cyan. We can have any number of selectors in a style sheet.

The CSS selectors are mapped to the HTML via the class attribute. That is, any element in the HTML document that specifies any selector as its class will inherit all the characteristics specified in that selector.

phpajaxstyle1.php

```
<html>
    <head>
        <script type="text/JavaScript" src="phpajaxstyle1.js"></script>
        <link href="styles1.css" type="text/css" rel="stylesheet"/>
    </head>
        <body>
            Enter your Name: <input type="text" onblur="showdata(this.value)"/>
<div class="name" id="info"></div>
</body>
</html>
```

As we can see in the above program, we are referencing the CSS style sheet styles1.css (so as to use the characteristics of the CSS selectors defined in it).

Since the <div> element specifies the selector name (defined in CSS style sheet) as its class, it will inherit its characteristics i.e. the text within the <div> tag will have the characteristics of the CSS selector named `name` i.e. it will appear in Verdana font of size 20 points in bold and its background colour will be cyan.

phpajaxstyle1.js

```
function makeRequestObject(){
var xmlhttp=false;
```

```
        try {
            xmlhttp = new ActiveXObject('Msxml2.XMLHTTP');
        } catch (e) {
            try {
                xmlhttp = new
                ActiveXObject('Microsoft.XMLHTTP');
          } catch (E) {
            xmlhttp = false;
                }
          }
          if (!xmlhttp && typeof XMLHttpRequest!='undefined') {
              xmlhttp = new XMLHttpRequest();
          }
return xmlhttp;
}
function showdata(user)
{
var xmlhttp=makeRequestObject();
          var file = 'ajaxdata1.php?usernme=';
        xmlhttp.open('GET', file + user, true);
        xmlhttp.onreadystatechange=function() {
          if (xmlhttp.readyState==4) {
              var content = xmlhttp.responseText;
              if( content ){
                  document.getElementById('info').innerHTML = content;
              }
          }
          }
          xmlhttp.send(null)
}
```

This program is doing the same thing, that is making an XMLHttpRequest object and making a request to the server for the file ajaxdata1.php, sending the user name entered by the user to it. The ajaxdata1.php generates the Welcome message as the server response. The div element with id `info` is located in the web page and the server response is pasted at that element. The server response will appear in the style defined by the CSS selector `name`.

ajaxdata1.php

```
<?php
echo "Welcome ".$_GET['usernme']. "to our Shopping Mall" ;
?>
```

The output of the program phpajaxstyle1.php may appear as shown in Figure 6.14.

Output:

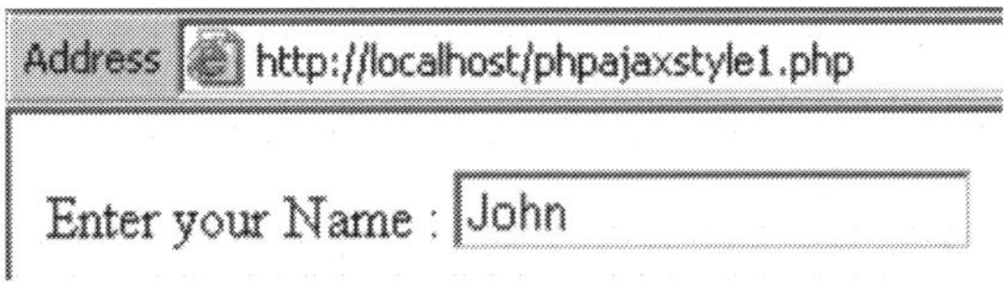

Figure 6.14 *User Name is Entered*

The user name appears in the applied style (Figure 6.15).

Figure 6.15 *Welcome Message is Displayed in Applied Styles*

6.11 SENDING DATA FROM COMBOBOX TO SERVER ASYNCHRONOUSLY

Let us see how the items selected in the combobox can be sent to the server asynchronously. That is, without a need to press any submit button, just selecting an item from the combobox will display the desired result. Let's make three files named comboajax.php, comboajax.js and showcat.php with the contents below in the `htdocs` subfolder of the `apache` directory.

comboajax.php

```
<html>
<head>
<script language="JavaScript" type="text/JavaScript" src="comboajax.js"></
script>
</head>
<body>
```

```
Category:
        <select name="Category" onChange='itemdisplay(this.value)' >
            <option value="" selected>Select Products Category</option>
            <option value="Camera">Camera</option>
            <option value="Mobile">Mobile</option>
            <option value="Book">Book</option>
        </select><br><br>

<div id="info"></div></body>
</html>
```

This program just creates a combobox named "Category" with three items Camera, Mobile and Book displayed in it. If any change takes place, that is if any item is selected from this combobox, a method `itemdisplay()` is invoked and the selected item is passed to it as argument. Also a <div> element is defined with id `info` for displaying the server response.

comboajax.js

```
function makeRequestObject(){
var xmlhttp=false;
            try {
                   xmlhttp = new ActiveXObject('Msxml2.XMLHTTP');
            } catch (e) {
                   try {
                          xmlhttp = new
                          ActiveXObject('Microsoft.XMLHTTP');
              } catch (E) {
                   xmlhttp = false;
                          }
            }
            if (!xmlhttp && typeof XMLHttpRequest!='undefined') {
                   xmlhttp = new XMLHttpRequest();
        }
return xmlhttp;
}

function itemdisplay(cat)
{
```

```
var xmlhttp=makeRequestObject();
    xmlhttp.open('GET', 'showcat.php?&Category='+cat, true);
        xmlhttp.onreadystatechange=function() {
                if (xmlhttp.readyState==4 && xmlhttp.status == 200) {
                        var content = xmlhttp.responseText;
                        if( content ){
                                document.getElementById('info').innerHTML = content;
                        }
        }
        }
        xmlhttp.send(null)
}
```

This program is doing the same thing, that is making an XMLHttpRequest object and making a request to the server (by GET method) for the file showcat.php, sending the category of item selected by the user (from the combobox) to it. This category is retrieved in showcat.php file using `$_GET` array.

Since an asynchronous request is made to the server, the state of the request and the response to the request is checked. If the value of *readyState* property becomes 4 (meaning the request is complete) and the value of the status of the HTTP Request is 200 (which means there is no error), the response is then retrieved from the response stream and is assigned to variable content which is then applied to the innerHTML property (property used to display results) of the element with id `info`. It is the same <div> element with id `info` we have defined in the web page for displaying the server response. Hence, the response retrieved from the server is displayed at the place of element `info`.

Note the response generated by the server is based on the execution of the file showcat.php. Let's analyse what it returns.

showcat.php

```
<?php
echo "Category selected is: " . $_GET['Category'] ;
?>
```

This file returns the text "Category selected is " and the category name selected by the user. The category selected by the user is passed while making the XMLHttpRequest for the file showcat.php in the following command:

```
xmlhttp.open('GET', 'showcat.php?&Category='+cat, true);
```

The output of the program comboajax.php may appear as shown in Figure 6.16.

Output:

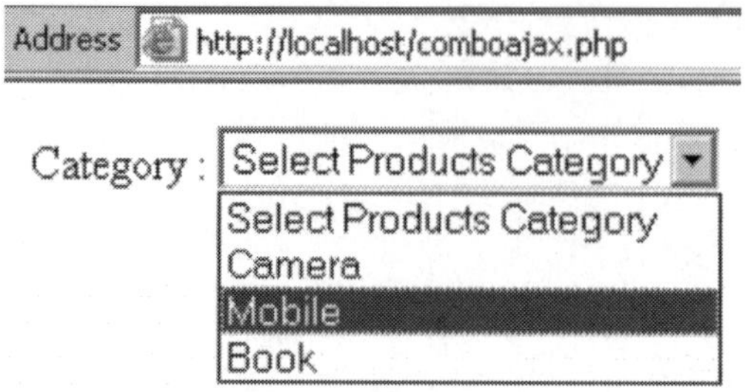

Figure 6.16 *Combobox Displaying Various Items*

The moment we select an item from the combobox, the message displaying the selected option appears on the screen (Figure 6.17).

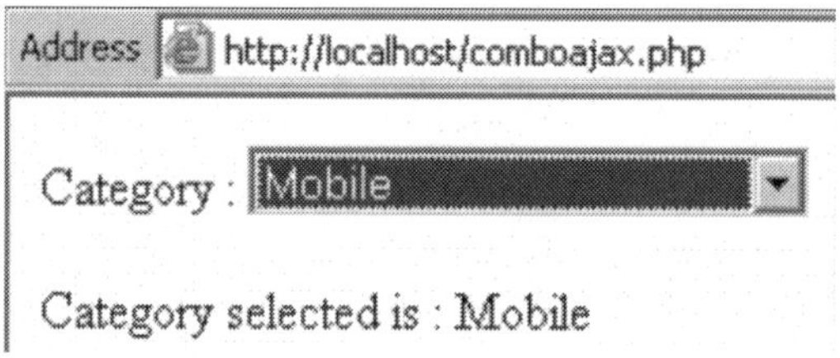

Figure 6.17 *The Selected Item is Displayed on the Screen*

6.12 SENDING MULTIPLE ITEMS SELECTED FROM LISTBOX TO THE SERVER ASYNCHRONOUSLY

In the following example we demonstrate how multiple items selected from the listbox are sent to the server asynchronously. Let's make three files named listajax.php, listajax.js and showlistdata.php with the contents below in the `htdocs` subfolder of the `apache` directory.

listajax.php

```
<html>
<head>
<script language="JavaScript" type="text/JavaScript" src="listajax.js"></
script>
</head>
<body>
Choose one or more category: <br>
<select name="Category" multiple="multiple" size="4" onblur='itemdisplay()' >
```

```
        <option value="Camera" selected>Camera</option>
        <option value="Mobile">Mobile</option>
        <option value="Book">Book</option>
        <option value="Computer">Computer</option>
        <option value="Washing Machine">Washing Machine</option>
        <option value="Refrigerator">Refrigerator</option>
        </select><br><br>

<div id=info></div></body>
</html>
```

This program creates a listbox named "Category" with six items: Camera, Mobile and Book, Computer, Washing Machine and Refrigerator displayed in it. The multiselect feature of the listbox is set with the help of `"multiple"` attribute. So, the user can select more than one item from the listbox (by pressing `Ctrl` or shift key). After selecting the item(s), the moment user presses `tab` key or clicks anywhere else on the web page i.e. when the focus of the listbox is lost, a method `itemdisplay()` is invoked. Beside this, a <div> element is defined with id `info` for displaying the server response.

listajax.js

```
function makeRequestObject(){
var xmlhttp=false;
try {
xmlhttp = new ActiveXObject('Msxml2.XMLHTTP');
} catch (e) {
try {
xmlhttp = new
ActiveXObject('Microsoft.XMLHTTP');
} catch (E) {
xmlhttp = false;
}
}
if (!xmlhttp && typeof XMLHttpRequest!='undefined') {
xmlhttp = new XMLHttpRequest();
}
return xmlhttp;
```

```
}

function itemdisplay()
{
var xmlhttp=makeRequestObject();
optionsArray=document.getElementById(‘Category’).options;
var selectedArray = new Array();
var x=0;
for(var i=0; i< optionsArray.length; i++)
{
if(optionsArray[i].selected)
{
selectedArray[x]=optionsArray[i].value;
x++;
}
}
var cat="";
for(var i=0;i<selectedArray.length;i++)
{
if( i!=selectedArray.length -1) {
cat +=selectedArray[i]+",";
}
else
{
cat+=selectedArray[i];
}
}
xmlhttp.open(‘GET’, ‘showlistdata.php?&Category=’+cat, true);
xmlhttp.onreadystatechange=function() {
if (xmlhttp.readyState==4 && xmlhttp.status == 200) {
var content = xmlhttp.responseText;
if( content ){
```

```
48. document.getElementById('info').innerHTML = content;
49. }
50. }
51. }
52. xmlhttp.send(null)
53. }
```

Explanation of listajax.js program

Statements 1–17 are making an XMLHttpRequest object.

```
21. optionsArray=document.getElementById('Category').options;
```

The element in the web page named "Category" (our listbox) is searched and all the items available in it are assigned to an array `optionsArray`.

```
22. var selectedArray = new Array();
23. var x=0;
24. for(var i=0; i< optionsArray.length; i++)
25. {
26. if(optionsArray[i].selected)
27. {
28. selectedArray[x]=optionsArray[i].value;
29. x++;
30. }
31. }
```

With the help of a loop, all the elements in the `optionsArray` are checked one by one and all the items selected by the user are stored in a separate array `selectedArray`.

```
32. var cat="";
33. for(var i=0;i<selectedArray.length;i++)
34. {
35. if( i!=selectedArray.length -1) {
36. cat +=selectedArray[i]+",";
37. }
38. else
39. {
40. cat+=selectedArray[i];
41. }
42. }
```

All the items stored in array `selectedArray` (containing only the list of items selected by the user) are retrieved and stored in a variable `cat` (after separating them with commas except the last one).

```
xmlhttp.open('GET', 'showlistdata.php?&Category='+cat, true);
xmlhttp.onreadystatechange=function() {
if (xmlhttp.readyState==4 && xmlhttp.status == 200) {
var content = xmlhttp.responseText;
if( content ){
document.getElementById('info').innerHTML = content;
}
}
}
```

XMLHttpRequest request is made to the server (by GET method) for the file showlistdata.php, sending all the item(s) selected by the user (stored in variable `cat`) to it. The selected item list sent to the requested file will be retrieved in showlistdata.php file using `$_GET` array.

The state and the response to asynchronous request is checked. If the value of readyState property becomes 4 (meaning the request is complete) and the value of the status of the HTTP request is 200 (which means there is no error), the response is then retrieved from the response stream and is assigned to variable `content` which is then applied to the innerHTML property (property used to display results) of the element with id `info` to display all the items that are selected by the user in the listbox.

Again the response generated by the server is based on the execution of the file showlistdata.php. Let's analyse what it returns.

showlistdata.php

```
<?php
echo "The categories of items selected are: " . $_GET['Category'] ;
?>
```

This file returns the text: "The categories of items selected are " and the category name(s) selected by the user. The categories selected by the user are passed to this file while making the XMLHttpRequest for the file by following command:

```
xmlhttp.open('GET', 'showlistdata.php?&Category='+cat, true);
```

The output of the program listajax.php may appear as shown in Figure 6.18.

Output:

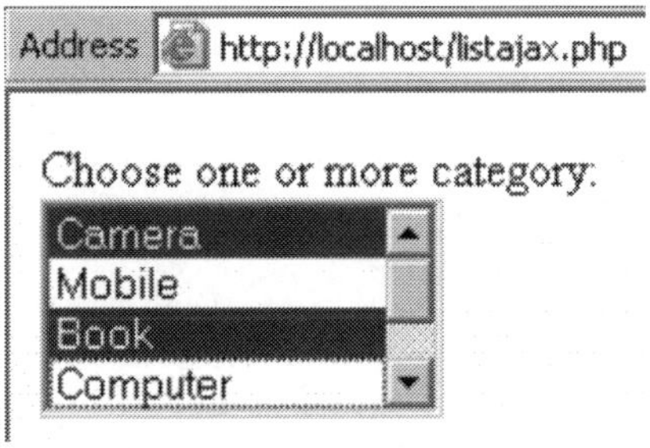

Figure 6.18 ***Selection of Various Items by Pressing Tab Key***

We can select as many categories of items as we want followed by pressing the tab key. All the categories selected are displayed separated by commas as shown in Figure 6.19.

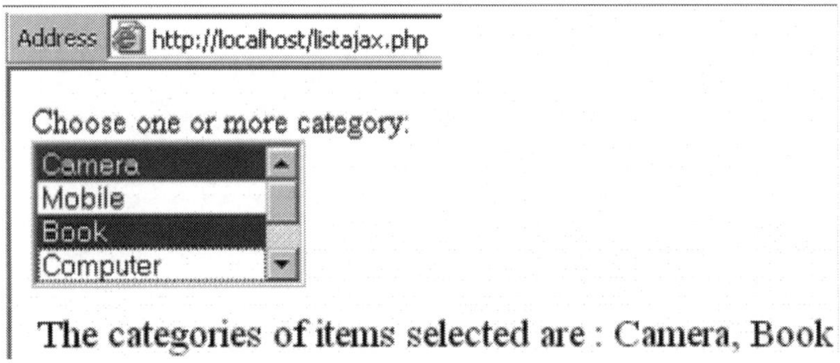

Figure 6.19 ***Items Selected are Displayed***

6.13 SENDING ITEMS SELECTED FROM RADIO AND CHECK BOX TO SERVER ASYNCHRONOUSLY

In usually every web application, listboxes, comboboxes, checkboxes and radio buttons play a major role in getting information from the user. So, after understanding how the messages from combobox and listbox are sent to the server asynchronously, it is time to demonstrate how to send the asynchronous messages of the selected checkboxes and radio boxes to the server. Let's make three files named checkboxradioajax.php, checkboxradioajax.js and checkboxradiodata.php with the following contents in the `htdocs` subfolder of the `apache` directory.

checkboxradioajax.php

```
<html>
<head>
<script language="JavaScript" type="text/JavaScript" src="checkboxradioajax.js"></script>
```

```
</head>
<body>
Choose one: <br>
<input type="radio" name="drink" value ="Hot Coffee" onClick='display()'> Hot Coffee <br>
<input type="radio" name="drink" value ="Cold Coffee" onClick='display()'> Cold Coffee <br>
<input type="radio" name="drink" value ="Soft Drink" onClick='display()'> Soft Drink <br><br>

Choose all the options that you want to have: <br>
<input type="checkbox" name="food" value ="Hot Dog" onClick='display()'> Hot Dog <br>
<input type="checkbox" name="food" value="Pizza" onClick='display()'>Pizza <br>
<input type="checkbox" name="food" value="Noodles" onClick='display()'>Noodles <br>
<input type="checkbox" name="food" value="Chips" onClick='display()'>Chips <br><br>

<div id=info></div>
</body>
</html>
```

This program defines three radio buttons with options Hot Coffee, Cold Coffee and Soft Drink and four checkboxes with options Hot Dog, Pizza, Noodles and Chips. The name assigned to the radio buttons is "drink" and if any of the radio button is selected, `display()` method will be invoked. Similarly the checkboxes are named "food" and if any of the checkboxes is selected, the same `display()` method will be invoked. Beside this, a <div> element is defined with id `info` for displaying the server response. Remember, we can select only one radio button in a group whereas any number of checkboxes can be selected in a group.

checkboxradioajax.js

```
function makeRequestObject(){
var xmlhttp=false;
try {
xmlhttp = new ActiveXObject('Msxml2.XMLHTTP');
} catch (e) {
try {
xmlhttp = new
ActiveXObject('Microsoft.XMLHTTP');
} catch (E) {
xmlhttp = false;
}
```

```
}
if (!xmlhttp && typeof XMLHttpRequest!=’undefined’) {
xmlhttp = new XMLHttpRequest();
}
return xmlhttp;
}

function display()
{
var xmlhttp=makeRequestObject();
ControlsArray=document.getElementsByTagName(‘input’);
var fooditms=””;
var drinkitms=””;
for(var i=0; i< ControlsArray.length; i++)
{
if(ControlsArray[i].type==”checkbox” && ControlsArray[i].checked)
{
fooditms+=ControlsArray[i].value + “ “;
}
if(ControlsArray[i].type==”radio” && ControlsArray[i].checked)
{
drinkitms+=ControlsArray[i].value + “ “;
}
}

xmlhttp.open(‘GET’,‘checkradiodata.php?SelectedDrink=’+drinkitms+’&SelectedFood=’+fooditms, true);
xmlhttp.onreadystatechange=function() {
if (xmlhttp.readyState==4 && xmlhttp.status == 200) {
var content = xmlhttp.responseText;
if( content ){
document.getElementById(‘info’).innerHTML = content;
}
}
}
xmlhttp.send(null)
}
```

Explanation of checkboxradioajax.js program

Statements 1–17 are making an XMLHttpRequest object.

```
21. ControlsArray=document.getElementsByTagName('input');
```

The elements in the web page named `input` (usually all the elements in a web page come under this category) are searched and all the items with this name are assigned to an array ControlsArray.

```
22. var fooditms="";
23. var drinkitms="";
24. for(var i=0; i< ControlsArray.length; i++)
25. {
26. if(ControlsArray[i].type=="checkbox" && ControlsArray[i].checked)
27. {
28. fooditms+=ControlsArray[i].value + " ";
29. }
30. if(ControlsArray[i].type=="radio" && ControlsArray[i].checked)
31. {
32. drinkitms+=ControlsArray[i].value + " ";
33. }
34. }
```

With the help of a loop, all the elements in the `ControlsArray` are checked one by one and the value of all the elements in the array which are of type "checkbox" and are checked (selected) are stored in a variable `fooditms`. Similarly, for all of the elements of type "radio" which are checked, their values is assigned to variable `drinkitms`.

```
35. xmlhttp.open('GET','checkradiodata.php?SelectedDrink='+drinkitms+'&
    SelectedFood='+fooditms, true);
36. xmlhttp.onreadystatechange=function() {
37. if (xmlhttp.readyState==4 && xmlhttp.status == 200) {
38. var content = xmlhttp.responseText;
39. if( content ){
40. document.getElementById('info').innerHTML = content;
41. }
42. }
43. }
44. xmlhttp.send(null)
45. }
```

An XMLHttp request is made to the server (by GET method) for the file checkboxradiodata.php, sending all the selected drink items and selected food items (stored in variables `drinkitms` and `fooditms` respectively) to it.

The state and the response to asynchronous request is checked. If the value of readyState property becomes 4 and the value of the status of the HTTP Request is 200, the response is then retrieved from the response stream and is assigned to variable `content` which is then applied to the innerHTML property of the element with id `info` to display the response from the server (i.e. to display all the items selected from the checkbox and radio buttons).

The instruction `xmlhttp.send(null)` is used to actually send the request to the server. And if we don't want to pass any query string to the requested file, the argument passed to this method is null or else it contains the query string.

Remember, the response generated by the server is based on the execution of the file checkboxradiodata.php. Let's analyse what it returns.

checkboxradiodata.php

```
<?php
$food=$_GET['SelectedFood'];
$drink=$_GET['SelectedDrink'];
if($drink=="")
{
echo "You have not selected any drink <br><br>";
}
else
{
echo "The drink selected is: " . $drink . "<br><br>";
}
if($food=="")
{
echo "You have not selected food <br><br>";
}
else
{
echo "The types of Food selected are: " . $food . "<br><br>";
}
?>
```

The selected food items and selected drink items are retrieved from `$_GET` array and stored in variables `$food`, and `$drink` respectively. The list of items selected from checkboxes and radio buttons are passed to this file while making the XMLHttp request for the file using the following command:

```
35. xmlhttp.open('GET', 'checkradiodata.php? SelectedDrink='+drinkitms+'
&SelectedFood='+ fooditms, true);
```

We can see in the above instruction that the selected drink item and the selected food items are passed to the checkboxradiodata.php file. The retrieved items in `$food` and `$drink` variables are displayed on the screen (if the contents of the variable are non blank or else the message: "You have not selected" food or drink is displayed).

Output:

The initial screen may appear as shown in Figure 6.20.

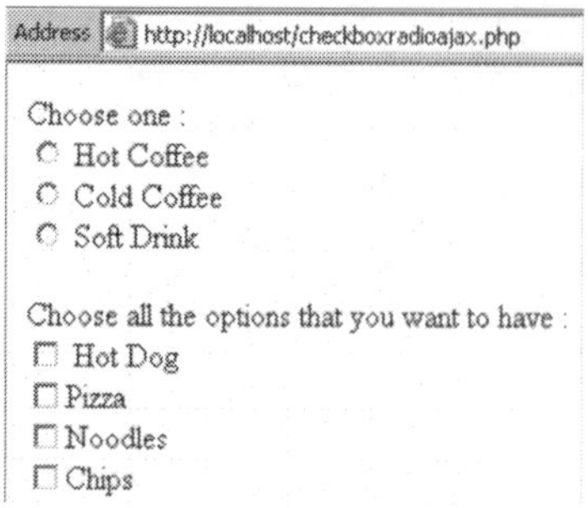

Figure 6.20 *Output of Checkbox Program*

If only drink item is selected, the output will as shown in Figure 6.21.

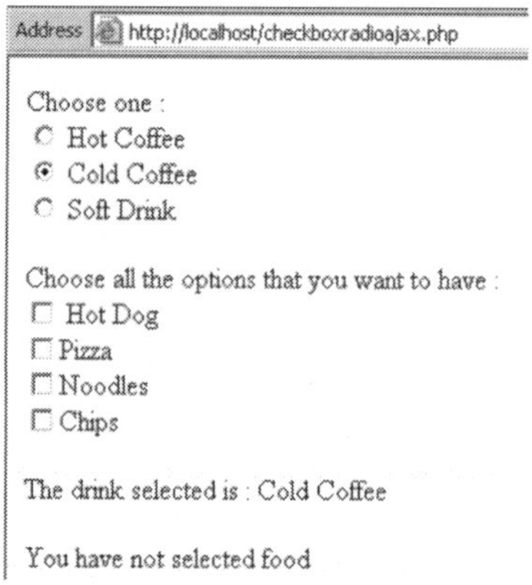

Figure 6.21 *Output if Only Drink Item is Selected*

If only food item is selected, the output may appear as shown in Figure 6.22.

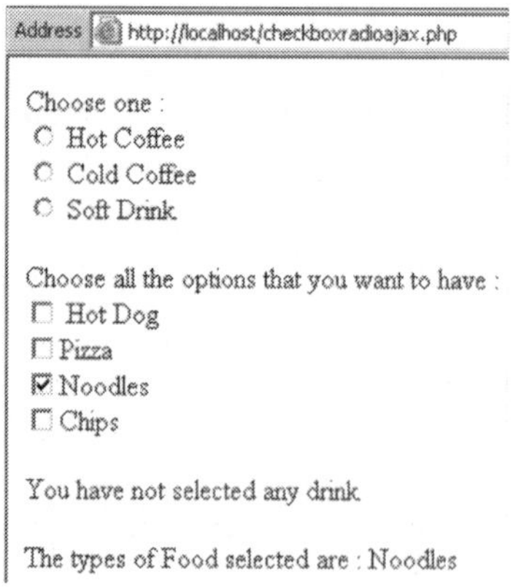

Figure 6.22 *Output if Only Food Item is Selected*

If both drink as well as food items are selected, the output may appear as shown in Figure 6.23.

Figure 6.23 ***Output if Both Drink and Food Items are Selected***

6.14 AJAX, PHP AND MYSQL ALL COMBINED FOR ACCESSING DATABASE

Let us place an asynchronous request to access the desired data from the database on server. In the following example, the user is provided two categories of items in the form of hyperlinks Camera and Mobile and he can select either of them to see the products available in that category. When the user selects any link, all the items in the `products` table (of shopping database) under the selected category will be displayed. That is, if the camera hyperlink is selected, all the cameras in the products table will be displayed. We are using the same shopping database and the same `products` table made in the Shopping Cart project included in Part I of this book. For reference purposes, the structure of the table is shown in Figure 6.24.

```
mysql> describe product;
+--------------+---------------+------+-----+---------+----------------+
| Field        | Type          | Null | Key | Default | Extra          |
+--------------+---------------+------+-----+---------+----------------+
| Item_code    | Int<4>        | NO   |     |         | auto_increment |
| item_name    | Varchar<50>   | NO   |     |         |                |
| Description  | varchar<255>  | NO   |     |         |                |
| quantity     | varchar<50>   | NO   |     |         |                |
| price        | int<4>        | NO   |     |         |                |
| image        | float         | YES  |     | NULL    |                |
| imagename    | blob          | YES  |     | NULL    |                |
| id           | varchar<50>   | YES  |     | NULL    |                |
|              | int<10>       | NO   |     | 0       |                |
+--------------+---------------+------+-----+---------+----------------+
9 rows in set <0.28 sec>
```

Figure 6.24 ***Structure of Table Products***

Let's make three files named ajaxform8.php, ajaxform8.js and ajaxdata8.php with the following contents in the `htdocs` subfolder of the `apache` directory.

ajaxform8.php

```
<head>
<script language="JavaScript" type="text/JavaScript" src="ajaxform8.js" >
</script>
</head>
<body>
<div id="links">
<a href="javascript:showdata('Camera')">Camera</a><a href="javascript: showdata
('Mobile')">Mobile</a>
</div>
<div id="content">
</div>
</body>
</html>
```

This program first includes the JavaScript file ajaxform8.js (so that methods in it can be invoked from this web page). It is defining two <div> elements with id `links` and `content` respectively. The two hyperlinks Camera and Mobile are placed inside the `links` element and the `content` element is left for displaying the server response. If either link is selected, a JavaScript method `showdata()` is executed and the name of the link selected (category of item selected) is passed to it as argument.

ajaxform8.js

```
function makeRequestObject(){
var xmlhttp=false;
       try {
                  xmlhttp = new ActiveXObject('Msxml2.XMLHTTP');
       } catch (e) {
                  try {
                         xmlhttp = new
                         ActiveXObject('Microsoft.XMLHTTP');
              } catch (E) {
                  xmlhttp = false;
                            }
       }
       if (!xmlhttp && typeof XMLHttpRequest!='undefined') {
                  xmlhttp = new XMLHttpRequest();
       }
return xmlhttp;
}
function showdata(cat)
{
var xmlhttp=makeRequestObject();
var file = 'ajaxdata8.php?Category=';
       xmlhttp.open('GET', file + cat, true);
    xmlhttp.onreadystatechange=function() {
    if (xmlhttp.readyState==4) {
document.getElementById('content').innerHTML = xmlhttp.responseText;
}
}
xmlhttp.send(null);
return;
}
```

This program is doing the same thing, that is making an XMLHttpRequest object and making request to the server (by GET method) for the file ajaxdata8.php, sending the category of item selected by the user (through hyperlink) to it. This category is retrieved in ajaxdata8.php file using `$_GET` array.

The state of the request is checked. If the value of *readyState* property becomes 4 (meaning the request is complete), the response is then retrieved from the response stream and is assigned to the innerHTML property (property used to display results) of the element with id `content`.

Since the response generated by the server is based on the execution of the file ajaxdata8.php, let's analyse what it returns.

ajaxdata8.php

```
<?php
mysql_connect("localhost", "root", "mce");
mysql_select_db("shopping");
$cat = $_GET["Category"];
$sql = "SELECT * FROM products WHERE Category like '$cat'";
$query = mysql_query($sql) or die(mysql_error());
echo '<table border="1">';
echo '<th>Item Code</th><th>Name of Item</th><th>Description</th><th>Price</
   th>';
while ($r = mysql_fetch_array($query)) {
echo '<tr><td>' . $r["item_code"] . '</td><td>' . $r["item_name"] . '< td>
   <td>' . $r["description"] . '</td><td>' . $r["price"] . '</td></tr>';
}
echo '</table>';
?>
```

This program is connecting to the MySQL server with user id "root" and password "mce". Then the database `"shopping"` is selected (as our `products` table is in this database). The category of the item selected by the user is retrieved using `$_GET` array and stored in variable `$cat`. Then, a SQL statement is executed to fetch all the rows from the `products` table with the category specified in **$cat** variable. The rows retrieved from the products table are then returned in the form of a table to be displayed on the client.

Output:

The user is provided two hyperlinks each designating a category of items (Figure 6.25).

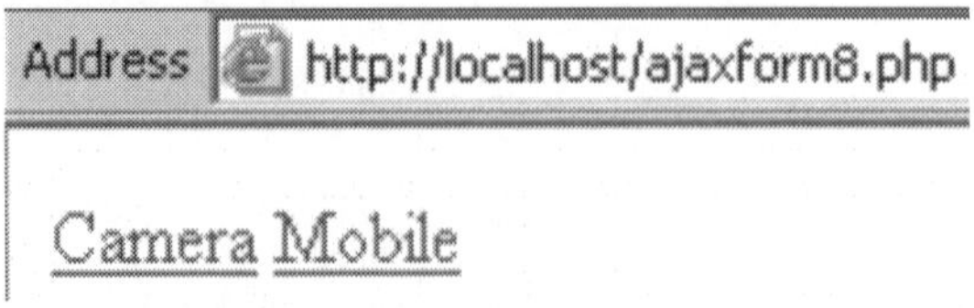

Figure 6.25 ***Output Displaying Hyperlinks***

If Camera link is selected, all the products under the camera category will be displayed as shown in Figure 6.26.

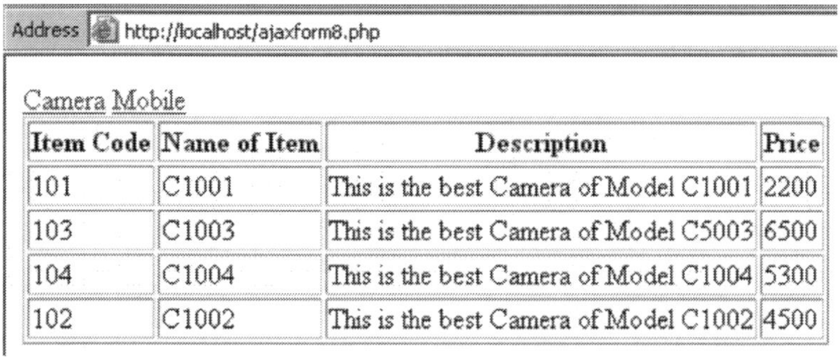

Item Code	Name of Item	Description	Price
101	C1001	This is the best Camera of Model C1001	2200
103	C1003	This is the best Camera of Model C5003	6500
104	C1004	This is the best Camera of Model C1004	5300
102	C1002	This is the best Camera of Model C1002	4500

Figure 6.26 ***Description of All Items Under Camera Category if Selected***

If Mobile link is selected, all the products under the mobile category are displayed (Figure 6.27).

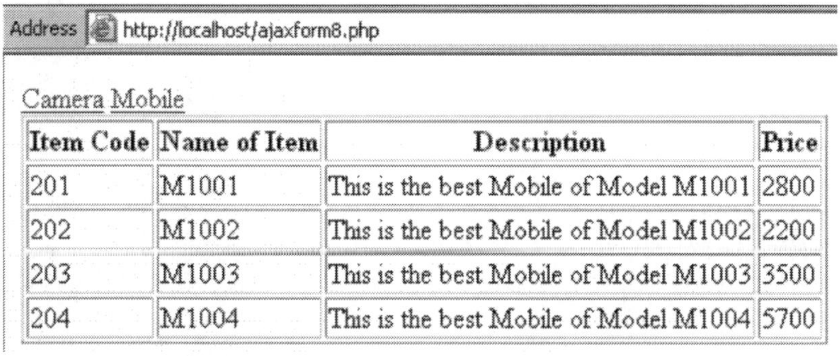

Item Code	Name of Item	Description	Price
201	M1001	This is the best Mobile of Model M1001	2800
202	M1002	This is the best Mobile of Model M1002	2200
203	M1003	This is the best Mobile of Model M1003	3500
204	M1004	This is the best Mobile of Model M1004	5700

Figure 6.27 ***All Products Under Mobile Category are Shown if Selected***

6.15 ACCESSING DATABASE IN AJAX—SECOND EXAMPLE

In this example, there is a limitation that the user can see products of only one category at a time. That is, if he selects "Camera" hyperlink then only the products under the camera category are displayed and if the user selects "Mobile" hyperlink, all the items under the mobile category are displayed. What if the user wishes to see the products of both categories together? So, in the following example, we provide the user a set of checkboxes each designating a category of products and the user can select any number of checkboxes to see the products of one or more categories together.

Again, the `shopping` database and the `products` table created in the Shopping Cart project explained in Part I of this book are used in this example. Let's make three files named accessdatabase1.php, accessdatabase1.js and retrievedata.php with the following contents in the `htdocs` subfolder of the `apache` directory.

accessdatabase1.php

```
<html>
<head>
<script language="JavaScript" type="text/JavaScript" src="accessdatabase1.
js"></script>
</head>
<body>
Choose all the categories of items you want to see: <br>
<input type="checkbox" name="cat" value ="Camera" onClick='display()'> Camera
<br>
<input type="checkbox" name="cat" value="Mobile" onClick='display()'>Mobile
<br>
<input type="checkbox" name="cat" value="Book" onClick='display()'>Book
<br><br>
<div id="itminfo"></div>
</body>
</html>
```

This program includes the JavaScript file accessdatabase1.js (so that its methods can be invoked from the current web page). Three checkboxes are created named "cat" and each of them designates a category of product. If any of the checkboxes is selected, it will result in execution of `display()` method specified in accessdatabase1.js file.

Also, a <div> element with id `itminfo` is defined for displaying the server response.

accessdatabase1.js

```
function makeRequestObject(){
var xmlhttp=false;
try {
xmlhttp = new ActiveXObject('Msxml2.XMLHTTP');
} catch (e) {
try {
xmlhttp = new
ActiveXObject('Microsoft.XMLHTTP');
} catch (E) {
xmlhttp = false;
```

```
}
}
if (!xmlhttp && typeof XMLHttpRequest!='undefined') {
xmlhttp = new XMLHttpRequest();
}
return xmlhttp;
}

function display()
{
var xmlhttp=makeRequestObject();
ControlsArray=document.getElementsByTagName('input');
var selectedcat="";
for(var i=0; i< ControlsArray.length; i++)
{
if(ControlsArray[i].type=="checkbox" && ControlsArray[i].checked)
{
selectedcat+=ControlsArray[i].value + " ";
}
}
xmlhttp.open('GET', 'retrievedata.php?SelectedCategory='+selectedcat,
  true);
xmlhttp.onreadystatechange=function() {
if (xmlhttp.readyState==4 && xmlhttp.status == 200) {
var content = xmlhttp.responseText;
if( content ){
document.getElementById('itminfo').innerHTML = content;
}
}
}
xmlhttp.send(null)
}
```

Explanation of accessdatabase1.js program

Statements 1–17 are making an XMLHttpRequest object.

```
21. ControlsArray=document.getElementsByTagName('input');
```

The elements in the web page with tag name `input` (usually all the elements in a web page come under this category) are searched and all the items with this tag name are assigned to an array: `ControlsArray`.

```
22. var selectedcat="";
23. for(var i=0; i< ControlsArray.length; i++)
24. {
25. if(ControlsArray[i].type=="checkbox" && ControlsArray[i].checked)
26. {
27. selectedcat+=ControlsArray[i].value + " ";
28. }
29. }
```

With the help of a loop, all the elements in the `ControlsArray` are checked one by one and the values of all the elements in the array which are of type "checkbox" and are checked (selected) are stored in a variable `selectedcat` (separated by a space).

```
30. xmlhttp.open('GET', 'retrievedata.php?SelectedCategory='+selectedcat, true);
31. xmlhttp.onreadystatechange=function() {
32. if (xmlhttp.readyState==4 && xmlhttp.status == 200) {
33. var content = xmlhttp.responseText;
34. if( content ){
35. document.getElementById('itminfo').innerHTML = content;
36. }
37. }
38. }
39. xmlhttp.send(null)
40. }
```

An XMLHttp request is made to the server (by GET method) for the file retrievedata.php, sending names of the categories selected by the user to it. The state and the response to asynchronous request is checked. If the value of readyState property becomes 4 and the value of the status of the HTTP Request is 200, the response is then retrieved from the response stream and is assigned to variable content which is then applied to the innerHTML property of the element with id `itminfo` to display the response from the server (i.e. to display all the products of the selected categories).

The instruction `xmlhttp.send(null)` is used to actually send the request to the server. And if we don't want to pass any query string to the requested file, the argument passed to this method is null or else it contains the query string.

The response generated by the server is based on the execution of the file retrievedata.php. Let's analyse what it returns.

retrievedata.php

```
<?php
mysql_connect("localhost", "root", "mce");
mysql_select_db("shopping");
$categories = $_GET["SelectedCategory"];
$catArray=explode(" ", $categories);
$prod="";
for($i=0;$i<sizeof($catArray);$i++)
{
if( $i!=sizeof($catArray) -1) {
$prod = $prod . "'" . $catArray[$i] . "', ";
}
else
{
$prod= $prod . "'" . $catArray[$i] . "'";
}
}
$sql = "SELECT * FROM products WHERE Category in (" . $prod . ") order by item_code";
$query = mysql_query($sql) or die(mysql_error());
echo '<table border="1">';
echo '<th>Item Code</th><th>Name of Item</th><th>Description</th><th>Price</th>';
while ($r = mysql_fetch_array($query)) {
echo '<tr><td>' . $r["item_code"] . '</td><td>' . $r["item_name"] . '</td>
<td>' . $r["description"] . '</td><td>' . $r["price"] . '</td></tr>';
}
echo '</table>';
?>
```

Explanation of retrievedata.php program

This program is connecting to the MySQL server with user id "root" and password "mce". Then the database "shopping" is selected (as our `products` table is in this database). The categories of the items selected by the user are retrieved using `$_GET` array and stored in variable `$categories` (it contains all the categories of the items selected by the user each separated by a space).

```
$catArray=explode(" ", $categories);
```

The `$categories` variable is exploded (split). That is, the values stored in this variable are separated on the basis of space (i.e. wherever a space occurs, it marks the beginning of another value) and stored in an array `$catArray`.

```
$prod="";
for($i=0;$i<sizeof($catArray);$i++)
{
if( $i!=sizeof($catArray) -1) {
$prod = $prod . "'" . $catArray[$i] . "', ";
}
else
{
$prod= $prod . "'" . $catArray[$i] . "'";
}
}
```

A `for` loop is used to extract all the elements from the array `$catArray` and stored in a variable `$prod` and each element except the last one is separated by a comma.

```
$sql = "SELECT * FROM products WHERE Category in (" . $prod . ") order by item_code";
$query = mysql_query($sql) or die(mysql_error());
```

An SQL statement is executed to fetch all the rows from the products table with the categories specified in `$prod` variable.

```
echo '<table border="1">';
echo '<th>Item Code</th><th>Name of Item</th><th>Description</th><th>Price</th>';
while ($r = mysql_fetch_array($query)) {
echo '<tr><td>' . $r["item_code"] . '</td><td>' . $r["item_name"] . '</
  td><td>' . $r["description"] . '</td><td>' . $r["price"] . '</td></tr>';
}
echo '</table>';
```

The rows retrieved from the products table are then returned in the form of a table to be displayed to the client.

Output:

The user is provided with three checkboxes each designating a category of item (Figure 6.28).

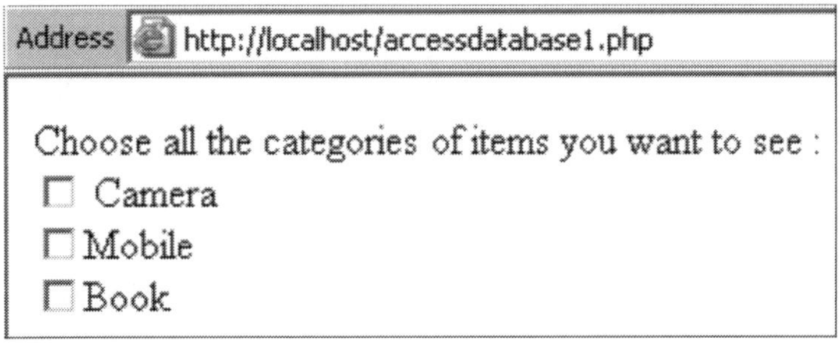

Figure 6.28 ***Three Checkboxes to Select***

If the checkbox of Camera category is selected, all the products under the camera category are displayed (Figure 6.29).

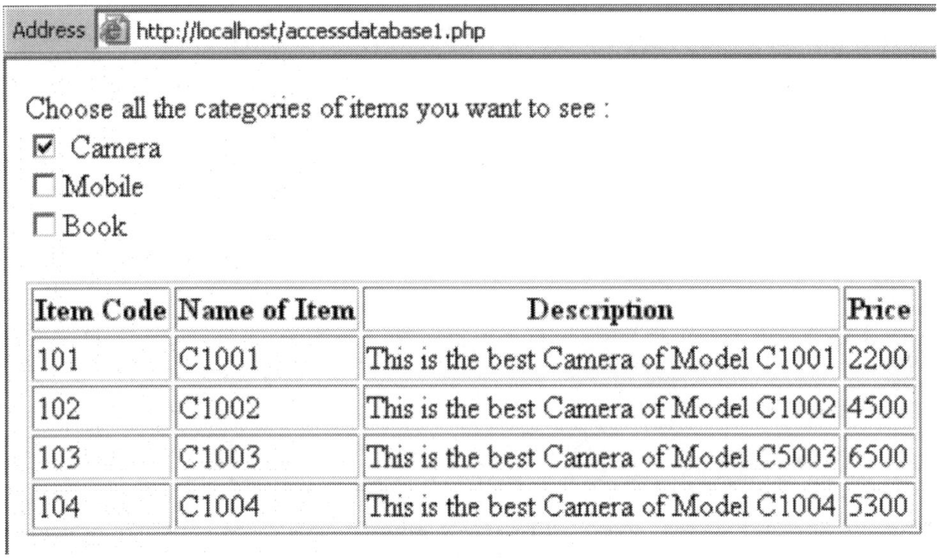

Figure 6.29 ***Description of Camera Products if its Checkbox is Marked***

If more than one checkbox is selected, for example the checkboxes of Mobile and Book category are both selected, then all the products belonging to these two categories are displayed as shown in Figure 6.30.

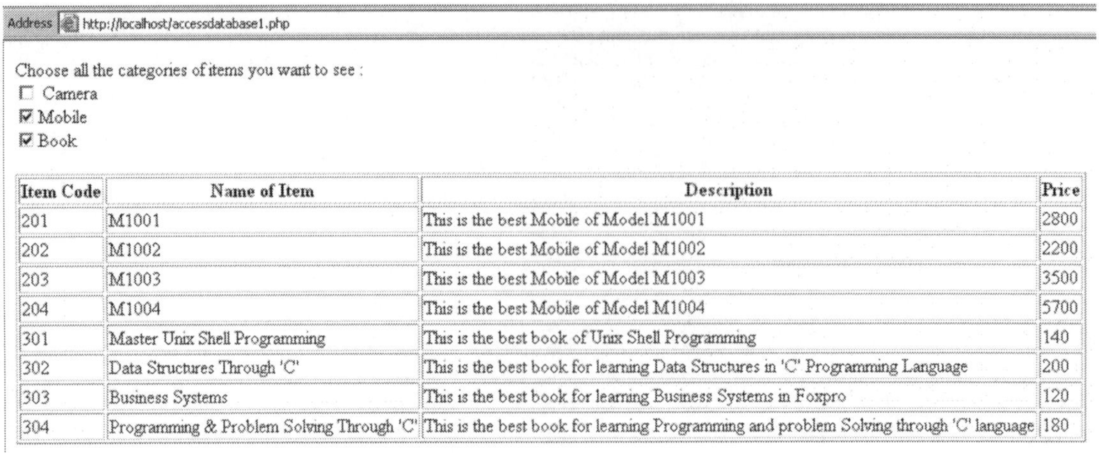

Item Code	Name of Item	Description	Price
201	M1001	This is the best Mobile of Model M1001	2800
202	M1002	This is the best Mobile of Model M1002	2200
203	M1003	This is the best Mobile of Model M1003	3500
204	M1004	This is the best Mobile of Model M1004	5700
301	Master Unix Shell Programming	This is the best book of Unix Shell Programming	140
302	Data Structures Through 'C'	This is the best book for learning Data Structures in 'C' Programming Language	200
303	Business Systems	This is the best book for learning Business Systems in Foxpro	120
304	Programming & Problem Solving Through 'C'	This is the best book for learning Programming and problem Solving through 'C' language	180

Figure 6.30 ***Descriptions of Both Mobile and Book Category are Displayed***

SUMMARY

In this chapter, we have learnt several things. A summary follows:

- JavaScript is a lightweight interpreted language that can be easily embedded in an `html` program.
- There are two ways of including JavaScript in a web page. One way is by writing its statements in `<head>` element and the second way is of writing JavaScript code in a separate file with extension .js and including the file by using `<script>` element.
- An HTML page is represented in the form of a document tree that is composed of elements or nodes and child nodes that can be manipulated using JavaScript code.
- Document Object Model is an object by which all the elements in an HTML document can be accessed by a JavaScript engine.
- The root node of the web page is accessed by a global variable called `document`.
- The method used for searching a web page for an object with the specified id is `document.getElementById()`.
- The object that is used for making asynchronous calls to the web server is known as XMLHttpRequest object. It is using this object that we can make HTTP requests, receive responses and update a region of the page completely in the background.
- The keydown event fires only when a character key is pressed.
- Since in some browsers XMLHttpRequest is a native object whereas in others it is implemented as an ActiveX control, the method of making its instance is different for each browser.

- To watch for the state of the request and also response to the request (since the request made to the server is an asynchronous request), we take the help of event handler `onreadystatechange` which fires at every state change.
- To actually send the request to the server, the statement used is `xmlhttp.send(null)`
- In POST requests, the information is passed in the form of a query string.
- In the query string, the name and the value of each parameter must be URL-encoded in order to avoid data loss during transmission. This encoding is done with the help of a built-in function in JavaScript called `encodeURIComponent()`.
- The CSS style sheet is a collection of font styles stored in a separate file with extension .css and is considered as the most favourable method of applying consistent styles to the elements on a web page.

In the next chapter, we will look at different validation checks. We will check whether any essential field is left blank, whether any field has less data then required. Also, we will see three different methods of validating email ids. We will also see how a userid can be validated i.e. checking whether the specified userid already exists in the database or not. Finally, we will see how a form is validated and storing the record in the table (if data in the form is found valid).

7

Validation

In this chapter we will look at the following validation checks:

- Checking if any field is left blank
- Checking if any field has less data then required
- Three different methods of validating email id
- Validating userid—checking if it already exists
- Validating the form and storing the record in the table (if data is valid)

Validation means confirming whether the data entered by the user is correct (in terms of type and value). If not, the data must not be processed and the user must be asked to correct the mistake.

In a traditional web application, form validation is performed on the click of the submit button i.e. when all the data has been entered by the user, but on application of AJAX, every field can be validated individually and that too as and when data is entered.

There are certain fields in a web form which must be validated immediately before proceeding with the rest of the fields, like userid (checking whether the userid entered already exists or not), emailid (whether the email id is correct or not) etc.

7.1 CHECKING IF ANY FIELD IS LEFT BLANK

While asking the user to fill up a form, a common problem that is faced is that some important fields are left blank by the user. So, through AJAX, we can make sure that certain required fields are not left blank. Let's check it with the following example. We make two files named validatefield.php and checkfield.js with the following contents in the `htdocs` subfolder of the `apache` directory.

validatefield.php

```
<html>
<head>
```

```
<script language="JavaScript" type="text/JavaScript" src="checkfield.js"></script>
</head>
<body>
Userid: <input size="20" type="text" name="userid" onblur = "validatefield (this)">
</body>
</html>
```

This program is including JavaScript file checkfield.js file in the current page so that methods defined in it can be accessed from this web page. The user is prompted to enter userid and after feeding it, the moment tab key is pressed or the user clicks anywhere else on the form (meaning if the focus of that field is lost), `validatefield()` method specified in the included JavaScript file is executed and the userid entered by the user is passed to it as argument (in order to confirm that it is not left blank).

checkfield.js

```
function validatefield(obj)
{
    if(obj.value.length ==0)
    {
    alert("This field cannot be left blank");
    obj.focus();
}
}
```

This method is checking whether the length of the object (userid) sent to it is 0 or not. If yes, it means the user has left this field blank, and an alert message is displayed to him and focus is set to the userid field so that the user can enter userid in it.

Output:

If the user keeps that field blank and presses tab key, an alert message is displayed (Figure 7.1).

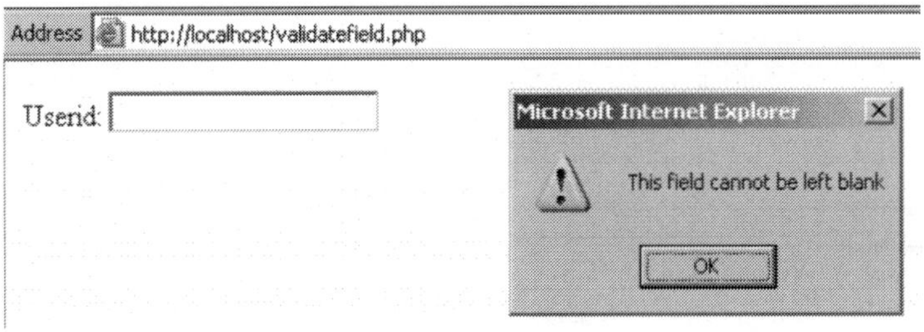

Figure 7.1 ***Alert Message is Displayed if Field is Left Blank***

If the user enters something in the userid field, then no error message is displayed (Figure 7.2).

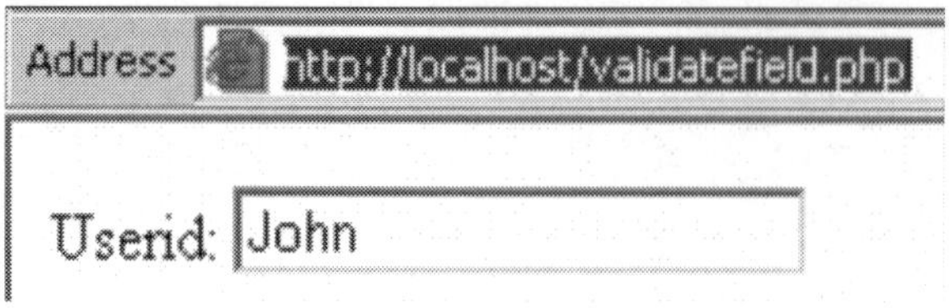

Figure 7.2 ***No Error Message is Displayed if User Enters Something in the Field***

7.1.1 Second Method of the Same Program

In the following example instead of directly attaching onblur event to the web page element, we are using window.onload event handler (which is automatically called when the browser completes loading of the web page) to access the element (userid) on the web page and execute a set of statements if the onblur event has occurred on that element. Let's make two files named validatefield1.php and checkfield1.js with the following contents in the `htdocs` subfolder of the `apache` directory.

validatefield1.php

```
<html>
<head>
<script language="JavaScript" type="text/JavaScript" src="checkfield1.js"></
script>
</head>
<body>
   Userid: <input size="20" type="text" name="userid">
</body>
</html>
```

We can see that onblur event handler is not there in the program above.

checkfield1.js

```
window.onload=function()
        {
        var obj=document.getElementById("userid");
        obj.onblur=function()
        {
        if(this.value.length ==0)
```

```
{
alert("This field cannot be left blank");
this.focus();
}
}
}
```

When the web page is loaded, window.onload event handler is automatically executed. We access the element on the document (web page) with name "userid" (with the help of `getElementById()` method) and check if onblur event has occurred on this element. If yes, then a function is executed which checks whether the length of the value entered for this element is 0 or not. If yes, then an alert message is displayed on the screen.

7.2 CHECKING IF ANY FIELD HAS LESS DATA THAN REQUIRED

Sometimes we want that the data entered in a given element should be of at least specified width (in the case of passwords, we want them to be of minimum 6 characters). In the following example, we are going to ask the user to enter userid (which cannot be left blank) and password which cannot be of less than 6 characters. We make two files named validatefields.php and checkfield2.js with the following contents in the `htdocs` subfolder of the `apache` directory.

validatefields.php

```
<html>
<head>
<script language="JavaScript" type="text/JavaScript" src="checkfield2.js"></
script>
</head>
<body>
   Userid: <input size="20" type="text" name="userid" onblur
="validatefield(this)"><br>
   Password: <input size="20" type="password" name="password" onblur
="if(this.value !='') {validatefield(this)}">
</body>
</html>
```

A JavaScript file checkfield2.js is included in the current page so the methods defined in it can be accessed from the current web page. The user is first prompted to enter userid. The moment the user presses the tab key after entering userid, `validatefield()` method is executed with userid entered by the user passed to it as argument. Similarly, after userid, the user is prompted for password too and the moment focus on that element is lost either by pressing tab key or by clicking mouse elsewhere on the web page, again `validatefield()` method is executed and the password entered is passed to it as argument.

Note: `validatefield()method` is executed only if password field is not left blank.

checkfield2.js

```
function validatefield(obj)
{
if(obj.name=="userid")
{
if(obj.value.length ==0)
{
alert("This field cannot be left blank");
obj.focus();
}
}

if(obj.name=="password")
{
if(obj.value.length <=5)
{
alert("The password should be of at least size 6");
obj.focus();
}
}
}
```

This method is checking if the object passed to it is userid. If it is so, then its length is checked and if it is 0, then an alert message is displayed to the user and the cursor is placed on userid field (using `focus()` method) so that the user can again feed it. And if the object passed to the method is password, and its length is less than 6 characters, then an alert message is displayed and again the cursor is set on the password field. In other words, focus is set on the password field for the user to re-enter the password of at least 6 characters.

Output:

If the user keeps userid field blank and presses the tab key, an alert message is displayed (Figure 7.3).

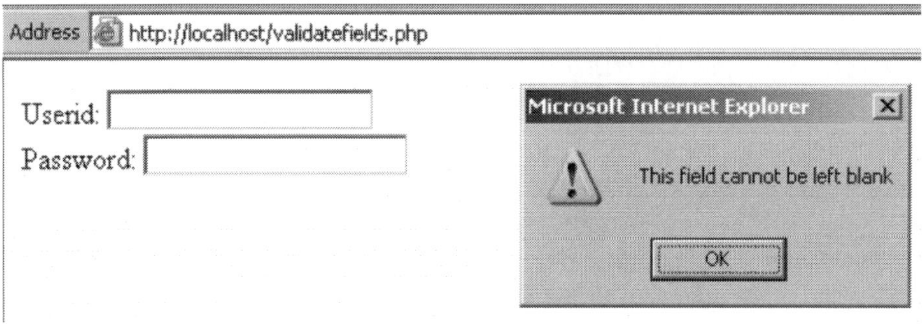

Figure 7.3 ***Alert Message is Displayed***

If the password entered is of less than 6 characters then an alert message is displayed (Figure 7.4).

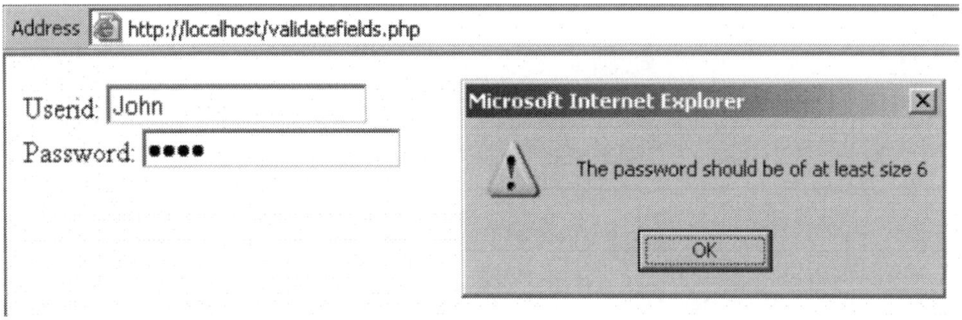

Figure 7.4 ***Alert Message is Displayed if Password is Less than 6 Characters Long***

7.3 VALIDATING EMAIL ID

The following example is for verifying whether the email id entered by user is a valid email id or not. To ensure the validity of the email id, we first check that the length of email id is not 0 (i.e. the user has not left the field blank). Then, we check for the presence of . (dot) and @ (at) in the email id entered by the user. Absence of either proves that invalid email id is entered.

We make two files named validateemail.php and checkemail.js with the following contents in the `htdocs` subfolder of the `apache` directory.

validateemail.php

```
<html>
<head>
<script language="JavaScript" type="text/JavaScript"
src="checkemail.js"></script>
```

```
</head>
<body>
Enter email id: <input size="20" type="text" name="emailid" onblur
="validatefield(this)">
   </form>
</body>
</html>
```

A JavaScript file checkemail.js is included in the current page so the methods defined in it can be accessed from the current web page. The user is prompted to enter email id. The moment the user presses the tab key after entering email id, `validatefield()` method is executed with email id entered by the user passed to it as argument.

checkemail.js

```
function validatefield(obj)
{
      if(obj.value.length==0||obj.value.indexOf(".")==-1 || obj.value.indexOf
      ("@") ==-1)
      {
      alert("email id is invalid");
      obj.focus();
}
}
```

This method is checking if the length of the object passed to it (email id) is 0. If its length is 0 (meaning the field is left blank) or the object doesn't contain . (dot) or @ (at) symbol, then an alert message is displayed and focus is set on it for the user to enter a valid email id.

Output:

If email id doesn't contain . (dot) or @ (at) symbol, then an alert message is displayed (Figure 7.5)

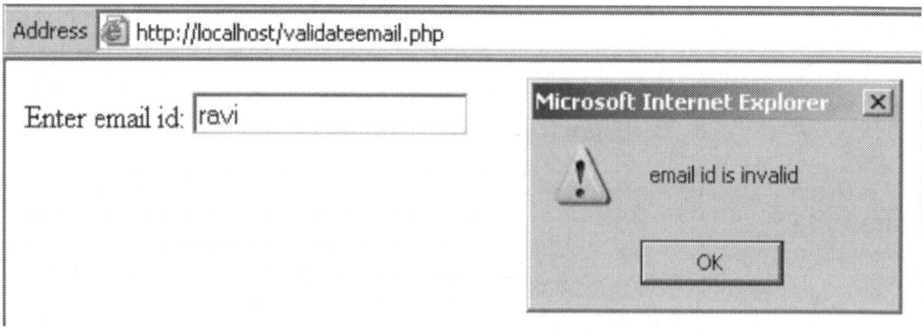

Figure 7.5 ***Alert Message is Displayed if Email id is Invalid***

If email id doesn't contain . (dot) symbol, still an alert message is displayed (Figure 7.6).

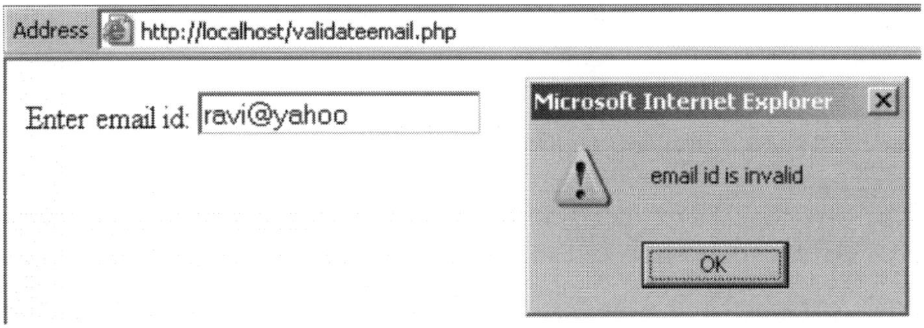

Figure 7.6 ***Alert Message is Displayed if dot(.) Not Added in the Address***

If the email id a valid email id, we find no errors (Figure 7.7).

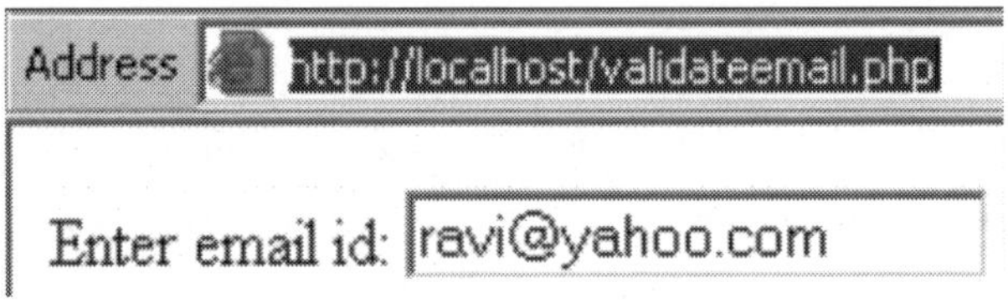

Figure 7.7 ***No Error Message is Displayed***

7.3.1 Validating email id—with Regular Expression

In this method, we check the validity of the email id with the help of regular expressions. We make two files named validateemail2.php and checkemail2.js with the following contents in the `htdocs` subfolder of the `apache` directory.

validateemail2.php

```
<html>
<head>
<script language="JavaScript" type="text/JavaScript" src="checkemail2.js"></
   script>
</head>
<body>
Enter email id: <input size="20" type="text" name="emailid" onblur
="validatefield(this)">
   </form>
```

```
</body>
</html>
```

This program is the same as the earlier program. It is invoking `validatefield()` method with email id entered by the user sent as argument to it.

checkemail2.js

```
function validatefield(obj)
{
        regex=/(^\w{2,}\@\w{2,}\.\w{2,})/;
        match=regex.exec(obj.value);
        if(!match)
        {
        alert("email id is invalid");
        obj.focus();
}
}
```

The object (email id) passed to the function is matched with a regular expression. If the email id doesn't match the regular expressions, an alert message is displayed. The regular expression:

```
regex=/(^\w{2,}\@\w{2,}\.\w{2,})/;
```

means that an email id must have two or more alphanumerical characters followed by @ (at) symbol and again two or more alphanumerical characters followed by . (dot) symbol which is again followed by two or more alphanumerical characters.

second way of writing `validatefield()` method:

```
function validatefield(obj)
{
            regex=/(^\w+\@\w+\.\w+)/;
            match=regex.exec(obj.value);
            if(!match)
            {
            alert("email id is invalid");
            obj.valid=false;
            obj.focus();
}
}
```

In this function, the regular expression is just changed. The regular expression:

```
regex=/(^\w+\@\w+\.\w+)/;
```

means that an email id must have one or more alphanumerical characters followed by a @ (at) symbol and again one or more alphanumerical characters followed by a . (dot) symbol which is again followed by one or more alphanumerical characters.

The output is the same as in the earlier example. For an invalid email, the error message: "email id is invalid" is displayed (Figure 7.8).

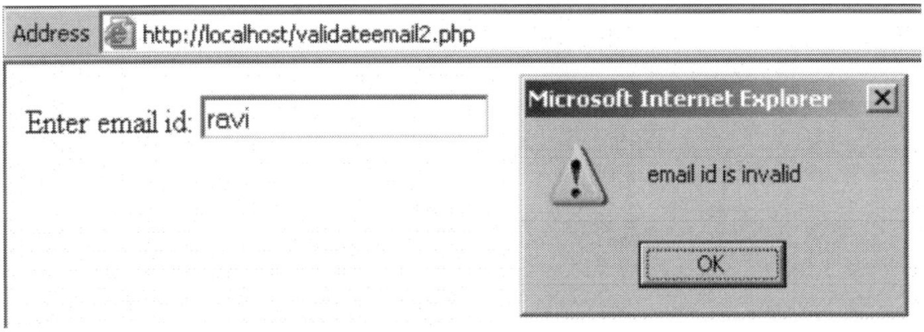

Figure 7.8 *Alert Message for Invalid Email id*

If . (dot) is missing, again the email id is considered to be an invalid email and hence, the error message: "email id is invalid" is displayed (Figure 7.9).

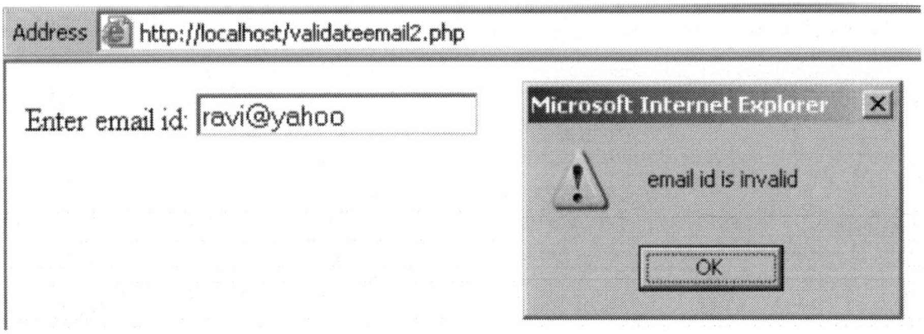

Figure 7.9 *Alert Message for Invalid Email id*

No error message is displayed for a valid email id and it is accepted (Figure 7.10).

Figure 7.10 *No Error Message is Displayed*

7.3.2 Validating email id—Using DOM

In the following example, instead of displaying error in the form of an alert message, we display it as text on the web page. That is, we define a <div> element on the web page which will be used for displaying error or other feedback messages to the user. We make two files named validateemail3.php and checkemail3.js with the following contents in the `htdocs` subfolder of the `apache` directory.

validateemail3.php

```
<html>
<head>
<script language="JavaScript" type="text/JavaScript"
src="checkemail3.js"></script>
</head>
<body>
Enter email id: <input size="20" type="text" name="emailid" onblur
="validatefield(this)"> <div id="emailmsg">
</body>
</html>
```

A JavaScript file checkemail3.js is included in the current page so the methods defined in it can be accessed from the current web page. The user is prompted to enter email id. The moment the user presses the tab key after entering email id, `validatefield()` method is executed with email id entered by the user passed to it as argument. Beside this, a <div> element with id `emailmsg` is defined where error or feedback messages will be displayed.

checkemail3.js

```
function validatefield(obj)
{
        var div=document.getElementById("emailmsg");
        div.style.color="red";
        if(div.hasChildNodes())
        {
        div.removeChild(div.firstChild);
        }
        regex=/(^\w+\@\w+\.\w+)/;
        match=regex.exec(obj.value);
```

```
if(!match)
{
div.appendChild(document.createTextNode("Invalid Email"));
obj.focus();
}
}
```

In the above program, we first search for the element named `emailmsg` in the document (web page). The div element `emailmsg` is made for displaying error messages. Set that element's colour to "red" (error messages are usually displayed in red to draw the user's attention). Then, we check if there are already some child nodes of the current element (i.e. if there is already some message displayed at the current element). If so, then that child node is removed (that is the earlier message if any is removed). After that, the object value i.e. email id passed as argument to this method is matched with the regular expression provided. If the email id doesn't match the regular expression, then a child in the form of text node displaying the message: "Invalid email" is added (appended) to the element `emailmsg` and focus is set to the email id field so that the user can enter a valid email id.

Output:

If an invalid email id is entered, an error message is displayed at the place of `<div>` element "emailmsg" instead of in the form of an alert message (Figure 7.11).

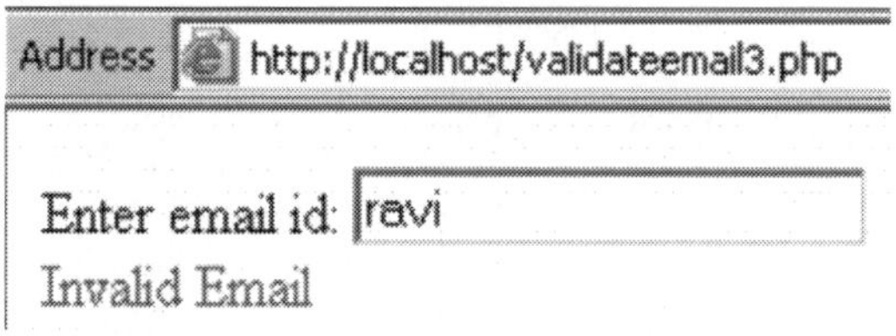

Figure 7.11 ***Error Message is Displayed in Place of Alert Message***

If . (dot) is not present in the email id, again an error message is displayed (Figure 7.12).

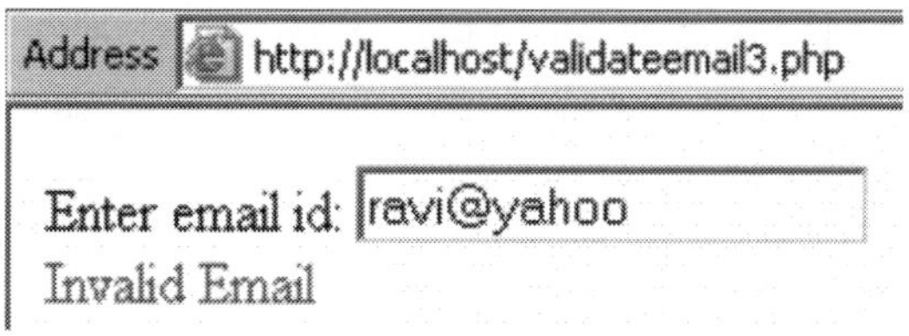

Figure 7.12 ***Error Message is Displayed***

If the email id has both @ (at) and . (dot) that means, the email id is valid and hence no error messages arise (Figure 7.13).

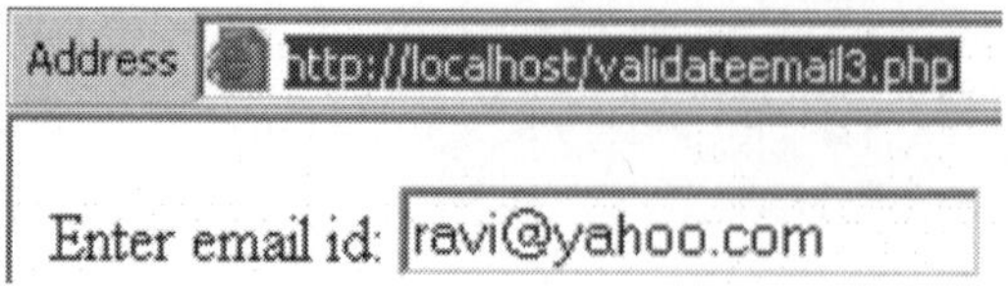

Figure 7.13 ***No Error Message is Displayed***

7.4 VALIDATING USERID—CHECKING IF IT ALREADY EXISTS

In the following example, we ask the user to enter a userid and if that userid already exists (that is found in the `customers` table of shopping database), an error message is displayed and the user is asked to enter another userid. The `shopping` database and `customers` table were created in "Shopping Cart Project" in Part I of this book. For reference, the structure of the `customers` table is provided (Figure 7.14).

mysql> describe customers;

Field	Type	Null	Key	Default	Extra
userid_code	Varchar<50>	NO	PRI		
first_name	Varchar<50>	YES		NULL	
last_name	Varchar<50>	YES		NULL	
add1	varchar<255>	YES		NULL	
add2	varchar<255>	YES		NULL	
city	Varchar<50>	YES		NULL	
state	Varchar<50>	YES		NULL	
zipcode	Varchar<12>	YES		NULL	
emailid	varchar<50>	YES		NULL	
password	Varchar<50>	YES		NULL	
phone_no	Varchar<50>	YES		NULL	
country	Varchar<50>	YES		NULL	

12 rows in set <0.28 sec>

Figure 7.14 ***Structure of the Table Customers***

We make two files named validateuserid.php and checkuserid.js with the following contents in the `htdocs` subfolder of the `apache` directory.

validateuserid.php

```
<html>
<head>
<script language="JavaScript" type="text/JavaScript" src="checkuserid.js"></script>
</head>
<body>
```

```
Enter user id: <input size="20" type="text" name="userid" onblur
="validatefield(this.value)"> <div id="uidmsg">
</body>
</html>
```

A JavaScript file checkuserid.js is included in the current page for using the methods defined in it from the current web page. The user is prompted to enter userid which is then validated with the help of `validatefield()` method that is invoked and userid entered by the user is passed to it as argument. Also, a <div> element with id `uidmsg` is defined where error or feedback messages can be displayed.

checkuserid.js

```
function makeRequestObject(){
var xmlhttp=false;
try {
xmlhttp = new ActiveXObject('Msxml2.XMLHTTP');
} catch (e) {
try {
xmlhttp = new
ActiveXObject('Microsoft.XMLHTTP');
} catch (E) {
xmlhttp = false;
}
}
if (!xmlhttp && typeof XMLHttpRequest!='undefined') {
xmlhttp = new XMLHttpRequest();
}
return xmlhttp;
}

function validatefield(user)
{
var div=document.getElementById("uidmsg");
div.style.color="red";
```

```
22. if(div.hasChildNodes())
23. {
24. div.removeChild(div.firstChild);
25. }
26. var xmlhttp=makeRequestObject();
27. xmlhttp.open('GET', 'ajaxcheckuser.php?userid='+user, true);
28. xmlhttp.onreadystatechange=function() {
29. if (xmlhttp.readyState==4 && xmlhttp.status == 200) {
30. var content = xmlhttp.responseText;
31. if( content ){
32. div.innerHTML = content;
33. }
34. }
35. }
36. xmlhttp.send(null);
37. }
```

Explanation of checkuserid.js program

Statements 1–17 are making an XMLHttpRequest object.

```
20. var div=document.getElementById("uidmsg");
21. div.style.color="red";
22. if(div.hasChildNodes())
23. {
24. div.removeChild(div.firstChild);
25. }
```

We first find the element in the document (web page) with id `uidmsg` (the <div> element defined for displaying error messages). Set that element's colour to "red" (error messages are usually displayed in red to draw the user's attention). Then, we check if it has already some child nodes (i.e if there is already some message displayed at this element). If it is so, then that child node is removed (that is, the earlier message if any is removed).

```
27. xmlhttp.open('GET', 'ajaxcheckuser.php?userid='+user, true);
28. xmlhttp.onreadystatechange=function() {
```

```
if (xmlhttp.readyState==4 && xmlhttp.status == 200) {
var content = xmlhttp.responseText;
if( content ){
div.innerHTML = content;
}
}
}
xmlhttp.send(null);
}
```

An XMLHttp request is made to the server (by GET method) for the file ajaxcheckuser.php, sending the userid entered by the user to it. The state and the response to asynchronous request are checked. If the value of `readyState` property becomes `4` and the value of the status of the HTTP Request is `200`, the response is then retrieved from the response stream and is assigned to variable `content` which is then applied to the innerHTML property of the element with id `uidmsg` to display the response from the server (i.e. to display the error message if the userid already exists in the `customers` table).

The instruction `xmlhttp.send(null)` is used to actually send the request to the server. If we don't want to pass any query string with the requested file, the argument passed to this method is null or else it contains the query string.

Remember, the actual checking of the userid is done in the file ajaxcheckuser.php (on server). And it is this file which returns the error message to the client if the userid already exists. Let's analyse how this file works.

ajaxcheckuser.php

```
<?php
$uid = $_GET["userid"];
mysql_connect("localhost", "root", "mce");
mysql_select_db("shopping");
$sql = "SELECT * FROM customers WHERE userid like '" . $uid . "'";
$result = mysql_query($sql) or die(mysql_error());
if (mysql_num_rows($result) == 1) {
echo "User already exist. Try another userid";
}
?>
```

In the above program, the userid passed is stored in a variable `$uid`. Then, a connection with MySQL server is established by user name `root` and password `mce`. Thereafter, the "shopping" database is selected and a SQL query is executed to find all the rows in the table `customers` with userid = `$uid` (that is, the userid entered by the user). If the query results in even a single row, it means there is already a record of a user in the `customers` table with the given userid. Hence an error message is returned to the client which is then pasted at the <div> element `uidmsg`.

Output:

If we enter a userid which already exists in the `customers` table, we get an error (Figure 7.15).

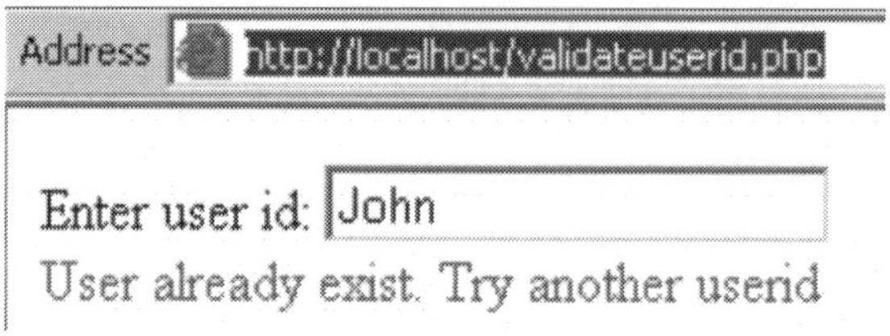

Figure 7.15 ***An Error Message is Displayed if Userid Already Exists***

If the userid entered doesn't exist already, no error appears (Figure 7.16).

Figure 7.16 ***No Error Message is Displayed if Userid Doesn't Exist Already***

7.5 VALIDATING FORM AND STORING THE RECORD IN THE TABLE (IF DATA IS VALID)

This is the best example to understand how validation is implemented in commercial web applications, because here instead of validating one element, we are validating three elements together and not only that, if the values in these elements are validated, that data will be stored in the `customers` table of shopping database (used in the earlier example).

validateform.php

```
<html>
<head>
<script language="JavaScript" type="text/JavaScript"
src="checkform.js"></script>
```

```
</head>
<body>
   Userid: <input size="20" type="text" name="userid" onblur
="validateuid(this)"> <div id="uidmsg"></div><br>
   Password: <input size="20" type="password" name="password" onblur
="if(this.value !='') {validatepwd(this)}"> <div id="pwdmsg"></div><br>
Enter email id: <input size="20" type="text" name="emailid" onblur
="if(this.value !='') {validateemail(this)}"> <div id="emailmsg"></div>
<div id="info"></div>
</body>
</html>
```

This program is including checkform.js file so as to invoke validation methods (stored in it) from this web page. This form asks the user to provided the following information: userid, password and email id. Since we don't want to display alert message for any mistake committed by the user, instead we want the error messages to be displayed in the form of text on the web page, so we define three <div> elements named `uidmsg`, `pwdmsg` and `emailmsg` to display error message for each element and place them adjacent to their respective elements on the form. Beside this, an element with id `info` is also defined in order to display any other server response.

checkform.js

```
function validateuid(obj)
{
var div=document.getElementById("uidmsg");
div.style.color="red";
if(div.hasChildNodes())
{
div.removeChild(div.firstChild);
}
if(obj.name=="userid")
{
if(obj.value.length ==0)
{
div.appendChild(document.createTextNode("User id cannot be blank"));
obj.focus();
```

```
}
}
}

function validatepwd(obj)
{
div=document.getElementById("pwdmsg");
div.style.color="red";
if(div.hasChildNodes())
{
div.removeChild(div.firstChild);
}
if(obj.name=="password")
{
if(obj.value.length <=5)
{
div.appendChild(document.createTextNode("The password should be of at least size 6"));
obj.focus();
}
}
}

function validateemail(obj)
{
div=document.getElementById("emailmsg");
div.style.color="red";
if(div.hasChildNodes())
{
div.removeChild(div.firstChild);
}
regex=/(^\w+\@\w+\.\w+)/;
match=regex.exec(obj.value);
```

```
if(!match)
{
div.appendChild(document.createTextNode("Invalid Email"));
obj.focus();
}
else
{
insertrec();
}
}

function makeRequestObject(){
var xmlhttp=false;
try {
xmlhttp = new ActiveXObject('Msxml2.XMLHTTP');
} catch (e) {
try {
xmlhttp = new
ActiveXObject('Microsoft.XMLHTTP');
} catch (E) {
xmlhttp = false;
}
}
if (!xmlhttp && typeof XMLHttpRequest!='undefined') {
xmlhttp = new XMLHttpRequest();
}
return xmlhttp;
}

function insertrec()
{
var xmlhttp=makeRequestObject();
user=document.getElementById('userid').value;
```

```
76. pswd=document.getElementById('password').value;
77. eml=document.getElementById('emailid').value;
78. xmlhttp.open('GET', 'insertdata.php?uid='+user+'&pwd='+pswd+'&email='+eml,
    true);
79. xmlhttp.onreadystatechange=function() {
80. if (xmlhttp.readyState==4 && xmlhttp.status == 200) {
81. var content = xmlhttp.responseText;
82. if( content ){
83. document.getElementById('info').innerHTML = content;
84. }
85. }
86. }
87. xmlhttp.send(null)
88. }
```

Explanation of checkform.js program

Meaning of statements 1–17

These instructions are finding an element in the document (web page) with id `uidmsg` (the <div> element defined for displaying error messages). The colour of this element is set to "red" and we check if it has already some child nodes (meaning if there is already some message displayed at this element). If it is so, it is removed (i.e. the earlier message if any is removed). Thereafter, it is checked if the object sent to this function is userid and if yes, its length is checked. If the length of userid is 0 (meaning the user hasn't entered anything in that field), then a text node containing a text message: "User id cannot be blank" is appended to this `uidmsg` <div> element so that the text appears at this element and focus is set on the userid element so the user can re-enter a valid userid.

Meaning of statements 18–34

These instructions are finding an element in the document with id `pwdmsg` and its colour is set to "red". It is checked whether there is already any message displayed in this element (whether it has any ChildNodes). If yes, then the message is deleted (ChildNode is removed). Then it is assured if the object sent to this function is password and if it is, then its length is checked. If the length of password is less than 6 characters, then a text node containing a text message: "The password should be of at least size 6" is appended to this `pwdmsg` <div> element so that the error message appears at this element and focus is set on password element so that the user can re-enter a valid password.

Meaning of statements 35–54

These instructions are finding an element in the document with id `emailmsg` and again its colour is set to “red”. Any earlier message displayed in this element is deleted (i.e. its ChildNodes if any are removed). The email id passed to this method is matched with a regular expression. The regular expression:

```
regex=/(^\w+\@\w+\.\w+)/
```

means that an email id must have one or more alphanumerical characters followed by a @ (at) symbol and one or more alphanumerical characters followed by a . (dot) symbol which is again followed by one or more alphanumerical characters. If the email id matches with the regular expression, then `insertrec()` method is executed for inserting the valid information passed by the user in the `customers` table and if email id doesn’t match with the regular expression, then a text node containing a text message “Invalid email” is appended to the `emailmsg` <div> element so that an error message is displayed at this element and focus is set on the email id element allowing the user to enter a valid email id.

Statements 55–87 are making an XMLHttpRequest object.

```
72. function insertrec()
73. {
74. var xmlhttp=makeRequestObject();
75. user=document.getElementById(‘userid’).value;
76. pswd=document.getElementById(‘password’).value;
77. eml=document.getElementById(‘emailid’).value;
78. xmlhttp.open(‘GET’, ‘insertdata.php?uid=’+user+’&pwd=’+pswd+’&email=’+eml,
    true);
79. xmlhttp.onreadystatechange=function() {
80. if (xmlhttp.readyState==4 && xmlhttp.status == 200) {
81. var content = xmlhttp.responseText;
82. if( content ){
83. document.getElementById(‘info’).innerHTML = content;
84. }
85. }
86. }
87. xmlhttp.send(null)
88. }
```

All the values entered by the user in form elements userid, password and emailid are retrieved and stored in variables `user`, `pswd` and `eml` respectively. Then an XMLHttp request is made to the server (by GET method) for the file insertdata.php, sending these three values to it (it is this file that will insert the information passed by the user into the `customers` table). The state and the response to asynchronous request are checked. If the value of readyState property becomes 4 and the value of the status of the HTTP Request is 200, the response is then retrieved from the response stream and is assigned to variable `content` which is then applied to the innerHTML property of the element with id `info` to display the response from the server. The instruction `xmlhttp.send(null)` is used to actually send the request to the server and since we don't want to pass any query string to this method, its argument is set to null.

Remember, the actual inserting of user information and returning of server response is done in file insertdata.php. Let's analyse how this file works.

insertdata.php

```
<?php
mysql_connect("localhost", "root", "mce");
mysql_select_db("shopping");
$uid = $_GET["uid"];
$pwd = $_GET["pwd"];
$email = $_GET["email"];
$sql = "insert into customers(userid, password, emailid) values('" . $uid . "',
'" . $pwd . "', '" . $email . "')";
$query = mysql_query($sql) or die(mysql_error());
echo 'Record Inserted';
?>
```

This program is first establishing connection with the MySQL server and then "shopping" database is selected. The userid, password and email id passed to this file are retrieved using `$_GET` array and stored in variables `$uid`, `$pwd` and `$email` respectively. An SQL statement is executed to insert the information passed by the user in `customers` table. If the insertion is successful, the server response in the form of text "Record Inserted" is passed to the client which is then displayed on the web page at the place of <div> element of id: `info`.

Output:

If user id is left blank, we get an error "User id cannot be blank" (Figure 7.17).

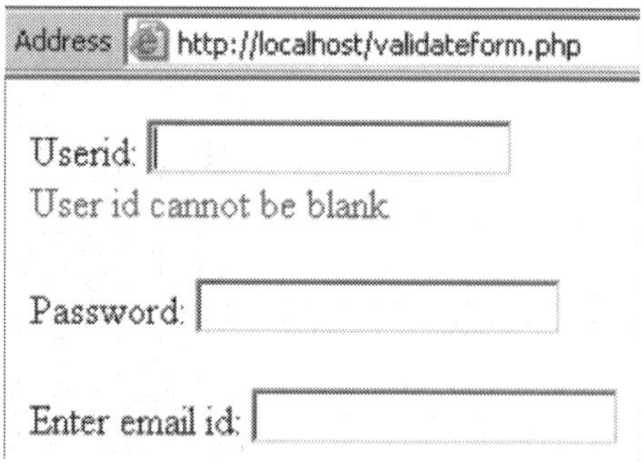

Figure 7.17 ***Error Message is Displayed if Userid is Left Blank***

If password entered is of less than 6 characters, we get an error "The password should be of at least size 6" (Figure 7.18).

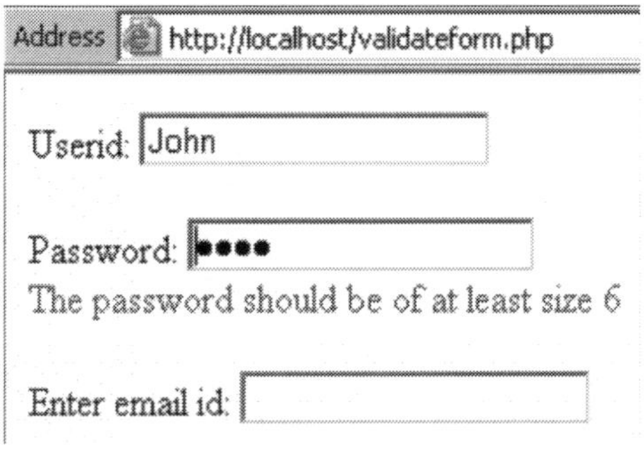

Figure 7.18 *Error Message is Displayed if the Password is Less than 6 Characters*

If email id is of length 0 or doesn't have . (dot) or @ (at) symbol in it, an error message: "Invalid Email" is displayed (Figure 7.19).

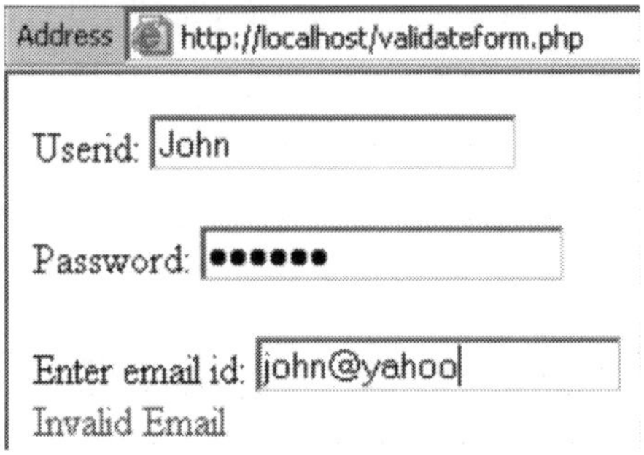

Figure 7.19 *Error Message is Displayed if Invalid email id is Given*

If all the information passed is valid, the record is inserted in the `customers` table and the message "Record Inserted" is displayed (Figure 7.20).

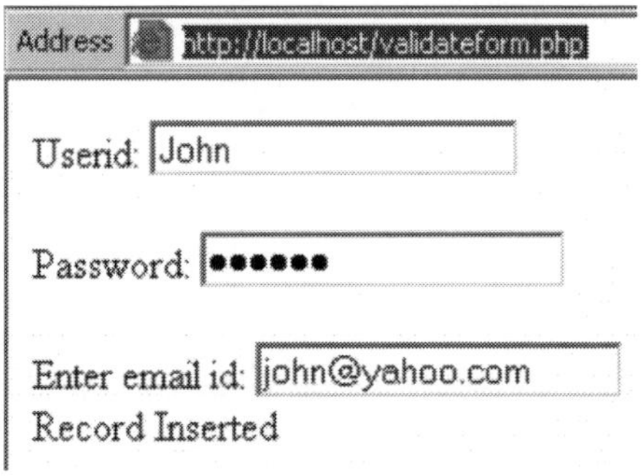

Figure 7.20 *If No Errors then Record Inserted is Displayed*

SUMMARY

In this chapter, we saw the role of validation in assuring that the information entered by the user is correct. We have seen the method of confirming that no essential field is left blank by the user while entering information. We also saw how to ensure that a field has enough data (minimum length). Also, we have seen the three different methods of validating email ids. We also saw the technique of validating a userid i.e. confirming that the specified userid exists in the given database. Finally, we saw the method of validating a form and storing the information in the table (if data in the form is found valid).

In the next chapter we will see the different types of response data retrieved from the server. Also, we will look at different DOM Node tree methods and properties and how XML response is received. We will study several programs that include the technique to display the contents of the first child, values (text) of all the child nodes of the given node, contents of the all the child nodes along with the names of the child nodes and contents of the selected nodes. We will have a good understanding of JSON i.e. what it is and how it is installed, how to receive data in JSON format, how to access the response through iteration, how to use library for encoding, how to convert data entered by user to JSON format and finally how to access database and display its contents in JSON format.

8

Receiving XML and JSON

XML is a W3C Recommendation that stands for EXtensible Markup Language. It is much like HTML and allows us to create our own markup to accommodate specific data. That is, XML gives us flexibility to define our own tags. It is designed to be self-descriptive and is very easy to maintain.

JSON is a lightweight data interchange format built on JavaScript. Being in a text-based format, JSON is easy to write and to understand for both humans and computers. JSON data structures consume less bytes when compared with XML structures.

In this chapter we will look at the following:

- Types of response data
- Different DOM node tree methods and properties
- Receiving XML response
- Display contents of the first child
- Display values (text) of all the child nodes of the given node
- Display values (text) of all the child nodes of the given node—2nd method
- Display contents of all the child nodes along with the names of the child nodes
- Display contents of the selected nodes
- What is JSON
- Installing JSON
- Receiving data in JSON format
- Accessing the response through iteration
- Using the library for encoding
- Converting data fed by the user to JSON format
- Accessing database and displaying in JSON format

Before we understand how to receive server response in XML format, let us first understand different types of response data.

8.1 TYPES OF RESPONSE DATA

Instead of just displaying, sometimes we need to process the response data retrieved from the server. The data is retrieved from the response stream (after the request is completed) with the help of the following properties:

- responseText
- responseXML

responseText

This property returns all the data that is a part of the response as a single string.

responseXML

This property returns all the data that is a part of the response as an XML document object. This object can be parsed using DOM node tree methods and properties.

Table 8.1 ***Different DOM Node Tree Manipulation Methods***

Methods	Description
createAttribute (Name);	Creates an attribute node with the given name.
createComment (comment);	Creates a comment node using the supplied comment string.
createDocumentFragment ( );	Creates a document fragment to hold a collection of nodes.
createElement (tagName);	Creates an element of the type specified by the tagName parameter.
createTextNode (text);	Creates a text node with the supplied text as its contents.
insertBefore (newChild, Node);	Inserts the nodes referenced by the newChild before the node referenced by the Node parameter in the document tree.
appendChild (newChild);	Append the node referenced by newChild to the end of the list of child nodes.
removeChild(childNode);	Removes the child node referenced by the childNode parameter from the list of children.
replaceChild(newNode,oldNode);	Replace the child node referenced by the oldNode parameter with the node referenced by the newNode parameter.
cloneNode(boolean);	Returns a reference to a copied or cloned version of the node. If the boolean parameter is true, then all the children are also included in the copy/cloning process.

Table 8.2 ***Different Node Properties***

DOMNode Object Properties	Description
nodeName	Contains the name of the node.
nodeValue	Contains the value of the node (applicable only to text nodes).
nodeTypes	Contains a number corresponding to the type of node. The node type can be: Element, Attribute, Text etc.
parentNode	A reference to the parent node of the current node is returned.
childNode	A reference to a list of child nodes is returned.
firstchild	A reference of first child node of a current object is returned.
lastchild	A reference to last child node of the current object is returned.
previousSibling	A reference to previous sibling node is returned.
nextSibling	A reference to the next sibling node is returned.
attributes	An array of attributes for the current nodeis returned.
ownerDocument	A reference to the containing document to which the node belongs is returned.

8.2 RECEIVING XML RESPONSE

To understand how to retrieve server response in terms of an XML document object and how the given node methods and properties can be applied to retrieve desired data, let us try a practical example. We will make three files named ajaxphpxml.html, ajaxxml1.js and school.xml file with the following contents in the `htdocs` folder of the `apache` directory.

ajaxphpxml.html

```
<!DOCTYPE html PUBLIC "-//W3C//DTD XHTML 1.1//EN" "http://www.w3.org/TR/xhtml11/DTD/xhtml11.dtd">
<html>
<head>
<script type="text/JavaScript" src="ajaxxml1.js"></script>
</head>
<body onload="showdata()">
The child nodes of Root node are <br>
<div id="info" />
</body>
```

```
</html>
```

This program is first importing the JavaScript file ajaxxml1.js to the current web page so that methods defined in it can be invoked from the current page. The event handler `onload()` function is used in the body tag to invoke `showdata()` method (present in ajaxxml1.js JavaScript file) when the page is all rendered. Also, `<div>` element (block element used for specifying the location for displaying the results) is defined with id `info`.

ajaxxml1.js

```
var xmlHttp;
function makeRequestObject(){
try {
xmlHttp = new ActiveXObject(‘Msxml2.XMLHTTP’);
} catch (e) {
try {
xmlHttp = new
ActiveXObject(‘Microsoft.XMLHTTP’);
} catch (E) {
xmlHttp = false;
}
}
if (!xmlHttp && typeof XMLHttpRequest!=’undefined’) {
xmlHttp = new XMLHttpRequest();
}
return xmlHttp;
}

function showdata()
{
var xmlHttp=makeRequestObject();
xmlHttp.open(“GET”, “school.xml”, true);
xmlHttp.onreadystatechange =function(){
if (xmlHttp.readyState == 4 && xmlHttp.status == 200)
```

```
24. {
25. try
26. {
27. readXML();
28. }
29. catch(e)
30. {
31. alert(“Error reading the response: ” + e.toString());
32. }
33. }
34. };
35. xmlHttp.send(null);
36. }

37. function readXML()
38. {
39. var xmlResponse = xmlHttp.responseXML;
40. xmlRoot = xmlResponse.documentElement;
41. var html=””;
42. for (var i=0; i<xmlRoot.childNodes.length; i++)
43. {
44. html+=xmlRoot.childNodes[i].nodeName+”<br>”;
45. }
46. document.getElementById(“info”).innerHTML = html;;
47. }
```

Explanation of ajaxxml1.js program

Statements 1–17 are used in building an XMLHttpRequest object.

```
21. xmlHttp.open(“GET”, “school.xml”, true);
22. xmlHttp.onreadystatechange =function(){
23. if (xmlHttp.readyState == 4 && xmlHttp.status == 200)
24. {
```

```
try
{
readXML();
}
catch(e)
{
alert("Error reading the response: " + e.toString());
}
}
};
xmlHttp.send(null);
}
```

An XMLHttpRequest request is made to the server (by GET method) for the file school.xml (the file containing data in XML format to be returned by the server). The state and the response to asynchronous request are checked. If the value of readyState property becomes 4 (meaning the request is complete) and the value of the status of the HTTP Request is 200 (which means there is no error), then `readXML()` method is executed (which extracts the data from XML file and assigns it to the innerHTML property of the <div> element `info` (to be displayed as server response).

```
function readXML()
{
var xmlResponse = xmlHttp.responseXML;
xmlRoot = xmlResponse.documentElement;
var html="";
for (var i=0; i<xmlRoot.childNodes.length; i++)
{
html+=xmlRoot.childNodes[i].nodeName+"<br>";
}
document.getElementById("info").innerHTML = html;;
}
```

The response is retrieved from the server in the form of an XML document object. This object can now be parsed using DOM node tree methods and properties. A reference to the root object (i.e. `school`) in the document tree is assigned to `xmlRoot` (refer to school.xml file). A loop is repeated equal to the number of child nodes of the root object to get the names of the child nodes. Since there are two child nodes of the root element student, the loop will run twice and the names of both the child nodes are stored in a variable `html` with a line break between them. The contents in the `html` variable (names of the child nodes) are assigned to the innerHTML property of the element on the web page with id `info`.

school.xml

```
<?xml version="1.0" encoding="UTF-8"?>
<school>
    <student>
        <roll>101</roll>
        <name>
            <first-name>Anil</first-name>
            <last-name>Sharma</last-name>
        </name>
        <address>
            <street>
                22/10 Sri Nagar Road
            </street>
            <city>
                Ajmer
            </city>
            <state>
                Rajasthan
            </state>
        </address>
        <marks>
            85
        </marks>
    </student>
    <student>
        <roll>102</roll>
        <name>
            <first-name>Manoj</first-name>
            <last-name>Arora</last-name>
        </name>
```

```
        <address>
            <street>
                H.No 11-B Alwar Gate
            </street>
            <city>
                Ajmer
            </city>
            <state>
                Rajasthan
            </state>
        </address>
        <marks>
            92
        </marks>
    </student>
</school>
```

This is an XML file whose data is retrieved and returned to the client as server response.

Output:

Both the child nodes of the root element `school` are displayed (Figure 8.1).

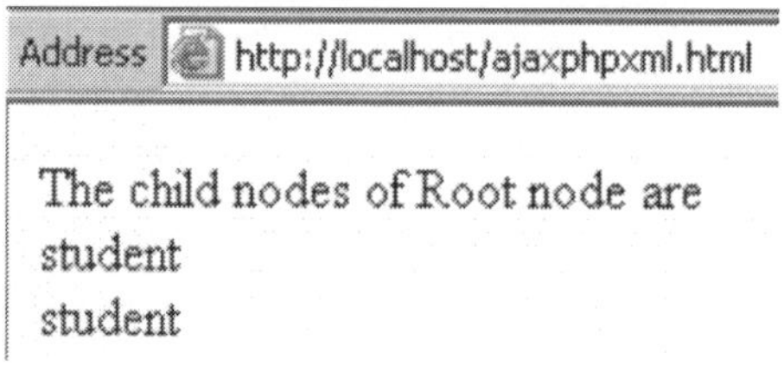

Figure 8.1 ***Child Nodes of the Root Node are Displayed***

8.3 DISPLAY CONTENTS OF THE FIRST CHILD

Suppose we want to see the value of the first child of all the child nodes of the root node, then replace `readXML()` method of the above example with the following contents:

```
    function readXML()
{
    var xmlResponse = xmlHttp.responseXML;
    xmlRoot = xmlResponse.documentElement;
    var html="";
    for (var i=0; i<xmlRoot.childNodes.length; i++)
    html += xmlRoot.childNodes[i].firstChild.text+"<br>";
    document.getElementById("info").innerHTML = html;;
}
```

The response is retrieved from the server in the form of an XML document object and is used to access the root element of the XML document (school). A loop is repeated equal to the number of child nodes of the root element to get the values of the first child of each child node of the root. The statement: xmlRoot.childNodes[i].firstChild.text retrieves the value (text) of the first child (roll) of the selected child node of the root `(student)`. These text values of the first child of both child nodes are separated with a line break and stored in a variable `html`. The contents of the `html` variable are assigned to the innerHTML property of the element on the web page with id `info` in order to display the first child values.

Output:

The values of all the sub-children of the child nodes of the root are displayed (Figure 8.2).

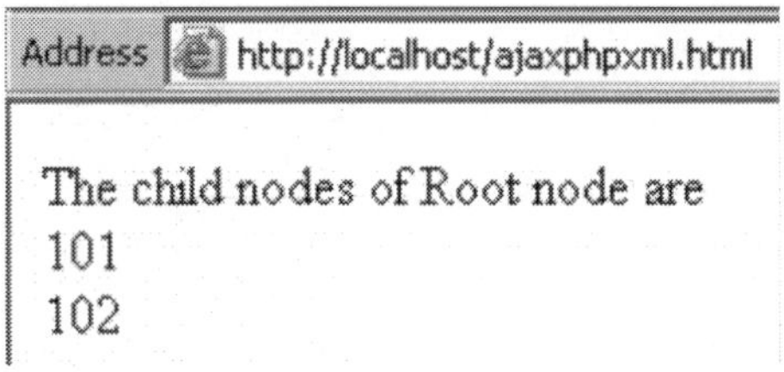

Figure 8.2 ***The Values of All the Sub-children are Displayed***

8.4 DISPLAY VALUES (TEXT) OF ALL THE CHILD NODES OF THE GIVEN NODE

Suppose we want to see all the matter stored in a particular child node, that is, if the values of all the child nodes of the given node are to be retrieved, then replace `readXML()` method of the example above with the following contents:

```
function readXML()
{
    var xmlResponse = xmlHttp.responseXML;
    xmlRoot = xmlResponse.documentElement;
    var html="";
    for (var i=0; i<xmlRoot.childNodes.length; i++)
    html += xmlRoot.childNodes[i].text+"<br>";
    document.getElementById("info").innerHTML = html;;
}
```

The response is retrieved from the server in the form of an XML document object which is used to access the root element of the XML document (school). A loop is repeated equal to the number of child nodes of the root element to get the complete text (xmlRoot.childNodes[i].text retrieves the values of all the sub-child nodes of the selected node). These values of the two child nodes are separated with a line break and stored in a variable `html`. The contents of the `html` variable (names of the child nodes) are assigned to the innerHTML property of the element on the web page with id `info`.

Output:

The values of all the sub-children of the child nodes of the root are displayed (Figure 8.3).

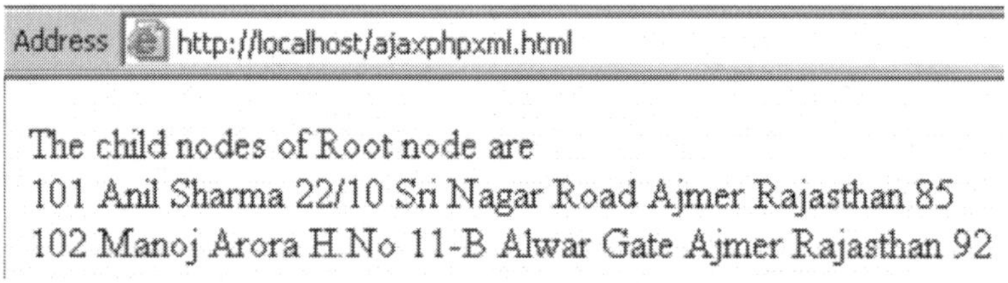

Figure 8.3 *The Values of All the Sub-children of the Child Nodes of the Root are Displayed*

8.5 DISPLAY VALUES (TEXT) OF ALL THE CHILD NODES OF THE GIVEN NODE—2ND METHOD

This method uses nested loops in order to see the values of all the child nodes of the given node. That is, there are two loops, one inside another. The outer loop runs for all the child nodes of the root node (school) i.e. it selects one child node of the root node i.e. student at a time, and the inner loop executes to display the values (text) of all the child nodes (roll, name, address and marks) of the selected child node of the root (student). To see its effect, replace `readXML()` method of the above example with the following contents:

```
function readXML()
{
```

```
    var xmlResponse = xmlHttp.responseXML;
    xmlRoot = xmlResponse.documentElement;
    var html="";
    for (var i=0; i<xmlRoot.childNodes.length; i++)
    {
    nod= xmlRoot.childNodes[i];
    for (var j=0; j<nod.childNodes.length; j++)
    {
    html += nod.childNodes[j].text+"<br>";
    }
    }
    document.getElementById("info").innerHTML = html;;
}
```

The response is retrieved from the server in the form of an XML document object and the object is used to access the root element of the XML document (i.e. `school`. Refer to school.xml file). A loop is repeated equal to the number of child nodes of the root element and one child node at a time i.e. student is assigned to variable `nod`. Again, a loop is repeated equal to the number of child nodes in `nod` (student node) and the value (text) of all its child nodes i.e. roll, name, address and marks are retrieved and stored in a variable `html`. That is the values of child nodes of both the student node are retrieved and assigned to `html` variable. The contents of the html variable are assigned to the innerHTML property of the element on the web page with id `info` in order to display the complete information of both the students' data.

Output:

The values of all the child nodes (roll, name, address and marks) of both child nodes of the root (student) are displayed (Figure 8.4).

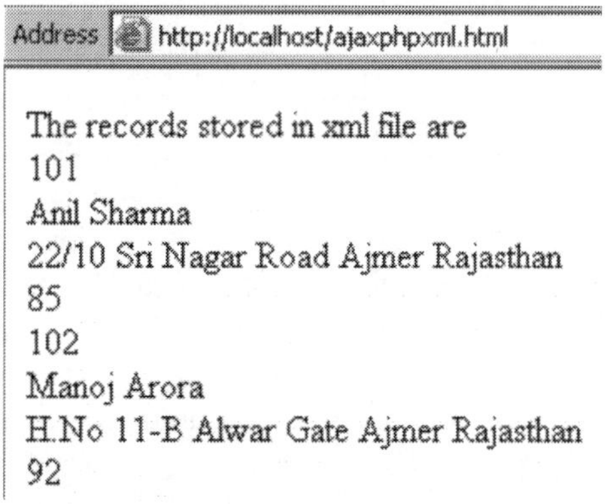

Figure 8.4 ***The Values of All the Child Nodes of Both Child Nodes of the Root are Displayed***

8.6 DISPLAY CONTENTS OF THE ALL THE CHILD NODES ALONG WITH THEIR NAMES

The only difference in the following and earlier example is that this displays the name of the node along with its values (text). To see its effect, replace `readXML()` method of the example above with the following contents:

```
function readXML()
{
    var xmlResponse = xmlHttp.responseXML;
    xmlRoot = xmlResponse.documentElement;
    var html="";
    for (var i=0; i<xmlRoot.childNodes.length; i++)
    {
    nod= xmlRoot.childNodes[i];
    for (var j=0; j<nod.childNodes.length; j++)
    {
    html+=nod.childNodes[j].nodeName+": ";
    html += nod.childNodes[j].text+"<br>";
    }
    }
    document.getElementById("info").innerHTML = html;;
}
```

The response is retrieved from the server in the form of an XML document object and the object is used to access the root element of the XML document (i.e. school). A loop is repeated equal to the number of child nodes of the root element and one child node at a time i.e. student is assigned to variable `nod`. Again, a loop is repeated equal to the number of child nodes in `nod` (student node) and the names of all the child nodes along with their values (text) i.e. roll, name, address and marks are retrieved and stored in a variable `html`. The contents of the `html` variable are assigned to the innerHTML property of the element on the web page with id `info` in order to display the complete information of both the students' data along with the names of the nodes.

Output:

The values of all the child nodes (roll, name, address and marks) of both child nodes of the root (student) are displayed along with the names of the nodes (Figure 8.5).

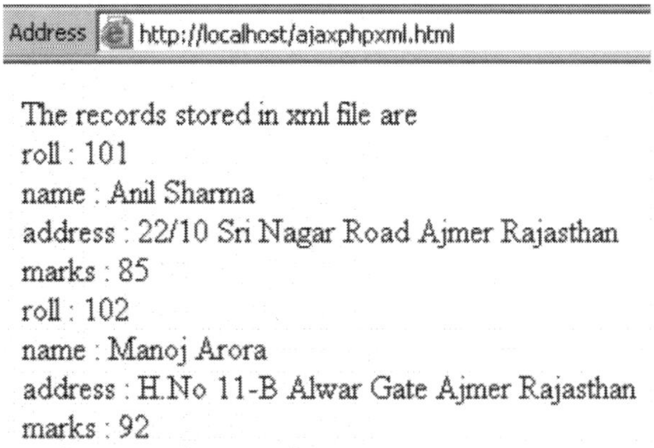

Figure 8.5 ***The Values of All the Child Nodes of Both Child Nodes of the Root are Displayed Along with the Names of the Nodes***

8.7 DISPLAY CONTENTS OF THE SELECTED NODES

Sometimes we don't want to display or process all the nodes of an XML document object, instead we just want to access or process certain specified nodes. The following example does exactly this i.e. it just accesses all the first names and last names from the XML document and displays them. To see how it's done, replace `readXML()` method of the example above with the following contents:

```
function readXML()
{
   var xmlResponse = xmlHttp.responseXML;
   xmlRoot = xmlResponse.documentElement;
   firstnameArray = xmlRoot.getElementsByTagName("first-name");
   lastnameArray = xmlRoot.getElementsByTagName("last-name");
   var html = "";
   for (var i=0; i<firstnameArray.length; i++)
      html += firstnameArray.item(i).firstChild.data +
            " " + lastnameArray.item(i).firstChild.data + "<br/>";
   document.getElementById("info").innerHTML = html;;
}
```

The response is retrieved from the server in the form of an XML document object and the object is used to access the root element of the XML document (i.e. school). All the nodes named "first-name" and "last-name" are searched and retrieved from the document and stored in the arrays: `firstnameArray` and `lastnameArray` respectively. The first name and last names are accessed from the two `arrays` and pasted along with a space in between and stored in a variable `html`. The first name and last name pairs of the two students (because there are two child nodes of the root) are separated with a line break and then stored in variable `html`. The contents of the `html` variable are assigned to innerHTML property of the element on the web page with id `info` in order to display the names.

Output:

The first name and last name pairs of both the child nodes (student) are displayed (Figure 8.6).

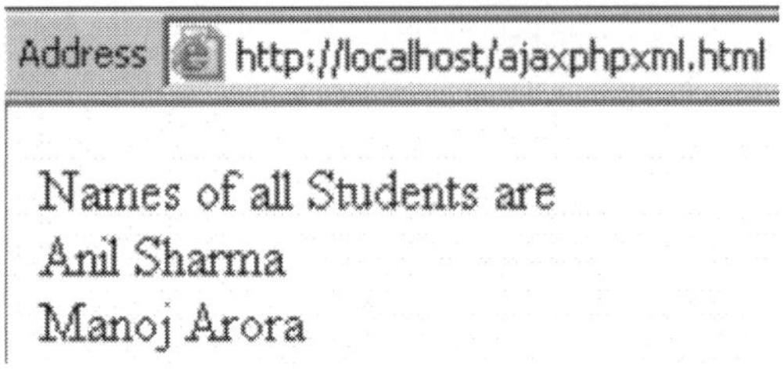

Figure 8.6 ***The First Name and Last Name Pairs of Both the Child Nodes are Displayed***

8.8 JSON (JAVASCRIPT OBJECT NOTATION)

JSON is a lightweight data interchange format built on JavaScript. Being in a text-based format, JSON is easy to write and to understand for both humans and computers. JSON data structures consume less bytes when compared with XML structures.

JSON is becoming more popular than XML because it has the following two characteristics:

- JSON is a data format preferred for exchanging information between a JavaScript client and a PHP server script as it consumes less bandwidth (its structure consumes less bytes).
- JSON is a text-based format that is easy to write and to understand for both humans and computers. That is, it is easy for machines to parse and generate JSON.

To compare the structure of XML and JSON, let's see how the two records of students are represented in XML and JSON.

8.8.1 XML Format

```
<?xml version="1.0" encoding="UTF-8"?>
<school>
    <student>
    <roll>101</roll>
    <name>Anil Sharma </name>
    <marks>85 </marks>
```

```
    </student>
    <student>
    <roll>102</roll>
    <name>Manoj Arora </name>
    <marks>92</marks>
    </student>
</school>
```

The same student structure can be represented in JSON as:

8.8.2 JSON Format

```
[
    "school":
    [
        {"student":
         {"roll":"101",
          "name": "Anil Sharma"},
          "marks":"85"}
        },
        {"student":
         {"roll":"102",
          "name": "Manoj Arora"},
          "marks":"92"}
        }
    ]
]
```

We can see that JSON format is smaller than XML and hence consumes lesser bytes. Let us compare a slightly more complex structure.

```
<?xml version="1.0" encoding="UTF-8"?>
<school>
```

```
<student>
    <roll>101</roll>
    <name>
        <first-name>Anil</first-name>
        <last-name>Sharma</last-name>
    </name>
    <address>
        <street>
            22/10 Sri Nagar Road
        </street>
        <city>
        Ajmer
    </city>
    <state>
        Rajasthan
    </state>
    </address>
    <marks>
        85
    </marks>
</student>
<student>
    <roll>102</roll>
    <name>
        <first-name>Manoj</first-name>
        <last-name>Arora</last-name>
    </name>
    <address>
        <street>
            H.No 11-B Alwar Gate
        </street>
        <city>
            Ajmer
```

```
            </city>
            <state>
               Rajasthan
            </state>
         </address>
         <marks>
            92
         </marks>
      </student>
</school>
```

This XML structure can be represented in JSON format as follows:

```
[
   "school":
    [
      {"student":
        {"roll":"101",
          "name":
             {"first-name": "Anil",
             "last-name": "Sharma"},
          "address":
             {"street": "22/10 Sri nagar Road",
             "city": "Ajmer",
             "state": "Rajasthan"},
          "marks":"85"}
      },
      {"student":
       {"roll":"102",
        "name":
             {"first-name": "Manoj",
             "last-name": "Arora"},
          "address":
```

```
            {"street": "H.No 11-B Alwar Gate",
            "city": "Ajmer",
            "state": "Rajasthan"},
        "marks":"92"}
      }
   ]
]
```

We can clearly see that JSON format is smaller in size.

JSON is a subset of JavaScript because it contains two basic structures:

1. array
2. object literals

8.8.3 Array

In JavaScript arrays are specified using square brackets ([]) in which values are enclosed delimited by comma.

Example:

```
var products=["Camera", "Mobile", "Book"];
```

We can even store values of different data types in an array:

```
var student=[101, "John", "11 Hill View Street", 85];
```

8.8.4 Object Literals

The object literals are used for storing information in terms of name-value pairs enclosed within curly braces ({ }). The name value pairs are separated by : (colon)

Syntax:

```
{ name1:value1, name2:value2, ... }
```

The type of the value can be an object, a string, a number, an array, true, false, or null.

Example:

```
var student = { “roll”: “101”, “name”: “John”, “marks”: “85”};
```

8.9 INSTALLING JSON

JSON libraries are available for most programming languages like ActionScript, C, C++, C#, Perl, PHP, Python, Ruby etc. For implementing JSON for PHP, a library, JSON.php is used. Just download this library from the net and copy it into the application's folder and refer it in the application by using the require_once directive.

Example:

```
require_once(‘JSON.php’);
```

While using JSON, encode and decode methods are used to encode a PHP object into JSON format and to decode a JSON string into a PHP object.

Let us write a program to build a simple JSON structure in PHP. Create a file phpjsondata.php file with the following contents in the `htdocs` subfolder of `apache` directory:

```
<?php
require_once(‘JSON.php’);
$json = new Services_JSON();
$students = array( array (‘roll’ => ‘101’,
            ‘name’ => ‘Anil Sharma’,
            ‘marks’ => ‘85’),
    array (‘roll’ => ‘102’,
            ‘name’ => ‘Manoj Arora’,
            ‘marks’ => ‘92’)
);
echo $json->encode($students);
?>
```

When we run this program, the JSON structure may appear as shown in Figure 8.7.

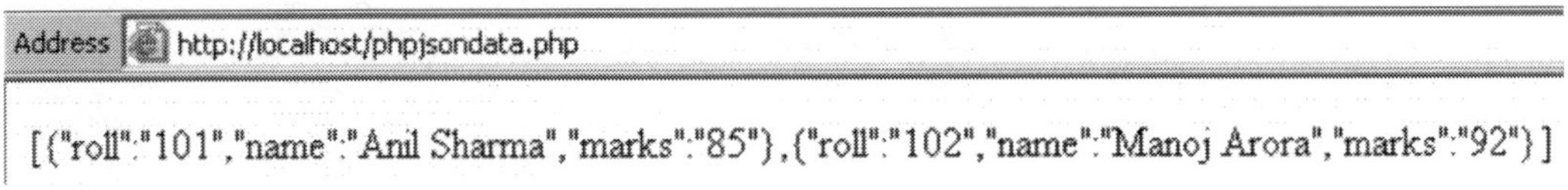

Figure 8.7 ***JSON Structure***

We can also create this JSON structured data as follows:

```
<?php
require_once(‘JSON.php’);
$json = new Services_JSON();
$students = array (‘student’ =>
    array(
        array (‘roll’ => ‘101’,
                ‘name’ => ‘Anil Sharma’,
                ‘marks’ => ‘85’),
        array (‘roll’ => ‘102’,
                ‘name’ => ‘Manoj Arora’,
                ‘marks’ => ‘92’)
));
echo $json->encode($students);
?>
```

When we run this program, the JSON structure may appear as shown in Figure 8.8.

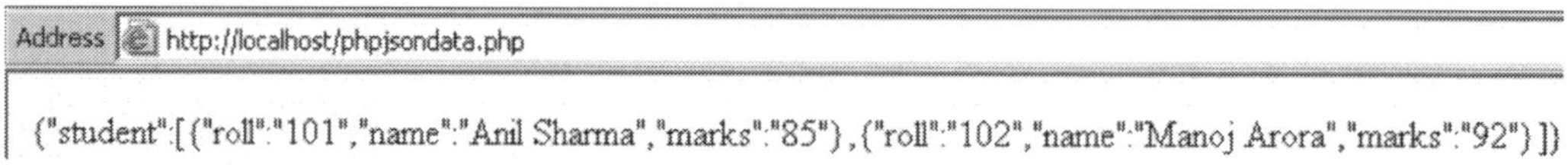

Figure 8.8 ***JSON Structure after Running the Program***

8.9.1 eval()

To parse JSON-formatted data, the easiest way is to use the built-in JavaScript `eval()` function. The syntax of `eval()` to read a JSON structure in JavaScript is:

```
variable = eval (‘(‘ + JSON encoded data + ‘) ‘);
```

The parentheses are necessary to inform JavaScript that the code is an expression to be evaluated instead of a statement to be run.

Example:

```
var p = eval("(" + JSON encoded data + ")");
```

If the JSON encoded data contains say roll, name, marks etc. they can be retrieved by p.roll, p.name and p.marks.

8.10 RECEIVING DATA IN JSON FORMAT

How the data is actually exchanged in JSON format, can be better explained with the help of a few running examples. The following example receives the data from the server in JSON structure and displays it on the client's screen. We have embedded the JavaScript code in this PHP script (but we can always make a separate file for keeping JavaScript code). Let's make two files named ajaxphpjson1.php and ajaxjsondata.php with the following contents in the `htdocs` subfolder of the `apache` directory.

ajaxphpjson1.php

```
<head>
<script language="JavaScript" type="text/JavaScript">

function makeRequestObject(){
var xmlhttp=false;
try {
xmlhttp = new ActiveXObject('Msxml2.XMLHTTP');
} catch (e) {
try {
xmlhttp = new
ActiveXObject('Microsoft.XMLHTTP');
} catch (E) {
xmlhttp = false;
}
}
if (!xmlhttp && typeof XMLHttpRequest!='undefined') {
xmlhttp = new XMLHttpRequest();
}
return xmlhttp;
```

```
}

function showdata()
{
var xmlhttp=makeRequestObject();
var file = 'ajaxjsondata.php';
xmlhttp.open('GET', file, true);
xmlhttp.onreadystatechange=function() {
if (xmlhttp.readyState==4 && xmlhttp.status == 200) {
var html="";
var content = eval(" (" + xmlhttp.responseText + ")" );
if( content ){
html+=" Roll:" + content.roll+"<br>"+"Name:"+content.name+"<br>"+"Address:"+content.address+"<br>"+"Marks:"+content.marks+"<br>";
document.getElementById('info').innerHTML = html;
}
}
}
xmlhttp.send(null)
}
</script>
</head>

<body onload="showdata()" >
The details of the student are <br>
<div id="info"></div>
</body>
</html>
```

ajaxjsondata.php

```
<?php
echo "{'roll': '101', 'name': 'John', 'address': '11 Hill View Street', 'marks': '85'}";
?>
```

Explanation of ajaxphpjson1.php program

Statements 3–19 are used for building an XMLHttpRequest object.

```
23. var file = 'ajaxjsondata.php';
24. xmlhttp.open('GET', file, true);
25. xmlhttp.onreadystatechange=function() {
26. if (xmlhttp.readyState==4 && xmlhttp.status == 200) {
```

An XMLHttpRequest request is made to the server (by GET method) for the file ajaxjsondata.php (the file containing data in JSON format to be returned by the server). The state and the response to asynchronous request is checked. If the value of readyState property becomes 4 (meaning the request is complete) and the value of the status of the HTTP Request is 200 (which means there is no error), then JSON formatted data is parsed.

```
28. var content = eval(" (" + xmlhttp.responseText + ")" );
```

This statement is parsing JSON formatted data. The server response is retrieved in the form of text, surrounded with parentheses and is then passed to `eval()` method. Recall that the parentheses are necessary to inform JavaScript that the code is an expression to be evaluated instead of a statement to be run. `eval()` method acts like a JavaScript interpreter and the result of this method is a JavaScript object which is assigned to a variable `content`.

In other words, the parsed JSON formatted data containing roll, name, address and marks (this is what been sent by the file ajaxjsondata.php on server) is assigned to variable `content`.

```
29. if( content ){
30. html+=" Roll:" + content.roll+"<br>"+"Name:"+content.name+"<br>"+"Address:"
    +content.address+"<br>"+"Marks:"+content.marks+"<br>";
31. document.getElementById('info').innerHTML = html;
32. }
33. }
34. }
35. xmlhttp.send(null)
36. }
```

The roll, name, address and marks assigned to variable `content` can be retrieved using commands like content.roll, content.marks etc. So, the data in `content` variable is retrieved and titles such as Roll, Name, Address and line breaks are added and stored in a variable `html`. The information in `html` variable is assigned to the innerHTML property of the <div> element `info` (defined on the web page to display server response). The instruction `xmlhttp.send(null)` is for actually sending the request to the server and since we don't want to pass any query string to the file being invoked (ajaxjsondata.php), its argument is set to null.

Remember, the server response i.e. JSON formatted data is actually generated by file ajaxjsondata.php. Let us see its contents:

Explanation of the ajaxjsondata.php program

ajaxjsondata.php

```
<?php
echo "{'roll': '101', 'name': 'John', 'address': '11 Hill View Street',
 'marks': '85'}";
?>
```

This just returns the data (roll, name, address and marks) in JSON format to the client.

Output:

The JSON formatted data returned by server is displayed (Figure 8.9).

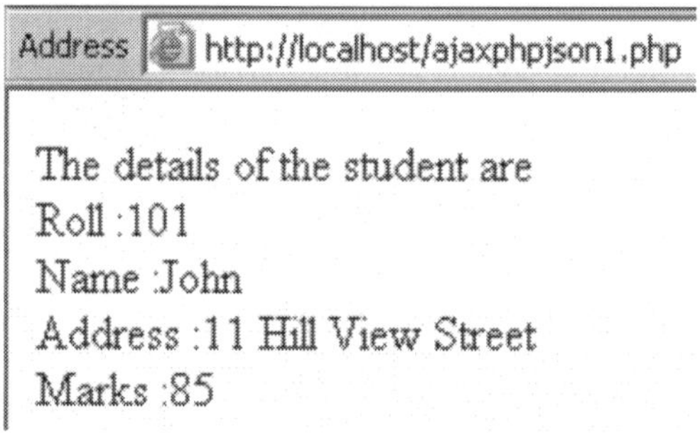

Figure 8.9 ***Display of JSON Formatted Data Returned by Server***

8.11 ACCESSING THE JSON RESPONSE THROUGH ITERATION

We observe that in `showdata()` method of the ajaxphpjson1.php program, the titles Roll, Name, Address etc. have been added before the actual data, content.roll, content.name etc. It may be tedious if the information sent by server is very large.

So, `showdata()` method in the program above can be modified as shown below:

```
function showdata()
{
var xmlhttp=makeRequestObject();
```

```
4. var file = 'ajaxjsondata.php';
5. xmlhttp.open('GET', file, true);
6. xmlhttp.onreadystatechange=function() {
7. if (xmlhttp.readyState==4 && xmlhttp.status == 200) {
8. var html="";
9. var content = eval(" (" + xmlhttp.responseText + ")" );
10. if( content ){
11. for(var key in content)
12. html+=key+": "+content[key]+"<br>";
13. document.getElementById('info').innerHTML = html;
14. }
15. }
16. }
17. xmlhttp.send(null)
18. }
```

Since the JSON formatted data is usually a sort of associative array i.e. in the form of key:value pair, this statement

```
11. for(var key in content)
```

loops through all the keys in the content variable i.e. variable `key` will be assigned one key from `content` variable at a time i.e. it will be assigned roll, name, address etc. at a time and the value corresponding to a key is retrieved by using content[key].

Hence in the following statement:

```
12. html+=key+": "+content[key]+"<br>";
```

key will display roll, name etc. and content[key] will retrieve the value associated with that key

The output of the program ajaxphpjson1.php is as shown in Figure 8.10.

Output:

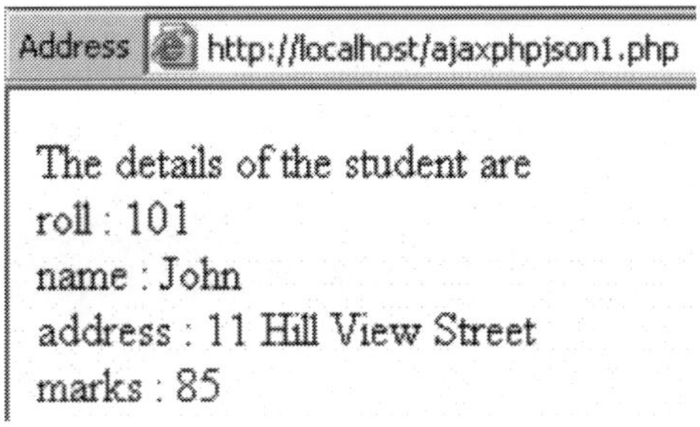

Figure 8.10 ***Output of Showdata Function***

8.12 USING THE LIBRARY FOR ENCODING

The response generated by the server can also be encoded using the library JSON.php. So, let's modify the contents of the file ajaxjsondata.php as shown:

ajaxjsondata.php

```
<?php
require_once "JSON.php";
$json = new Services_JSON();
//convert php object to json
$value = array('roll' => '101', 'name' => 'John', 'address' => '11 Hill View Street', 'marks' => '85');
echo $json->encode($value);
?>
```

Remember, the library file JSON.php must be present in the `htdocs` subfolder of the `apache` directory (application's folder). We refer this library file in our application using the require_once directive:

```
require_once('JSON.php');
```

In order to start using it effectively, we need to instantiate the class:

```
$json= new Services_JSON();
```

The encode and decode methods allow us to encode a PHP object into JSON format and to decode a JSON string into a PHP object.

The following statement encodes the PHP object into JSON format:

```
echo $json->encode($value);
```

There will be no change in the output.

8.13 CONVERTING DATA ENTERED BY THE USER TO JSON FORMAT

In the examples above, the values for roll, name, address etc were not entered by the user; instead we have taken fixed values for them. In the following example, we prompt the user to provide his/her information and that information is converted to JSON format and returned by the server. Let us make three files ajaxphpjson3.php, ajaxphpjson3.js and ajaxjsondata3.php with the following contents in the `htdocs` subfolder of the `apache` directory.

ajaxphpjson3.php

```
<html>
<head>
<script language="JavaScript" type="text/JavaScript" src="ajaxphpjson3.js"></
script>
</head>
<body>
Enter Name: <input size="20" type="text" name="name"><br>
Enter Email id: <input size="20" type="text" name="emailid"><br>
Enter contact no: <input size="20" type="text" name="contactno"><br>
   <input type="button" onclick="showdata()" value="Submit">
<div id="info"></div>
</body>
</html>
```

This program is importing the JavaScript file ajaxphpjson3.js to the current web page so that the methods defined in it can be invoked from here. Three text boxes are provided for the user to fill in name, email and contact no. A button is provided and an event handler onclick is attached to it so that when the user clicks on the button, the `showdata()` method specified in the JavaScript file is invoked. A <div> element with id `info` is defined to display server response at the place of this element.

ajaxphpjson3.js

```
function makeRequestObject(){
var xmlhttp=false;
try {
xmlhttp = new ActiveXObject('Msxml2.XMLHTTP');
} catch (e) {
try {
xmlhttp = new
ActiveXObject('Microsoft.XMLHTTP');
} catch (E) {
xmlhttp = false;
```

```
11. }
12. }
13. if (!xmlhttp && typeof XMLHttpRequest!='undefined') {
14. xmlhttp = new XMLHttpRequest();
15. }
16. return xmlhttp;
17. }

18. function showdata()
19. {
20. var xmlhttp=makeRequestObject();
21. nme=document.getElementById('name').value;
22. email=document.getElementById('emailid').value;
23. contact=document.getElementById('contactno').value;
24. xmlhttp.open('GET', 'ajaxjsondata3.php?name='+nme+'&emailid=' +email+'
    &contactno='+contact, true);
25. xmlhttp.onreadystatechange=function() {
26. if (xmlhttp.readyState==4 && xmlhttp.status == 200) {
27. var html="";
28. var content = eval(" (" + xmlhttp.responseText + ")" );
29. if( content ){
30. for(var key in content)
31. html+=key+": "+content[key]+"<br>";
32. document.getElementById('info').innerHTML = html;
33. }
34. }
35. }
36. xmlhttp.send(null)
37. }
```

Explanation of ajaxphpjson3.js program

Statements 1–17 are used for building an XMLHttpRequest object.

```
20. var xmlhttp=makeRequestObject();
21. nme=document.getElementById('name').value;
22. email=document.getElementById('emailid').value;
23. contact=document.getElementById('contactno').value;
```

The information (name, emailid and contactno) fed by the user on client machine (through ajaxphpjson3.php file) are retrieved using `getElementById(element name/id).value` method and stored in variables `nme`, `email` and `contact` respectively. The method `getElementById(element name/id)` is for searching for an element in the document (web page) with the specified element name or id and value property is for accessing the data entered in that element.

```
24. xmlhttp.open('GET', 'ajaxjsondata3.php?name='+nme+'&emailid='+email+'
    &contactno='+contact, true);
```

An XMLHttpRequest request is made to the server (by GET method) for the file ajaxjsondata3.php (the file on the server meant for returning information in JSON format to the client). While making the request for ajaxjsondata3.php file, the information consisting of name, email and contact number entered by the user is passed to this file.

```
25. xmlhttp.onreadystatechange=function() {
26. if (xmlhttp.readyState==4 && xmlhttp.status == 200) {
```

The state and the response to asynchronous request are checked. If the value of readyState property becomes 4 (meaning the request is complete) and the value of the status of the HTTP Request is 200 (which means there is no error), then JSON formatted data is parsed.

```
28. var content = eval(" (" + xmlhttp.responseText + ")" );
```

This statement is parsing JSON formatted data. The server response is retrieved in the form of text, surrounded with parentheses (parentheses are to inform JavaScript that the code is an expression to be evaluated instead of to be run) and is then passed to `eval()` method. `eval()` method acts like a JavaScript interpreter and the result of this method is a JavaScript object which is assigned to a variable `content`.

In other words, the parsed JSON formatted data containing name, email and contact no (sent by the file ajaxjsondata3.php placed on server) is assigned to variable `content`.

```
30. for(var key in content)
31. html+=key+": "+content[key]+"<br>";
```

Since the JSON formatted data is usually a sort of associative array i.e. in the form of key:value pair, this statement loops through all the keys in the `content` variable i.e. variable `key` will be assigned one key from content variable at a time i.e. it will be assigned name, email id, contact no etc. one at a time and the value corresponding to a key is retrieved by using `content[key]`. So, `key` will display name, email id and contact no and `content[key]` will retrieve the value associated with that key. These keys and values are retrieved and assigned to a variable `html` with a line break in between.

```
32. document.getElementById('info').innerHTML = html;
```

The information in `html` variable is assigned to the innerHTML property of the <div> element `info` (defined on the web page to display server response).

```
36. xmlhttp.send(null)
```

This instruction is for actually sending the request to the server and since we don't want to pass any query string to the file being invoked (ajaxjsondata3.php), its argument is set to null.

Remember, the server response i.e. JSON formatted data is actually generated by file ajaxjsondata3.php. Let's see its contents:

ajaxjsondata3.php

```
<?php
require_once "JSON.php";
$json = new Services_JSON();
$name = $_GET["name"];
$emailid = $_GET["emailid"];
$contactno = $_GET["contactno"];

//convert php object to json
$value = array('name' => $name, 'emailid' => $emailid, 'contactno' =>
$contactno);
echo $json->encode($value);
?>
```

The library file JSON.php is referenced in this program using the require_once directive (so that it can be used in encoding data in JSON format). Also, in order to use it effectively, we need to instantiate the class by the following statement:

```
$json= new Services_JSON();
```

We retrieve the name, email id and contact no sent by the client and assign them to variables `$name`, `$emailid` and `$contactno` respectively. The information in these variables is used to form an associative array named `$value`.

The information in associative array `$value` is encoded from a PHP object into JSON format and sent to the client using the following statement:

```
echo $json->encode($value);
```

Output:

The user is prompted to enter his/her information followed by clicking the Submit button (Figure 8.11).

Figure 8.11 *The User is Prompted to Enter Details and Click the Submit Button*

On clicking the Submit button, server response is generated displaying all the information entered by the user (Figure 8.12).

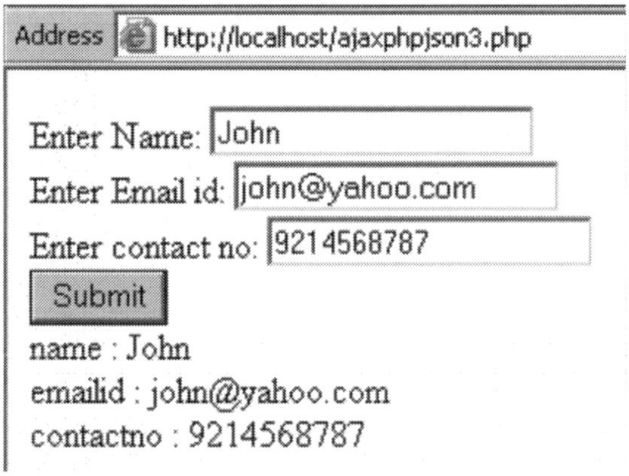

Figure 8.12 *Server Response is Generated Displaying all the Information*

8.14 ACCESSING DATABASE AND DISPLAYING IN JSON FORMAT

In the following example, the user is given a list of Categories (of items available) in the form of a combobox and the user is supposed to select one. Then, all the items in `products` table under the selected Category are returned to the client for display.

Let's make three files ajaxphpjson4.php, ajaxphpjson4.js and ajaxjsondata4.php with the following contents in the `htdocs` subfolder of the `apache` directory.

ajaxphpjson4.php

```
<html>
<head>
<script language="JavaScript" type="text/JavaScript" src="ajaxphpjson4.js"></
script>
```

```
</head>
<body>
Select Category of item:
<?php
$connect = mysql_connect("localhost", "root", "mce") or die("Please, check your
server connection.");
mysql_select_db("shopping");
$query = "SELECT distinct category FROM products ";
$results = mysql_query($query) or die(mysql_error());
?>
        <select name="Category" onChange='showdata(this.value)' >
            <option value="" selected>Select Products Category</option>
        <?php
        while ($row = mysql_fetch_array($results)) {
        extract($row);
?>
            <option value="<?php echo $category; ?>"><?php echo $category;
        ?></option>
        <?php
        }
        ?>
        </select><br><br><br>
        <div id="info"></div>
        </body>
        </html>
```

Explanation of ajaxphpjson4.php program

This program is importing the JavaScript file ajaxphpjson4.js to the current web page so that the methods defined in it can be invoked from here. To display the categories of items available, all the unique categories from the `products` table are fetched and displayed in the form of a combobox to the user. Line-by-line explanation is as follows:

```
$connect = mysql_connect("localhost", "root", "mce") or die("Please, check your
server connection.");
```

Connection to the local MySQL server is established with the user name "root" and password "mce".

```
mysql_select_db("shopping");
```

The database "shopping" is selected as the products table from where categories of items are to be fetched exists in this database.

```
$query = "SELECT distinct category FROM products ";
```

An SQL query is written to fetch all the distinct categories present in the products table.

```
$results = mysql_query($query) or die(mysql_error());
```

The SQL query is executed and different categories present in the products table are retrieved and stored in $results array.

```
<select name="Category" onChange='showdata(this.value)' >
        <option value="" selected>Select Products Category</option>
    <?php
    while ($row = mysql_fetch_array($results)) {
    extract($row);
    ?>
        <option value="<?php echo $category; ?>"><?php echo $category;
    ?></option>
    <?php
    }
    ?>
    </select>
```

A combobox named "Category" is made in which all the rows (categories) present in $results array are fetched and displayed as options. If any of the options (category) are selected from this combobox, it will result in invoking showdata() method and the option selected is passed to it as argument.

```
<div id="info"></div>
```

A <div> element with id info is defined to display server response.

ajaxphpjson4.js

```
function makeRequestObject(){
var xmlhttp=false;
try {
```

```
xmlhttp = new ActiveXObject(‘Msxml2.XMLHTTP’);
} catch (e) {
try {
xmlhttp = new
ActiveXObject(‘Microsoft.XMLHTTP’);
} catch (E) {
xmlhttp = false;
}
}
if (!xmlhttp && typeof XMLHttpRequest!=’undefined’) {
xmlhttp = new XMLHttpRequest();
}
return xmlhttp;
}
function showdata(cat)
{
var xmlhttp=makeRequestObject();
xmlhttp.open(‘GET’, ‘ajaxjsondata4.php?Category=’+cat, true);
xmlhttp.onreadystatechange=function() {
if (xmlhttp.readyState==4 && xmlhttp.status == 200) {
eval(“var response = (“ + xmlhttp.responseText + “)”);
var msg = ‘<TABLE BORDER=”1" CELLSPACING=”0" CELLPADDING=”0">’;
msg += ‘<TR>’;
msg += ‘<TH align=”left”>Item Code</TH>’;
msg += ‘<TH align=”left”>Name of Item</TH>’;
msg += ‘<TH align=”left”>Description</TH>’;
msg += ‘<TH align=”left”>Price</TH>’;
msg += ‘</TR>’;
for(var i in response)
{
msg += ‘<TR>’;
msg += ‘<TD>’ + response[i].item_code + ‘</TD>’;
```

```
36. msg += '<TD>' + response[i].item_name + '</TD>';
37. msg += '<TD>' + response[i].description + '</TD>';
38. msg += '<TD>' + response[i].price + '</TD>';
39. msg += '</TR>';
40. }
41. msg += '</TABLE>';
42. document.getElementById('info').innerHTML = msg;
43. }
44. }
45. xmlhttp.send(null);
46. }
```

Explanation of ajaxphpjson4.js program

Statements 1–17 are used for building an XMLHttpRequest object.

```
21. xmlhttp.open('GET', 'ajaxjsondata4.php?Category='+cat, true);
22. xmlhttp.onreadystatechange=function() {
23. if (xmlhttp.readyState==4 && xmlhttp.status == 200) {
```

An XMLHttpRequest request is made to the server (by GET method) for the file ajaxjsondata4.php (the file on the server meant for returning information in JSON format to the client). While making the request for the file, the Category of item selected by user (through combobox in ajaxphpjson4.php file) is passed to this file.

The state and the response to asynchronous request are checked. If the value of readyState property becomes 4 (meaning the request is complete) and the value of the status of the HTTP Request is 200 (which means there is no error), then JSON formatted data is parsed.

```
24. eval("var response = (" + xmlhttp.responseText + ")");
25. var msg = '<TABLE BORDER="1" CELLSPACING="0" CELLPADDING="0">';
26. msg += '<TR>';
27. msg += '<TH align="left">Item Code</TH>';
28. msg += '<TH align="left">Name of Item</TH>';
29. msg += '<TH align="left">Description</TH>';
30. msg += '<TH align="left">Price</TH>';
31. msg += '</TR>';
```

The statement: 24 is parsing JSON formatted data. The server response is retrieved in the form of text, surrounded with parentheses (parentheses are to inform JavaScript that the code is an expression to be evaluated instead of to be run) and is then passed to `eval()` method. `eval()` method acts like a JavaScript interpreter and the result of this method is a JavaScript object which is assigned to a variable `response`.

In other words, the parsed JSON formatted data containing rows of the products under the specified category (sent by the file ajaxjsondata4.php) is assigned to variable `response` and a variable named `msg` is initialised to contain a table with headings Item Code, Name of Item, Description and Price.

```
for(var i in response)
{
msg += '<TR>';
msg += '<TD>' + response[i].item_code + '</TD>';
msg += '<TD>' + response[i].item_name + '</TD>';
msg += '<TD>' + response[i].description + '</TD>';
msg += '<TD>' + response[i].price + '</TD>';
msg += '</TR>';
}
msg += '</TABLE>';
```

Since the JSON formatted data returned by the server consists of an array of items of the selected category, a loop is used to retrieve one row at a time and the attributes item_code, item_name, description and price of every row (containing the respective information of a product) are retrieved and stored in the form of a table in `msg` variable.

```
document.getElementById('info').innerHTML = msg;
```

The table of products (having the rows of products of the selected category) in `msg` variable is assigned to the innerHTML property of the <div> element `info` (defined on the web page to display server response). And the statement `xmlhttp.send(null)` is for actually sending the request to the server and since we don't want to pass any query string to the file being invoked (ajaxjsondata4.php), its argument is set to null.

Remember, the server response i.e. JSON formatted data is actually generated by file ajaxjsondata4.php. Let's see its contents:

ajaxjsondata4.php

```
<?php
require_once "JSON.php";
$json = new Services_JSON();
$cat = $_GET["Category"];
mysql_connect("localhost", "root", "mce");
```

```
mysql_select_db("shopping");
$sql = "SELECT * FROM products WHERE Category like '" . $cat . "' order by
item_code";
$resultSet = mysql_query($sql) or die(mysql_error());
while($obj = mysql_fetch_object($resultSet)) { $arr[] = $obj; }
echo( $json->encode( $arr ) );
?>
```

The library file JSON.php is referenced using the require_once directive (so that it can be used in encoding data in JSON format). Then, we instantiate the class. The category of the item selected by the user sent by the client program is retrieved and stored in `$cat` variable. Connection to the local MySQL server is established with the user name "root" and password "mce". The database `"shopping"` is selected as the `products` table from where products of the selected category are to be fetched exists in this database. An SQL query is written to fetch all the products whose category matches the category specified in `$cat` variable. The SQL query is executed and all the products of the selected category are retrieved from the `products` table and stored in `$resultSet` array.

The following loop fetches one row (product) at a time from the resultSet array and stores it in an array `$arr` in the form of a PHP object:

```
while($obj = mysql_fetch_object($resultSet)) { $arr[] = $obj; }
```

The array of PHP objects `$arr` is encoded from a PHP object into JSON format and sent to client using the following statement:

```
echo( $json->encode( $arr ) );
```

Output:

A combobox is provided showing all the categories of items available (Figure 8.13).

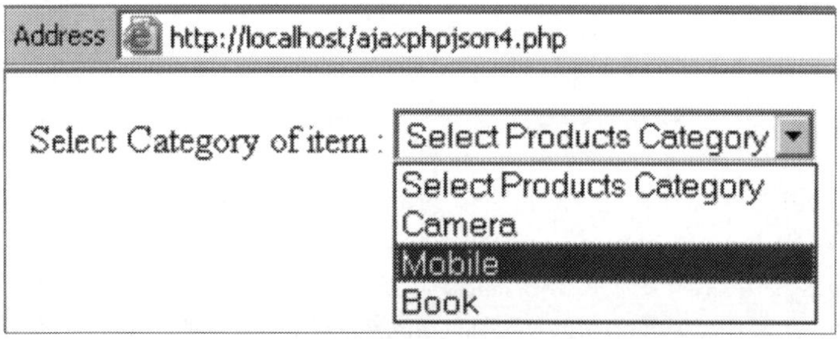

Figure 8.13 ***A Combobox Displaying All the Categories of Items Available***

If the user selects a category, say, Mobile, then all the items under Mobile category in the products table are displayed (Figure 8.14).

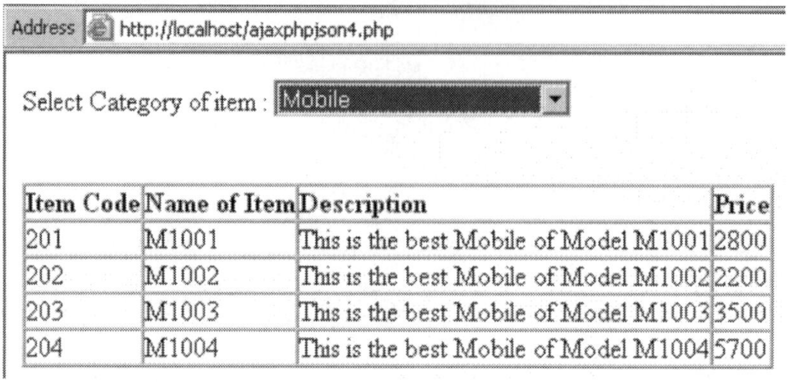

Item Code	Name of Item	Description	Price
201	M1001	This is the best Mobile of Model M1001	2800
202	M1002	This is the best Mobile of Model M1002	2200
203	M1003	This is the best Mobile of Model M1003	3500
204	M1004	This is the best Mobile of Model M1004	5700

Figure 8.14 ***Description of Details of Mobile Category***

Similarly, if the user selects a category, say, Book, then all the items under the Book category in the `products` table are displayed (Figure 8.15).

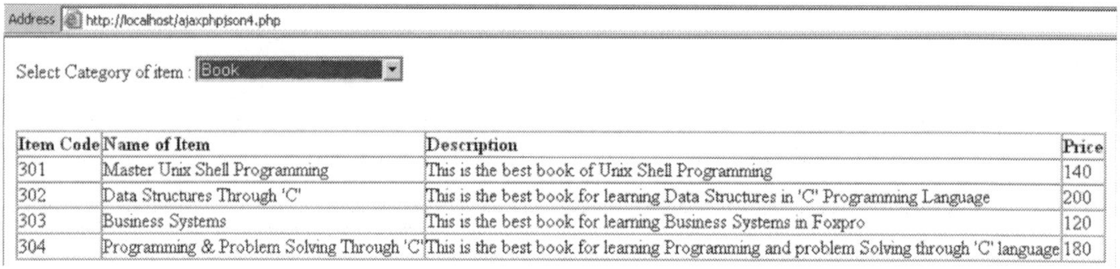

Item Code	Name of Item	Description	Price
301	Master Unix Shell Programming	This is the best book of Unix Shell Programming	140
302	Data Structures Through 'C'	This is the best book for learning Data Structures in 'C' Programming Language	200
303	Business Systems	This is the best book for learning Business Systems in Foxpro	120
304	Programming & Problem Solving Through 'C'	This is the best book for learning Programming and problem Solving through 'C' language	180

Figure 8.15 ***Items of Books Category are Displayed***

SUMMARY

In this chapter we dealt with two types of response data retrieved from the server, responseXML and responseText. We viewed different DOM Node tree methods and properties. We saw running examples of how XML response is received, the technique to display the contents of the first child, values (text) of all the child nodes of the given node, contents of the all the child nodes along with the names of the child nodes, contents of the selected nodes. We also had an introduction to JSON and the steps to install it. We have also seen how to receive data in JSON format, how to access the response through iteration, how to use the library for encoding, how to convert data entered by the user to JSON format and finally how to access database and display its contents in JSON format.

In the next chapter, we are going to see the sample output of the AJAX based Shopping Cart, that is, how its different modules behave on execution. The working of each link is displayed step by step.

9

Introduction to Web Services

In this chapter we are going to learn:

- What are web services
- XML
- Introduction to techniques used for web services like SOAP, XML-RPC and REST

9.1 WHAT ARE WEB SERVICES?

Web service is a technique by which two applications can communicate with each other in a platform and programming language independent manner. A web service consists of several methods advertised for use by the general public. To make it possible for every application to access a web service, it uses XML based protocols. Note that XML is accepted as a standard format for data exchange among applications in order to avoid data type mismatch problems.

Web services are gaining popularity today, as they are a successful shortcut to adding the maximum features in any web application in the shortest possible time. That is, instead of building a feature for any application from scratch, it is a better option to invoke a publicly available web service (providing that feature) directly from our application. Suppose I want to provide a search facility for the visitors to my website, then instead of making a search application from scratch (which may need a lot of work ranging from making a database of information and developing different indexing and hashing features), I can directly use the "Google Search" web service in my website which will access the database of information provided by Google and return the desired results to the visitor.

Before we delve deep into how web services work internally, let's first understand a similar term, RPC.

9.1.1 RPC (Remote Procedure Call)

RPC (remote procedure call) is a programming model which enables systems to communicate in a distributed architecture environment. Distributed architecture is a networked system in which databases and applications are not placed on one server (as in a centralised system) but are spread on all the connected systems. As the name suggests, RPC means a procedure or method invocation on the remote system.

Note: For web services, RPC communication is implemented using the SOAP protocol. That is, the client and the server must communicate using SOAP (SOAP provides a standard framework for exchanging packets in XML format), in which the client invokes the method on the server.

The service provider after developing the service provides a WSDL document which describes all the methods available in the service and their parameter types so that the application which is supposed to invoke the web service will have complete information of all the methods along with their parameter types. To make people aware of the web service, the service provider advertises it by registering it in UDDI (Figure 9.1).

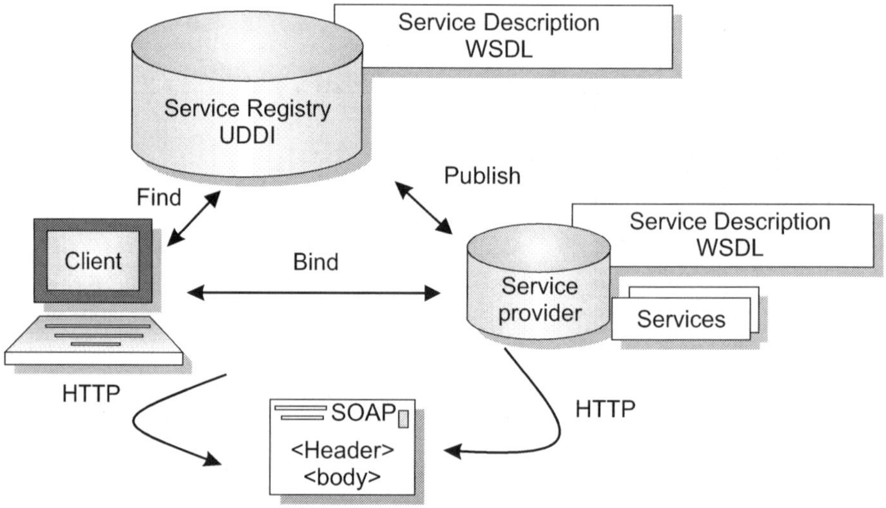

Figure 9.1 ***The Web Service Model***

Figure 9.1 demonstrates that the service provider after developing the service, publishes its WSDL on UDDI for public viewing. Any client looking for a particular service searches for it in UDDI and if found, that service is invoked and the message passing takes place as SOAP.

9.2 TERMS RELATED TO WEB SERVICE

Before delving deeper into understanding web services let's get an idea of different terms that we will be using frequently:

9.2.1 WSDL (Web Services Description Language)

It is an XML file that gives a complete description of a web service, its methods exposed for public usage, the format of the XML messages etc. A WSDL definition serves as a contract between the service provider and service consumer.

9.2.2 UDDI (Uniform Description, Discovery and Integration)

UDDI is a XML-based protocol which is a sort of distributed directory of publicly available web services. The organisations which want their web services to be used by general public register their web services in this directory.

9.2.3 Interoperability

Web service has become the choice of developers because it supports interoperability. Interoperability is the concept by which an application can interface and communicate with other applications deployed on dissimilar systems. To implement interoperability, XML is used.

9.2.4 XML

XML (Extensible Markup Language) is a popular and widely-implemented standard used to create documents and data records that are fully portable and platform-independent. It is a markup language for documents containing structured information. A markup language is a mechanism to identify structures in a document. Let's see what an XML document looks like:

```
<?xml version="1.0"?>
<student>
<roll>101</roll>
<name>John</name>
<marks>85</marks>
</student>
```

The first line is the XML declaration. All XML documents can optionally begin with an XML declaration that provides at a minimum the version of XML in use:

```
<?xml version="1.0"?>
```

The XML declaration can also specify the character encoding used in the document:

```
<?xml version="1.0" encoding="UTF-8"?>
```

All XML parsers are required to support the Unicode "UTF-8" and "UTF-16" encodings; many XML parsers support other encodings, such as "ISO-8859-1", as well.

Note: The XML declaration is case sensitive. If the XML declaration appears at all, it must be the very first thing in the XML document: not even white space or comments may appear before it.

There are two different kinds of information in this example:

- markup, like "<roll>" , "<name>" etc.
- text, like "101", "John" etc.

XML documents mix markup and text together in a single file: the markup describes the structure of the document, while the text is the document's content.

9.2.5 SOAP (Simple Object Access Protocol) Framework

For exchanging data among applications, the standard format used is XML. That is, web service requests and responses are sent as XML messages and SOAP provides a standard framework for packaging and exchanging XML messages over a computer network, normally using HTTP.

Once again, how all the above terms are connected to a web service is demonstrated in Figure 9.2.

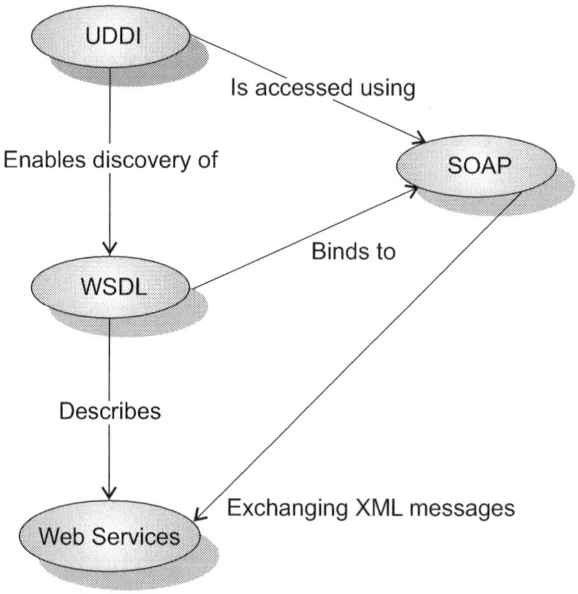

Figure 9.2 ***The SOAP Framework***

We can see in this figure that the WSDL of a web service is registered in UDDI and the web application which needs to invoke the web service discovers its WSDL from UDDI and communicates with it using SOAP.

9.3 METHODS OF PRODUCING AND CONSUMING WEB SERVICES

There are three methods of producing and consuming web services:

- XML-RPC
- REST and
- SOAP

Of these three, we will be using the SOAP method in the examples used in the book.

Characteristics of these three methods are as follows:

9.3.1 XML-RPC

- Developed by UserLand Software (http://www.userland.com/) in April 1998.
- is a specification and a set of implementations that allow software running on dissimilar operating systems, running in different environments, to make procedure calls over the Internet.
- Popular RPC implementations are DCOM and CORBA. XML-RPC is an established implementation of RPC that allows the transport of XML encoded data between two servers using HTTP.
- To enable PHP XML-RPC functionality, we must download the XML-RPC toolkit.
- is implemented by including two files: xmlrpc.inc (the base class library) and xmlrpcs.inc (the server class library).
- is considered a simpler alternative to SOAP.

9.3.2 REST (Representational State Transfer)

- The term was coined by Roy Fielding in his Ph.D. dissertation to describe an architecture style of networked systems.
- is not a standard but just an architectural style. We can only understand it, and design our web services in that style.
- is a simpler approach than XML-RPC or SOAP to send and retrieve XML data. It uses standard HTTP methods like GET, POST and PUT. We can use tools like PHP DOM, SAX, or even XSL to do the parsing. The disadvantage is that everything has to be built by hand.
- is easy to implement and has many highly desirable architectural properties: scalability, performance, security, reliability, and extensibility.
- is an alternative to SOAP. REST calls are made over HTTP, and parameters are specified in the query string.

9.3.3 SOAP (Simple Object Access Protocol)

- is a W3C standard protocol that defines the format for exchanging data with the web service.
- is a object-oriented protocol that exists in over 80 implementations on every popular platform, including AppleScript, JavaScript, and Cocoa.
- is a RPC (Remote Procedure Call) method which is XML based and can be transmitted on HTTP protocol, FTP, SMTP etc. which do not require special ports. Note: Other protocols which have RPC methods require special ports, for example, DCOM, CORBA, and Java, require special ports.
- provides a sort of a platform independent communication layer between applications. That is, if both the remote application and the client speak SOAP, they can communicate with each other.
- deals in a standard way of representing data. That is, the calling application translates the data to be passed to the remote application into SOAP format (so that the remote application can translate the data in SOAP format into the data type it requires). Similarly, the remote application returns the result in SOAP format which the client application can convert into its data type.

Figure 9.3 demonstrates how a client communicates with a web service using SOAP.

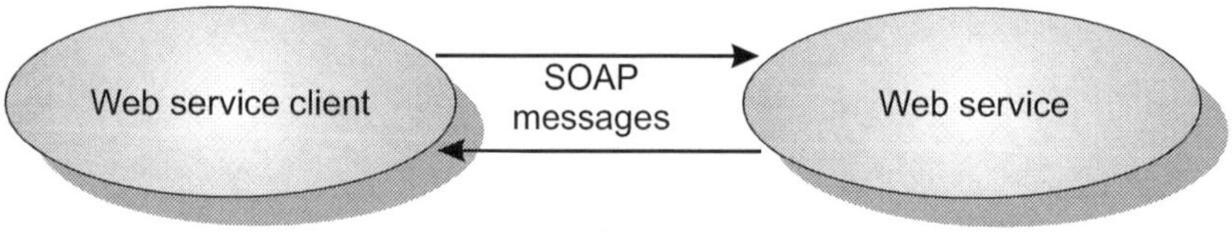

Figure 9.3 ***Client Communicates with a Web Service Using SOAP***

The preferred method of communication for web services is the SOAP protocol, but there's nothing built into PHP that handles this protocol. There are two tools for adding SOAP functionality to PHP.

9.4 TOOLS FOR ADDING SOAP FUNCTIONALITY TO PHP

There are two tools for adding SOAP functionality to PHP:

- NuSOAP and
- PEAR:SOAP

9.4.1 NuSOAP

One of the most popular SOAP implementations of PHP is NuSOAP (formerly known as SOAPx4) consisting of several PHP classes that allow us to create and consume SOAP web services. It has built-in WSDL support. That is, the server script made in NuSOAP automatically creates a WSDL document for us.

9.4.2 PEAR:SOAP

PEAR:SOAP is based on the NuSOAP implementation, and supports the same functionality as NuSOAP but with some extensions. It supports method-overloading and the SOAP message can be transported with both HTTP and SMTP protocol.

A disadvantage is that it is slightly more complex than NuSOAP.

SUMMARY

We have learnt the following things in this chapter:

- Web services allow us to share data across different platforms and hardware configurations. For example, a PHP web service can be consumed by a .NET client.
- Web services use protocols based on XML language.
- XML is a popular markup language used for creating portable and platform-independent documents.
- SOAP provides a standard framework for packaging and exchanging XML messages.
- WSDL—Provides the list of methods in a web service available for public use.
- UDDI—Used for discovering web services.

10
NuSOAP

In this chapter, we are going to see several things including:

- How to use toolkit: NuSOAP to build web services using SOAP.
- Installation of NuSOAP.
- What are the different elements of a WSDL document
- Developing and testing several sever as well as client web services like:
- CurrencyConverter—for converting pounds into dollars
- Web service that asks the user to enter his name and greets him with a welcome message
- Web services that access information from the database
- Displaying the price of the product on supplying its item code
- Web services dealing with complex data type—fetching complete information of the product (item code, item name, description and price) with the supplied item code.
- Modifying the client interface to display the item codes in the form of a dropdown list
- Displaying only the item names of the products of the selected category
- Displaying all fields of the product of a particular category

One of the most popular SOAP implementations of PHP is NuSOAP (formerly known as SOAPx4) that was provided by NuSphere and Dietrich Ayala. It consists of a set of PHP classes that allow us to create and consume SOAP web services.

Characteristics

1. NuSOAP is a toolkit which provides a powerful API developed for PHP for building web services using SOAP.
2. It has built-in WSDL support. That is, the server script automatically creates a WSDL document for us.

For installing the API, the first thing that we need is a PHP enabled server (I have used Apache Server ver 2.2.8). Secondly, we need to get PHP up and running. All the libraries required for NuSOAP are contained in a file called nusoap.php. So, the third step is to download both the toolkit and the documentation from the link: `http://deitrich.ganx4.com/nusoap/`.

10.1 STEPS TO INSTALL NuSOAP

- Download the package from the Internet.
- Unzip it to get a file nusoap.php, which contains the actual PHP classes.
- To use them, place nusoap.php in our PHP path and include it in the scripts.

NuSOAP is a component-based web services toolkit. It employs a base class that provides utility methods and helps classes to accomplish the sending and receiving of SOAP messages.

10.2 FIRST WEB SERVICE

Let's make a SOAP server web service. This web service consists of a method, CurrencyConverter which will ask the client to specify some amount in pounds and that amount will be then converted into dollars (assuming that 1 pound = 40$). So let's create a file named server1.php in the `htdocs` subfolder of our `apache` directory with the following contents:

server1.php

```
1. <?php
2. require_once('nusoap.php');
3. $server = new soap_server();
4. $server->configureWSDL('Currency Converter','urn:server1');
5. $server->register('CurrencyConverter', array('amount' => 'xsd:string'),
   array('return' => 'xsd:string'), 'urn:server1');
6. function CurrencyConverter($amount){
7. $dollar=$amount*40;
8. return 'Amount in Dollar is ' . $dollar;
9. }
10. $server->service($HTTP_RAW_POST_DATA);
11. ?>
```

Explanation of server1.php program

```
2. require_once('nusoap.php');
```

It is used to include the file nusoap.php in the current script. Recall that all the libraries required for NuSOAP are contained in the file called nusoap.php which contains several helper classes to accomplish the sending and receiving of SOAP messages. The require_once command assures that the functions are added only once in our script.

```
3. $server = new soap_server();
```

Instantiate the soap_server class.

```
4. $server->configureWSDL('Currency Converter','urn:server1');
```

Define the settings for our WSDL file (which the NuSOAP library will automatically create for us). We specify the server service name: Currency Converter and the namespace (urn:server1) of our service. Each of the web services has to be assigned a distinctive URI.

```
5. $server->register('CurrencyConverter', array('amount' => 'xsd:string'),
   array('return' => 'xsd:string'), 'urn:server1');
```

We are registering our method: `CurrencyConverter` so that the server comes to know that there exists a method by this name. Also we need to specify the data types of the argument passed to the method and returned by it. In the above command we are specifying that the argument passed to the method is an `amount` and is of string data type. Similarly, the returned parameter is "return" of string data type. We specify the arguments in the form of an array where the key of the array represents the name of the parameter and the value specifies the data type of the parameter. Following the array of arguments, we specify the namespace we are operating in.

Note: Every method must be registered separately.

```
6. function CurrencyConverter($amount){
7. $dollar=$amount*40;
8. return 'Amount in Dollar is ' . $dollar;
9. }
```

The value passed to the function `CurrencyConverter` is assigned to the `$amount` parameter which is then multiplied by 40 to convert it into dollars (assuming that the value passed is in pounds and 1 pound=40$). The string that is returned to the client consists of "Amount in dollars is " along with the converted amount in dollars.

```
10. $server->service($HTTP_RAW_POST_DATA);
```

The web request is passed to the service by the `$HTTP_RAW_POST_DATA` variable i.e. the service is invoked by this command.

Now, let's make a client web service which will consume the server web service made just now. We create a file client1.php in the `htdocs` subfolder of the `apache` directory with the following contents:

client1.php

```
1. <?php
2. require_once(‘nusoap.php’);
3. $client=new soapclient(‘http://localhost/server1.php?wsdl’, true);
4. $param=array(‘amount’ => ’15.00');
5. echo $client->call(‘CurrencyConverter’, $param);
6. ?>
```

The `soapclient` class takes the URL of the WSDL file as an argument to its constructor, and uses the WSDL class to parse the WSDL file and extract all the data. The boolean value `true` is passed to inform NuSOAP that WSDL is being used. The WSDL class has methods that extract data on a per-operation or per-binding basis.

The soapclient uses this data from the WSDL file to encode parameters and create the SOAP envelope when the user executes a call to a service. When the call is executed, the soapclient class uses the soap_transport_http class to send the outgoing message and receive the incoming message. The incoming message is parsed using soap_parser class.

Explanation of client1.php program

```
3. $client=new soapclient(‘http://localhost/server1.php?wsdl’, true);
```

We first instantiate the soapclient object and pass the URL of our web service's WSDL file to it. The boolean value `true` is passed to inform NuSOAP that WSDL is being used.

```
4. $param=array(‘amount’ => ’15.00');
```

We create an array containing the parameter(s) name and the value to be passed to the web service.

```
5. echo $client->call(‘CurrencyConverter’, $param);
```

By using the `call()` method, we inform the soapclient object which service to access. We also pass parameters to it. We are invoking the `CurrencyConverter` method by the above statement and passing parameters stored in `$param`.

Time for testing

Let's run the client web service now. Open the browser and invoke the client web service by writing: http://localhost/client1.php in the address bar. We get the output as shown in Figure 10.1.

Figure 10.1 ***Output on Running Client Web Service***

We get the output as 600 because the amount passed to the web service is 15 pounds. Assuming 1 pound = 40$, the output in dollars is 15 × 40 = 600 dollars.

Now let us run the server web service. In the browser write: http://localhost/server1.php in the address bar. We get the output as shown in Figure 10.2.

Figure 10.2 ***Output on Running the Server Web Service***

If we select the method CurrencyConverter of our web service, we get the screen showing various details of the method (Figure 10.3).

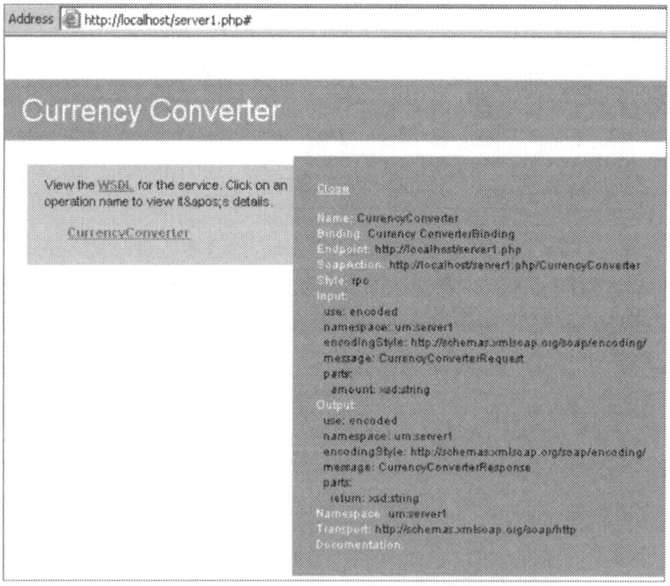

Figure 10.3 ***Screen of Currency Converter***

If we select the WSDL link to see the automatically generated WSDL of our web service, we get the complete WSDL document generated as shown below:

10.3 WSDL DOCUMENT

```
<?xml version="1.0" encoding="ISO-8859-1" ?>
- <definitions xmlns:SOAP-
ENV="http://schemas.xmlsoap.org/soap/envelope/"
xmlns:xsd="http://www.w3.org/2001/XMLSchema"
xmlns:xsi="http://www.w3.org/2001/XMLSchema-instance" xmlns:SOAP-
ENC="http://schemas.xmlsoap.org/soap/encoding/"
xmlns:tns="urn:server1"
xmlns:soap="http://schemas.xmlsoap.org/wsdl/soap/"
xmlns:wsdl="http://schemas.xmlsoap.org/wsdl/"
xmlns="http://schemas.xmlsoap.org/wsdl/"
targetNamespace="urn:server1">
-   <types>
-   <xsd:schema targetNamespace="urn:server1">
    <xsd:import namespace="http://schemas.xmlsoap.org/soap/encoding/" />
    <xsd:import namespace="http://schemas.xmlsoap.org/wsdl/" />
    </xsd:schema>
    </types>
-   <message name="CurrencyConverterRequest">
    <part name="amount" type="xsd:string" />
    </message>
-   <message name="CurrencyConverterResponse">
    <part name="return" type="xsd:string" />
    </message>
-   <portType name="Currency ConverterPortType">
-   <operation name="CurrencyConverter">
    <input message="tns:CurrencyConverterRequest" />
    <output message="tns:CurrencyConverterResponse" />
    </operation>
    </portType>
-   <binding name="Currency ConverterBinding" type="tns:Currency
    ConverterPortType">
```

```
<soap:binding style="rpc" transport="http://schemas.xmlsoap.org/soap/http"
/>
- <operation name="CurrencyConverter">
<soap:operation soapAction="http://localhost/server1.php/CurrencyConverter"
style="rpc" />
- <input>
<soap:body use="encoded" namespace="urn:server1"
encodingStyle="http://schemas.xmlsoap.org/soap/encoding/" />
</input>
- <output>
<soap:body use="encoded" namespace="urn:server1"
encodingStyle="http://schemas.xmlsoap.org/soap/encoding/" />
</output>
</operation>
</binding>
- <service name="Currency Converter">
- <port name="Currency ConverterPort" binding="tns:Currency
ConverterBinding">
<soap:address location="http://localhost/server1.php" />
</port>
</service>
</definitions>
```

Explanation of WSDL Code Generated Above

WSDL is a XML description of the service i.e. it is a document written in XML format to describe the type of services offered by the web service. This document contains all the required information of the service like data types of data in message, service name, parameters exchanged, protocol bindings etc. Any application can process the WSDL file (as it is in XML format) to get all the details required for operating a web service.

Recall that web service requests and responses are sent as XML messages and SOAP provides a standard framework for packaging and exchanging XML messages. The SOAP protocol not only moves XML data to the target system but also specifies a set of rules for the application on the target system to initiate some action upon the delivery of XML data.

The elements included in a WSDL file are as shown in Figure 10.4.

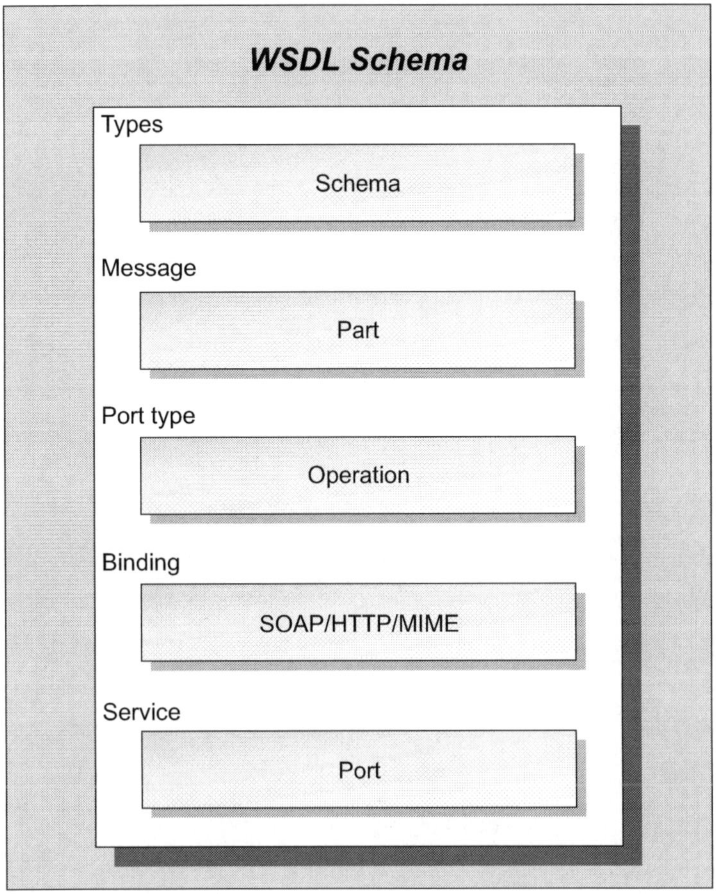

Figure 10.4 ***Elements of a WSDL File***

From this figure, we can get an outline of the structure of the WSDL document:

```
<definitions>
   <types>
      <!– which provides data type definitions used to describe the
         messages exchanged. –>
   </types>
   <message>
      <!– represents an abstract definition of the data being
         transmitted. A message consists of logical parts, each of which
         is associated with a definition within some type system. –>
   </message>
```

```
    <portType>
        <!– a set of abstract operations. Each operation refers to an input
            message and output messages. –>
    </portType>
    <binding>
        <!– specifies concrete protocol and data format specifications
            for the operations and messages defined by a particular
            portType. –>
    </binding>
    <service>
        <!– used to aggregate a set of related ports. –>
        <port>
            <!– specifies an address for a binding, thus defining a single
                communication endpoint. –>
        </port>
    </service>
</definitions>
```

10.3.1 Description of the WSDL Elements

WSDL element	Description
definitions	It is root element of a WSDL document.
types	A container for abstract type definitions for the messages exchanged by the web service defined using the XML schema.
messages	A definition of an abstract message that may consist of multiple parts, each part may be of a different type.
portstypes	An abstract set of operations supported by one or more endpoints (interface).
operation	An action (method) supported by the service. Each operation consists of input and output messages.
input	Specifies a message format for the request.
output	Specifies a message format for the response.
binding	a concrete protocol and data format specification for a particular port type. Binding is used to attach a particular protocol or data format to an abstract message or endpoint.
service	A collection of related endpoints, where an endpoint is defined as a combination of a binding and an address (URI). It specifies a group of ports.
port	a single endpoint defined as a combination of a binding and a network address.

For communication with a web service, the application requires a point of contact for a service. This point of contact of a web service also known as the *service endpoint* is described by the WSDL document.

WSDL service description is separated into two parts:

- abstract description
- concrete description

10.3.2 Abstract Description

It is the definition of the interface characteristics of the web service and has nothing to do with the actual technology used in hosting the web service or used in transmission of messages. The reason for this isolation with the underlying technology is that the changes made in technology (if any) should not affect the description of interfaces. The three main parts that comprise an abstract description are the portType, operation, and message.

portType	provides a high-level view of the service interface.
Message	is the actual information communicated by a web service.
Operation	represents a specific action performed by the service. It is a group of functions which collectively do some processing. An operation consists of a set of input and output messages.

The other elements like binding, port and service describe the concrete details of how the abstract interface maps to the actual messages transmitted.

10.3.3 Concrete Description

Until and unless the abstract web service interface is connected to a physical transport protocol, communication cannot be implemented in a web service. This connection is defined in the concrete description portion of the WSDL file, and consists of three parts: binding, port, and service.

binding	describes the requirements for a service to establish physical connections. It represents the transport technology used by the service to communicate. SOAP is the most common form of binding.
port	represents the physical address at which a service can be accessed with a specific protocol.
service	is used to refer to a group of related endpoints.

Let us understand the generated WSDL line by line:

```
1. <?xml version="1.0" encoding="ISO-8859-1" ?>
```

```
2. <definitions xmlns:SOAP-ENV="http://schemas.xmlsoap.org/soap/envelope/"
   xmlns:xsd="http://www.w3.org/2001/XMLSchema"
   xmlns:xsi="http://www.w3.org/2001/XMLSchema-instance"
   xmlns:SOAP-ENC="http://schemas.xmlsoap.org/soap/encoding/"
   xmlns:tns="urn:server1" xmlns:soap="http://schemas.xmlsoap.org/wsdl/soap/"
   xmlns:wsdl="http://schemas.xmlsoap.org/wsdl/"
   xmlns="http://schemas.xmlsoap.org/wsdl/" targetNamespace="urn:server1">
```

Since WSDL is an XML description of the service, the document begins with an optional XML declaration which provides the version of XML in use as well as the character encoding used in the document.

All XML parsers usually support the Unicode "UTF-8" and "UTF-16" encodings and a few parsers also support other encodings, such as "ISO-8859-1".

10.3.4 Definitions

This is the root element of every WSDL document. It contains all other parts of the service definition, along with the namespaces used within the WSDL document. We know that SOAP provides a standard framework for packaging and exchanging XML messages and a SOAP message must have an envelope element associated with the http://schemas.xmlsoap.org/soap/envelope/" namespace. If a message is received by a SOAP application in which the SOAP envelope element is associated with a different namespace, the application assumes that a version error has occurred resulting in discarding of the message.

10.3.5 What are Namespaces?

Namespaces are applied on elements to avoid any naming conflicts and also to enable the document to refer multiple external specifications like WSDL specification, the SOAP specification, and the XML Schema specification.

Namespaces are also used for better naming conventions. A namespace representation consists of two parts: a naming prefix and an associated URI (Uniform Resource Identifier). Each namespace is declared by a namespace attribute which then acts as a shorthand for that namespace.

For example, consider the following namespace declaration:

```
xmlns:xsd="http://www.w3.org/2001/XMLSchema"
```

Here, "xmlns:xsd" defines a shorthand (xsd) for the namespace: `http://www.w3.org/2001/XMLSchema`

This means we can refer to this namespace by simply prefixing a name with "xsd:". For example: "xsd:int"

Note: The term Uniform Resource Identifier (URI) is a string of characters which identifies an Internet resource. The most common URI is the Uniform Resource Locator (URL) which identifies an Internet domain address. Another type of URI is the Universal Resource Name (URN).

10.3.6 What is XML Schema?

We know that the data communicated between the two applications in a web service is in XML format, and to ensure that the XML data is free from syntactic as well as semantic errors, certain document constraining is applied. There are two types of document constraining techniques:

- DTD (Document Type Definition)
- XSD (XML Schema Definition)

DTD is the schema specification definition for XML documents but because of its serious limitations in document constraining, the XML schema system was designed to replace it.

An XML document must understand the schema of the data and therefore the schema definition is placed at the beginning of the XML document and the document uses these definitions for enforcing semantic correctness in the XML data.

XML Schema Definition Language is an XML language for describing and constraining the content of XML documents. WSDL data typing is based on "XML Schema: Data types" (XSD). There are three different versions of this document (1999, 2000/10, and 2001), and declaring it as one of the namespace attributes in the <definitions> element specifies which version is used in a particular WSDL file:

```
xmlns:xsd="http://www.w3.org/2001/XMLSchema"
```

This statement means that all elements within the WSDL that belong to the XML Schema Definition Language need to be prefixed with the xsd: qualifier.

The following prefixes or namespace shorthand is used:

Prefix	Equivalent Namespace	Description
soapenc	http://schemas.xmlsoap.org/soap/encoding	SOAP 1.1 encoding
wsdl	http://schemas.xmlsoap.org/wsdl/soap	WSDL 1.1
xsd	http://www.w3.org/2001/XMLSchema	XML Schema

The xmlns attribute also defines a default namespace:

```
xmlns="http://schemas.xmlsoap.org/wsdl/"
```

This statement means that all of the elements that belong to the WSDL language do not need prefixes (or qualifiers) to associate them with the WSDL specification.

The xmlns:soap namespace declaration:

```
xmlns:soap="http://schemas.xmlsoap.org/wsdl/soap/"
```

establishes the soap: prefix used by elements in the bindings construct (where the WSDL definition associates its abstract operations to concrete SOAP bindings).

The structure also defines several attributes for direct use in any XML documents. These attributes are in a different namespace, which has the namespace name:http://www.w3.org/2001/XMLSchema-instance. The text and examples in this specification use the prefix xsi:.

10.3.7 Encoding

The SOAP encodings style attribute is used to indicate the serialisation rules used in a SOAP message. The attribute value is a URI identifying the serialisation rule or rules that can be used to deserialise the SOAP message.

```
xmlns:SOAP-ENC="http://schemas.xmlsoap.org/soap/encoding/"
```

The definitions element also specifies a targetNamespace attribute. The targetNamespace is a convention of the XML schema that enables the WSDL document to refer to itself. Anything that we name in the WSDL definition (like a message, portType, binding, etc.) automatically becomes part of the WSDL definition's target namespace defined by the targetNamespace attribute.

```
xmlns:tns="urn:server1"
```

Here, "xmlns:tns" defines a shorthand (tns) for the namespace "urn:server1". This means anything defined with tns attribute belongs to the current WSDL document.

```
3. <types>
4. <xsd:schema targetNamespace="urn:server1">
5. <xsd:import namespace="http://schemas.xmlsoap.org/soap/encoding/" />
6. <xsd:import namespace="http://schemas.xmlsoap.org/wsdl/" />
7. </xsd:schema>
8. </types>
```

10.3.8 Types

This element is used to specify the data type definitions required for the exchange of messages. WSDL prefers the use of XSD type system to define the types in a message to avoid any problem occurring in binding the messages.

XSD

It is a type definition language used for describing message format. It is a rich type system that supports XML schema specification and is platform independent.

To import definitions from external namespaces, first, we define the namespace as usual.

Then W3C XML schema needs to be informed of the location at which it can find the schema corresponding to the namespace. This is done using an import element. For example:

```
xmlns:wsdl="http://schemas.xmlsoap.org/wsdl/"
<xsd:import namespace="http://schemas.xmlsoap.org/wsdl/" />
```

```
<message name="CurrencyConverterRequest">
<part name="amount" type="xsd:string" />
</message>
<message name="CurrencyConverterResponse">
<part name="return" type="xsd:string" />
</message>
```

The WSDL message element defines an abstract message that can serve as the input or output of an operation. Messages consist of one or more part elements, where each part is associated with either an element (when using document style) or a type (when using RPC style).

If we are defining an RPC style service, the message parts represent the method's parameters. In this case, the name of the part becomes the name of an element in the concrete message and its structure is determined by the supplied type attribute. If we are defining a document style service, the parts simply refer to the XML elements that are placed within the body (referenced by the element attribute).

Note: The message and type definitions in WSDL are considered to be abstract definitions and these abstract contents are mapped into a concrete format (described by message binding). The SOAP messages bind to a protocol and are sent out on the network. The message is then routed along a so-called "message path" to the ultimate destination.

```
<portType name="Currency ConverterPortType">
<operation name="CurrencyConverter">
<input message="tns:CurrencyConverterRequest" />
<output message="tns:CurrencyConverterResponse" />
</operation>
</portType>
```

10.3.9 portTypes (interfaces)

The WSDL portType element defines a group of operations, also known as an interface. It may contain zero or more operation elements. Each portType must be given a unique name. Each operation element contains a combination of input and output elements and the order of these elements defines the message exchange pattern (MEP) supported by the given operation.

For example, an input element followed by an output element defines a request-response operation, while an output element followed by an input element defines a solicit-response operation. An operation that only contains an input element defines a one-way operation, while an operation that only contains an output element defines a notification operation.

MEP	Description
One-way	The endpoint receives a message (only an input element).
Request-response	The endpoint receives a message and sends a related message (input followed by output element).
Solicit-response	The endpoint sends a message and receives a related message (output followed by input element).
Notification	The endpoint sends a message (contains only on output element).

The input and output elements specify the abstract message format for the request and response, respectively.

```
<binding name="Currency ConverterBinding" type="tns:Currency
ConverterPortType">
<soap:binding style="rpc" transport="http://schemas.xmlsoap.org/soap/http" /
>
<operation name="CurrencyConverter">
<soap:operation soapAction="http://localhost/server1.php/CurrencyConverter"
style="rpc" />
<input>
<soap:body use="encoded" namespace="urn:server1" encodingStyle="http://
schemas.xmlsoap.org/soap/encoding/" />
</input>
<output>
<soap:body use="encoded" namespace="urn:server1" encodingStyle="http://
schemas.xmlsoap.org/soap/encoding/" />
</output>
</operation>
</binding>
```

The WSDL binding element describes message format and protocol details for operations and messages defined by a particular portType. There may be any number of bindings for a given portType. A binding references the portType that it binds using the type attribute.

The WSDL specification provides some binding elements for describing SOAP bindings, although they're in a different namespace.

10.3.10 soap:binding

The purpose of the SOAP binding element is to signify that the binding is bound to the SOAP protocol format: envelope, header and body. It also indicates the default style of service (document or RPC). If the style attribute is omitted, it is assumed to be "document".

Using document style in SOAP indicates that the body will contain an XML document, and that the message parts specify the XML elements that will be placed there.

Using RPC style in SOAP indicates that the body will contain an XML representation of a method call and that the message parts represent the parameters to the method.

The transport attribute indicates the transport protocol this binding corresponds to. The URI value http://schemas.xmlsoap.org/soap/http corresponds to the HTTP binding in the SOAP specification. Other URIs indicate other transports such as SMTP, FTP, etc.

10.3.11 soap:operation

The soap:operation element provides information for the operation as a whole. The style attribute indicates whether the operation is RPC-oriented (messages containing parameters and return values) or document-oriented (message containing document(s)). This information may be used to select an appropriate programming model. If the attribute is not specified, it defaults to the value specified in the soap:binding element.

- If the operation style is RPC each part is a parameter or a return value and appears inside a wrapper element within the body. The wrapper element is named identically to the operation name and its namespace is the value of the namespace attribute.
- If the operation style is document there are no additional wrappers, and the message parts appear directly under the SOAP body element.

The soapAction attribute specifies the value of the SOAPAction header for this operation. This URI value should be used directly as the value for the SOAPAction header.

10.3.12 soap:body

This element defines how the message parts appear inside of the SOAP body element (literal or encoded form). The `use` attribute specifies the encoding that should be used to translate the abstract message parts into a concrete representation. Two options:

- encoded

In this case, the abstract definitions are translated into a concrete format by applying the SOAP encoding rules specified by the encodingStyle attribute.

- literal

In this case, the abstract type definitions become the concrete definitions themselves (they're 'literal' definitions). In this case, we inspect the XML schema type definitions to determine the concrete message format.

```
<service name=”Currency Converter”>
<port name=”Currency ConverterPort” binding=”tns:Currency ConverterBinding”>
<soap:address location=”http://localhost/server1.php” />
</port>
</service>
</definitions>
```

The WSDL service element defines a collection of ports, or endpoints, that expose a particular binding. We must give each port a name and assign it a binding. Then, within the port element, we use an extensibility element to define the address details specific to the binding. The service element completes the WSDL definition.

A port defines an individual endpoint by specifying a single address for a binding.

The name attribute provides a unique name among all ports defined within the enclosing WSDL document.

10.4 SECOND WEB SERVICE

Let us make another server web service. This web service contains a method: `WelcomeMsg` which will ask the user to enter his name and will then return a welcome message to him. So let's create two files named demoserver2.php and democlient2.php in the `htdocs` subfolder of our `apache` directory with the following contents:

demoserver2.php

```
<?php
require_once('nusoap.php');
$s= new soap_server();
$s->configureWSDL('Displaying Welcome Message','urn:demoserver2');
$s->wsdl->schemaTargetNamespace = 'urn:demoserver2';
$s->register('WelcomeMsg',array('name' => 'xsd:string'), array('result' =>
  'xsd:string'), 'urn:demoserver2');
```

```
7.  function WelcomeMsg($name) {
8.  return "Hello " . $name;
9.  }
10. $s->service($HTTP_RAW_POST_DATA);
11. ?>
```

Explanation of demoserver2.php program

```
2.  require_once('nusoap.php');
```

Include the file: nusoap.php in the current script as it contains all the libraries required for NuSOAP. It also contains several helper classes to accomplish the sending and receiving of SOAP messages. The require_once command ensures that the functions are added only once in our script.

```
3.  $s= new soap_server();
```

Instantiate the soap_server class.

```
4.  $s->configureWSDL('Displaying Welcome Message','urn:demoserver2');
5.  $s->wsdl->schemaTargetNamespace = 'urn:demoserver2';
```

These statements define the settings for our WSDL file (which the NuSOAP library will automatically create for us). We specify the server service name: `Displaying Welcome Message` and the namespace `(urn:demoserver2)` of our service. Each of the web services has to be assigned a distinctive URI.

```
6.  $s->register('WelcomeMsg',array('name' => 'xsd:string'), array('result' =>
    'xsd:string'), 'urn:demoserver2');
```

We are registering our method: `WelcomeMsg` and also specifying the data types of the argument passed as well as returned by the method. In the above command we are specifying that the argument passed to the method is `name` and is of string data type. Similarly, the returned parameter is `"result"` of string data type. Following the array of arguments, we specify the namespace we are operating in.

Note: Every method must be registered separately.

```
7.  function WelcomeMsg($name) {
8.  return "Hello " . $name;
9.  }
```

The string passed to the function `WelcomeMsg` is assigned to the `$name` parameter which is then returned to the client along with the Hello message.

```
10. $s->service($HTTP_RAW_POST_DATA);
```

The service is invoked by this command.

democlient2.php

```
<?php
require_once("nusoap.php");
if (isset($_POST['submit'])) {
    $string =$_POST['strng'];
    $param = array('name'=>$string);
    $s= new soapclient('http://localhost/demoserver2.php?wsdl', true);
    $result =$s->call ('WelcomeMsg',$param);
    if(!$error = $s->getError()) {
        echo $result;
    }
    else {
        echo 'Error:' . $error;
    }
}
else
{
?>

    <form action="democlient2.php" method="post">
        Enter your name: <input type="text" name="strng">
        <input type="submit" name="submit" value="Enter">
    </form>
    <?php
}
?>
```

The client is asked to enter his name (which is assigned to variable: `strng`). On clicking the submit button, the form elements are submitted to itself (i.e. to democlient2.php file). Using `$_POST` array, the name entered by the client is accessed and stored in `$string` variable.

Create an array by name `$param` containing the parameter name and the value to be passed to the web service. The parameter name specified is "name" and the value passed is `$string` variable (containing the name entered by the client).

Then instantiate the soapclient object and pass the URL of our web service's WSDL file to it i.e.'http://localhost/demoserver2.php?wsdl' . The boolean value `true` is passed to inform NuSOAP that WSDL is being used.

With the help of the `call()` method, we inform the soapclient object to access `WelcomeMsg` method and pass parameters (`$param` array) to it. The welcome message returned by the web service is stored in `$result` variable which is then displayed on the screen.

Output:

When we run the client program, we get a screen to enter a name (Figure 10.5).

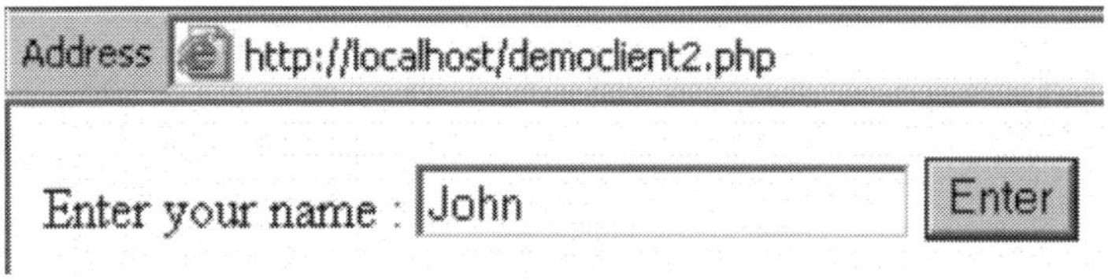

Figure 10.5 ***Screen to Enter Name***

After entering a name, when we press the Enter key, we get a welcome message from the web service (Figure 10.6).

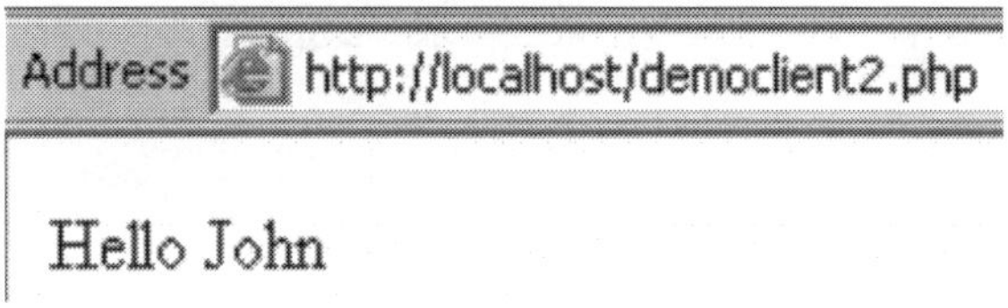

Figure 10.6 ***Welcome Message***

When we run the server web service, we get a screen as shown in Figure 10.7.

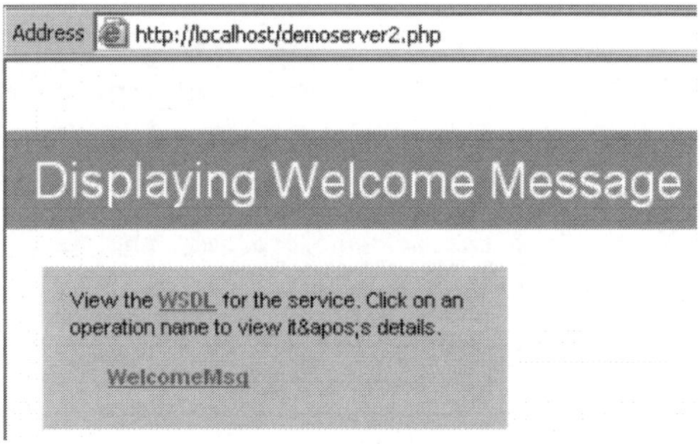

Figure 10.7 ***Screen on Running Server Web Service***

If we select the method: WelcomeMsg of the web service, we get the screen showing various details of the method (Figure 10.8).

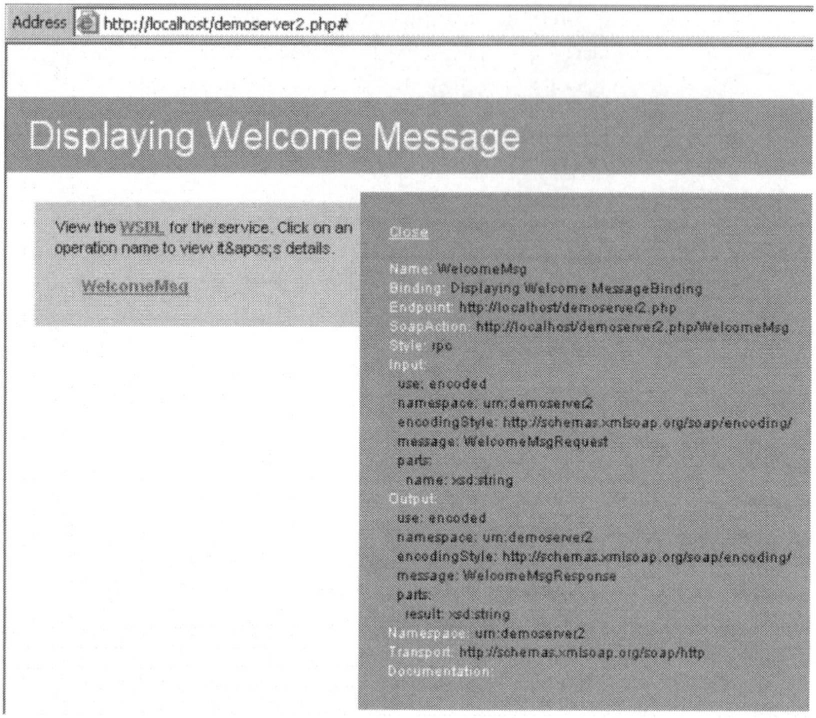

Figure 10.8 ***Screen on Selecting WelcomeMsg***

If we select the WSDL link to see the automatically generated WSDL of our web service, we get the complete WSDL document generated as shown below:

```
<?xml version="1.0" encoding="ISO-8859-1" ?>
- <definitions xmlns:SOAP-ENV="http://schemas.xmlsoap.org/soap/envelope/"
  xmlns:xsd="http://www.w3.org/2001/XMLSchema"
  xmlns:xsi="http://www.w3.org/2001/XMLSchema-instance"
  xmlns:SOAP-ENC="http://schemas.xmlsoap.org/soap/encoding/"
  xmlns:tns="urn:demoserver2"
  xmlns:soap="http://schemas.xmlsoap.org/wsdl/soap/"
  xmlns:wsdl="http://schemas.xmlsoap.org/wsdl/"
  xmlns="http://schemas.xmlsoap.org/wsdl/"
  targetNamespace="urn:demoserver2">
- <types>
- <xsd:schema targetNamespace="urn:demoserver2">
  <xsd:import namespace="http://schemas.xmlsoap.org/soap/encoding/" />
```

```
<xsd:import namespace="http://schemas.xmlsoap.org/wsdl/" />
</xsd:schema>
</types>
- <message name="WelcomeMsgRequest">
<part name="name" type="xsd:string" />
</message>
- <message name="WelcomeMsgResponse">
<part name="result" type="xsd:string" />
</message>
- <portType name="Displaying Welcome MessagePortType">
- <operation name="WelcomeMsg">
<input message="tns:WelcomeMsgRequest" />
<output message="tns:WelcomeMsgResponse" />
</operation>
</portType>
- <binding name="Displaying Welcome MessageBinding" type="tns:Displaying
   Welcome MessagePortType">
<soap:binding style="rpc"
transport="http://schemas.xmlsoap.org/soap/http" />
- <operation name="WelcomeMsg">
<soap:operation
soapAction="http://localhost/demoserver2.php/WelcomeMsg"
style="rpc" />
- <input>
<soap:body use="encoded" namespace="urn:demoserver2"
   encodingStyle="http://schemas.xmlsoap.org/soap/encoding/" />
</input>
- <output>
<soap:body use="encoded" namespace="urn:demoserver2"
encodingStyle="http://schemas.xmlsoap.org/soap/encoding/" />
</output>
</operation>
</binding>
```

```
- <service name="Displaying Welcome Message">
- <port name="Displaying Welcome MessagePort"
  binding="tns:Displaying Welcome MessageBinding">
  <soap:address location="http://localhost/demoserver2.php" />
  </port>
  </service>
  </definitions>
```

10.5 MODIFYING THE CLIENT PROGRAM OF CURRENCY CONVERTER WEB SERVICE

In the client web service of our first web service: Currency Converter, we find one constraint that the amount in pounds is hard coded in the client program. That is, if the user wishes to specify some other amount in pounds, he has make changes in the client program. So, we modify the client program so that it prompts the user to enter amount in pounds (instead of making changes in the client code) and it will be converted into dollars.

client1.php

```
<?php
require_once('nusoap.php');

if (isset($_POST['submit'])) {
$amt =$_POST['amt'];
$client=new soapclient('http://localhost/server1.php?wsdl', true);
$param=array('amount' => $amt);
echo $client->call('CurrencyConverter', $param);
}
else
{
?>
<form action="client1.php" method="post">
Enter amount in Pounds: <input type="text" name="amt">
<input type="submit" name="submit" value="Submit">
 </form>
```

```
<?php
}
?>
```

The client is asked to enter amount in pounds (which is assigned to variable: `amt`). On clicking the submit button, the form elements are submitted to itself (i.e. to client1.php file). Using `$_POST` array, the amount entered by the client is accessed and stored in `$amt` variable.

An array named `$param` is created consisting of the parameter name as "amount" and value as `$amt` - the amount entered by the client.

Then instantiate the soapclient object and pass the URL of the web service's WSDL file to it i.e.'http://localhost/server1.php?wsdl'. The boolean value `true` is passed to inform NuSOAP that WSDL is being used.

With the help of the `call()` method, we inform the soapclient object to access CurrencyConverter method and pass parameters (`$param` array carrying the amount entered by the user) to it. The value returned in dollars by the web service is echoed on the screen.

Output:

When we run the client web service by directing the browser to http://localhost/client1.php, we get a screen which prompts the client to enter amount in pounds (Figure 10.9).

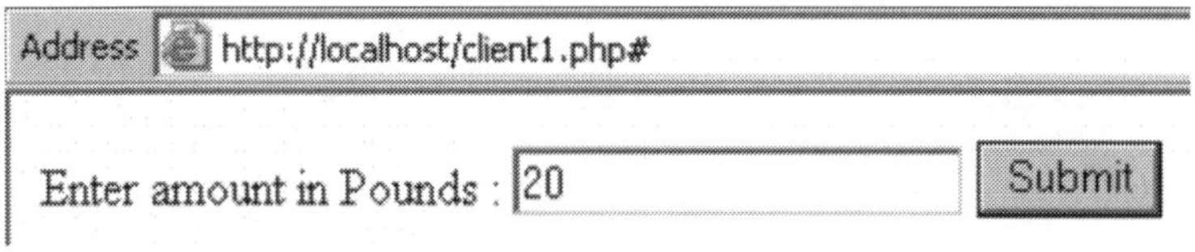

Figure 10.9 ***Screen on Running Client Web Service***

After entering amount in pounds, we get the amount converted into dollars (assuming 1 pound=40$) (Figure 10.10).

Figure 10.10 ***Amount Converted into Dollars***

10.6 WEB SERVICE ACCESSING DATABASE

Usually all the web services publicly available around us consist of a database containing the information to be supplied to the client. When the client asks for particular data, the desired data is fetched from database and is returned to the client.

So, let us do it practically. The following web service asks the user to specify the item code of a product and that item code is searched for in the `products` table (we are using the same products table (in the `shopping` database) made while making the Shopping Cart web application in Part I of this book) and the `price` of that product is returned to the client. This web service contains a method: `getprice` which searches the product with the supplied item code and returns its price. So let us create two files named server2.php and client2.php in the `htdocs` subfolder of our `apache` directory with the following contents:

server2.php

```
1.  <?php
2.  require_once(‘nusoap.php’);
3.  $server = new soap_server();
4.  $server->configureWSDL(‘Get Price’,’urn:server2');
5.  $soap->wsdl->schemaTargetNamespace = ‘urn:server2’;
6.  $server->register(‘getprice’, array(‘icode’ => ‘xsd:string’), array(‘result’
=> ‘xsd:string’), ‘urn:server2’);

7.  function getprice($icode) {
8.  $connect = mysql_connect(“localhost”, “root”, “mce”)
9.  or die(“Please, check your server connection.”);
10. mysql_select_db(“shopping”);
11. $query = “select price from products where item_code = “ . $icode;
12. $result = mysql_query($query);
13. $data = mysql_fetch_array($result);
14. return $data[‘price’];
15. }
16. $server->service($HTTP_RAW_POST_DATA);
17. ?>
```

Explanation of server2.php program

```
4. $server->configureWSDL(‘Get Price’,’urn:server2');
```

Defining the settings for our WSDL file (which the NuSOAP library will automatically create for us). We specify the service name: Get Price and the namespace (urn:server2) of our service.

```
5. $soap->wsdl->schemaTargetNamespace = 'urn:server2';
```

The TargetNamespace is a convention that enables the WSDL document to refer to itself. The TargetNamespace is set to the namespace (urn:server2).

```
6. $server->register('getprice', array('icode' => 'xsd:string'), array('result'
=> 'xsd:string'), 'urn:server2');
```

We are registering our method: getprice. Also we specify the data types of the arguments passed as well as returned by the method. In the above command we are specifying that the argument passed to the method is "icode" (for itemcode) and is of string data type. Similarly, the returned parameter is "result" of string data type. We specify the arguments in the form of an array where the key of the array represents the name of the input/output parameter and the value specifies the data type of the input/output parameter. Following the array of arguments, we specify the namespace we are operating in.

```
7.  function getprice($icode) {
8.  $connect = mysql_connect("localhost", "root", "mce")
9.  or die("Please, check your server connection.");
10. mysql_select_db("shopping");
11. $query = "select price from products where item_code = " . $icode;
12. $result = mysql_query($query);
13. $data = mysql_fetch_array($result);
14. return $data['price'];
15. }
```

The value passed to the function getprice is assigned to `$icode` parameter. Then a connection with the MySQL server is established as a user `root`. After that, the `shopping` database is selected and an SQL statement is written to retrieve the `price` of the product with item_code=$icode from the `products` table. The query is executed and the fetched price from the `products` table is stored in `$result` array. The `price` of the product is fetched from the `$result` array and stored in `$data` variable which is returned to be displayed on the client.

client2.php

```
<?php
    require_once('nusoap.php');
    $param = array('icode'=>'102');
    $client=new soapclient('http://localhost/server2.php?wsdl', true);
```

```
    $rec = $client->call('getprice',$param);
    if (isset($fault)) {
        print "Error: ". $fault;
    }
    else {
        echo "The price of product with item code ". $param[icode] ." is ".
            $rec;
    }
    unset($client);
?>
```

We are supplying the item code in the coded form i.e. an array by name `$param` is created consisting of the parameter name as "icode" and value as "102".

Then instantiate the soapclient object and pass the URL of the web service's WSDL file to it i.e. 'http://localhost/server2.php?wsdl'. The boolean value `true` is passed to inform NuSOAP that WSDL is being used.

With the help of the `call()` method, we inform the soapclient object to access `getprice` method and pass parameters (`$param` array carrying the item code of the product whose price is desired) to it. The `price` of the product is returned by the web service and is displayed on the screen.

Output:

Let's run the client web service first. Open the browser and invoke the client web service by writing: http://localhost/client2.php in the address bar. We get the price of the product in the form of output (Figure 10.11).

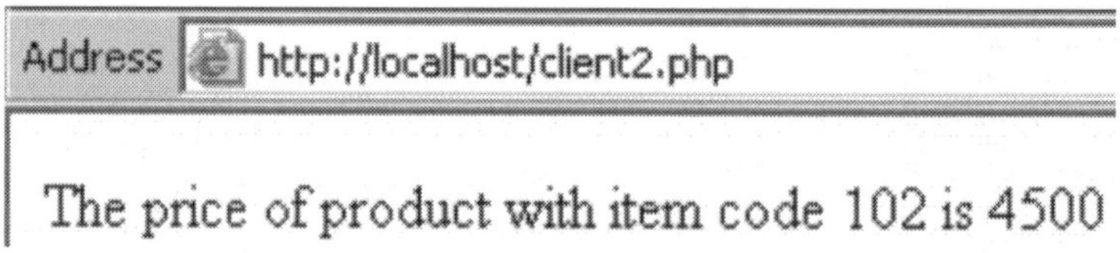

Figure 10.11 ***Output as Price of the Product***

Now let us run the server web service. Direct the browser to the following address: http://localhost/server2.php. We get the following output (Figure 10.12).

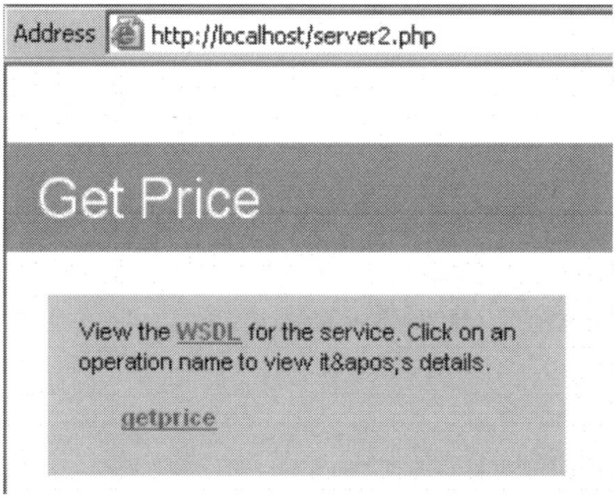

Figure 10.12 ***Output on Running Server Web Service***

If we select the method: `getprice` of our web service, we get the screen showing various details of the method (Figure 10.13).

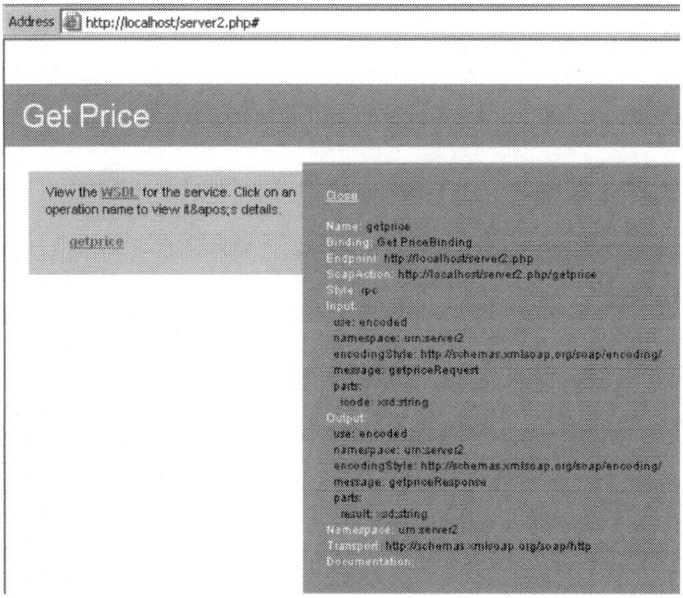

Figure 10.13 ***Screen on Selecting GetPrice Method***

If we select the WSDL link to see the automatically generated WSDL of our web service, we get the complete WSDL document generated as shown below:

```
http://localhost/server2.php?wsdl

<?xml version="1.0" encoding="ISO-8859-1" ?>
- <definitions xmlns:SOAP-
  ENV="http://schemas.xmlsoap.org/soap/envelope/"
  xmlns:xsd="http://www.w3.org/2001/XMLSchema"
  xmlns:xsi="http://www.w3.org/2001/XMLSchema-instance"
  xmlns:SOAP-ENC="http://schemas.xmlsoap.org/soap/encoding/"
  xmlns:tns="urn:server2"
  xmlns:soap="http://schemas.xmlsoap.org/wsdl/soap/"
  xmlns:wsdl="http://schemas.xmlsoap.org/wsdl/"
  xmlns="http://schemas.xmlsoap.org/wsdl/"
  targetNamespace="urn:server2">
- <types>
- <xsd:schema targetNamespace="urn:server2">
  <xsd:import namespace="http://schemas.xmlsoap.org/soap/encoding/" />
  <xsd:import namespace="http://schemas.xmlsoap.org/wsdl/" />
  </xsd:schema>
  </types>
- <message name="getpriceRequest">
  <part name="icode" type="xsd:string" />
  </message>
- <message name="getpriceResponse">
  <part name="result" type="xsd:string" />
  </message>
- <portType name="Get PricePortType">
- <operation name="getprice">
  <input message="tns:getpriceRequest" />
  <output message="tns:getpriceResponse" />
  </operation>
  </portType>
- <binding name="Get PriceBinding" type="tns:Get PricePortType">
  <soap:binding style="rpc"
```

```
    transport="http://schemas.xmlsoap.org/soap/http" />
- <operation name="getprice">
  <soap:operation soapAction="http://localhost/server2.php/getprice"
    style="rpc" />
- <input>
  <soap:body use="encoded" namespace="urn:server2"
    encodingStyle="http://schemas.xmlsoap.org/soap/encoding/" />
  </input>
- <output>
  <soap:body use="encoded" namespace="urn:server2"
    encodingStyle="http://schemas.xmlsoap.org/soap/encoding/" />
  </output>
  </operation>
  </binding>
- <service name="Get Price">
- <port name="Get PricePort" binding="tns:Get PriceBinding">
  <soap:address location="http://localhost/server2.php" />
  </port>
  </service>
  </definitions>
```

10.7 DEALING WITH COMPLEXTYPE

Complex type is a data type that includes structures and arrays.

This web service will contain a method: `getdetails` which will ask the client to specify the `item code` and then it will search the table named `products` in the database `shopping` for that item code and full details of the `product` i.e. item code, item name, its description and price. So let's create a file named `server3.php` in the `htdocs` subfolder of our `apache` directory with the following contents:

server3.php

```
<?php
require_once('nusoap.php');
$server = new soap_server();
```

```
$server->configureWSDL('Get Product Details','urn:server3');
$server->wsdl->schemaTargetNamespace = 'urn:server3';
$server->wsdl->addComplexType(
'ItemData',
'complexType',
'struct',
'all',
'',
array(
'item_code' => array('item_code'=>'item_code', 'type'=>'xsd:int'),
'item_name' => array('item_name'=>'item_name', 'type'=>'xsd:string'),
'description' => array('description'=>'description', 'type'=>'xsd:string'),
'price' => array('price'=>'price', 'type'=>'xsd:int')
)
);
$server->register('getdetails', array('icode' => 'xsd:string'), array
  ('return' => 'tns:ItemData'), 'urn:server3');
function getdetails($icode) {
$connect = mysql_connect("localhost", "root", "mce")
or die("Please, check your server connection.");
mysql_select_db("shopping");
$query = "select item_code, item_name, description, price from products where
  item_code = " . $icode;
$result = mysql_query($query);
$data = mysql_fetch_array($result, MYSQL_ASSOC);
return $data;
}
$server->service($HTTP_RAW_POST_DATA);
?>
```

Explanation of server3.php program

```
6. $server->wsdl->addComplexType(
7. ‘ItemData’,
8. ‘complexType’,
9. ‘struct’,
10. ‘all’,
11. ‘’,
12. array(
13. ‘item_code’ => array(‘item_code’=>’item_code’, ‘type’=>’xsd:int’),
14. ‘item_name’ => array(‘item_name’=>’item_name’, ‘type’=>’xsd:string’),
15. ‘description’ => array(‘description’=>’description’, ‘type’=>’xsd:string’),
16. ‘price’ => array(‘price’=>’price’, ‘type’=>’xsd:int’)
17. )
18. );
```

There are two different kinds of data types:

- Built-in types
- Complex data type

Complex data type includes the following:

- structures and
- arrays.

In the above statements, we are adding a complex data type called `ItemData` to our SOAP server. This ItemData complex type is a SOAP struct. The SOAP struct in NuSOAP is represented using associative array. So, we define our `ItemData` struct in the form of an associative array consisting of four simple elements that can be included in any order: `item_code (int)`, `item_name(string)`,`description (string)`,`price(int)`. Line by line explanation is as follows:

```
7. ‘ItemData’,
```

It is the name of data type we are defining.

```
8. ‘complexType’,
```

The data type is not simpleType but complexType.

```
9. ‘struct’,
```

It is a phpType and it can be: either array or struct. We are defining ItemData of type: struct

```
10. 'all',
```

It is a compositor which can be:

- all,
- sequence or
- choice.

The `compositor` is a way of defining how the subelements of the current element work, i.e. whether all optional elements to be included in any order (all), or only to be allowed in the given order (sequence) or only one of them is allowed at any one time (choice).

```
11. ' ',
```

This option is for specifying restrictionBase namespace. It is left blank as we don't want to specify any restrictions here. The restrictions can be imposed to specify the allowed values if:

we want to specify the `maximum size` of the allowed values in terms of length

we want to specify the `minimum size` of the allowed value

we want the output if it is in `fractions` be restricted to the specified number of digits after the decimal point

```
12. array(
13. 'item_code' => array('item_code'=>'item_code', 'type'=>'xsd:int'),
14. 'item_name' => array('item_name'=>'item_name', 'type'=>'xsd:string'),
15. 'description' => array('description'=>'description', 'type'=>'xsd:string'),
16. 'price' => array('price'=>'price', 'type'=>'xsd:int')
17. )
```

This array explains the structure of `ItemData` to NuSOAP i.e. we are defining the elements of ItemData structure. The elements item is an array containing a list of subelements, each of which has a name and a type.

```
19. $server->register('getdetails', array('icode' => 'xsd:string'),
    array('return' => 'tns:ItemData'), 'urn:server3');
```

This command registers the function `getdetails` as a SOAP function. The parameters of the function are defined in the form of an array. The input parameter states that an `icode` of type string will be passed. The output parameter states the `return` type as 'tns:Itemdata' meaning the returned data will be in the form of our complex type: ItemData. 'urn:server3' specifies the name of the WSDL.

```
20. function getdetails($icode) {
21. $connect = mysql_connect("localhost", "root", "mce")
22. or die("Please, check your server connection.");
23. mysql_select_db("shopping");
```

```
$query = "select item_code, item_name, description, price from products where
item_code = " . $icode;
$result = mysql_query($query);
$data = mysql_fetch_array($result, MYSQL_ASSOC);
return $data;
}
```

The value passed to the function `getdetails` is assigned to the `$icode` parameter. A connection with the MySQL server is established as a user `root` and the `shopping` database is selected. Then, an SQL statement is written to retrieve the attributes like: item_code, item_name, description and price of the product with item_code=$icode from the `products` table. The query is executed and the fetched row from the `products` table is stored in `$result` array. This array is converted in the form of associative array (an array in the form of key value pair i.e. values attached to different keys) and assigned to `$data`. `$data`, an associative array is returned for display to the client.

```
$server->service($HTTP_RAW_POST_DATA);
```

Passing incoming posted data to our SOAP service method.

client3.php

```
<?php
require_once('nusoap.php');
$param = array('icode'=>'102');
$client=new soapclient('http://localhost/server3.php?wsdl', true);
$rec = $client->call('getdetails',$param);
if (isset($fault)) {
print "Error: ". $fault;
}
else {
echo "The details of product with item code ". $param[icode] ." are ";
echo "<table border=1>";
echo "<th>Item Code</th><th>Name of Item</th><th>Description</th><th>Price</
  th>";
echo "<tr>";
```

```
14. echo "<td>";
15. echo $rec['item_code'];
16. echo "</td>";
17. echo "<td>";
18. echo $rec['item_name'];
19. echo "</td>";
20. echo "<td>";
21. echo $rec['description'];
22. echo "</td>";
23. echo "<td>";
24. echo $rec['price'];
25. echo "</td>";
26. echo "</tr></table>";
27. }
28. unset($client);
29. ?>
```

Explanation of client3.php program

```
3. $param = array('icode'=>'102');
```

Defining a parameter in the form of array to be sent to our web method: getdetails. We are setting the value of the argument icode as 102.

```
4. $client=new soapclient('http://localhost/server3.php?wsdl', true);
```

Creating an object for the client and passing the URL to the server as argument. We can call a public method with the help of a client object.

```
5. $rec = $client->call('getdetails',$param);
```

Invoking the web method: `getdetails` and passing the parameter (containing the argument `icode` set to value 102). The returned value (complex data type:Itemdata) will be stored in `$rec` for displaying the result.

```
6. if (isset($fault)) {
7. print "Error: ". $fault;
8. }
```

Checking for errors and if there are any, displaying those errors.

Output:

Let's run the client web service first. Open the browser and invoke the client web service by writing: http://localhost/client3.php in the address bar. We get the details of the product with item code 102 in the form of output as shown in Figure 10.14.

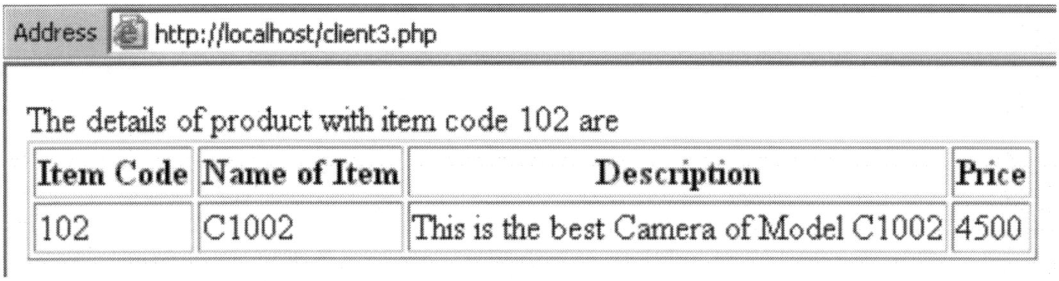

Figure 10.14 ***Details of a Product***

Now let us run the server web service. Direct the browser to the following address: http://localhost/server3.php. We get the following output (Figure 10.15).

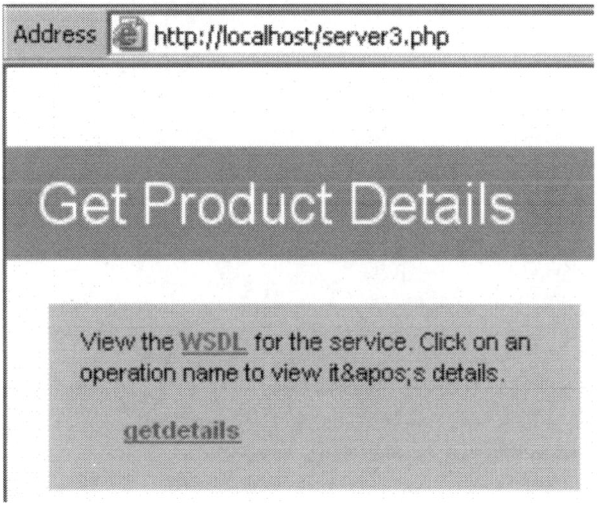

Figure 10.15 ***Screen for Get Product Details***

If we select the method: `getdetails` of our web service, we get a screen showing various details of the method (Figure 10.16).

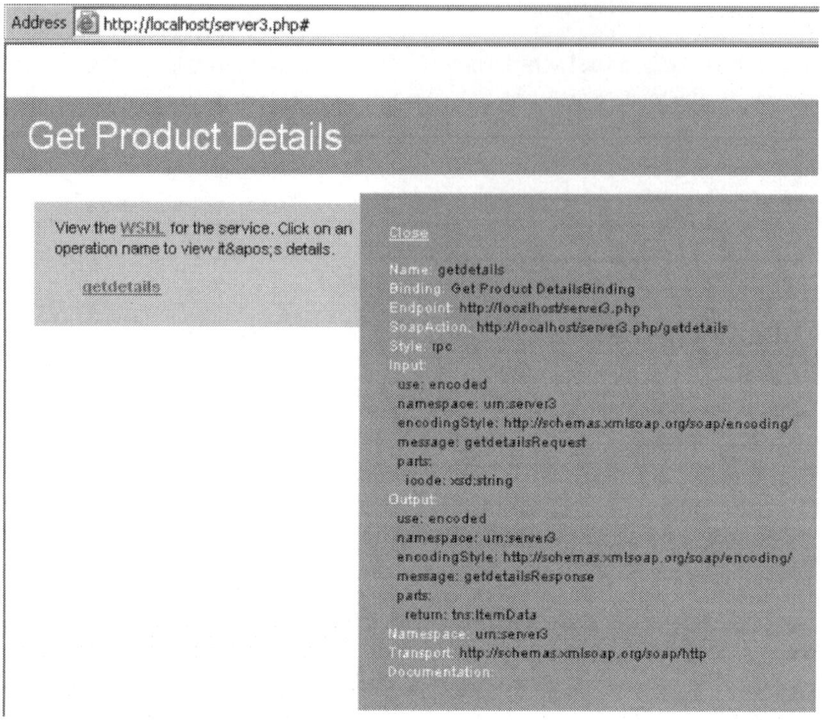

Figure 10.16 *Various methods of Get Product Details*

If we select the WSDL link to see the automatically generated WSDL of our web service, we get the complete WSDL document generated as shown below:

```
<?xml version="1.0" encoding="ISO-8859-1" ?>
- <definitions xmlns:SOAP-ENV="http://schemas.xmlsoap.org/soap/envelope/"
  xmlns:xsd="http://www.w3.org/2001/XMLSchema"
  xmlns:xsi="http://www.w3.org/ 2001/XMLSchema-instance" xmlns:SOAP-
  ENC="http://schemas.xmlsoap.org/soap/encoding/"
  xmlns:tns="urn:server3"
  xmlns:soap="http://schemas.xmlsoap.org/wsdl/soap/"
  xmlns:wsdl="http://schemas.xmlsoap.org/wsdl/"
  xmlns="http://schemas.xmlsoap.org/wsdl/"
  targetNamespace="urn:server3">
- <types>
- <xsd:schema targetNamespace="urn:server3">
  <xsd:import namespace="http://schemas.xmlsoap.org/soap/encoding/" />
  <xsd:import namespace="http://schemas.xmlsoap.org/wsdl/" />
- <xsd:complexType name="ItemData">
```

```
- <xsd:all>
  <xsd:element name="item_code" type="xsd:int" item_code="item_code" />
  <xsd:element name="item_name" type="xsd:string" item_name="item_name" />
  <xsd:element name="description" type="xsd:string" description="description"
  />
  <xsd:element name="price" type="xsd:int" price="price" />
  </xsd:all>
  </xsd:complexType>
  </xsd:schema>
  </types>
- <message name="getdetailsRequest">
  <part name="icode" type="xsd:string" />
  </message>
- <message name="getdetailsResponse">
  <part name="return" type="tns:ItemData" />
  </message>
- <portType name="Get Product DetailsPortType">
- <operation name="getdetails">
  <input message="tns:getdetailsRequest" />
  <output message="tns:getdetailsResponse" />
  </operation>
  </portType>
- <binding name="Get Product DetailsBinding" type="tns:Get Product
     DetailsPortType">
  <soap:binding style="rpc" transport="http://schemas.xmlsoap.org/soap/http"
     />
- <operation name="getdetails">
  <soap:operation soapAction="http://localhost/server3.php/getdetails"
     style="rpc" />
- <input>
  <soap:body use="encoded" namespace="urn:server3"
  encodingStyle="http://schemas.xmlsoap.org/soap/encoding/" />
  </input>
```

```
- <output>
  <soap:body use="encoded" namespace="urn:server3"
  encodingStyle="http://schemas.xmlsoap.org/soap/encoding/" />
  </output>
  </operation>
  </binding>
- <service name="Get Product Details">
- <port name="Get Product DetailsPort" binding="tns:Get Product
     DetailsBinding">
  <soap:address location="http://localhost/server3.php" />
  </port>
  </service>
  </definitions>
```

10.8 DISPLAYING ITEM CODES IN THE FORM OF A DROPDOWN LIST

In this example, we are providing a facility to the client that he can select the item code of the product whose details he might be interested in viewing. That is, we are using the same web service: `server3.php` but with a better client interface. We need to make two client programs: one is `callclient.php` and the other is `client4.php`. The `callclient.php` program fetches the `item codes` from the `products` table and displays them in the form of a dropdown list. The item code selected by the client is then passed to the `client4.php` program which does the main job. It invokes the method: `getdetails` of the web service and passes the item code selected by the client to it. The web service searches the table named `products` in the database: `shopping` for that item code and the full details of the product i.e. item code, item name, its description and price are displayed.

callclient.php

```
<html>
<head>
</head>
<body>
   <form action="client4.php" method="post">
   <?php
      $connect = mysql_connect("localhost", "root", "mce")
      or die("Please, check your server connection.");
      mysql_select_db("shopping");
```

```
        $query = "SELECT item_code " . "FROM products " .
            "where category like 'Camera' order by item_code";
        $results = mysql_query($query) or die(mysql_error());
    ?>
    Select item code
        <select name="itmcode">
            <option value="" selected>Select Item Code</option>
            <?php
                while ($row = mysql_fetch_array($results)) {
                    extract($row);
            ?>
    <option value=<?php echo $item_code ?> ><?php echo $item_code ?>
        </option>
            <?php
                }
            ?>
        </select>
    <input type="submit" name="Submit" value="Display Details">
    </form>
</body>
</html>
```

client4.php

```
<?php
    require_once('nusoap.php');
    $code=$_POST['itmcode'];
    $param = array('icode'=>$code);
    $client=new soapclient('http://localhost/server3.php?wsdl', true);
    $rec = $client->call('getdetails',$param);
    if (isset($fault)) {
        print "Error: ". $fault;
    }
    else {
        echo "The details of product with item code ". $param[icode] ." are ";
        echo "<table border=1>";
```

```
echo "<th>Item Code</th><th>Name of Item</th> <th>Description</th>
    <th>Price</th>";
        echo "<tr>";
    echo "<td>";
    echo $rec['item_code'];
    echo "</td>";
    echo "<td>";
    echo $rec['item_name'];
    echo "</td>";
    echo "<td>";
    echo $rec['description'];
    echo "</td>";
    echo "<td>";
    echo $rec['price'];
    echo "</td>";
        echo "</tr></table>";
    }
    unset($client);
?>
```

Output:

Let's run the client program `callclient.php` by pointing the browser to the following address: `http://localhost/client5.php`. This client program displays the `item codes` from the `products` table in the form of a dropdown list (Figure 10.17).

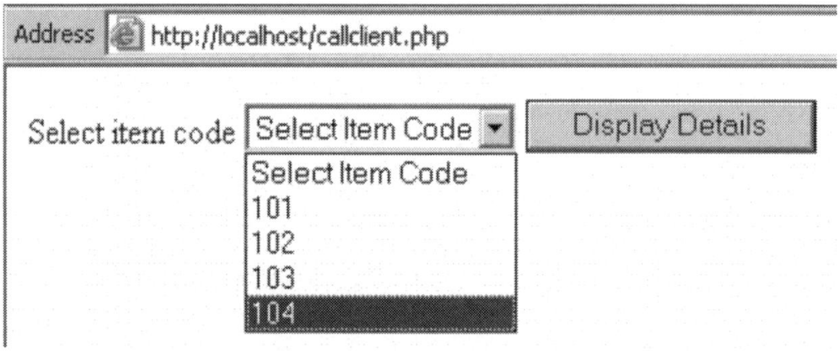

Figure 10.17 ***Screen for Selection of Item Code***

The item code selected by the client will be automatically passed to the client web service: `client4.php` which invokes the server web service and gets the details of the product with the selected item code in the form of a table (Figure 10.18).

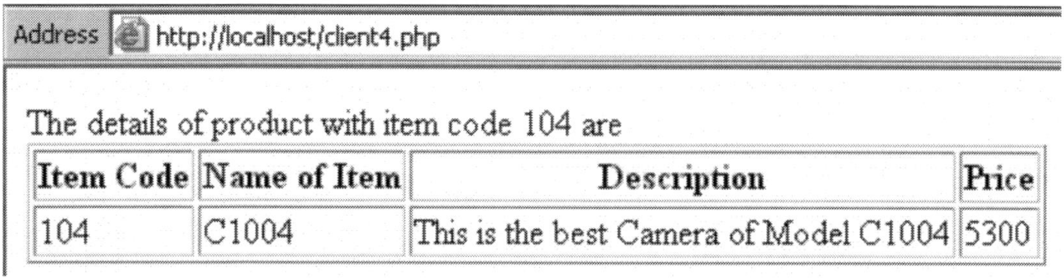

Item Code	Name of Item	Description	Price
104	C1004	This is the best Camera of Model C1004	5300

Figure 10.18 ***Details of the Selected Product***

10.9 DISPLAYING NAMES OF THE PRODUCTS OF THE SELECTED CATEGORY

In this example, we are going to make a server web service named `servergetnames.php`. It will have a method: `getnames` which will search the `products` table of the `shopping` database for the supplied category and the item names of the product falling in the supplied category will be displayed.

We will be making two client programs: `selectcategory.php` and `clientshownames.php`. The selectcategory.php program displays the different categories of products available in the form of a dropdown list and passes the selected category to the `clientshownames.php` program. The clientshownames.php does the main job of invoking the web service and passes the category selected by the client to its `getnames` method. The web service searches the `products` table of the `shopping` database and extracts the item names of the products falling in the supplied category and sends them to the client for display.

servergetnames.php

```
<?php
require_once('nusoap.php');
$server = new soap_server();
$server->configureWSDL('Get Item Names','urn:server4');
$server->wsdl->schemaTargetNamespace = 'urn:server4';
$server->wsdl->addComplexType(
'ItemNames',
'complexType',
```

```
‘array’,
‘ ’,
‘SOAP-ENC:Array’,
array(),
array(array(‘ref’=>’SOAP-ENC:arrayType’,’wsdl:arrayType’=>’string[]’)),
‘xsd:string’
);

$server->register(‘getnames’,
array(‘category’ => ‘xsd:string’),
array(‘return’ => ‘tns:ItemNames’),
‘urn:server4’,
‘urn:server4#getnames’,
‘rpc’,
‘encoded’,
‘Returns the item names’
);

function getnames($category) {
$connect = mysql_connect(“localhost”, “root”, “mce”)
or die(“Please, check your server connection.”);
mysql_select_db(“shopping”);
$query = “select item_name from products where category like ‘“ . $category .
“‘“;
$result = mysql_query($query);
$data = array();
while($r = mysql_fetch_array($result)){
array_push($data, $r[‘item_name’]);
}
return $data;
}
$server->service($HTTP_RAW_POST_DATA);
?>
```

Explanation of servergetnames.php program

```
6.  $server->wsdl->addComplexType(
7.  'ItemNames',
8.  'complexType',
9.  'array',
10. ' ',
11. 'SOAP-ENC:Array',
12. array(),
13. array(array('ref'=>'SOAP-ENC:arrayType','wsdl:arrayType'=>'string[]')),
14. 'xsd:string'
15. );
```

Adding a complex data type called ItemNames to our SOAP server. This `ItemNames` is an array of strings. Line by line explanation is as follows:

```
7.  'ItemNames',
```

It is the name of Complex data type that we are defining.

```
8.  'complexType',
```

The data type is not simpleType but a complexType.

```
9.  'array',
```

It is a phpType and it can be: either array or struct. We are defining ItemNames of type: array

```
10. ' ',
```

The compositor is left blank. A compositor can be:

- all,
- sequence or
- choice.

and is used to define how the subelements of an element work i.e. whether they have to be allowed in any order (all), allowed in the given order (sequence) or only one of them is allowed at any time(choice).

```
11. 'SOAP-ENC:Array',
```

restrictionBase is set to 'SOAP-ENC:Array'. This tells the system that our complex type is based on the array type defined within the soap-encoding namespace.

```
12. array(),
```

The elements parameter is set to blank array.

```
13. array(array('ref'=>'SOAP-ENC:arrayType','wsdl:arrayType'=>'string[]')),
```

The parameter is an array defining the type of the array and the type of the elements within the array which is string. That means our complexType `ItemNames` is an array of strings.

```
14. 'xsd:string'
```

The data type of the array is string.

```
16. $server->register('getnames',
17. array('category' => 'xsd:string'),
18. array('return' => 'tns:ItemNames'),
19. 'urn:server4',
20. 'urn:server4#getnames',
21. 'rpc',
22. 'encoded',
23. 'Returns the item names'
24. );
```

Registering the function `getnames` along with input and output parameters (in the form of an array).

```
17. array('category' => 'xsd:string'),
```

It is an input parameter which states that a category of type string will be passed to the `getnames` function.

```
18. array('return' => 'tns:ItemNames'),
```

The output parameter states the return type as 'tns:ItemNames' meaning the returned data will be in the form of our complex type: ItemNames.

```
19. 'urn:server4',
```

Defining the namespace. It designates the name of the WSDL document

```
20. 'urn:server4#getnames',
```

It is a soapaction. That is we are setting the action to the method name within the namespace.

```
21. 'rpc',
```

The style used is a Remote Procedure Call. Recall that, if we are defining an RPC style service, the message parts represent the method's parameters. In this case, the name of the part becomes the name of an element in the concrete message and its structure is determined by the supplied type attribute. If we're defining a document style service, the parts simply refer to the XML elements that are placed within the body (referenced by the element attribute).

```
22. 'encoded',
```

It means encoding is used. The SOAP encodingStyle global attribute can be used to indicate the serialisation rules used in a SOAP message.

Brief description of what the function is doing.

```
function getnames($category) {
$connect = mysql_connect(“localhost”, “root”, “mce”)
or die(“Please, check your server connection.”);
mysql_select_db(“shopping”);
$query = “select item_name from products where category like ‘“ . $category .
   “‘“;
$result = mysql_query($query);
$data = array();
while($r = mysql_fetch_array($result)){
array_push($data, $r[‘item_name’]);
}
return $data;
}
```

The category name selected passed to the function `getnames` is assigned to `$category` parameter. A connection with the MySQL server is established as a user root and the `shopping` database is selected. Then, an SQL statement is written to retrieve all the item_name of the products belonging to `$category` from the `products` table. The query is executed and the fetched item names from the `products` table are stored in the `$result` array. All the item_name stored in `$result` array are retrieved one by one and stored in a linear array: `$data` (mysql_fetch_array is for returning several rows of the entire result). This linear array `$data` consisting of all item_name of the products of the specified category is then returned for display to the client.

selectcategory.php

```
<html>
<head>
</head>
<body>
    <form action="clientshownames.php" method="post">
        Select Category
            <select name="category">
                <option value="" selected>Select a Category</option>
                <option value="Camera">Camera </option>
```

```
            <option value="Mobile">Mobile </option>
            <option value="Book">Book </option>
        </select>
    <input type="submit" name="Submit" value="Display Item Names">
  </form>
</body>
</html>
```

clientshownames.php

```
<?php
   require_once('nusoap.php');
   $cat=$_POST['category'];
   $param = array('category'=>$cat);
   $client=new soapclient('http://localhost/servergetnames.php?wsdl',
      true);
   $records = $client->call('getnames',$param);
   if (isset($fault)) {
      print "Error: ". $fault;
   }
   else {
      echo "The item names of the category ". $param[category] ." are ";
      echo "<table border=1>";
      echo "<th>Item Name</th>";
      foreach($records as $rec)
      {
         echo "<tr>";
         echo "<td>";
         echo $rec;
         echo "</td>";
         echo "</tr>";
      }
      echo "</table>";
   }
```

```
    unset($client);
?>
```

Output:

Let us run the client program `selectcategory.php` by pointing the browser at the following address: `http://localhost/selectcategory.php`. This client program displays the different categories of products in the form of a dropdown list (Figure 10.19).

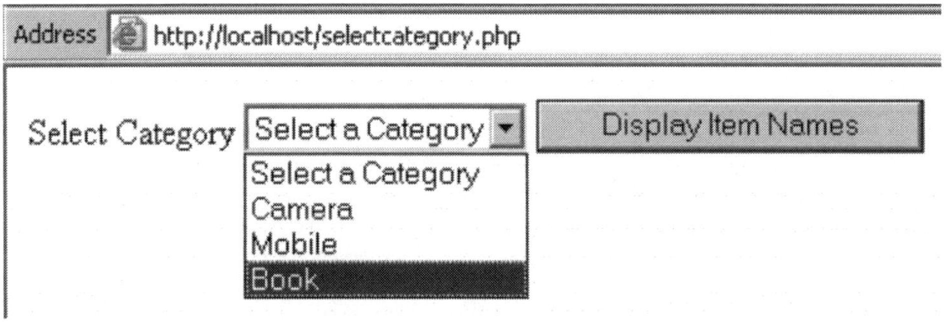

Figure 10.19 ***Selection of a Category***

The category selected by the client will be automatically passed to the client web service: `clientshownames.php` which invokes the server web service and gets the item names of the products falling in the selected category in the form of a table (Figure 10.20).

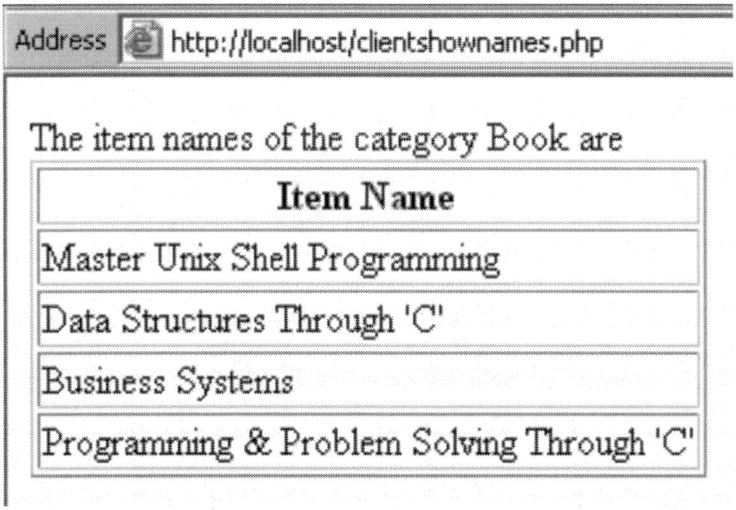

Figure 10.20 ***Description of the Selected Category***

Let us try selecting `Camera` category (Figure 10.21).

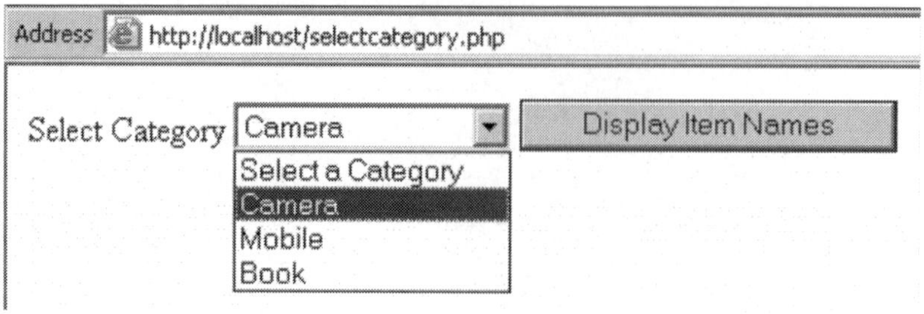

Figure 10.21 ***Selection of a Category***

All the products of Camera category will be displayed (Figure 10.22).

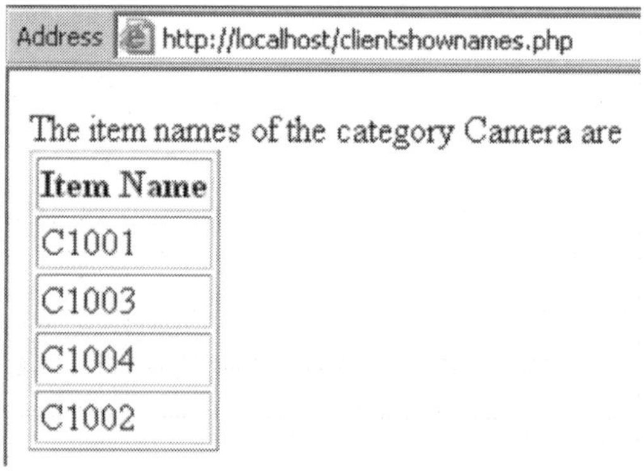

Figure 10.22 ***Item names of the Selected Category***

Now let us run the server web service. Direct the browser to the following address: `http://localhost/servergetnames.php`. We get the following output (Figure 10.23).

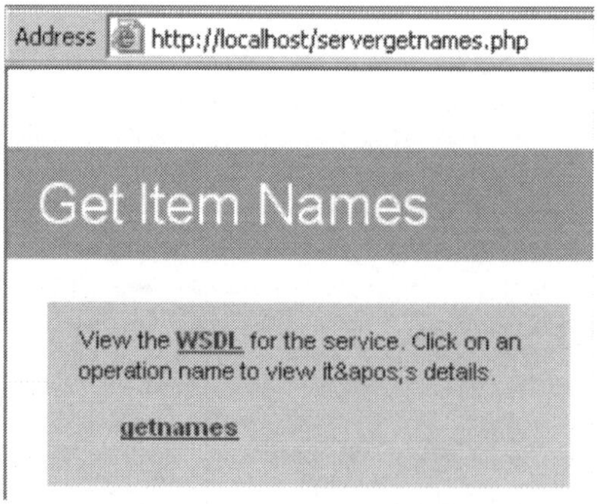

Figure 10.23 ***Screen for Get Item Names***

If we select the method: getnames of our web service, we get the screen showing various details of the method (Figure 10.24).

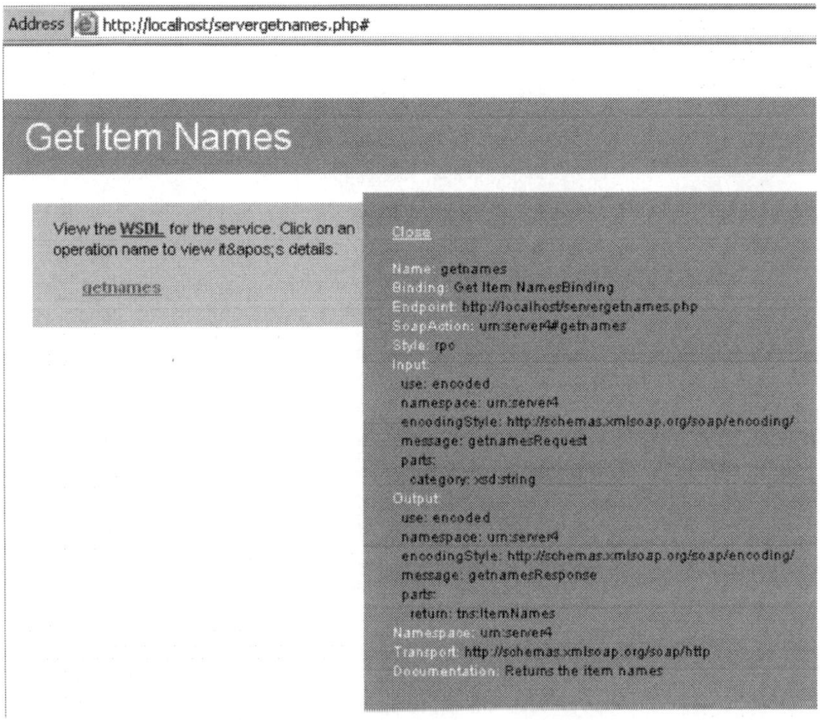

Figure 10.24 ***Various Methods of Getnames Option***

If we select the WSDL link to see the automatically generated WSDL of our web service, we get the complete WSDL document generated as shown below:

```
http://localhost/servergetnames.php?wsdl

<?xml version="1.0" encoding="ISO-8859-1" ?>
- <definitions xmlns:SOAP-ENV="http://schemas.xmlsoap.org/soap/envelope/"
  xmlns:xsd="http://www.w3.org/2001/XMLSchema"
  xmlns:xsi="http://www.w3.org/2001/XMLSchema-instance" xmlns:SOAP-
  ENC="http://schemas.xmlsoap.org/soap/encoding/"
  xmlns:tns="urn:server4"
  xmlns:soap="http://schemas.xmlsoap.org/wsdl/soap/"
  xmlns:wsdl="http://schemas.xmlsoap.org/wsdl/"
  xmlns="http://schemas.xmlsoap.org/wsdl/"
  targetNamespace="urn:server4">
```

```
- <types>
- <xsd:schema targetNamespace="urn:server4">
  <xsd:import namespace="http://schemas.xmlsoap.org/soap/encoding/" />
  <xsd:import namespace="http://schemas.xmlsoap.org/wsdl/" />
- <xsd:complexType name="ItemNames">
- <xsd:complexContent>
- <xsd:restriction base="SOAP-ENC:Array">
  <xsd:attribute ref="SOAP-ENC:arrayType" wsdl:arrayType="string[]" />
  </xsd:restriction>
  </xsd:complexContent>
  </xsd:complexType>
  </xsd:schema>
  </types>
- <message name="getnamesRequest">
  <part name="category" type="xsd:string" />
  </message>
- <message name="getnamesResponse">
  <part name="return" type="tns:ItemNames" />
  </message>
- <portType name="Get Item NamesPortType">
- <operation name="getnames">
  <documentation>Returns the item names</documentation>
  <input message="tns:getnamesRequest" />
  <output message="tns:getnamesResponse" />
  </operation>
  </portType>
- <binding name="Get Item NamesBinding" type="tns:Get Item
  NamesPortType">
  <soap:binding style="rpc"
  transport="http://schemas.xmlsoap.org/soap/http" />
- <operation name="getnames">
  <soap:operation soapAction="urn:server4#getnames" style="rpc" />
- <input>
```

```
<soap:body use="encoded" namespace="urn:server4"
encodingStyle="http://schemas.xmlsoap.org/soap/encoding/" />
</input>
- <output>
<soap:body use="encoded" namespace="urn:server4"
encodingStyle="http://schemas.xmlsoap.org/soap/encoding/" />
</output>
</operation>
</binding>
- <service name="Get Item Names">
- <port name="Get Item NamesPort" binding="tns:Get Item NamesBinding">
<soap:address location="http://localhost/servergetnames.php" />
</port>
</service>
</definitions>
```

10.10 DISPLAYING ALL FIELDS OF THE PRODUCTS OF A PARTICULAR CATEGORY

In this example, we are going to make a server web service named `server5.php`. It will have a method: `getallproducts` which will search the `products` table of the `shopping` database for a particular category and the complete information of the product i.e. item code, item name, description and price of the product of the given category will be returned. The client program name is `client5.php` that assumes that the category of the product as `'Camera'` (any) and invokes the web service and passes the `Camera` category to its `getallproducts` method. The information of the products returned by the web service method is then displayed on the screen.

server5.php

```
<?php
require_once('nusoap.php');
$server = new soap_server();
$server->configureWSDL('Get All Products ','urn:server5');
$server->wsdl->schemaTargetNamespace = 'urn:server5';
$server->wsdl->addComplexType(
'ItemData',
```

```
‘complexType’,
‘struct’,
‘all’,
‘’,
array(‘item_code’ => array(‘item_code’=>’item_code’,’type’=>’xsd:int’),
‘item_name’ => array(‘item_name’=>’item_name’,’type’=>’xsd:string’),
‘description’=>array(‘description’=>’description’,’type’=>’xsd:string’),
‘price’ => array(‘price’=>’price’, ‘type’=>’xsd:int’)
)
);
$server->wsdl->addComplexType(
‘ItemList’,
‘complexType’,
‘array’,
‘’,
‘SOAP-ENC:Array’,
array(),
array(array(‘ref’=>’SOAP-ENC:arrayType’,
 ‘wsdl:arrayType’=>’tns:ItemData[]’)),
‘tns:ItemData’
);
$server->register(‘getallproducts’,
array(‘cat’ => ‘xsd:string’),
array(‘return’ => ‘tns:ItemList’),
‘urn:server5’,
‘urn:server5#getallproducts’,
‘rpc’,
‘encoded’,
‘Returns the details for every product’
);
function getallproducts($cat) {
```

```
38. $connect = mysql_connect("localhost", "root", "mce")
39. or die("Please, check your server connection.");
40. mysql_select_db("shopping");
41. $query = "select item_code, item_name, description, price from products where
category like '" . $cat . "'";
42. $result = mysql_query($query);
43. $data = array();
44. while($r = mysql_fetch_array($result)){
45. $tempArray = array('item_code' => $r['item_code'],
46. 'item_name' => $r['item_name'],
47. 'description' => $r['description'],
48. 'price' => $r['price']);
49. array_push($data, $tempArray);
50. }
51. return $data;
52. }
53. $server->service($HTTP_RAW_POST_DATA);
54. ?>
```

Explanation of server5.php program

```
6.  $server->wsdl->addComplexType(
7.  'ItemData',
8.  'complexType',
9.  'struct',
10. 'all',
11. '',
12. array('item_code' => array('item_code'=>'item_code','type'=>'xsd:int'),
13. 'item_name' => array('item_name'=>'item_name','type'=>'xsd:string'),
14. 'description'=>array('description'=>'description','type'=>'xsd:string'),
15. 'price' => array('price'=>'price', 'type'=>'xsd:int')
16. )
17. );
```

Since the server service is supposed to return an array of structures, we are first adding a complex data type named: `ItemData` which is nothing but a structure of a few elements and thereafter we will define another ComplexType named `ItemList` which will be an array of struct: `ItemData`. We know that a SOAP struct in NuSOAP is represented using associative array. So, we define our ItemData struct in the form of associative array consisting of four simple elements that can be included in any order: item_code (int), item_name(string), description (string), price(int). Line by line explanation is as follows:

```
7.  'ItemData',
```

It is the name of data type we are defining.

```
8.  'complexType',
```

The data type is not simpleType but it is a complexType.

```
9.  'struct',
```

It is a phpType and it can be: either array or struct. We are defining ItemData of type: struct.

```
10. 'all',
```

It is a compositor which can be:

- all,
- sequence or
- choice.

The compositor is a way of defining how the subelements of the current element work, are they either all optional elements, to be included in any order (all), optional but only to be allowed in the given order (sequence) or only one of them is allowed at any one time (choice). The compositor: sequence defines an ordered sequence of sub-elements.

```
11. '',
```

This option is for specifying restrictionBase namespace. It is left blank as we don't want to specify any restrictions here. The restrictions can be imposed to specify the certain constraints like the maximum or minimum size of the allowed values etc.

```
12. array('item_code' => array('item_code'=>'item_code','type'=>'xsd:int'),
13. 'item_name' => array('item_name'=>'item_name','type'=>'xsd:string'),
14. 'description'=>array('description'=>'description','type'=>'xsd:string'),
15. 'price' => array('price'=>'price', 'type'=>'xsd:int')
```

This array explains the structure of `ItemData` to NuSOAP i.e. we are defining the elements of `ItemData` structure. The elements item is an array containing a list of subelements, each of which has a name and a type.

```
18. $server->wsdl->addComplexType(
19. 'ItemList',
20. 'complexType',
```

```
21. ‘array’,
22. ‘’,
23. ‘SOAP-ENC:Array’,
24. array(),
25. array(array(‘ref’=>’SOAP-ENC:arrayType’,
    ‘wsdl:arrayType’=>’tns:ItemData[]’)),
26. ‘tns:ItemData’
27. );
```

Adding another complex data type called ItemList to our SOAP server. This ItemList is an array of struct: ItemData (just defined above). Line by line explanation is as follows:

```
19. ‘ItemList’,
```

It is the name of Complex data type that we are defining.

```
20. ‘complexType’,
```

The data type is not simpleType but a complexType.

```
21. ‘array’,
```

It is a phpType and it can be: either array or struct. We are defining ItemList of type: array

```
22. ‘’,
```

The compositor is left blank. A compositor can be: all, sequence or choice.

```
23. ‘SOAP-ENC:Array’,
```

restrictionBase is set to ‘SOAP-ENC:Array’. This tells the system that our complex type is based on the array type defined within the soap-encoding namespace.

```
24. array(),
```

The elements parameter is set to blank array.

```
25. array(array(‘ref’=>’SOAP-ENC:arrayType’,
    ‘wsdl:arrayType’=>’tns:ItemData[]’)),
```

The attrs parameter is an array defining the type of the array and the parameter defines the type of the elements within the array which is nothing but an array of struct: Itemdata. That means our complexType ItemList is an array of structure: ItemData.

```
26. ‘tns:ItemData’
```

The data type of array is ItemData structure.

```
28. $server->register(‘getallproducts’,
29. array(‘cat’ => ‘xsd:string’),
30. array(‘return’ => ‘tns:ItemList’),
```

```
31. 'urn:server5',
32. 'urn:server5#getallproducts',
33. 'rpc',
34. 'encoded',
35. 'Returns the details for every product'
36. );
```

Registering the function getallproducts along with input and output parameters (in the form of an array).

```
29. array('cat' => 'xsd:string'),
```

It is an input parameter which states that a category of type string will be passed to the getallproducts function.

```
30. array('return' => 'tns:ItemList'),
```

The output parameter states the return type as 'tns:ItemList' meaning the returned data will be in the form of our complex type: ItemList (which is an array of struct: ItemData).

```
31. 'urn:server5',
```

Defining the namespace. It designates the name of the WSDL document

```
32. 'urn:server5#getallproducts',
```

It is a soapaction. That is we are setting the action to the method name within the namespace.

```
33. 'rpc',
```

Style used is a Remote Procedure Call. Recall that, if we're defining an RPC style service, the message parts represent the method's parameters. In this case, the name of the part becomes the name of an element in the concrete message and its structure is determined by the supplied type attribute. If we're defining a document style service, the parts simply refer to the XML elements that are placed within the body (referenced by the element attribute).

```
34. 'encoded',
```

It means encoding is used. The SOAP encodingStyle global attribute can be used to indicate the serialisation rules used in a SOAP message.

Brief description of what the function is doing [subhead level 1]

```
37. function getallproducts($cat) {
38. $connect = mysql_connect("localhost", "root", "mce")
39. or die("Please, check your server connection.");
40. mysql_select_db("shopping");
41. $query = "select item_code, item_name, description, price from products
    where category like '" . $cat . "'";
42. $result = mysql_query($query);
43. $data = array();
```

```
while($r = mysql_fetch_array($result)){
$tempArray = array(‘item_code’ => $r[‘item_code’],
‘item_name’ => $r[‘item_name’],
‘description’ => $r[‘description’],
‘price’ => $r[‘price’]);
array_push($data, $tempArray);
}
return $data;
}
```

The category name selected passed to the function getallproducts is assigned to the `$cat` parameter. A connection with the MySQL server is established as a user root and the `shopping` database is selected. Then, an SQL statement is written to retrieve the attributes: item_code, item_name, description and price of all the products belonging to category=`$cat` from the `products` table. The query is executed and the fetched rows from the products table are stored in the `$result` array. All the rows stored in the `$result` array are retrieved one by one along with the values of the attributes of each row and stored in an array `$data`. mysql_fetch_array is for returning several rows of the entire result). This array `$data` consisting of all rows of the products of the specified category is then returned for display to the client.

client5.php

```
<?php
require_once(‘nusoap.php’);
$param = array(‘cat’=>’Camera’);
$client=new soapclient(‘http://localhost/server5.php?wsdl’, true);
$records = $client->call(‘getallproducts’,$param);

if (isset($fault)) {
      print "Error: ". $fault;
      }
else {
   echo "The details of product with category ". $param[cat] ." are ";
echo "<table border=1>";
echo "<th>Item Code</th><th>Name of
Item</th><th>Description</th><th>Price</th>";
foreach($records as $rec)
```

```
{
echo "<tr>";
    echo "<td>";
    echo $rec['item_code'];
    echo "</td>";
        echo "<td>";
    echo $rec['item_name'];
    echo "</td>";
    echo "<td>";
    echo $rec['description'];
    echo "</td>";
    echo "<td>";
    echo $rec['price'];
    echo "</td>";
echo "</tr>";
}
echo "</table>";
        }
unset($client);
?>
```

Output:

Let's run the client web service first. Open the browser and invoke the client web service by writing: `http://localhost/client5.php` in the address bar. We get the details of the product with category `Camera` in the form of a table (Figure 10.25).

Address http://localhost/client5.php

The details of product with category Camera are

Item Code	Name of Item	Description	Price
101	C1001	This is the best Camera of Model C1001	2200
103	C1003	This is the best Camera of Model C5003	6500
104	C1004	This is the best Camera of Model C1004	5300
102	C1002	This is the best Camera of Model C1002	4500

Figure 10.25 ***Details of Product with Category Camera***

Now let us run the server web service. Direct the browser to following address: `http://localhost/server5.php`. We get the following output (Figure 10.26).

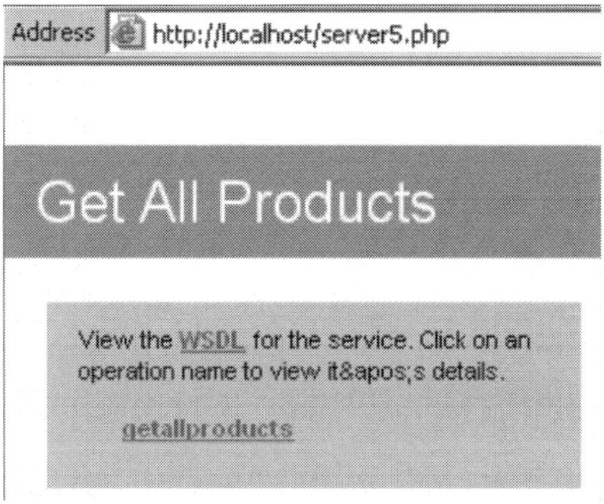

Figure 10.26 ***Screen for Get All Products***

If we select the method: getallproducts of our web service, we get the screen showing various details of the method (Figure 10.27).

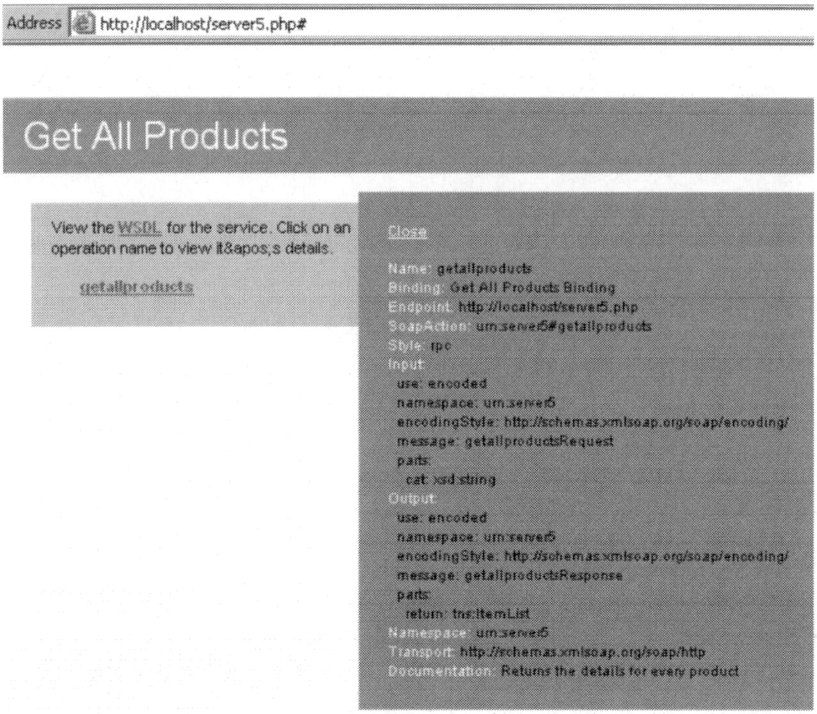

Figure 10.27 ***Various Methods of GetAllProducts***

If we select the WSDL link to see the automatically generated WSDL of our web service, we get the complete WSDL document generated as shown below:

```
<?xml version="1.0" encoding="ISO-8859-1" ?>
- <definitions xmlns:SOAP-
  ENV="http://schemas.xmlsoap.org/soap/envelope/"
  xmlns:xsd="http://www.w3.org/2001/XMLSchema"
  xmlns:xsi="http://www.w3.org/2001/XMLSchema-instance" xmlns:SOAP-
  ENC="http://schemas.xmlsoap.org/soap/encoding/"
  xmlns:tns="urn:server5"
  xmlns:soap="http://schemas.xmlsoap.org/wsdl/soap/"
  xmlns:wsdl="http://schemas.xmlsoap.org/wsdl/"
  xmlns="http://schemas.xmlsoap.org/wsdl/"
  targetNamespace="urn:server5">
- <types>
- <xsd:schema targetNamespace="urn:server5">
  <xsd:import namespace="http://schemas.xmlsoap.org/soap/encoding/" />
  <xsd:import namespace="http://schemas.xmlsoap.org/wsdl/" />
- <xsd:complexType name="ItemData">
- <xsd:all>
  <xsd:element name="item_code" type="xsd:int" item_code="item_code" />
  <xsd:element name="item_name" type="xsd:string" item_name="item_name" />
  <xsd:element name="description" type="xsd:string" description="description"
  />
  <xsd:element name="price" type="xsd:int" price="price" />
  </xsd:all>
  </xsd:complexType>
- <xsd:complexType name="ItemList">
- <xsd:complexContent>
- <xsd:restriction base="SOAP-ENC:Array">
  <xsd:attribute ref="SOAP-ENC:arrayType" wsdl:arrayType="tns:ItemData[]"
  />
  </xsd:restriction>
  </xsd:complexContent>
  </xsd:complexType>
  </xsd:schema>
```

```
  </types>
- <message name="getallproductsRequest">
  <part name="cat" type="xsd:string" />
  </message>
- <message name="getallproductsResponse">
  <part name="return" type="tns:ItemList" />
  </message>
- <portType name="Get All Products PortType">
- <operation name="getallproducts">
  <documentation>Returns the details for every product</documentation>
  <input message="tns:getallproductsRequest" />
  <output message="tns:getallproductsResponse" />
  </operation>
  </portType>
- <binding name="Get All Products Binding" type="tns:Get All Products
     PortType">
  <soap:binding style="rpc"
  transport="http://schemas.xmlsoap.org/soap/http" />
- <operation name="getallproducts">
  <soap:operation soapAction="urn:server5#getallproducts" style="rpc" />
- <input>
  <soap:body use="encoded" namespace="urn:server5"
  encodingStyle="http://schemas.xmlsoap.org/soap/encoding/" />
  </input>
- <output>
  <soap:body use="encoded" namespace="urn:server5"
     encodingStyle="http://schemas.xmlsoap.org/soap/encoding/" />
  </output>
  </operation>
  </binding>
- <service name="Get All Products">
- <port name="Get All Products Port" binding="tns:Get All Products Binding">
  <soap:address location="http://localhost/server5.php" />
```

```
</port>
</service>
</definitions>
```

SUMMARY

In this chapter, we saw how to use a NuSOAP toolkit to build web services using SOAP. We saw the installation of NuSOAP. We have seen different elements of a WSDL document. We developed and tested several sever as well as client web services that included: CurrencyConverter—for converting pounds into dollars, greeting the client with a welcome message, accessing information from the database—displaying the price of the product on supplying its item code, web services dealing with complex data types for fetching complete information of the product etc.

11

Consuming Public Web Services

In this chapter, we will learn the technique of consuming publicly available web services. There are several websites that display the web services deployed by their owners for public use. One of these website is: `XMethods.net` that not only displays the list of publicly available web services that we can use in our web application but also allows us to upload our own web services.

On opening the XMethods.net website, we get a list of web services that are available on it for public usage. When we select any web service, the details of that web service are displayed including a brief idea of what functions the web service can perform and also an example of how to access the web service. Out of the list of web services available, if we select the one provided by `http://www.foreclosuredatabank.com` (that displays the latest Bank Foreclosures on providing a zip code), the screen that we may get is as shown in Figure 11.1.

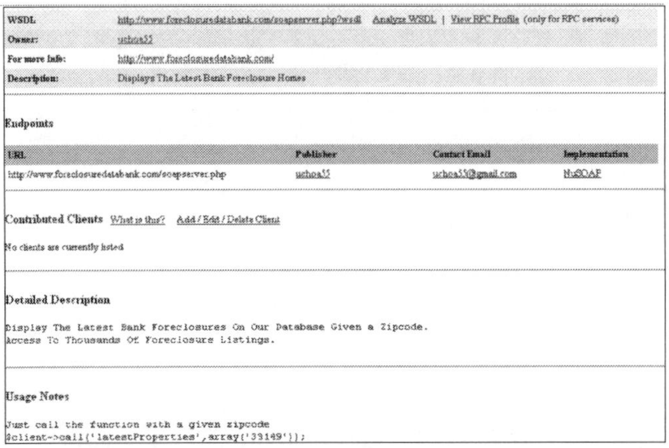

Figure 11.1 ***Screen for Latest Bank Foreclosures***

This figure gives a brief idea of what the web service is all about (look at title `Detailed Description`) and also at the bottom, it provides an example of how to access this web service with heading:

Usage Notes

```
Just call the function with a given zipcode
$client->call('latestProperties', array('33149'));.
```

If we select the link: `Analyze WSDL`, we get a screen that explains the command that can be used to see the WSDL of the web service and also the list of Operations/Methods that are provided by the web service for public use:

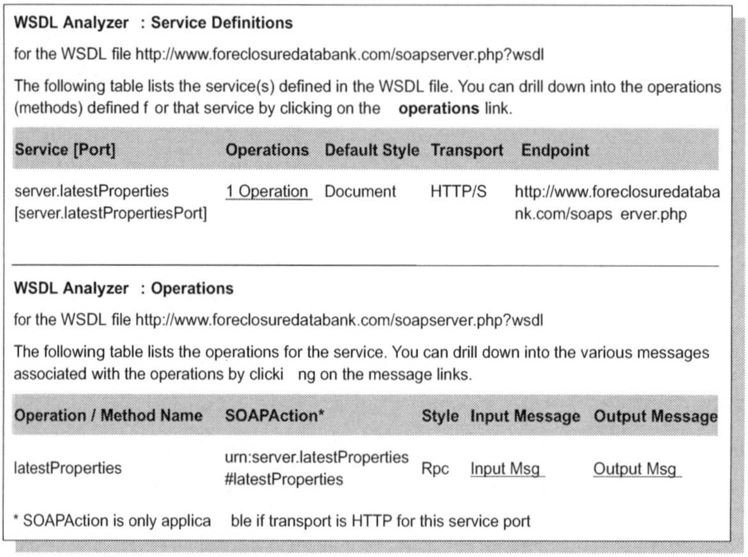

WSDL Analyzer : Service Definitions

for the WSDL file http://www.foreclosuredatabank.com/soapserver.php?wsdl

The following table lists the service(s) defined in the WSDL file. You can drill down into the operations (methods) defined f or that service by clicking on the **operations** link.

Service [Port]	Operations	Default Style	Transport	Endpoint
server.latestProperties [server.latestPropertiesPort]	1 Operation	Document	HTTP/S	http://www.foreclosuredatabank.com/soaps erver.php

WSDL Analyzer : Operations

for the WSDL file http://www.foreclosuredatabank.com/soapserver.php?wsdl

The following table lists the operations for the service. You can drill down into the various messages associated with the operations by clicki ng on the message links.

Operation / Method Name	SOAPAction*	Style	Input Message	Output Message
latestProperties	urn:server.latestProperties #latestProperties	Rpc	Input Msg	Output Msg

* SOAPAction is only applica ble if transport is HTTP for this service port

Figure 11.2 ***Operations of WSDL Analyzer***

If we select the link `Input Msg`, we get a brief explanation of the `Input Parameter` and its type that will be passed to the method (provided by the web service to access). In our example, the method name is: `latestProperties` and the input parameter is `Zipcode` of type `string` as shown below:

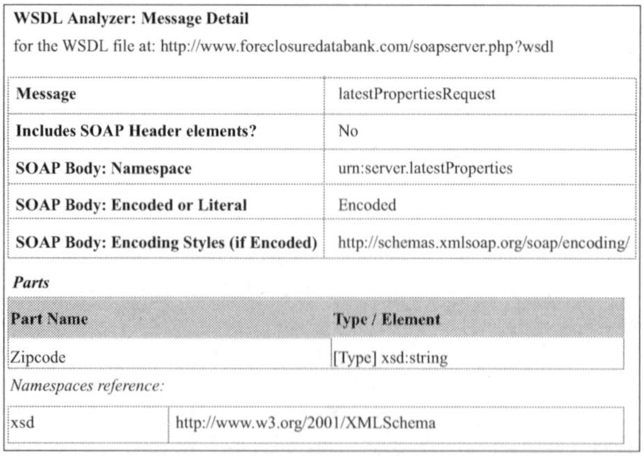

WSDL Analyzer: Message Detail

for the WSDL file at: http://www.foreclosuredatabank.com/soapserver.php?wsdl

Message	latestPropertiesRequest
Includes SOAP Header elements?	No
SOAP Body: Namespace	urn:server.latestProperties
SOAP Body: Encoded or Literal	Encoded
SOAP Body: Encoding Styles (if Encoded)	http://schemas.xmlsoap.org/soap/encoding/

Parts

Part Name	Type / Element
Zipcode	[Type] xsd:string

Namespaces reference:

xsd	http://www.w3.org/2001/XMLSchema

Figure 11.3 ***Brief Explanation of the Input Parameter and Its Type***

Similarly, if we select the link `OutputMsg`, we get a brief explanation of the `Output Parameter` and its type that will be passed by the method of our web service: `latestProperties`. The output of our method is a string and is named "`Return`" as shown below:

WSDL Analyzer: Message Detail

for the WSDL file at: http://www.foreclosuredatabank.com/soapserver.php?wsdl

Message	latestPropertiesResponse
Includes SOAP Header elements?	No
SOAP Body: Namespace	urn:server.latestProperties
SOAP Body: Encoded or Literal	Encoded
SOAP Body: Encoding Styles (if Encoded)	http://schemas.xmlsoap.org/soap/encoding/

Parts

Part Name	**Type / Element**
Return	[Type] xsd:string

Namespaces reference:

xsd	http://www.w3.org/2001/XMLSchema

Figure 11.4 ***Brief Explanation of the Output Parameter and its Type***

Now we have enough information to try this web service. Let's make a client program of the above web service named tryclient1.php with the following code:

tryclient1.php

```
<html>
<head><title>Forclosure Bank client</title></head>
<body>
<h2>Fore closure Bank client </h2>
<?php
require_once('nusoap.php');
$parameters = array('zipcode' => '33149');
$soapclient = new soapclient('http://www.foreclosuredatabank.com/
soapserver.php?wsdl', 'wsdl');
$data = $soapclient->call('latestProperties', $parameters);
echo "<br /><br />Output is $data";
?>
</body>
</html>
```

As we can see in the above client program, we provide any zip value to see the latest Bank Foreclosures (let us try it out with zipcode: 33149). To run this client program, I have uploaded it on my website http://www.bmharwani.com and when I run it, I get the information as shown in Figure 11.5.

Figure 11.5 ***Information on Running the Client Program***

Let us try one more web service provided by `http://www.neurofuzz.com` which encrypts the input string. The algorithm used for encrypting the string is `block-cipher-AES`. The first screen that we get on selecting that web service is shown in Figure 11.6.

Figure 11.6 gives a brief idea of what the web service is all about (refer `Detailed Description`) and also at the bottom, it provides some information of how to access this web service – refer `Usage Notes` in the figure that says:

Be sure to exchange the "key" data in some non-Internet based method (snail-mail, sneaker-net, POTS, etc) because that value is what makes the data generated by this service useful and as secure as it will be. Make the key complex because it will drive some of the strength.

If we select the link: `Analyze WSDL` at the top, we get a screen that explains the command that can be used to see the WSDL of the web service and also the list of Operations/ Methods that are provided by the web service for public use:

WSDL	https://sec.neurofuzz-software.com/paos/cryptoSOAP.php?wsdl Analyze WSDL | View RPC Profile (only for RPC services)
Owner:	aandreu
For more Info:	http://www.neurofuzz.com/
Description:	A simple demonstration of AES encryption and decryption via SOAP.

Endpoints

URL	Publisher	Contact Email	Implementation
http://neurofuzz.com/modules/cryptoService/cryptoSOAP.php	aandreu	andres@neurofuzz.com	NuSOAP

Contributed Clients What is this? Add / Edit / Delete Client

No clients are currently listed

Detailed Description

```
This is a free web based service to provide the public with an idea of
what strong encryption is.  The encryption algorithm implemented is
the block-cipher AES Rijndael with a 256-bit block size and 32-bit key
size.
```

Usage Notes

```
Be sure to exchange the "key" data in some non-Internet based method
(snail-mail, sneaker-net, POTS, etc) because that value is what makes
the data generated by this service useful and as secure as it will be.
Make the key complex because it will drive some of the strength
```

Figure 11.6 ***Screen on Selecting Neurofuzz.com Web Service***

WSDL Analyzer: Operations

For the WSDL file https://sec.neurofuzz-software.com/paos/cryptoSOAP.php?wsdl

The following table lists the operations for the service. You can drill down into the various messages associated with the operations by clicking on the message links.

Operation / Method Name	SOAPAction*	Style	Input Message	Output Message
Encrypt	Urn:encryptwsdl#encryptrpc		Input Msg	Output Msg
Decrypt	urn:decryptwsdl#decryptrpc		Input Msg	Output Msg

* SOAPAction is only applicable if transport is HTTP for this service port

Figure 11.7 ***Operations of WSDL Analyzer***

We can see that this web service provides two methods:

- Encrypt and
- Decrypt.

Both methods have one input and one output parameter. If we select the link `Input Msg` of `Encrypt` method, we get a brief explanation of the `Input Parameters` and their type that will be passed to the method (provided by the web service to access). In our example, the method name is: `Encrypt` and the input parameters are `String` and `Key` and both are of type `string` as shown below:

WSDL Analyzer: Message Detail	
for the WSDL file at: https://sec.neurofuzz-software.com/paos/cryptoSOAP.php?wsdl	
Message	encryptRequest
Includes SOAP Header elements?	No
SOAP Body: Namespace	urn:encryptwsdl
SOAP Body: Encoded or Literal	encoded
SOAP Body: Encoding Styles (if Encoded)	http://schemas.xmlsoap.org/soap/encoding/

Parts

Part Name	Type / Element
String	[Type] xsd:string
Key	[Type] xsd:string

Namespaces reference:

xsd	http://www.w3.org/2001/XMLSchema

Figure 11.8 ***Brief Explanation of the Input Parameters and their Type***

Similarly, if we select the link `OutputMsg` of our `Encrypt` method, we get a brief explanation of the `Output Parameter` and its type that will be passed by the method of our web service. The output of our method is a string and is named "`Return`" as shown below:

WSDL Analyzer: Message Detail	
for the WSDL file at: https://sec.neurofuzz-software.com/paos/cryptoSOAP.php?wsdl	
Message	encryptResponse
Includes SOAP Header elements?	No
SOAP Body: Namespace	urn:encryptwsdl
SOAP Body: Encoded or Literal	encoded
SOAP Body: Encoding Styles (if Encoded)	http://schemas.xmlsoap.org/soap/encoding/

Parts

Part Name	Type / Element
return	[Type] xsd:string

Namespaces reference:

xsd	http://www.w3.org/2001/XMLSchema

Figure 11.9 ***Brief Explanation of the Output Parameters and their Type***

Now, we have enough information to try this web service. Let us make a client program of the above web service named tryclient2.php with the following code:

tryclient2.php

```
<html>
<head><title>String Encryption</title></head>
<body>
<h2>Encrypting a string </h2>
<?php
require_once('nusoap.php');
$parameters = array('string' => 'India', 'key' => 'Gold');
$soapclient = new soapclient('https://sec.neurofuzz-software.com/paos/cryptoSOAP.php?wsdl ', 'wsdl');
$data = $soapclient->call('encrypt', $parameters);
echo "<br /><br />Encrypted format is  $data";
?>
</body>
</html>
```

In the above client program, we provide the values of the two input parameters: the input parameter: `string` is provided the value "India" and another input parameter: `key` is provided the value "Gold". To run this client program, I have uploaded it on my website http://www.bmharwani.com and when I run it, I get the encryption form of the string provided: India (Figure 11.10).

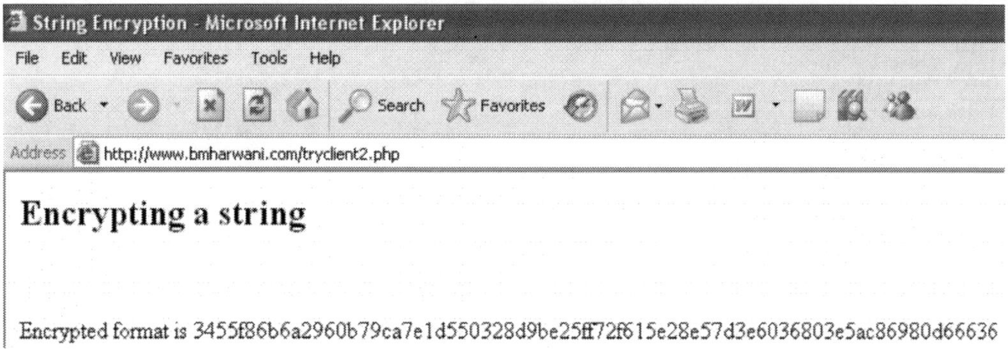

Figure 11.10 ***Screen for Encrypting a String***

SUMMARY

In this chapter we saw the step-by-step procedure to use the publicly available web services from XMethods.net website. We saw how to recognise the input and output parameters and their data types required for writing web service clients. We wrote the client web service to invoke the two web services: one from `http://www.foreclosuredatabank.com` that displays the latest Bank Foreclosures on providing a zip code and the other from `http://www.neurofuzz.com` which encrypts the input string.

12

PHP Frameworks

This chapter explains different PHP frameworks. Frameworks provide all facilities in one such as editor, compiler, database view etc. all in one place making the job of a software developer quite easy. In this chapter, we are going to learn:

- XAMPP (from Apache Friends)—a PHP Framework
- phpMyAdmin—software used for creating and maintaining MySQL databases
- CodeIgniter—a PHP Framework

12.1 APACHE FRIENDS

Apache Friends is a project meant to promote the Apache web server founded by Kai 'Oswald' Seidler and Kay Vogelgesang in 2002.

12.2 XAMPP

To develop any application with PHP, we require a web server, database and the PHP language installed on our computer. XAMPP is an Apache distribution that contains all three: MySQL, PHP and Perl. When XAMPP is installed (it is very easy to install as it doesn't require any manual configuration), it will automatically install Apache web server along with MySQL, PHP and Perl. Usually it is difficult to install Apache web server with MySQL, PHP and Perl.

12.3 XAMPP INSTALLATION

XAMPP is very easy to install. Just download the file from the net, available in four versions, one for each operating system: Linux systems, Windows, Solaris SPARC and for Mac OS X. I have downloaded the Windows version: XAMPP 1.6.7 and at the time of writing, this is the latest version on Windows platform available on the Internet. The downloaded file is named: xampp-win32-1.6.7-installer.exe. Just double click on this exe file to install it.

The first screen that we get is to decide in which language we want to install XAMPP. We select English and click the OK button (Figure 12.1).

Figure 12.1 ***Screen for Installer Language***

We get a welcome screen (Figure 12.2).

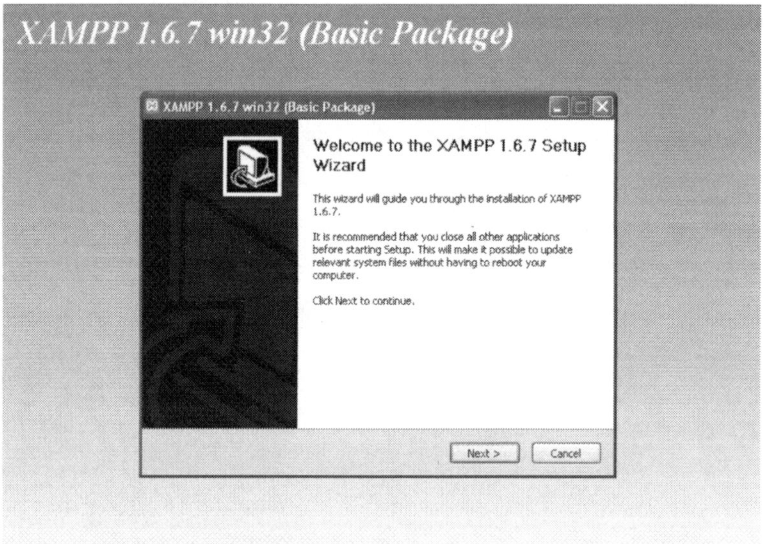

Figure 12.2 ***Welcome Screen of XAMPP***

Select the Next button. We will be prompted to specify the location to install XAMPP. We specify C:\xampp folder (Figure 12.3).

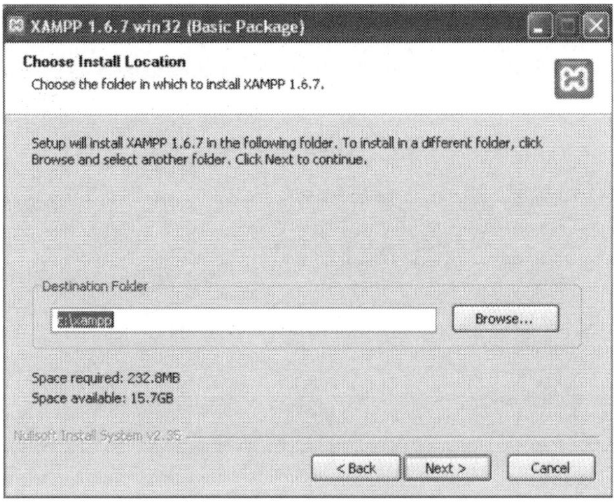

Figure 12.3 ***Specification of the Location to Install XAMPP***

Click the Next button. We get a dialog box to specify which are the services we want to install. Since we want Apache as well as MySQL, select the two checkboxes: Install Apache as service and Install MySQL as service (Figure 12.4).

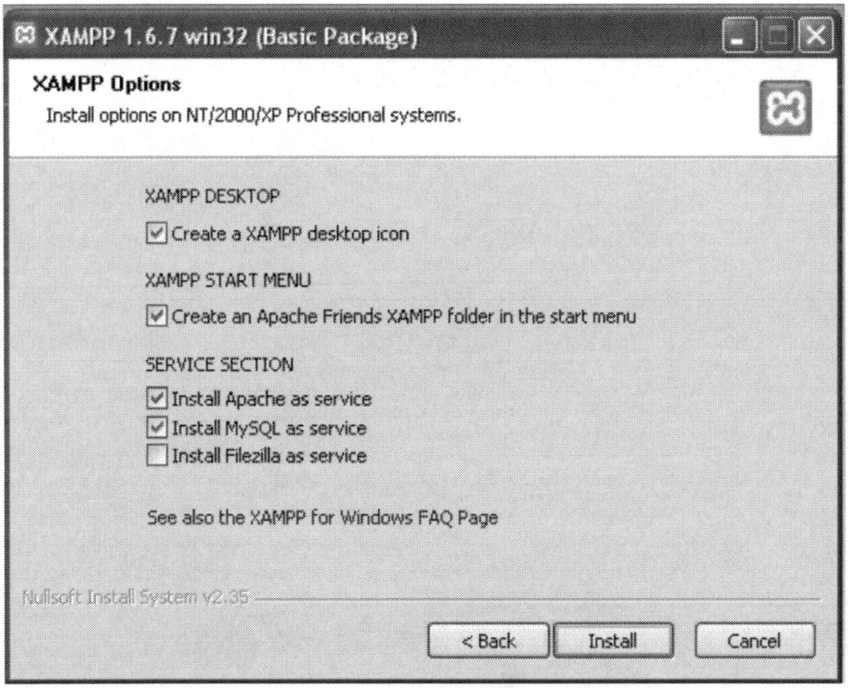

Figure 12.4 ***Dialog Box to Specify the Services to Install***

Click the Install button and XAMPP will start extracting the files (Figure 12.5).

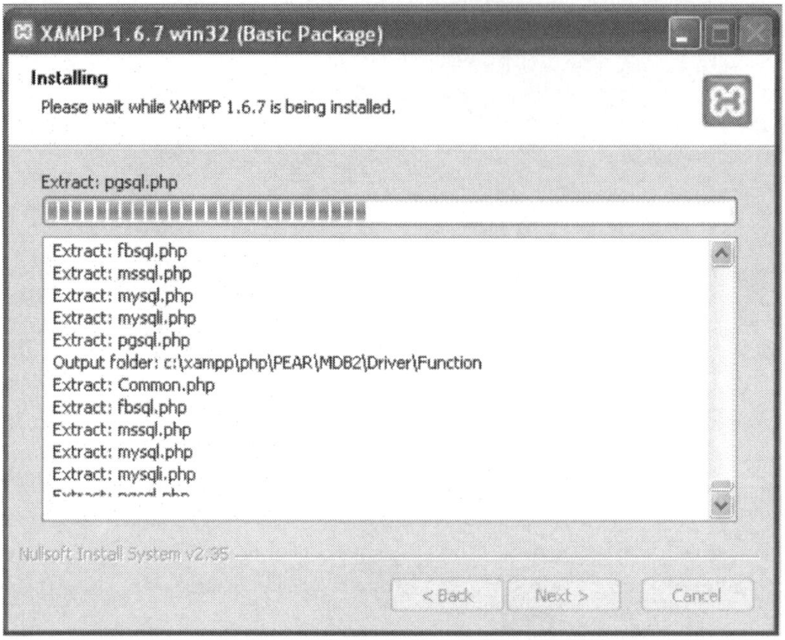

Figure 12.5 ***Selection of Install Button***

We get a splash window showing that it is configuring XAMPP (Figure 12.6).

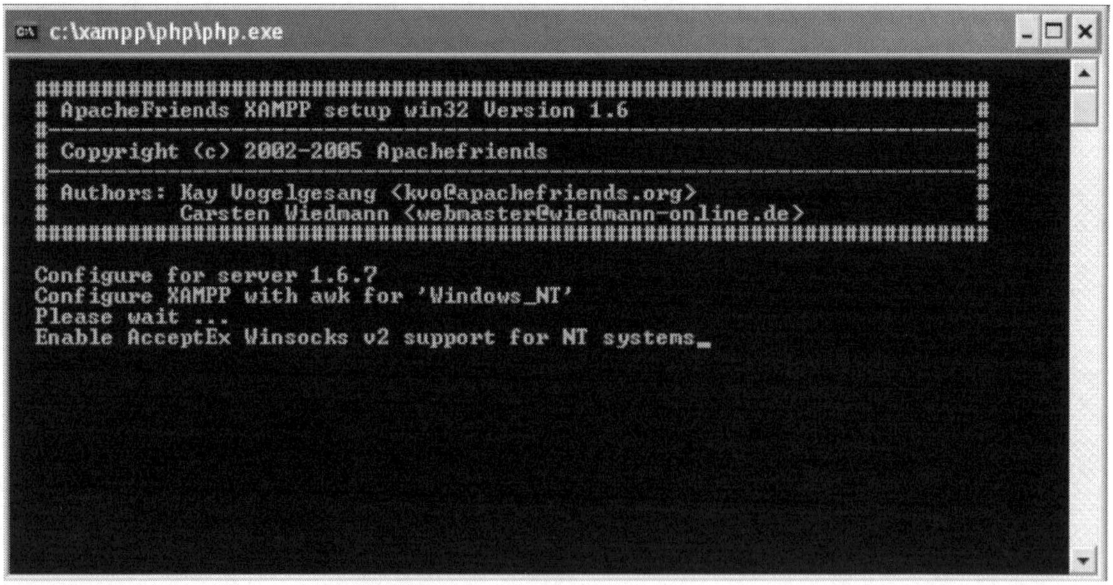

Figure 12.6 ***Configuration of XAMPP***

Finally, we get a screen showing that XAMPP installation is complete (Figure 12.7).

Figure 12.7 ***Installation Completed***

Click the Finish button to complete the installation. We get a dialog box asking whether to start XAMPP control panel (Figure 12.8). XAMPP control panel is the main steering panel from where we can control the working of Apache as well as MySQL. We can also work with phpMyAdmin through this panel (More about phpMyAdmin later).

Note: XAMPP comes packed with phpMyAdmin and an FTP server.

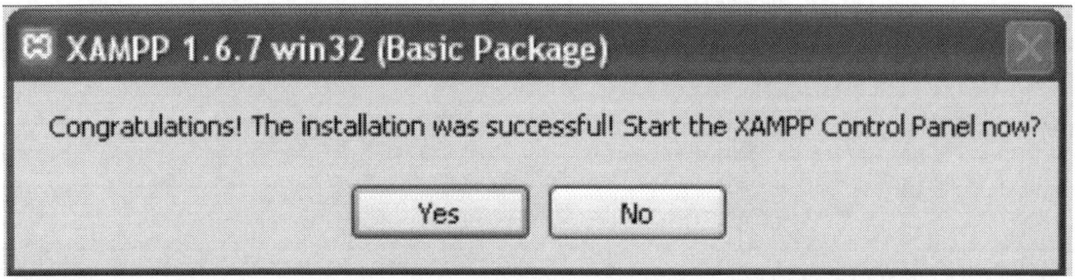

Figure 12.8 ***Dialog Box for XAMPP Control Panel***

We click the Yes button and the XAMPP Control panel is displayed (Figure 12.9).

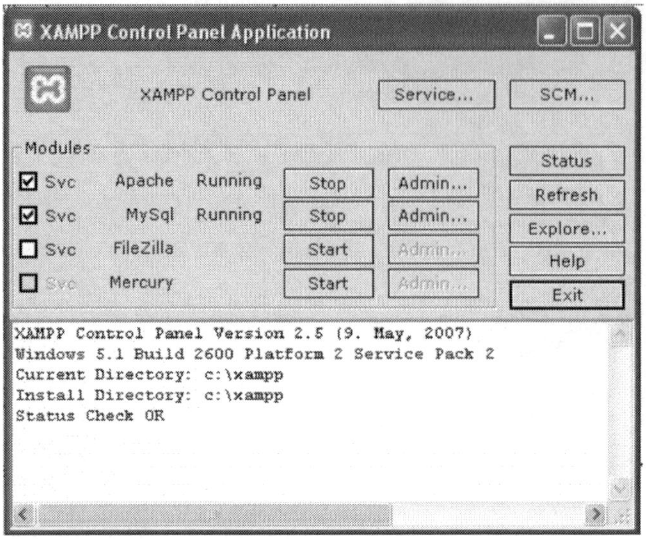

Figure 12.9 ***XAMPP Control Panel is Displayed***

We can see that both Apache as well as MySQL are displayed as running. (This is what we selected while installing XAMPP.)

If we click the Status button, we get the output shown in Figure 12.10.

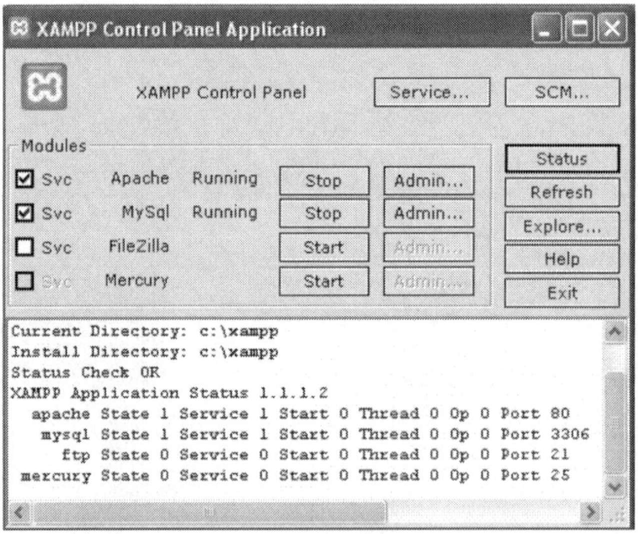

Figure 12.10 ***Output on Clicking the Status Button***

We get the folder name where XAMPP is installed and the ports numbers used by different modules: Apache, MySQL, ftp etc.

If we select Refresh button, we get the output shown in Figure 12.11.

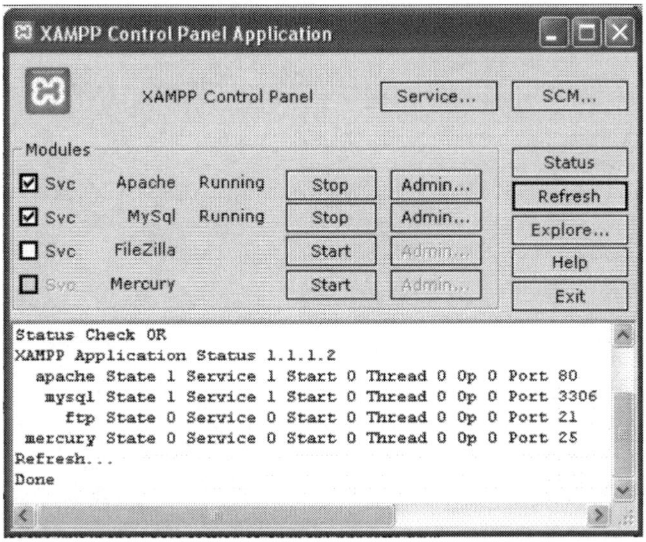

Figure 12.11 ***Output on Selecting Refresh Button***

The window refreshes the status of the modules i.e. re-initialises them and displays the message "Done" when refreshing is finished.

If we click the Explore button, we get the list of all the subfolders under `xampp` folder as well as files required to start and stop XAMPP (Figure 12.12).

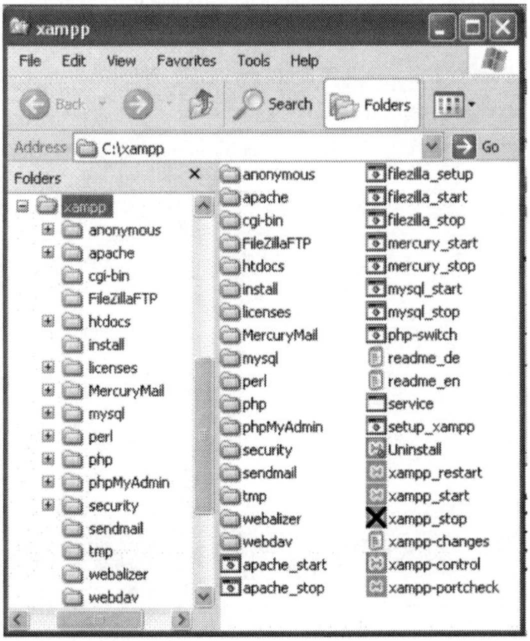

Figure 12.12 ***Output on Clicking the Explore Button***

If we click the help button, we get a dialog box with two buttons: one for online support and the other for displaying the ReadMe file (Figure 12.13).

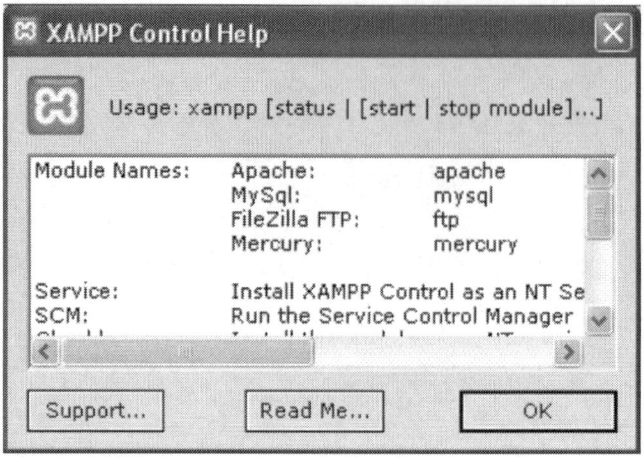

Figure 12.13 ***Screen on Clicking the Help Button***

If we click the Support button, we navigate to the site: http://www.nat32.com/xampp/index.htm which provides online support documentation. If we click the Read Me button, a readme file opens showing the list of basic packages available in XAMPP and the quick installation steps to install XAMPP etc.

If we click the Service button, we get a dialog box where we can Start or Stop any module (Figure 12.14).

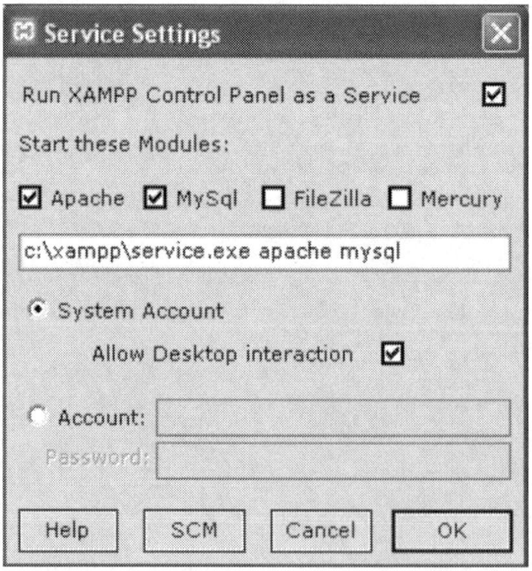

Figure 12.14 ***Screen on Selecting Service Button***

If we click the SCM button, we get the list of Services and their status on our computer (Figure 12.15). We can start and stop any service via this window too by right clicking on any service and selecting the desired option from the shortcut menu that pops up.

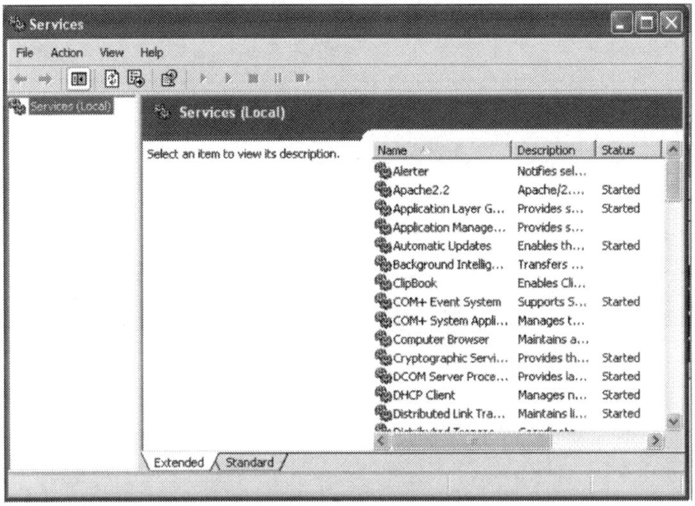

Figure 12.15 ***Screen on Clicking the SCM Button***

In the XAMPP control panel, if we click the Admin button of MySQL, we get a screen displaying the environment, server, client, host etc. information (Figure 12.16). We can administer MySQL and set its environment from this page.

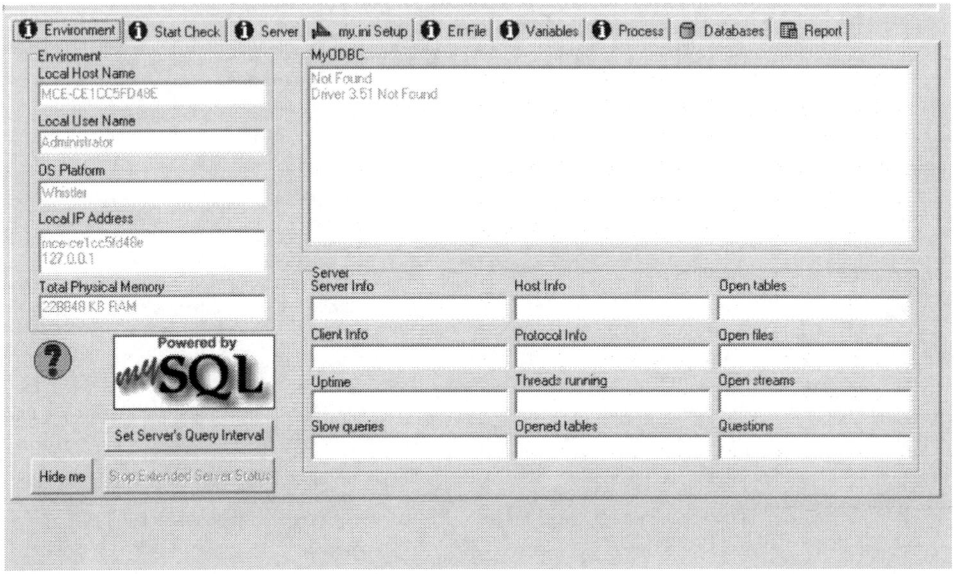

Figure 12.16 ***Screen on Clicking the Admin Button***

In the XAMPP control panel (refer Figure 12.9), if we click the Admin button of Apache, we get a screen asking for selecting a language in which we want to administer XAMPP (Figure 12.17).

Figure 12.17 ***Selection of a Language***

We click the English link to get the administration information window in English (Figure 12.18).

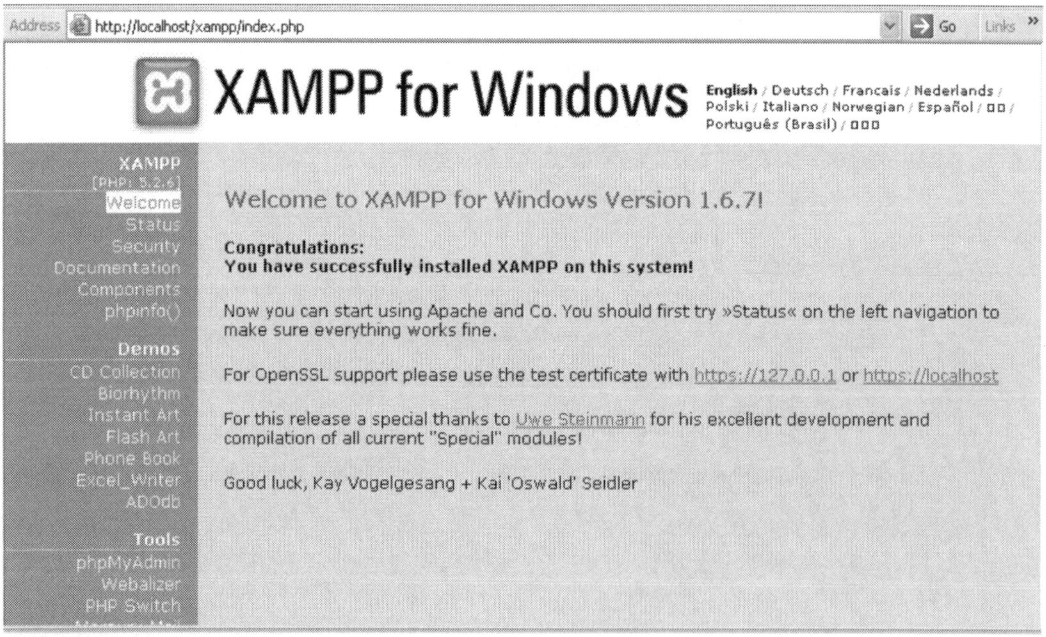

Figure 12.18 ***XAMPP Administration Windows***

If we click the `Status` button in the menu on the left, we get the status of the service(s) running on our computer (Figure 12.19).

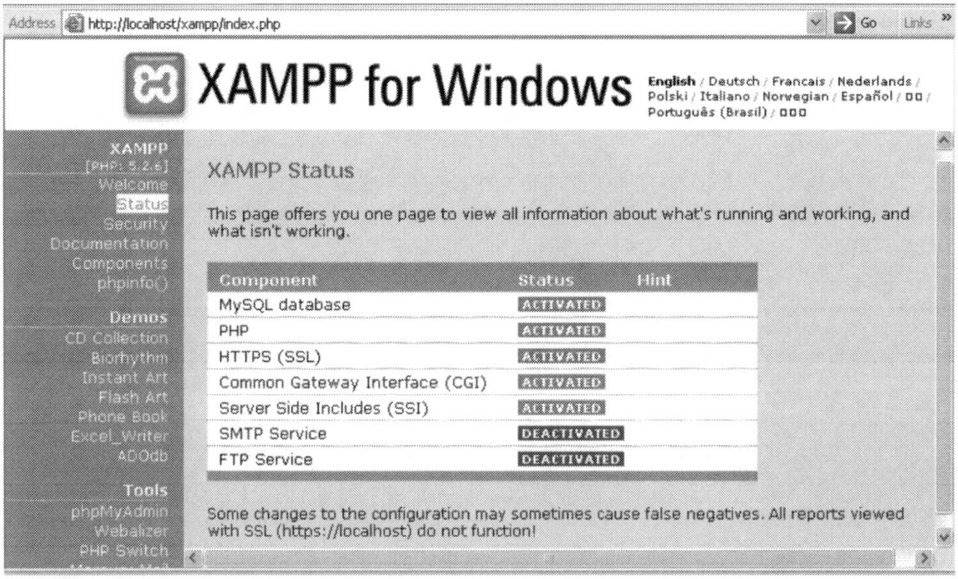

Figure 12.19 *Screen on Clicking the Status Button*

If we click the phpinfo() button from the menu, we get the complete information of all the attributes of PHP Version 5.2.6 (Figure 12.20).

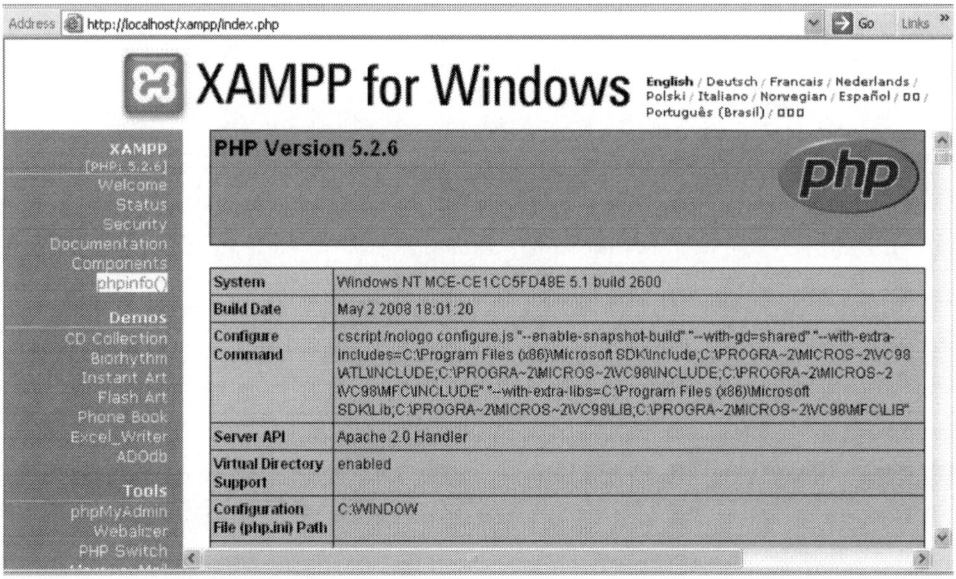

Figure 12.20 *Complete Information of all the Attributes of PHP*

In order to see the demos of certain applications supplied with XAMPP, select any demo application from the menu. If we select the `CD Collector` button, we may get its demo (Figure 12.21).

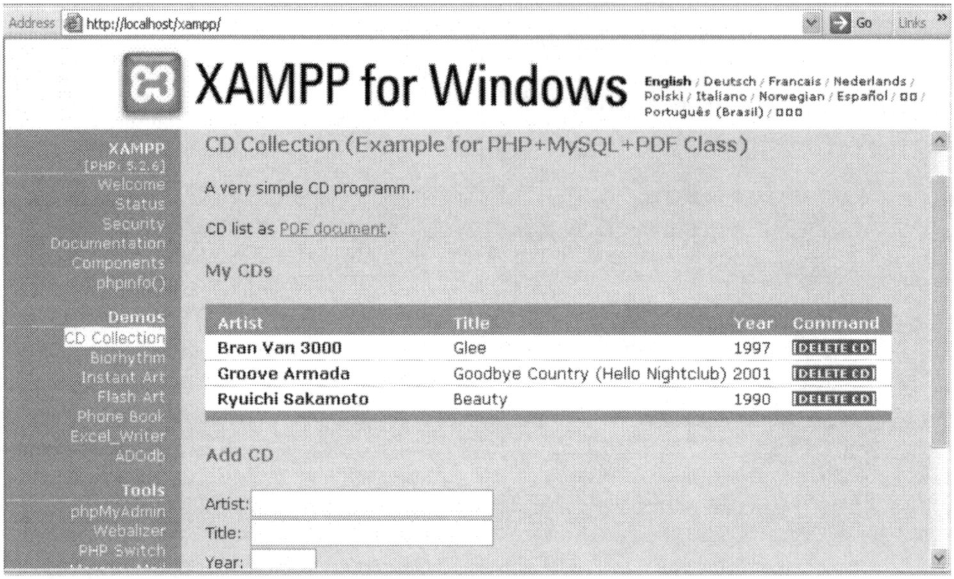

Figure 12.21 ***Demo of CD Collector Button***

There are a few sample programs provided by XAMPP that can be run to verify that the installation is successful. But we prefer writing our own small program and testing it.

Before we see how the PHP program is written and executed in XAMPP, let's see some of its characteristics:

12.4 CHARACTERISTICS OF XAMPP

- XAMPP is a compilation of free software and is free to copy under the terms of the GNU General Public License.
- XAMPP for Windows version contains: Apache, MySQL, PHP + PEAR, Perl, mod_php, mod_perl, mod_ssl, OpenSSL, phpMyAdmin, Webalizer, Mercury Mail Transport System for Win32 and NetWare Systems v3.32, Ming, JpGraph, FileZilla FTP Server, mcrypt, eAccelerator, SQLite, and WEB-DAV + mod_auth_mysql.
- To make it convenient for developers, XAMPP is configured with all features turned on.

12.5 RUNNING A PHP PROGRAM IN XAMPP

To run a PHP program, place it in XAMPP's `htdocs` folder. For example, let's write a file try.php with the following contents:

```
<html>
    <body>
        <?php
            $name="John";
            echo "Welcome " . $name . "<br>";
        ?>
    </body>
</html>
```

Save the file at location: C:\xampp\htdocs (because XAMPP is installed in C: drive). To test the PHP program, open the browser and point it at the following address:

http://localhost/try.php.

We get the output as shown in Figure 12.22.

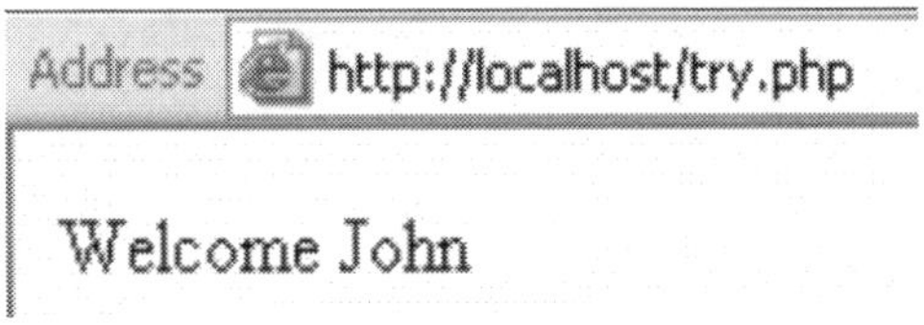

Figure 12.22 ***Output Displayed***

If you want to store the PHP file in any subfolder, create that subfolder in `htdocs` folder. Say, the subfolder name is ecomm (in `htdocs` folder), and the try.php file is placed in it, we can run the file by pointing the browser at the following address:

12.6 PHPMYADMIN

phpMyAdmin is software used for creating and maintaining MySQL databases.

When you are ready to work on your database, use the link in the Tools section http://localhost/ecomm/try.php (refer Figure 12.18) to open the phpMyAdmin database management interface.

We get the initial screen shown in Figure 12.23.

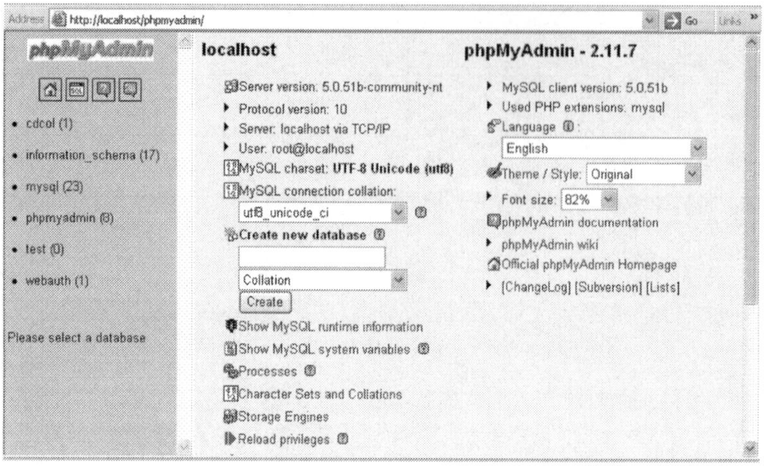

Figure 12.23 *Initial Screen of phpMyAdmin*

The left-hand frame in phpMyAdmin is used for navigation. The databases that we create are displayed in this area along with the tables (if any) under the respective database names. We can click on any database or table to work with it.

If we click the link "Show MySQL runtime information", we may get the output shown in Figure 12.24.

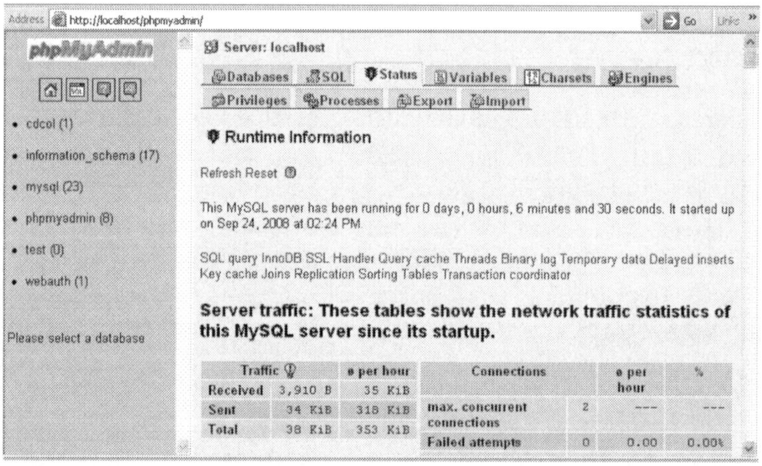

Figure 12.24 *Screen on Selecting Show MySQL Runtime Information*

We get the information on how long MySQL has been running and the network traffic details i.e., how many packets have been received or sent and similar information.

If we click the link "phpMyAdmin documentation", we may get the output shown in Figure 12.25.

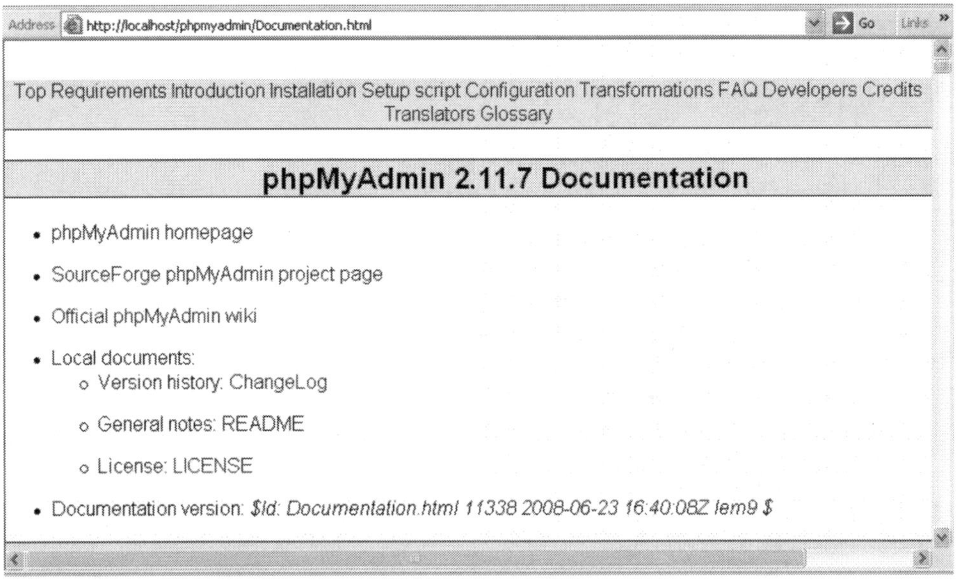

Figure 12.25 ***Screen on Selecting phpMyAdmin Documentation***

We can see that the documentation page contains links for the homepage, Readme and Licence to display the desired information.

If we click the link "Databases" (refer to Figure 12.24) at the top, we get a screen to specify the name of the database to be created (Figure 12.26).

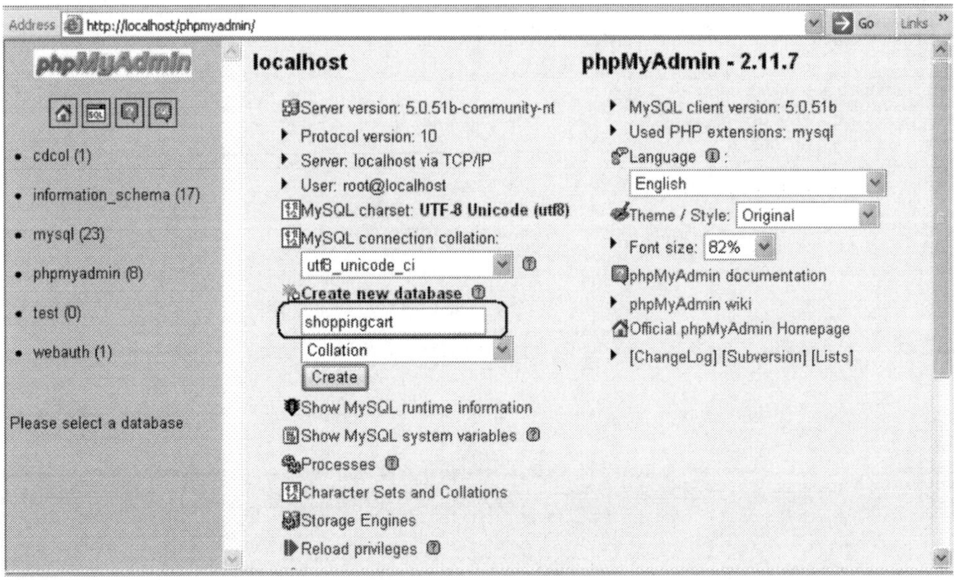

Figure 12.26 ***Screen on Selecting "Databases" Option***

Enter the database name say: `shoppingcart` and click the `Create` button to create it. The moment we create the database, its name is displayed in the navigation bar on the left side. We see the database name as: `shoppingcart(0)` in the navigation bar where `0` means it has 0 tables i.e. no table is yet created for this database. Also an SQL query statement which was automatically created and executed for creating the database is shown in Figure 12.27.

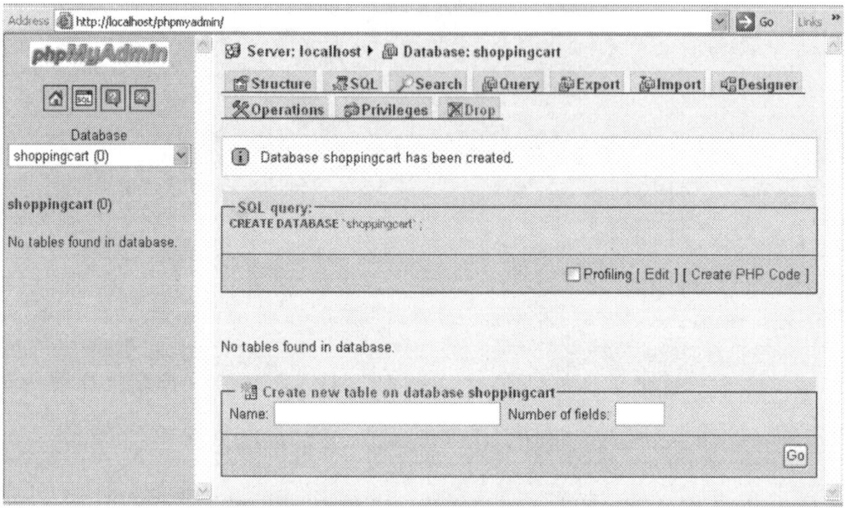

Figure 12.27 ***Creation of the Database***

In Figure 12.27, we also get a box to specify the name of the table if we want to create it in the given database. We also need to specify the expected number of fields in the table to be created (Figure 12.28).

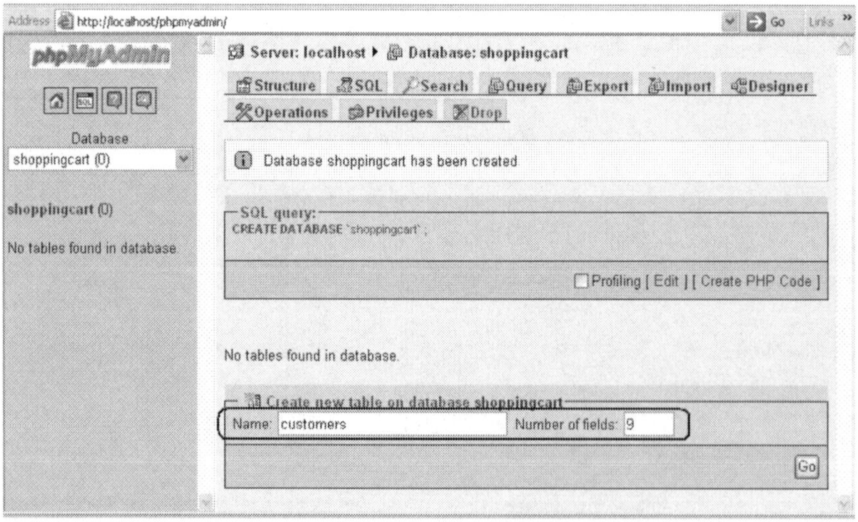

Figure 12.28 ***Creation of the Table***

Let us create a table named `customers` with nine fields. We enter the information in the respective boxes and click the `Go` button. We get a page to specify the field names, their data types and their length (Figure 12.29).

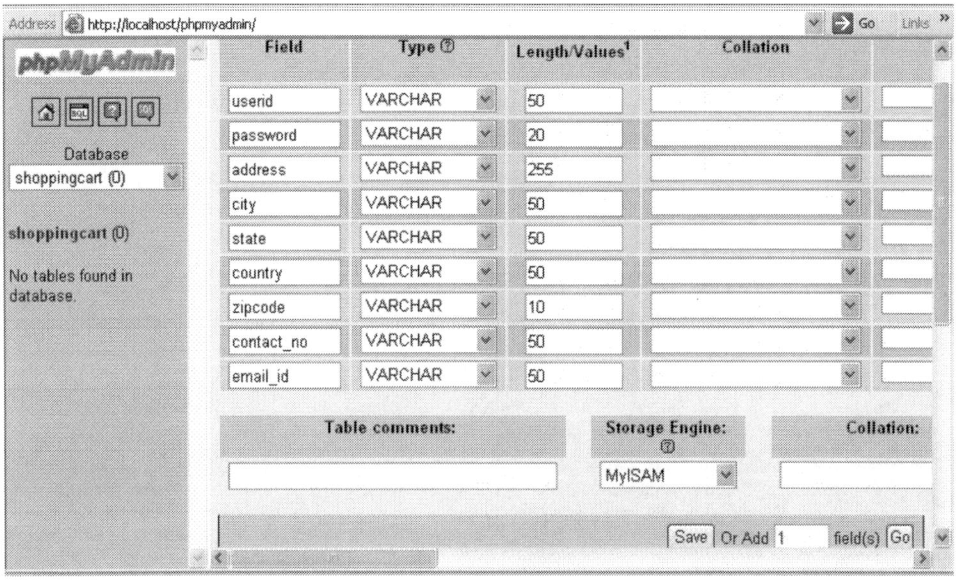

Figure 12.29 ***Page to Specify the Field Names, their Data Types and their Length***

After specifying the information of the fields, we click the `Save` button to save the structure of the table: `customers`. We get a confirmation page showing the table is created along with the SQL command that was automatically created and executed internally to create the table (Figure 12.30).

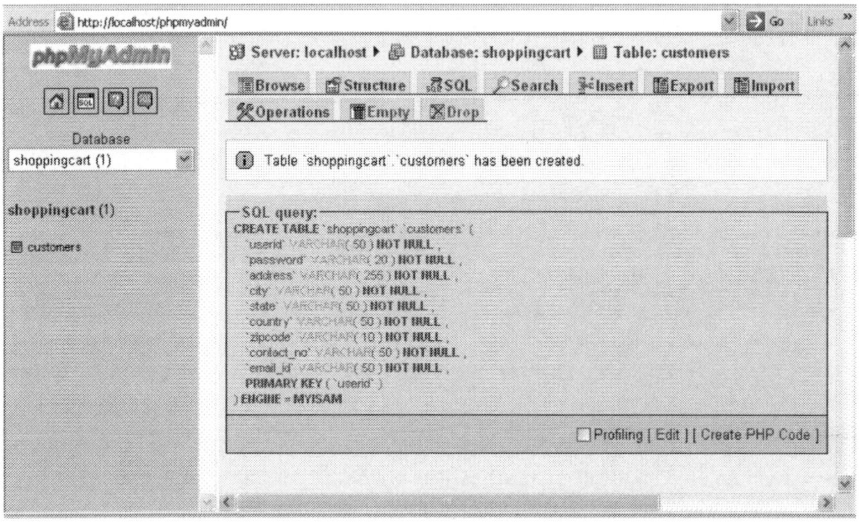

Figure 12.30 ***Creation of the Customer Table***

We can see in above page that the name of the database appears as `shoppingcart(1)` in the navigation bar where `1` shows that this database contains one table. Also we see that a few links appear at the top of the page to maintain the table. The links include:

Browse	To see/edit all the rows of the table
Structure	To see/modify the structure of the table
SQL	To execute the SQL statement (to maintain the table)
Search	To search rows (records) with the given criteria
Insert	To insert new rows in the table
Operations	To perform operations like renaming the table, moving it to another database, sorting it on a particular field etc.
Empty	To delete all the rows of the table
Drop	To drop the table along with its rows

If we click the the `Insert` link, we get a dialog box to enter the information of the new customer (Figure 12.31).

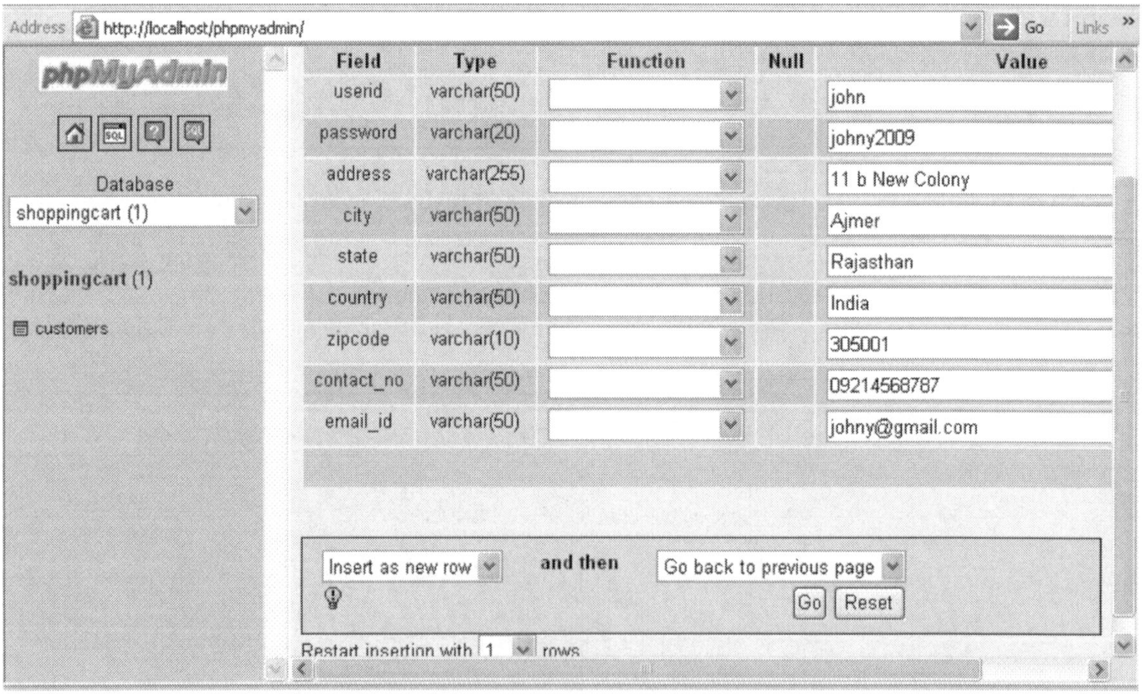

Figure 12.31 ***Dialog Box for Entering Information of a New Customer***

Let us insert the information of the new customer as shown in Figure 12.31 and click the `Save` button to save it. A SQL statement appears that was internally created and executed to insert the row with the given values in the `customers` table (Figure 12.32).

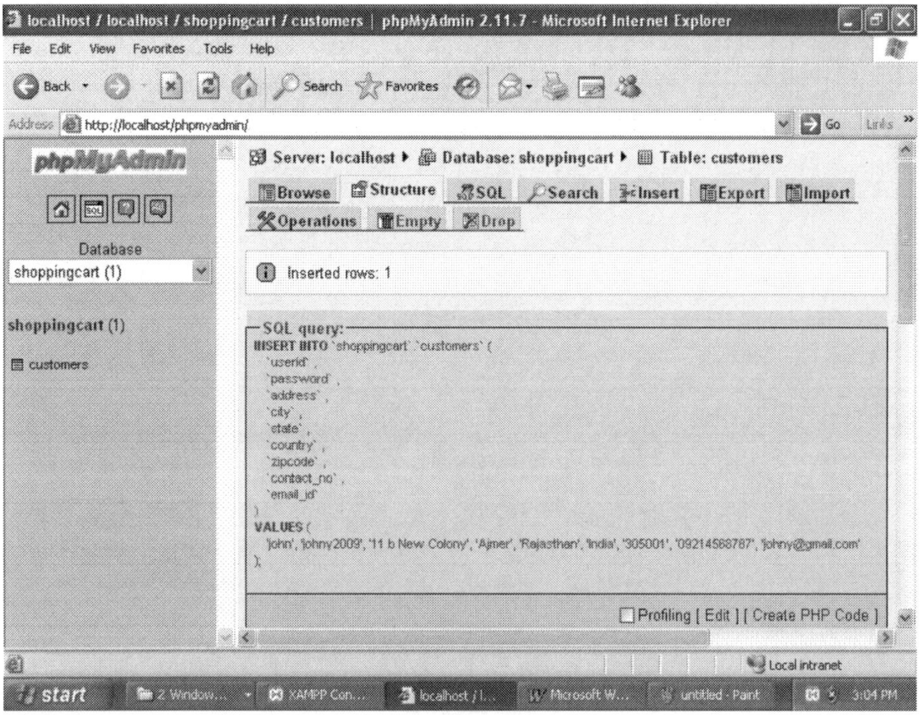

Figure 12.32 ***SQL Statement Appears to Insert the New Record in the Table***

If we click the the `Browse` link at the top, we get the row(s) in the given table (Figure 12.33).

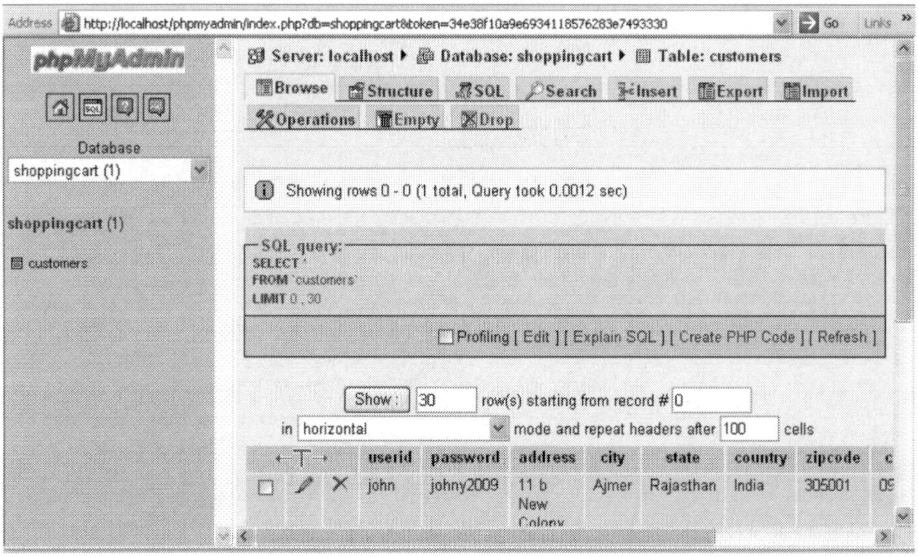

Figure 12.33 ***On Selecting Browse Link, We Get the Rows in the Table***

We can delete or edit any row by selecting the respective icon attached to each row. We can also set the rows to be displayed vertically instead of horizontally. Click the the option "`vertical`" from the "`mode`" dropdown list and click the `Show` button. We may get the rows of the table in the following format (Figure 12.34).

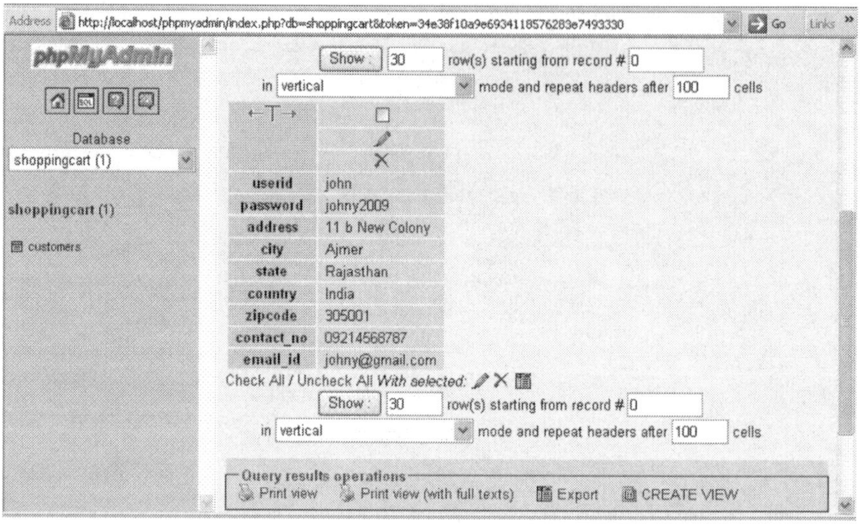

Figure 12.34 ***Selection of Vertical form and Dropdown List Mode***

If we click the the "`Structure`" link at the top, we get the complete structure of the selected table. We can check any field and can edit its name, data type or length. We can delete or insert a new field also. The screen that we may get is shown in Figure 12.35.

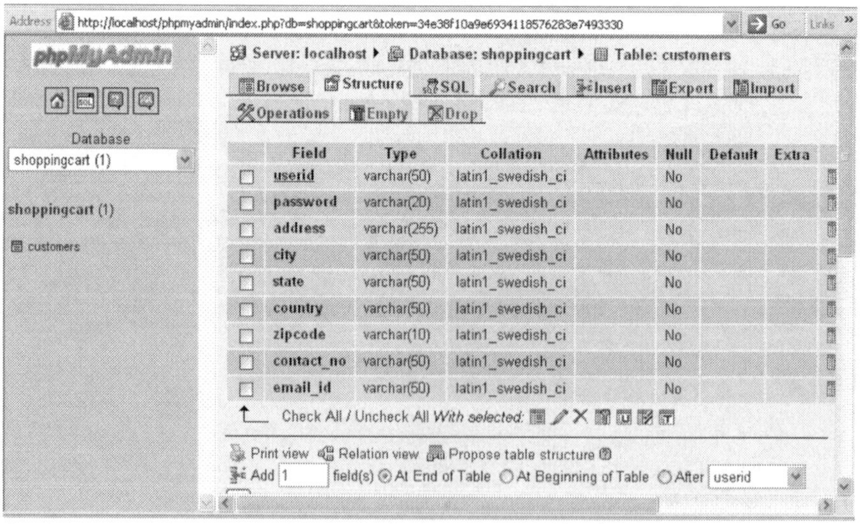

Figure 12.35 ***Selection of Structure Link to Make Modifications in the Table***

Suppose we want to modify the length of the field say: contact_no. We click the the field by checking its checkbox and selecting the `Change` icon (Figure 12.36).

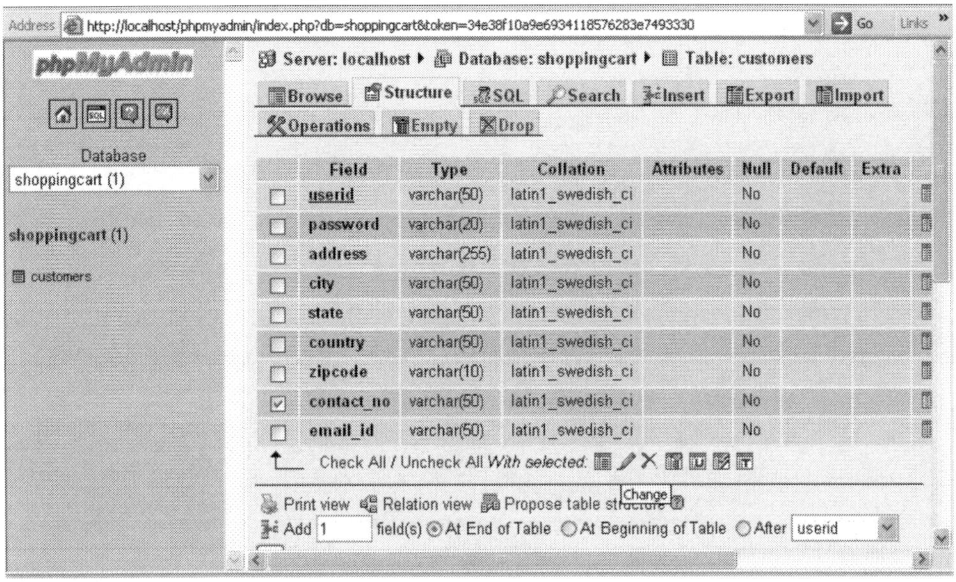

Figure 12.36 ***Modification of the Length of the Field***

We get a page displaying the complete information of the selected field and we can modify its data type, field name, length etc. and can save the changes by selecting the Save button (Figure 12.37).

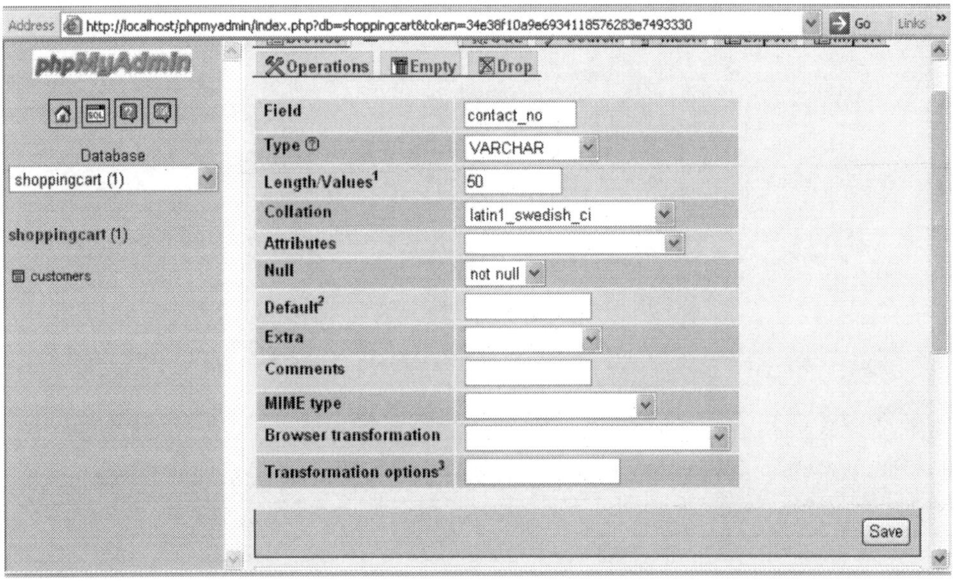

Figure 12.37 ***Modification of the Field***

Let's click the `Insert` link and insert three rows of customers. After inserting three rows, when we click the the `Browse` link, we may get the page shown in Figure 12.38.

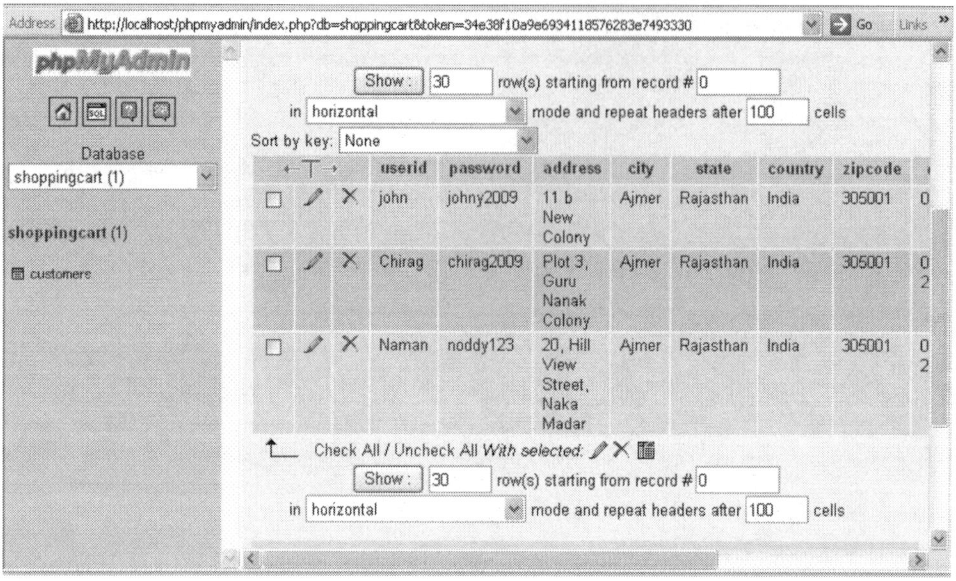

Figure 12.38 ***Insertion of Three Rows***

To execute an SQL statement on the given table in order to search, insert, delete or update any row in the table, we click the SQL link found at the top of the page. We get a page where we can type a SQL statement that we want to be executed on the selected table and click the `Go` button (Figure 12.39).

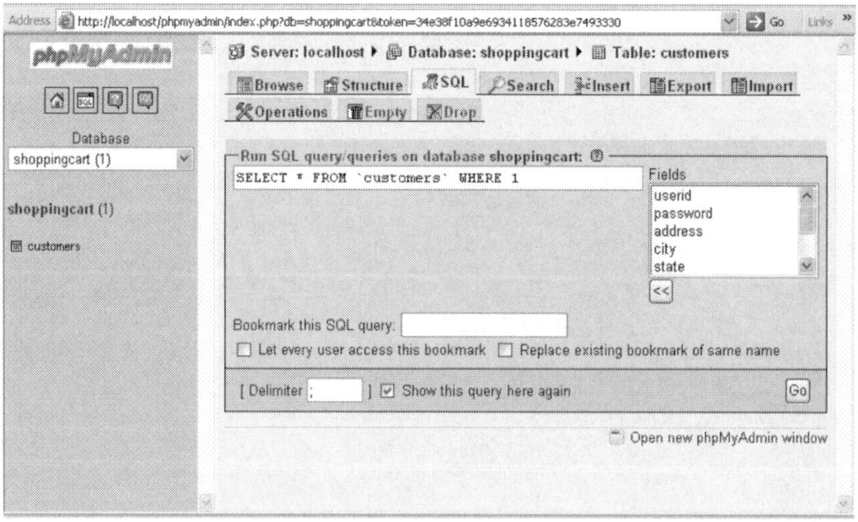

Figure 12.39 ***Click the SQL Link to Execute a SQL Statement***

Suppose we want to see the information of the customer with userid "Chirag". We can write the SQL statement as shown in Figure 12.40 and click the Go button:

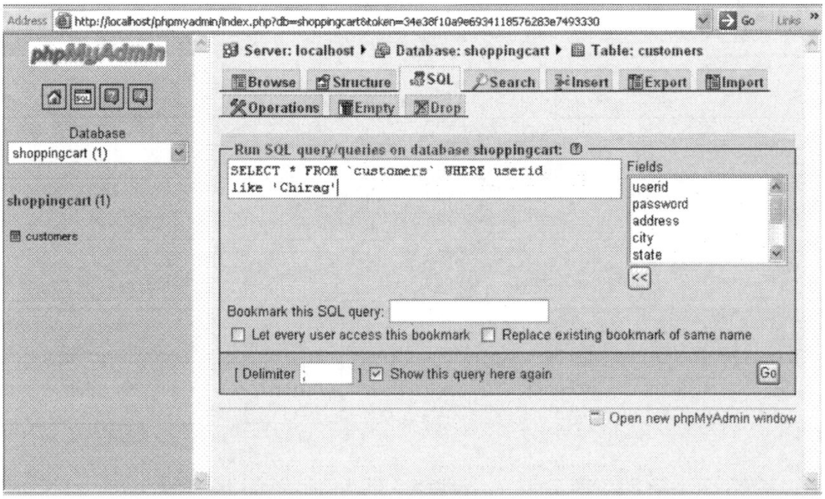

Figure 12.40 ***Selection of the GO Button***

We see that the information of the customer: "Chirag" is displayed. We can now edit it or delete it depending on our requirement. The screen that we may get is shown in Figure 12.41.

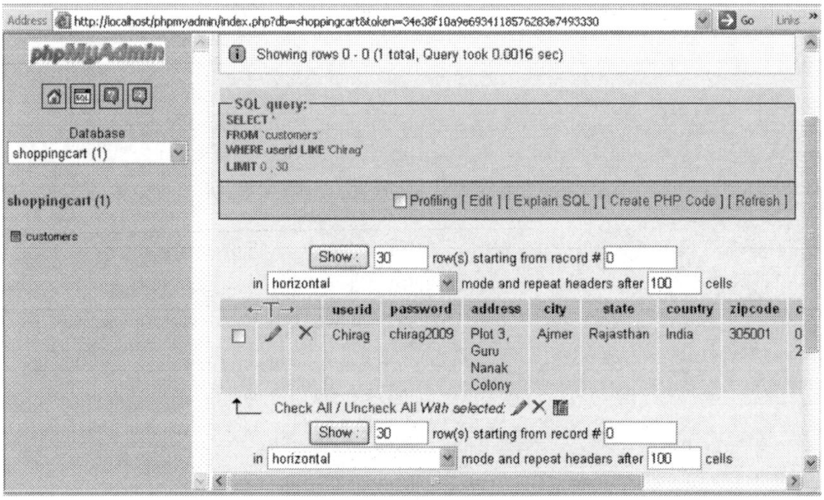

Figure 12.41 ***Information of the Customer is Displayed***

The SQL link explained above can be used to maintain the table i.e., we can delete, insert or update any row. But if we are not interested in maintenance of the table but to extract the desired information only, then just click the the Search link. We may get a screen to enter the criteria to search (Figure 12.42).

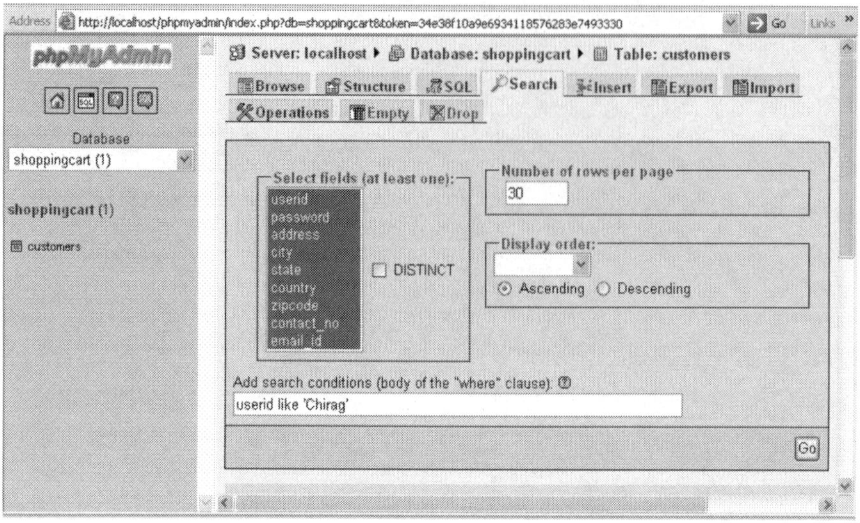

Figure 12.42 ***Click the the Search Link to Extract the Desired Information***

In the textbox given, we can write the criteria to get the desired row. Suppose we again want to see the information of the customer with userid "Chirag", write the criteria as shown in above figure and click the Go button to get the row that satisfies the given criteria.

If we click the the Operations link, we get the page that assists the user in doing operations like renaming the table, moving it to another database, setting it to be sorted in ascending or descending order of the particular field etc. (Figure 12.43).

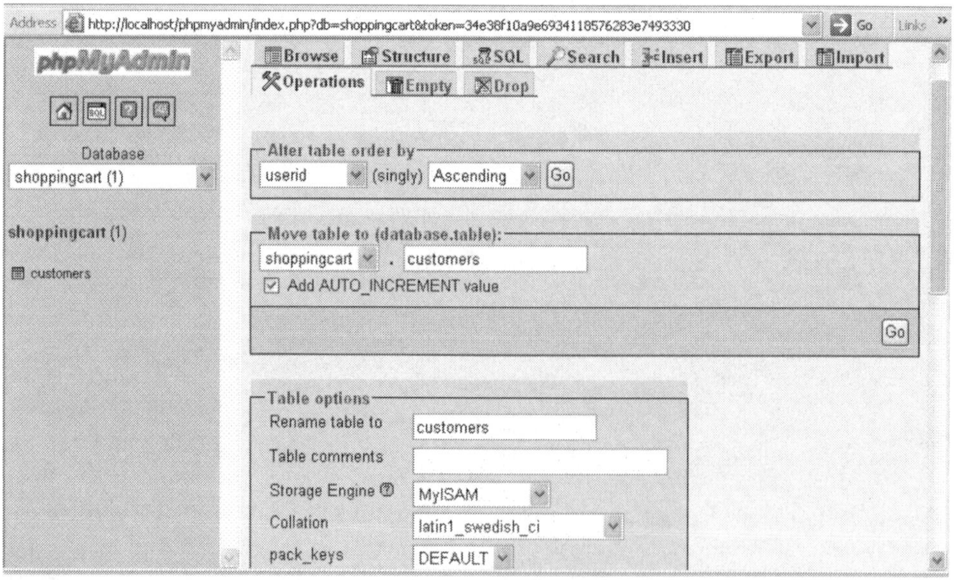

Figure 12.43 ***Selection of Operation Link to Make Alterations***

If we click the the Empty tab, it will delete all the rows of the selected table. We get a dialog box asking for confirmation (Figure 12.44).

Figure 12.44 *Dialog Box for Confirmation*

On selecting OK button, all the rows of the table will be deleted.

If we click the the Drop tab, the whole table along with its rows will be deleted. Again, we get a confirmation dialog box (Figure 12.45).

Figure 12.45 *Dialog Box for Confirmation of Deleting the Whole Table*

On selecting OK button, the table with its contents will be deleted.

12.7 CODEIGNITER

CodeIgniter is an Open Source Web Application Framework that has a simple and elegant toolkit to create fully featured web applications quickly. It uses the Model-View-Controller (MVC) approach similar to that of Ruby on Rails.

Characteristics of CodeIgniter

- It has great performance.
- It requires minimum configuration.
- User is not required to use the command line.

- It doesn't requires monolithic libraries
- User doesn't have to learn a templating language
- It is lightweight, i.e., it has just the basic libraries (but we can always load more if required).

Installing CodeIgniter

To install CodeIgniter framework, the following steps are taken:

- Download the zip file from the net. The downloaded file name may be: CodeIgniter_1.6.3.zip.
- Unzip it to any folder. Unzipped files consist of two folders:
- system and
- user_guide

and also two other files

- index.php and
- a text file named license
- Upload the CodeIgniter folders and files to the server. That is, copy the two folders and files to the `htdocs` folder of the server.

To check whether CodeIgniter is working, open the browser and point it at the following address: http://localhost/index.php. We may get the output shown in Figure 12.46.

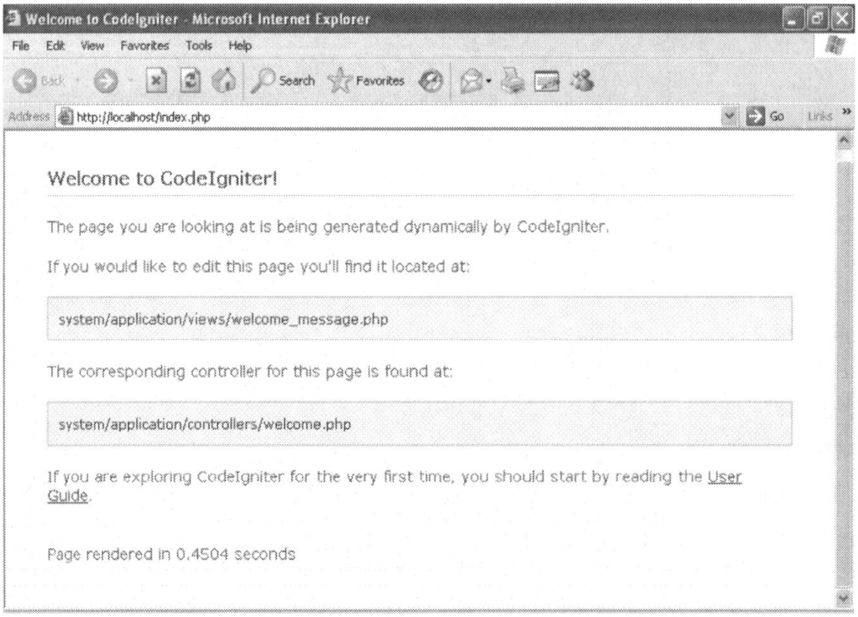

Figure 12.46 ***Welcome Screen of CodeIgniter***

This welcome page designates that CodeIgniter is successfully installed. If we click the the link: User guide, we may get the output shown in Figure 12.47.

Figure 12.47 ***Screen of CodeIgniter User Guide***

We can use this page to search for a particular command, function or class. We can also click the the Table of Contents link to see the list of topics. If we click the the Table of Contents link at the top, we may get the output shown in Figure 12.48.

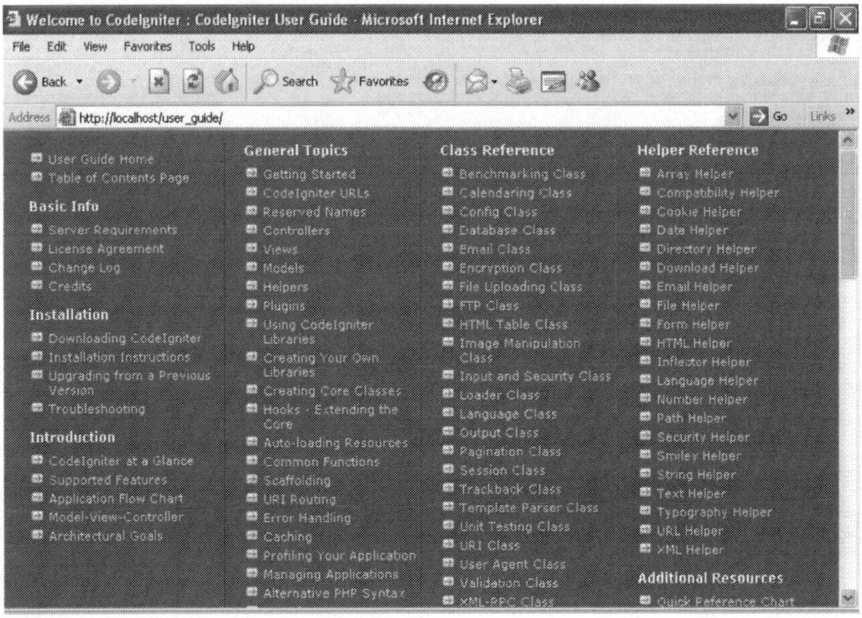

Figure 12.48 ***Screen of Table of Contents***

If we click the Application Flow Chart option from the Introduction section, we may get the output shown in Figure 12.49.

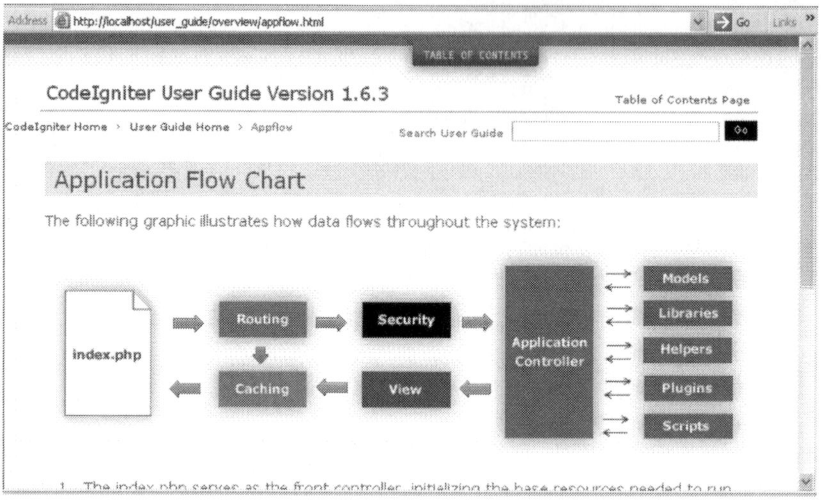

Figure 12.49 ***Screen on Selecting Application Flow Chart Option***

This page displays the relation between the PHP pages and the application controllers. That is how index.php file is routed to application controller where the help of different Libraries and Plugins is taken to execute the business logic and how the view is used for displaying results and is cached for better performance.

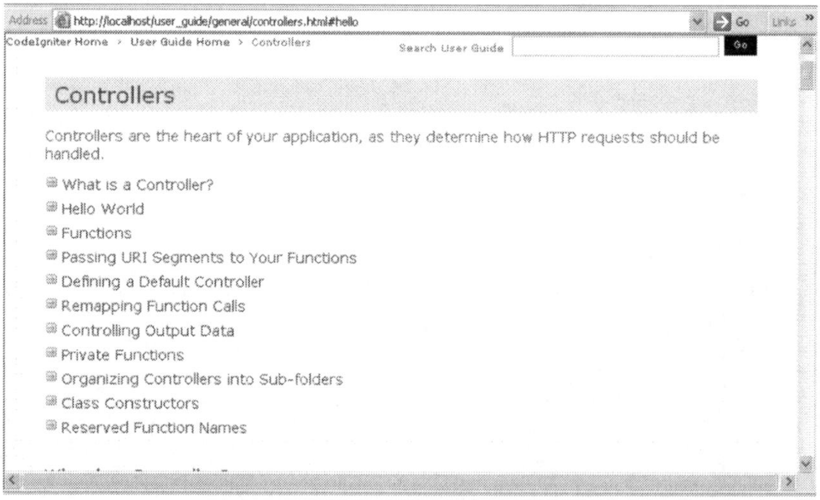

Figure 12.50 ***Screen of Controllers***

If we click the Controllers link from the General Topics section (refer Figure 12.48), we may get the output shown in Figure 12.50. The page displayed contains links for explaining several topics like:

- What is a Controller,
- How to make smallapplication like: Hello World,
- What are Functions,
- How to define default controller etc.

Controllers are the entry point of any application. We make our application in terms of controllers but we don't make it from scratch, we inherit the built-in Controller class and use its methods.

If we click the Hello World link from the above page, we may get the application named: Blog.php which is nothing but a controller that explains how to display "Hello World" text using the `index()` function (Figure 12.51).

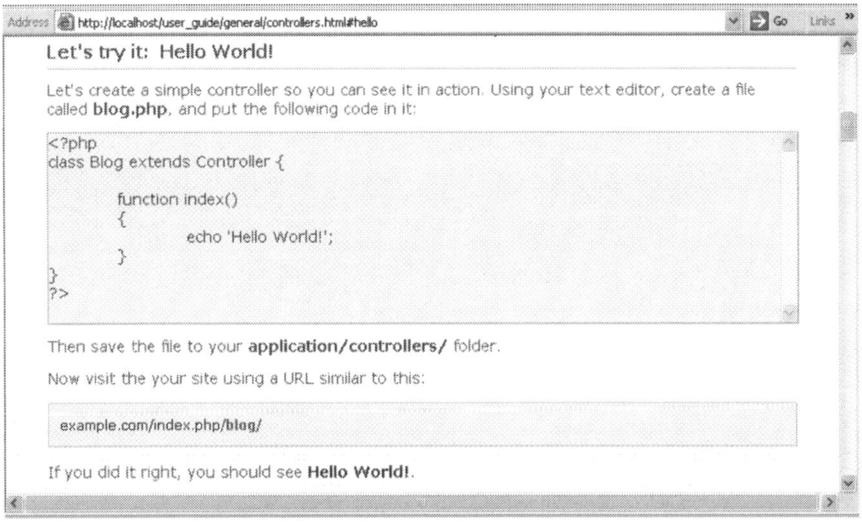

Figure 12.51 ***Screen on Selecting Hello Link World***

As explained earlier, the unzipped version of CodeIgniter includes two folders and two files. Of the two folders: system and user_guide, system folder is the most important one. It contains everything to work with CodeIgniter and consists of several folders. The most important subfolder in system folder is the application folder that contains all the views, controllers and models etc.

In application folder we have several other folders like :

Config	It deals with the setting up of the database connection, base URL, auto loader (which loads other classes and helper functions as well as plugins) and routes.
Controllers	Its main role is to forward requests to the correct models and views.
Errors	It deals with errors.
Models	It contains database functions in order to retrieve or insert information to the database.
Scripts	It is the folder where all the script includes and classes are stored.
Views	It contains the pages that will be displayed to the user. That is, the pages via which the user gets information displayed are placed in this folder

Before beginning with our first application in CodeIgniter, we need to make certain changes in the two files:

config.php and
autlooad.php

So, open the file config.php in config folder and modify the line:

```
$config['base_url'] = "http://127.0.0.1/CodeIgniter/";
```

to

```
$config['base_url'] = "http://127.0.0.1/";
```

This is done so that we can call our CodeIgniter application using following address:

http://localhost//index.php/intro1 and not http://localhost//CodeIgniter/index.php/intro1

Now, open autoload.php and add the following line:

```
$autoload['helper'] = array('url', 'form');
```

below the line:

```
$autoload['helper'] = array();
```

and save the file.

The statement is added so as to load the form methods automatically (we will be using several form methods in the view we are about to see).

12.8 FIRST APPLICATION IN CODEIGNITER

As said earlier, the applications in the CodeIgniter are in the form of controllers. So let us create our first controller. Create a PHP file named intro1.php with the following code and save it into the controllers folder.

```
<?php
    class Intro1 extends Controller {
        function index()
        {
                echo "Believe in God ";
        }
    }
?>
```

We can see in the above code that we make our own controller named intro1 by inheriting the built-in Controller class and overriding its `index()` function to display a text "Believe in God" on the screen.

To run the application, open the browser and point to the address: http://localhost//index.php/intro1, we get the following output (Figure 12.52).

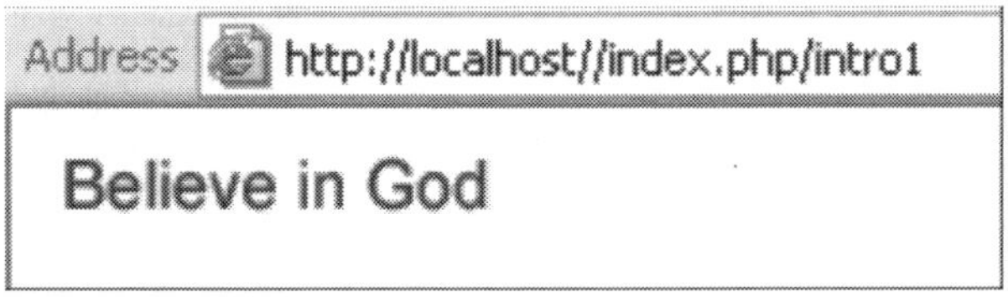

Figure 12.52 ***Output Displayed***

It looks awkward to include index.php in the URL while calling our application but it is the default way CodeIgniter handles URLs.

12.9 SECOND APPLICATION IN CODEIGNITER

In this application, we ask the user to enter userid and address. So we make a file named intro2.php in `controllers` folder with the following code in it:

intro2.php

```
<?php
class Intro2 extends Controller {
    function index()
    {
        $data['userid'] = array('name' => 'userid', 'id' => 'userid');
        $data['address'] = array('name' => 'address', 'id' => 'address');
        $this->load->view('intro2_view', $data);


    }
}
?>
```

In this file, we have created an array of variables which themselves contain an array of data which we will use in our view. The values in our `$data` arrays represent our variables and the attribute and value pairs in the respective arrays will be used to construct our form elements.

The line:

```
$this->load->view('intro2_view', $data);
```

deals with loading our view and importing our data array so that we can use our variables.

Let's make a file named intro2_view.php and store it in the `views` folder.

intro2_view.php

```
<!DOCTYPE html PUBLIC "-//W3C//DTD XHTML 1.0 Strict//EN" "http://www.w3.org/TR/
xhtml1/DTD/xhtml1-strict.dtd">
<html>
    <head>
        <meta http-equiv="content-type" content="text/html; charset=utf-8" />
        <title></title>
        <style type="text/css">
            body {
                font: small/2em Verdana, Arial, Helvetica, serif;
            }
        </style>
    </head>
    <body>
        <h1>Enter your details</h1>
        <?php echo form_open('dispresponse'); ?>
        <label for="userid">Userid: </label><?php echo form_input($userid); ?>
        <br />
        <label for="address">Address: </label><?php echo form_input($address);
        ?> <br />
        <?php echo form_submit('submit', 'Submit'); ?>
        <?php echo form_close(); ?>
    </body>
</html>
```

As explained earlier, the line added in autoload.php file:

```
$autoload['helper'] = array('url', 'form');
```

makes the CodeIgniter's form functions available to us and that's why we are able to use these functions in our view file. The meaning of other statements is as under:

$form_open('dispresponse)	creates an opening form element and the dispresponse represents the action attribute that we usually use in a <form> tag, with form being our controller and dispresponse being our function that deals with submitting our form. In other words, when we click the the submit button, we will be navigated to the disresponse.php file
form_input($userid)	creates an input field for our form with the attributes and values that we specified in our $data['userid'] array in our controller.
form_submit('submit', 'Submit')	a submit button is created with type attribute "submit" and value attribute "Submit".
form_close()	is for closing the form i.e. it represents </form>.

Let us run the application. Open the browser and point it at: http://localhost//index.php/intro2. We get the output as shown in Figure 12.53.

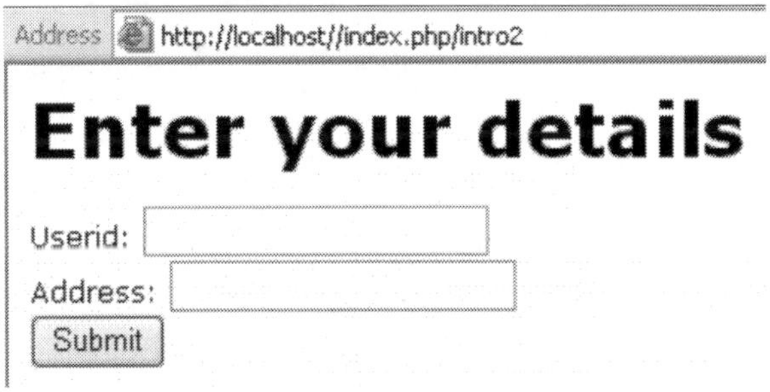

Figure 12.53 ***Output Displayed to Enter Information***

If we click the submit button after feeding userid and password, we get an error: "Object not found" as the file dispresonse.php is not yet made.

Let's make the file disresponse.php in the `controllers` folder with following code:

```
<?php
   class Dispresponse extends Controller {
      function index()
      {
         echo "You are Welcome ";
      }
   }
?>
```

We can see that dispresponse.php file just displays a welcome message.

Now if we run the above program and click the Submit button, we may get the output shown in Figure 12.54.

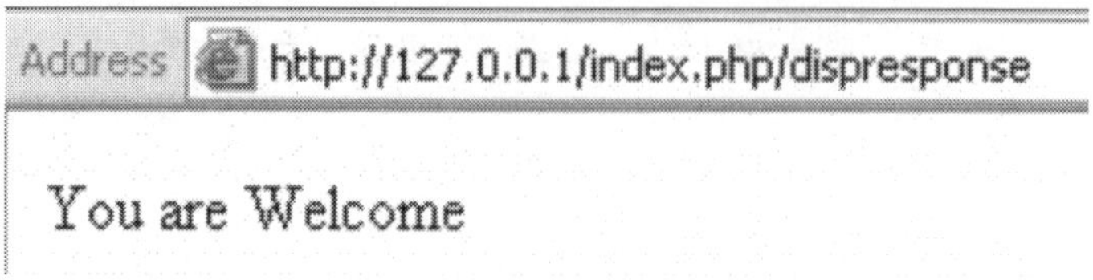

Figure 12.54 ***Welcome Message Displayed***

SUMMARY

In this chapter we had an introduction to two PHP frameworks: XAMPP and CodeIgniter. We have seen the step-by-step installation of XAMPP and CodeIgniter. We also saw the steps to run PHP programs using both frameworks. Also, we saw how to maintain MySQL database via phpMyAdmin. We saw the procedure to create a database, specifying the structure of a table and eventually creating a table in phpMyAdmin. We have seen how to insert rows in the table, how to edit or delete any row, how to alter the structure of the table and how to run SQL commands to see desired records.

Appendix A

Shopping Cart Project in PHP Script

Before we begin with understanding the code of different PHP programs used in this Shopping Cart website, let us first get a look and feel of the website on execution. We will see the output and the action taken on selecting different links and icons on the website. The first welcome screen that we get is as shown in Figure A.1.

Figure A.1 *First Screen on Executing Shopping Cart site*

We can see that at the top is a header which contains the title of our website and a `Show Cart` icon at the top right corner (a handy tool for the user to know what things he has placed in his cart). On the left is a menu which displays different categories of items that are available for sale on our website. Beside this, there are links provided for the user to create his account, allow him to log in to our website and a link "`Contact Us`" to display email and address information to the user so that he can interact with the organisation in future. On selecting the Category dropdown list, we will see different categories of products available for sale on our website (Figure A.2).

Figure A.2 ***Selection of Category Camera***

In Figure A.2, we can see that the dropdown list displays three Categories of products that are available for sale: `Camera, Mobile and Book` (more categories can also be added easily). From the dropdown list control, if we select the category "`Camera`" to see all the products falling in the Camera category, we may get the output as shown in Figure A.3.

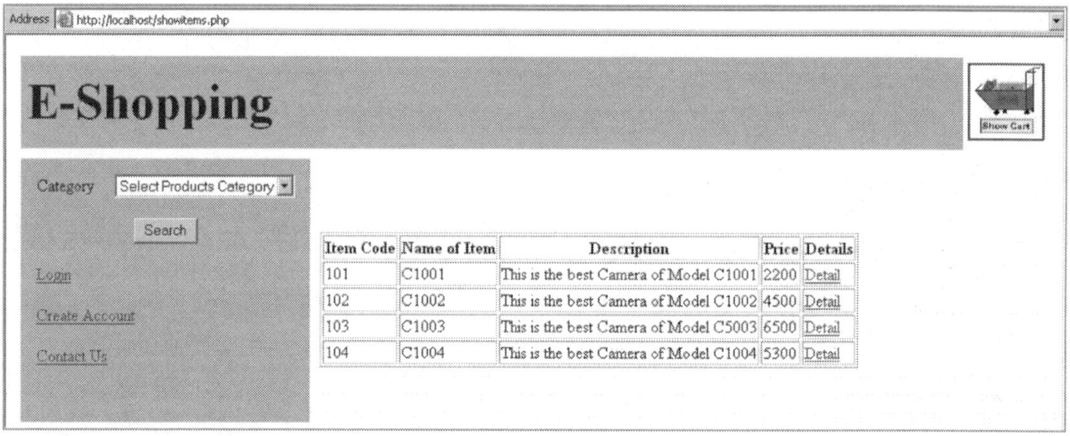

Figure A.3 ***Description of Category Camera in Detail***

The "`Detail`" link on the right of each product is meant to provide more information about the selected product. We can click the Detail link of any product before choosing it. Suppose we select the Detail link of the product with item code=101, we get the complete description of the product along with its image (Figure A.4).

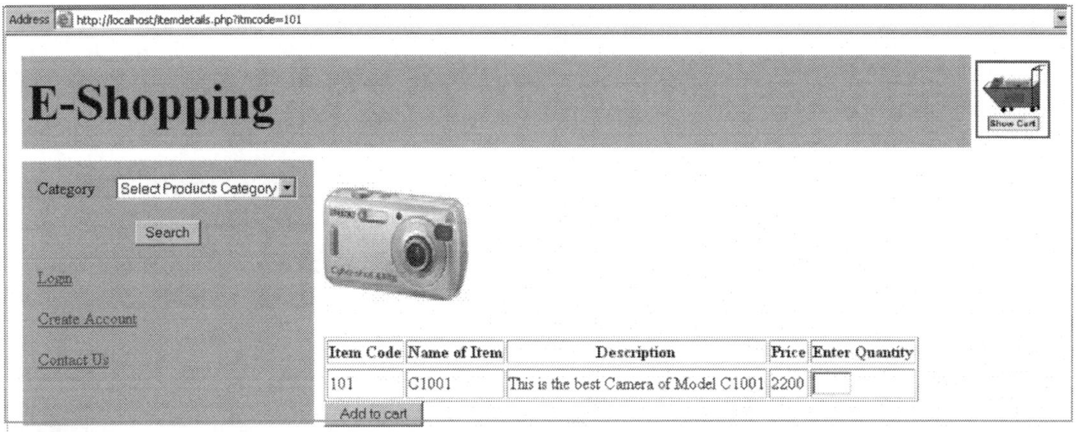

Figure A.4 ***Description of a Particular Item Code***

The textbox on the right under the column "`Enter Quantity`" is to enter the quantity of the selected product we want to purchase. If we leave this box blank and select `Add to cart` button, the default quantity assumed is `1`. Let us suppose we want to purchase 2 pieces of the product 101, we enter value 2 in the text box and then click the `Add to cart` button (Figure A.5).

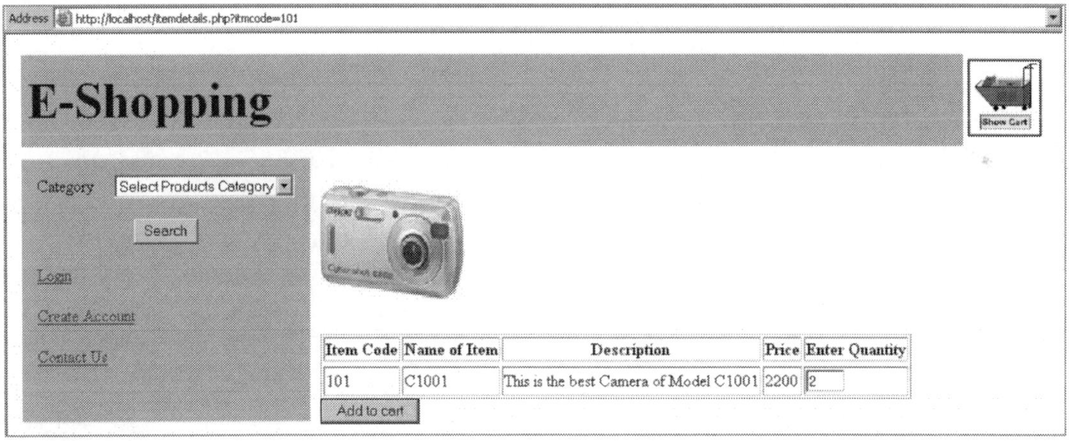

Figure A.5 ***Enter the Quantity Required***

On selecting `Add to cart` button, the selected item along with the specified quantity is added to our Shopping cart and the current status of the Shopping Cart will be displayed automatically. That is, all the items that are currently present in the Shopping Cart will be displayed (Figure A.6). We can see in the figure that the item with Item Name: `C1001` is displayed as being selected in the Shopping Cart along with its Item Code, Quantity, Name, Price and Total Price where Total Price is automatically computed as the multiplication of Quantity and Price. Along with the item(s) in the Shopping Cart four buttons will also be displayed: `Change Qty`, `Delete Item`, `Empty Cart`, and `Checkout`. Of these, `Change Qty` and `Delete Item` buttons will be attached with each row (product present) in the Shopping Cart.

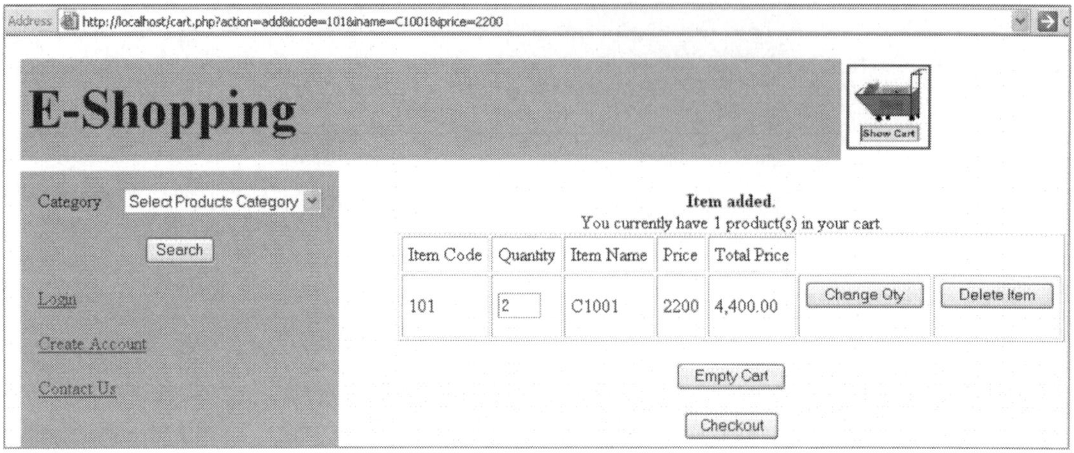

Figure A.6 ***The Selected Item Along with the Required Quantity is Added to the Cart***

- The Change Qty button is for changing the quantity of the product selected in the Shopping Cart. We can enter any desired value in the Quantity textbox of the related product and click the Change Qty button.
- Delete Item button appears along with every product (row) in the cart and clickng it will delete that product from the Shopping cart list.
- Empty cart button will erase all the products from the Shopping Cart and leave it completely empty.
- Checkout button takes us to the Order Form to place the order and to supply shipping information (address to which the ordered products have to be delivered). The pre-requisite condition for placing the order is that the visitor must be logged in to our website. So, before filling in the Order Form, we check whether the visitor is already logged in to our website or not. If he is not logged in, he will be provided two links: one is for logging in to our website and the second link is for creating an account if he is not already registered on our website. The user may choose the link accordingly. After creating an account and logging in, the user can place the order.

Before we click the **Checkout** button, let us choose some products belonging to some other category. Suppose we need to see all the items under **Mobile** category, we can select the category from the menu on the left (Figure A.7).

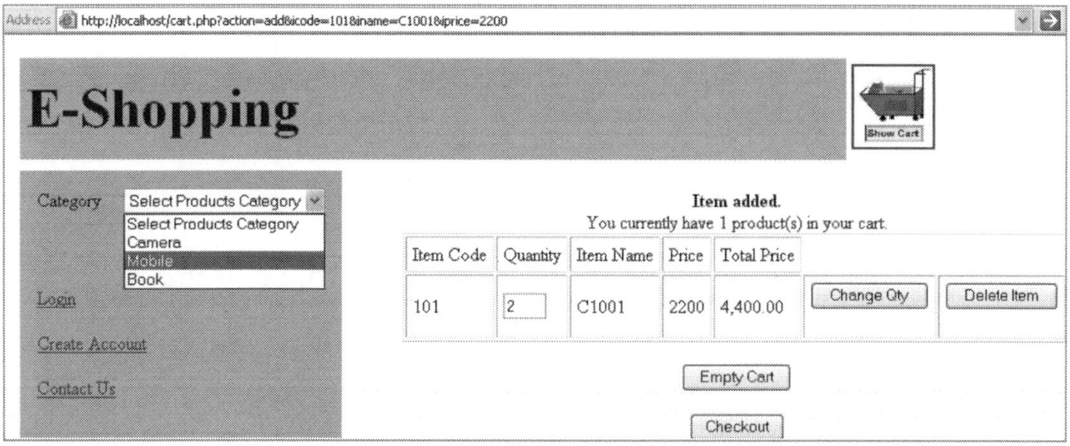

Figure A.7 *Selection of Mobile Category to add More Products to the Cart*

On selecting `Mobile` category from the dropdown list, all the products falling under the `Mobile` category will be displayed in tabular format (Figure A.8). These products are fetched from a table called `products` from `shopping` database (we will soon learn about different tables and their structure related to this project).

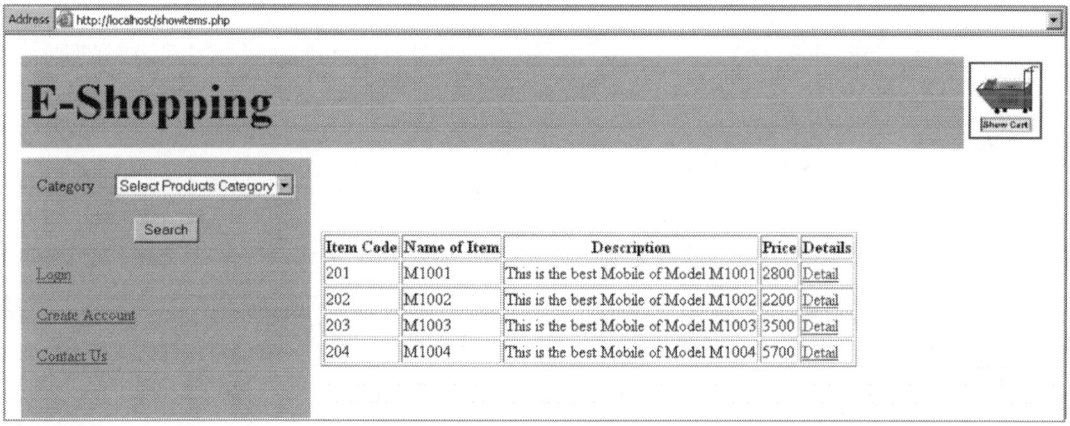

Figure A.8 *Products of Mobile Category*

Again, along with each product, a link "`Detail`" is provided which when clicked displays complete information about the selected product along with its image. If we select Detail link of a product, with code say 203, we will get its complete description along with its image (Figure A.9).

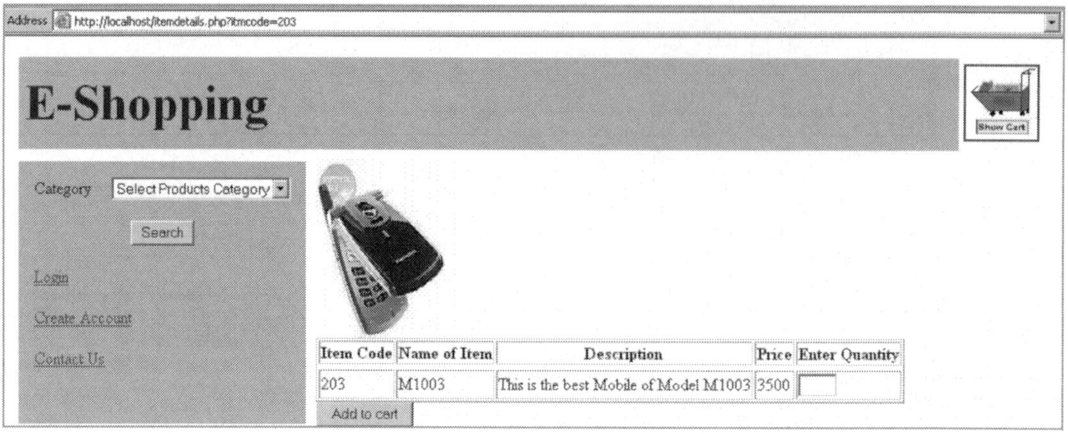

Figure A.9 ***Detailed Information of a Particular Item Code***

Again the textbox at the right under **"Enter Quantity"** column appears for specifying what quantity of the selected product we want to purchase (default value is 1). To purchase 3 pieces of this product, enter the **quantity** of this product as **3** and click the **Add to cart** button (Figure A.10).

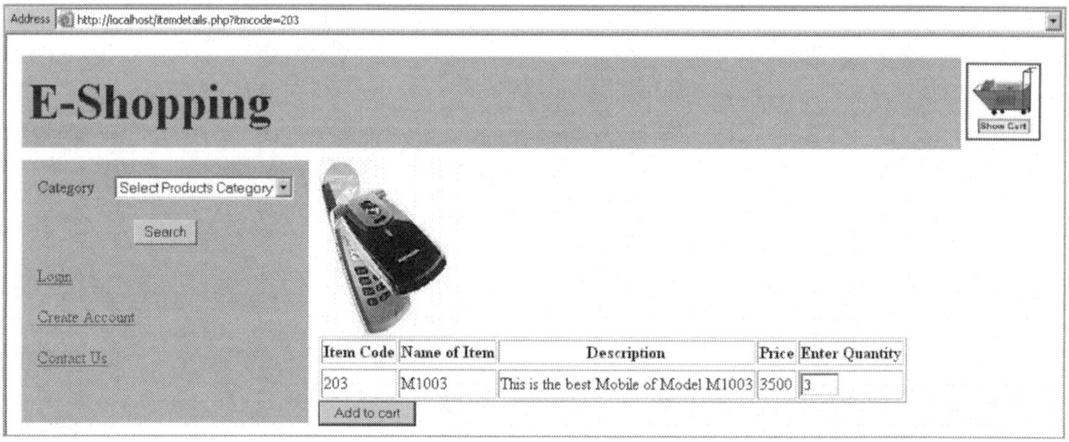

Figure A.10 ***Quantity Required is Entered***

On clicking the `"Add to cart"` button, all the products currently selected in the cart will be displayed automatically (Figure A.11). In the figure, we can see that now we have two products selected in the Shopping Cart, one with `Item Name: C1001` and the other with `Item Name: M1003`. Also, along with every product (row) in the Shopping Cart, two buttons: `Change Qty` and `Delete Item` are attached.

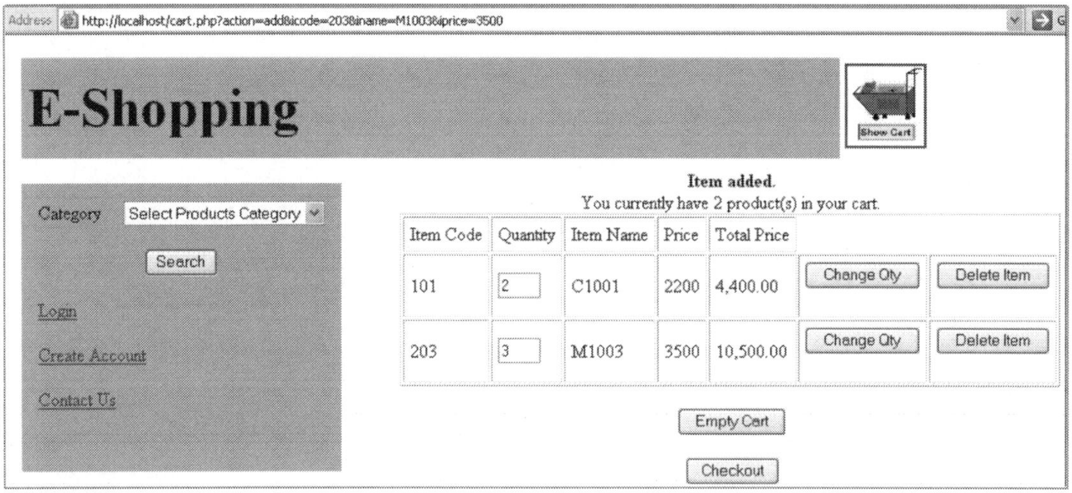

Figure A.11 ***Item of Mobile Category Added to the Cart***

We can change not just the quantity of the products in the cart but also delete an item from the cart. Let's update the quantity of the product with Item Name: "`C1001`" from 2 to 1. We just need to change the value from 2 to 1 in the text box under column "`Quantity`" of the related product followed by clicking the "`Change Qty`" button (Figure A.12).

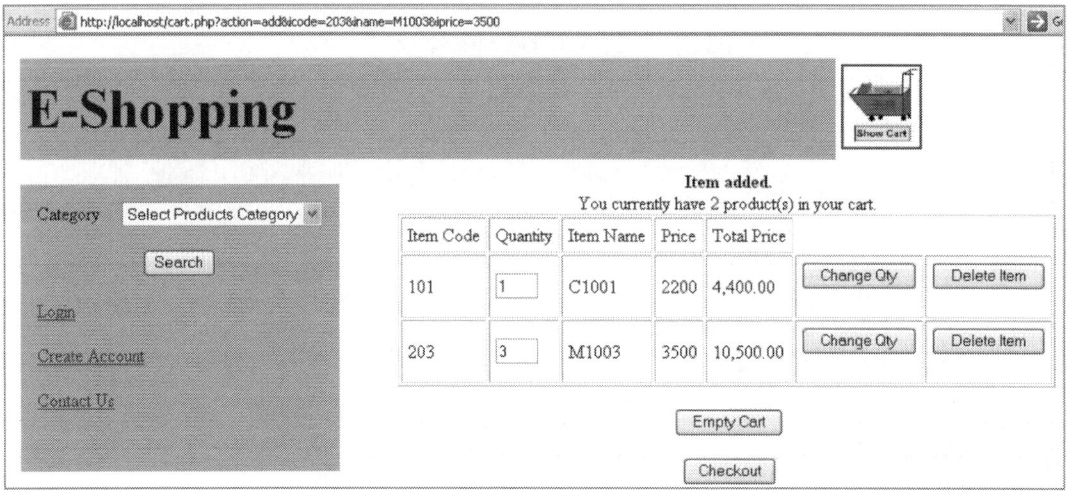

Figure A.12 ***Alteration in Quantity Required from the Cart***

The quantity of the selected product (with item name: C1001) will be changed in the Shopping Cart and information about the update is displayed in the form of a message: "`Quantity changed`" (Figure A.13). We can see in the figure that the value in the Total Price column also changes on changing the quantity of any product in the Shopping Cart to reflect the changes. (Formula of Total Price=Quantity * Price).

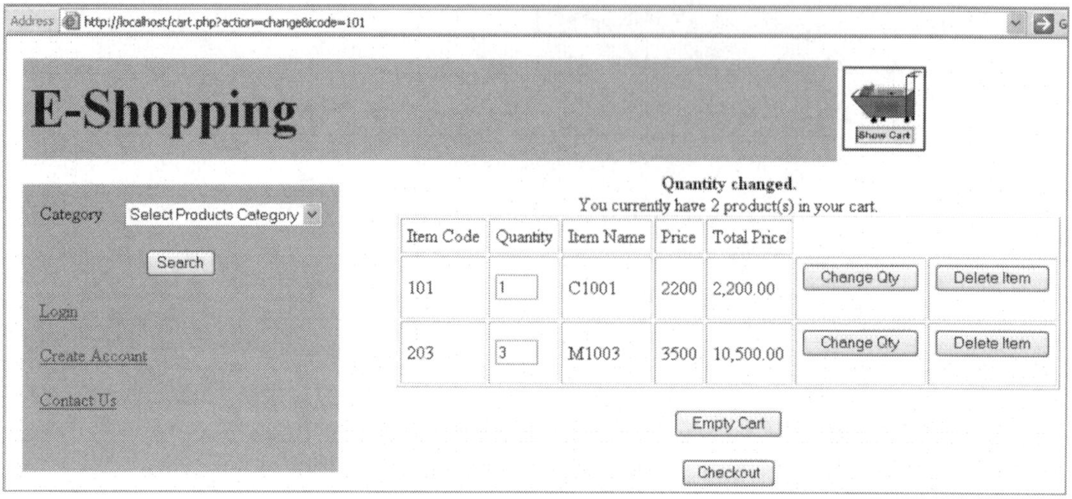

Figure A.13 ***Changes Seen in the Total Price Due to Change in Quantity***

We can even delete any product currently present in the Shopping Cart. For that, we just press the `Delete Item` button of the related product (i.e. Delete Item button of the respective row in which the product is been displayed is clicked). Let us click the `Delete Item` button of the product with Item Name "`M1003`" from the cart to erase it. Immediately, the product will be removed from the Shopping Cart and it will be left with a single item with Item Name: `C1001`. The updated Shopping Cart will be immediately displayed automatically (Figure A.14).

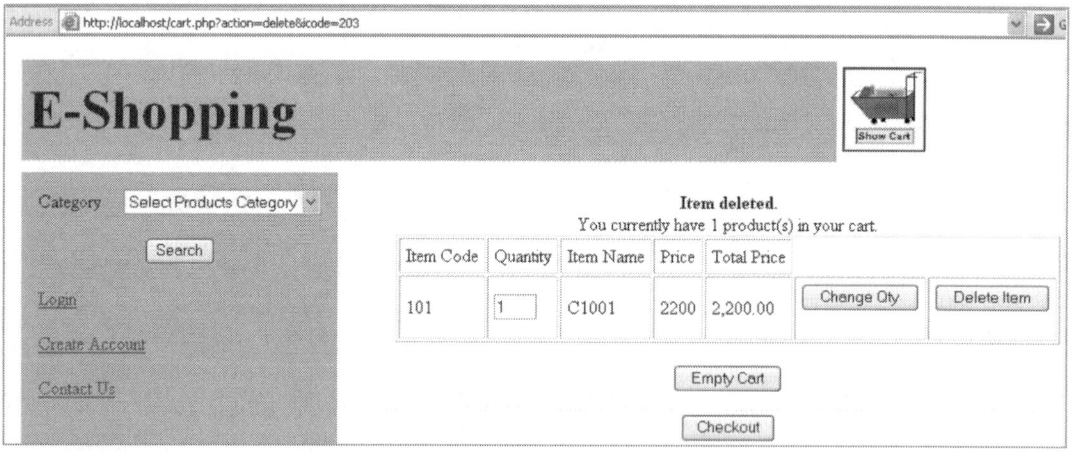

Figure A.14 ***Item Name M1003 Deleted from the Cart***

Note: Selecting "`Empty Cart`" button will delete all the products selected in the cart.

If we are done with choosing items, we can click the `Checkout` button to place the order. If before choosing items, we have created our account and have logged in to the website (by selecting `Login` link from the menu), then our details like name, address, contact number etc. will be automatically displayed (from the information that we entered while creating the Account) and we will be asked to enter just the shipping information (the location where purchased items have to be delivered). But if we haven't yet logged in, then we will get the following message on the screen (Figure A.15). The message says that we are not currently logged in to the system and we need to either select `Login link` (if we are already registered on our website) to login to the system or select `Create an Account` to create an account if we haven't yet created it.

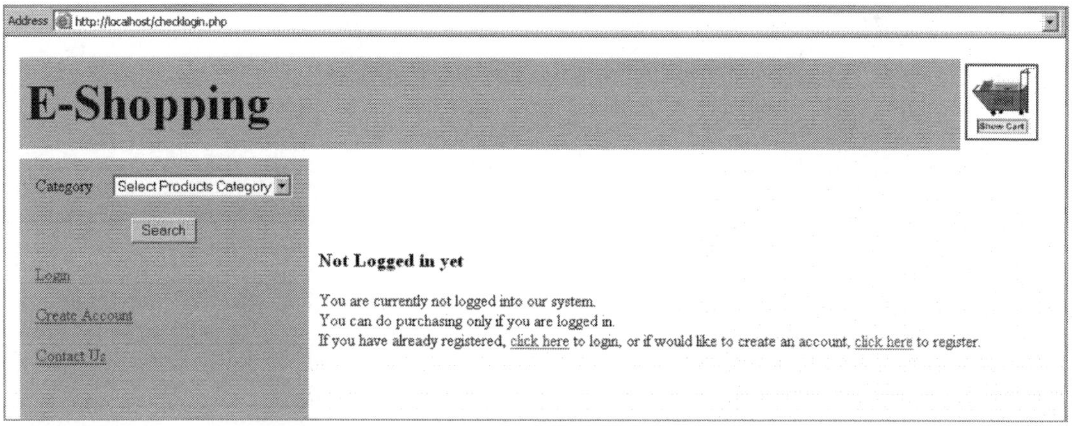

Figure A.15 ***Screen Indicating not Logged in Before***

Assuming that the visitor has not yet created an account on our website, he is prompted to do that first. On selecting the `Create Account` link, a screen will be provided where the visitor can fill in his information. The screen prompts the visitor to enter a unique userid, password, first name, last name, address, city, state, country, zip code, email id, phone number etc. (Figure A.16).

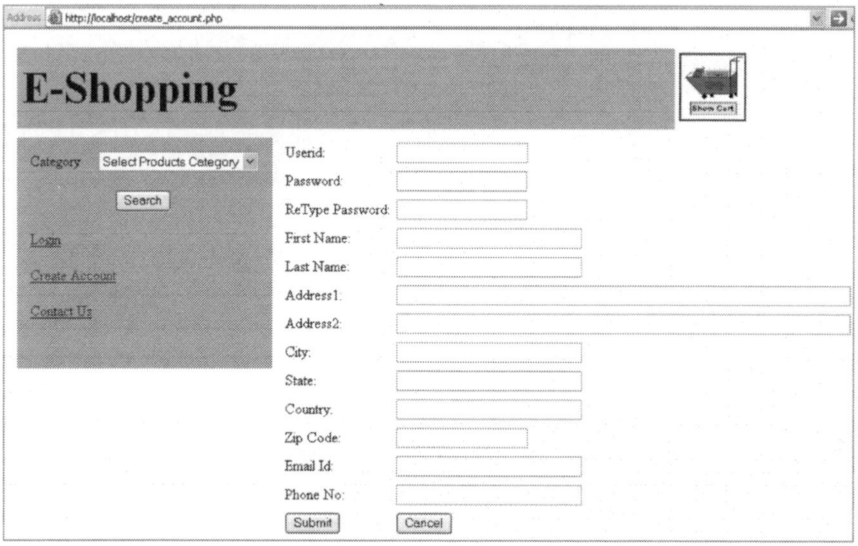

Figure A.16 ***Screen for Create Account Link***

While filling in the form, proper care has to be taken while filling the two fields: `Password` and `ReType Password`. The passwords entered in these two boxes must be exactly the same. If we make a mistake and there appears some difference in them (Figure A.17), we can see the difference in the size of the two passwords in the two fields: `Password` and `ReType Password`.

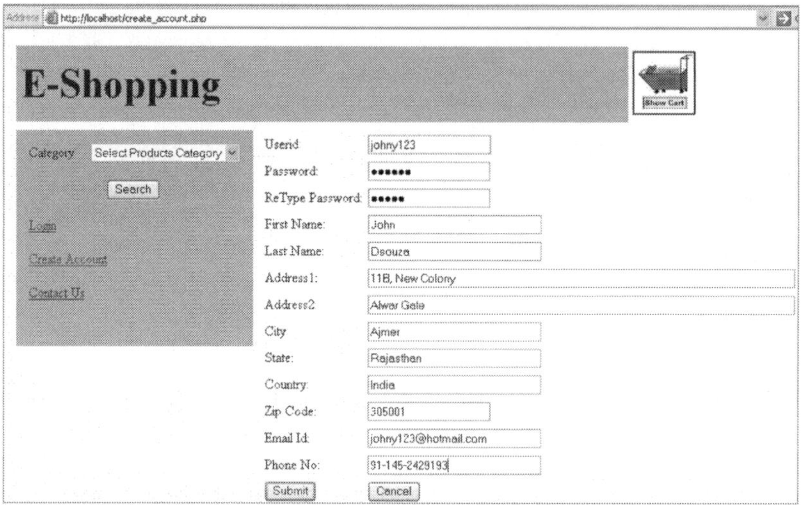

Figure A.17 ***Password and Retype Password Should be Exactly the Same***

If contents of both the fields: `Password` and `ReType Password` don't match, an error message: `"Your Passwords do not match. Try again"` is displayed and the user is asked to re-enter password in both of the fields (Figure A.18).

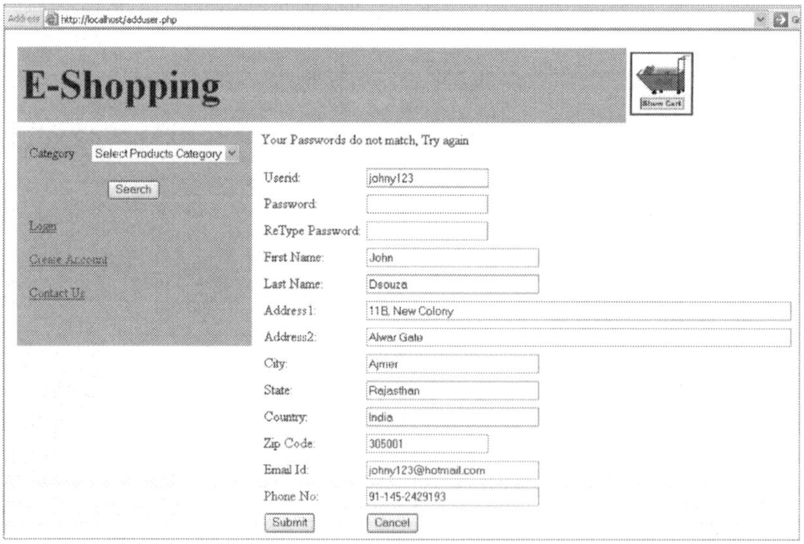

Figure A.18 ***If Both Didn't Match, Another Screen will Follow to Feed the Same Again***

Let us enter the passwords in both the fields: `Password` and `ReType Password` exactly the same (without any difference) and click the Submit button (Figure A.19).

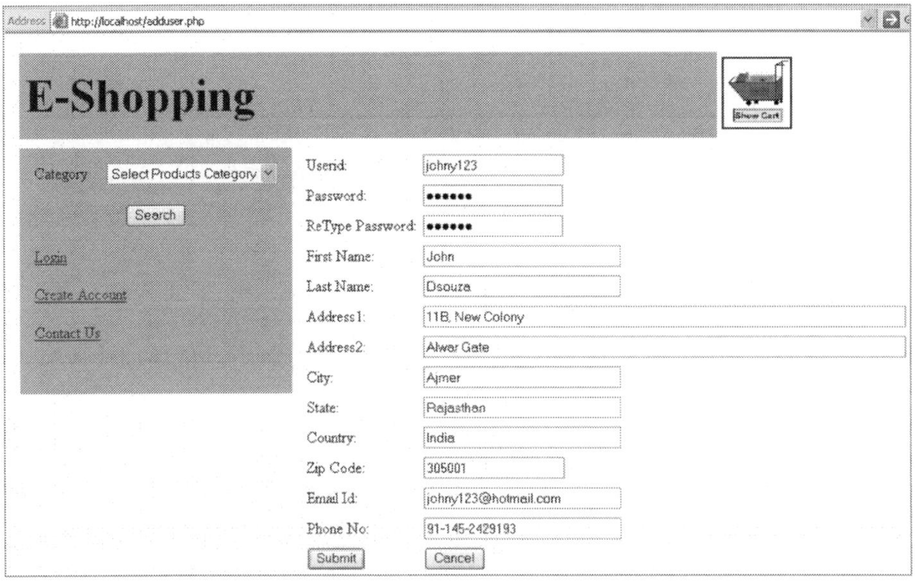

Figure A.19 ***Clicking the Submit Button After Entering the Same Password in Password and ReType Password Fields***

If the supplied information is correct, the visitor is registered on our website i.e. his account is created and he is asked to select a link to enter shipping information (address where product(s) have to be delivered) if purchasing is over (Figure A.20).

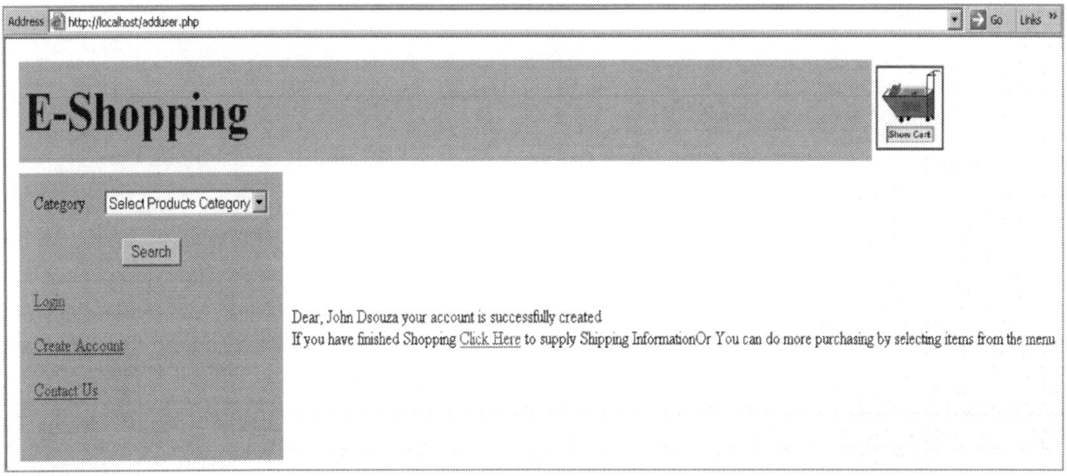

Figure A.20 ***User is Registered***

When we click the link for supplying shipping information, we get a few textboxes more to supply the details of the location where the products have to be delivered (Figure A.21). All the textboxes before the heading `Shipping Information` will appear already filled with the information that was entered while creating the account. We have to just fill in the textboxes after the heading "`Shipping Information`" to supply delivery details.

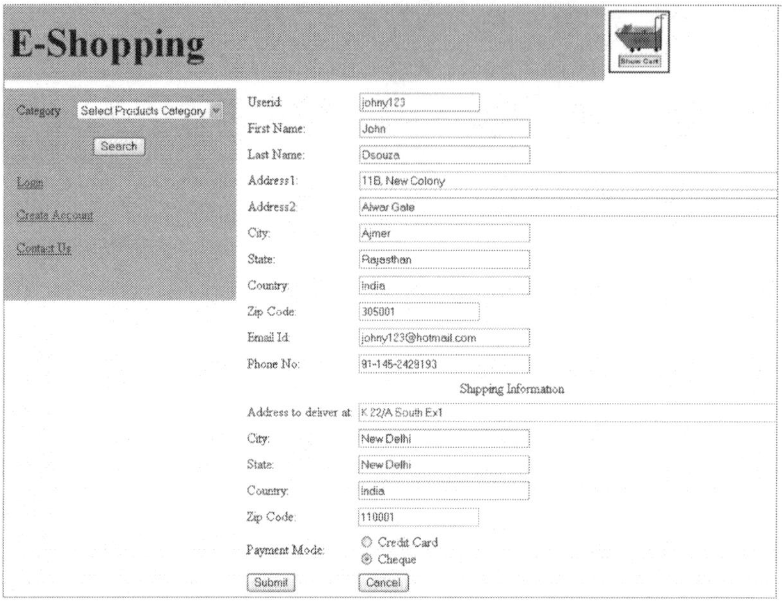

Figure A.21 ***Supply of Shipping Information***

After filling in the shipping information when we click the **Submit** button, our order details will be stored in the database with a unique order (successive) number. This order number is displayed to the user for future communication (Figure A.22).

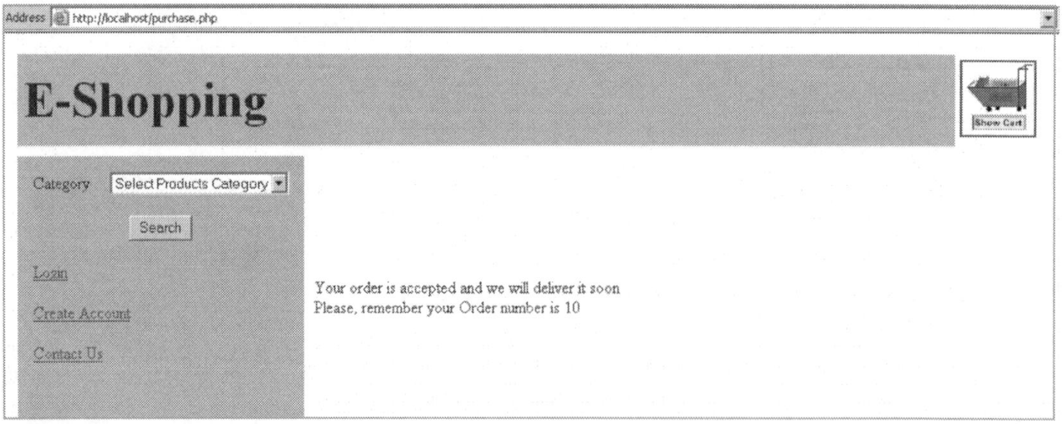

Figure A.22 ***Display of Order Number for Future Communication***

Appendix B

Source Code of the Project with Explanation

For this Shopping Cart project, we will create a database named "**shopping**" (any name) using the MySQL command: **create database** (refer to Chapter 2 for MySQL commands). In this database, we need to store the following information:

- Products of different categories
- Customer details
- Item details selected in shopping cart
- Order details

We need tables for storing the information of products available for sale on our website, information of the items selected by the visitor in the Shopping Cart, information of the customer placing the order and the information of the order placed by the visitor.

So, we will create five tables (in the shopping database) with the following names:

1. products
2. cart
3. customers
4. orders
5. orders_details

PRODUCTS TABLE

`Products` is the table that will store all the information of the products available for sale on our website. Its structure is shown in Figure B.1.

```
mysql> describe products;
+-------------+--------------+------+-----+---------+-------+
| Field       | Type         | Null | Key | Default | Extra |
+-------------+--------------+------+-----+---------+-------+
| item_code   | int<4>       | NO   |     |         |       |
| item_name   | varchar<50>  | NO   |     |         |       |
| description | varchar<255> | NO   |     |         |       |
| category    | varchar<50>  | NO   |     |         |       |
| quantity    | int<4>       | NO   |     |         |       |
| price       | float        | YES  |     | NULL    |       |
| imagename   | varchar<50>  | YES  |     | NULL    |       |
+-------------+--------------+------+-----+---------+-------+
7 rows in set <0.11 sec>
```

Figure B.1 *Structure of Products Table*

Usage of the fields

Fields	Usage
item_code	This field will store the unique item codes of every product. The first digit of the item code signifies the category it belongs to. For example, the item code of all cameras begins with digit 1 like: 101,102 and so on. Similarly, the item code of all mobiles begins with digit 2 i.e. 201, 202...
item_name	The name of the product or its model is stored in this field
description	All characteristics of the product which make it different from the rest are stored in this field
category	This field stores the category to which the item belongs. Since we are selling items of three categories in our website, we can store any of the following text in this field: `Camera, Mobile` or `Book` Note: We can include more categories of items by just appending them in our database
quantity	The quantity of the current item is stored here
price	Selling price of the item is stored in this field
imagename	The path and the filename of the picture of the product is stored in this field

CART TABLE

`Cart` is the table used for storing the information of the products selected for purchase by a particular visitor to our website. Its structure is shown in Figure B.2.

```
mysql> describe chart;
+-----------------+--------------+------+-----+---------+-------+
| Field           | Type         | Null | Key | Default | Extra |
+-----------------+--------------+------+-----+---------+-------+
| chart_sess      | char<50>     | NO   |     |         |       |
| chart_itmcode   | char<5>      | NO   |     |         |       |
| chart_qty       | int<3>       | NO   |     |         |       |
| chart_itme_name | varchar<50>  | YES  |     | NULL    |       |
| chart_price     | float        | YES  |     | NULL    |       |
+-----------------+--------------+------+-----+---------+-------+
5 rows in set <0.00 sec>
```

Figure B.2 ***Structure of Cart Table***

Usage of the fields

Fields	Usage
cart_sess	It will store the session id of the cart to uniquely identify the items selected by an individual visitor. The session mechanism is used to recognise whether the requests are generated by the same client. In other words, it helps in

	distinguishing the items selected by each visitor separately. The session id is automatically generated and will be stored in this field
cart_itmcode	In this field, the item code of the selected product will be stored
cart_qty	This field stores the quantity of the product selected in the Shopping Cart by the visitor
cart_item_name	The name of the item selected by the visitor in his Shopping Cart is stored here
cart_price	Selling price of the item selected in the Shopping Cart is stored in this field

CUSTOMERS TABLE

`Customers` is the table used for storing the information of the customers placing orders on our website. The information may be used for delivering the order and for future correspondence. Its structure is shown in Figure B.3.

```
mysql> describe customers;
+----------------+---------------+------+-----+---------+-------+
| Field          | Type          | Null | Key | Default | Extra |
+----------------+---------------+------+-----+---------+-------+
| userid         | Varchar<50>   | NO   | PRI |         |       |
| first_name     | varchar<50>   | YES  |     | NULL    |       |
| last_name      | varchar<50>   | YES  |     | NULL    |       |
| add1           | varchar<255>  | YES  |     | NULL    |       |
| add2           | varchar<255>  | YES  |     | NULL    |       |
| city           | varchar<50>   | YES  |     | NULL    |       |
| state          | varchar<50>   | YES  |     | NULL    |       |
| zipcode        | varchar<12>   | YES  |     | NULL    |       |
| emailid        | varchar<50>   | YES  |     | NULL    |       |
| password       | varchar<50>   | YES  |     | NULL    |       |
| phone_no       | varchar<50>   | YES  |     | NULL    |       |
| country        | varchar<50>   | YES  |     | NULL    |       |
+----------------+---------------+------+-----+---------+-------+
12 rows in set <0.03 sec>
```

Figure B.3 ***Structure of Table Customers***

Usage of the fields

Fields	**Usage**
userid	This field is a unique primary key with the help of which, the customer will be able to log in to our website later. No two users can have the same userid
first_name	It will store the first name of the customer
last_name	It will store the last name of the customer
add1	The address of the customer will be stored in this field
add2	If the address of the customer is large enough and cannot be accommodated in one field: add1, then we may use this field to store the next part of the address
city	Here, the name of the city to which customer belongs will be stored
state	The name of the state to which customer belongs will be stored in this field

zipcode	The zip code of the city to which customer belongs is stored here
emailid	The email address of the customer is stored here to inform him about the shipment details or about new arrivals etc.
password	The password of the customer is stored here. The password may be a collection of characters, digits and symbol and is known to the customer only
phone_no	It will store the phone number of the customer
country	In this field, the country to which customer belongs is stored

The information of the orders placed by the customers is divided in two tables: `orders` and `orders_details`. The `orders` table is used for storing the order number, order date, userid (of the customer placing the order) and the shipping information i.e. the location where the order has to be delivered. In the `order_details` table, the complete information of the ordered products, their item code, item name, quantity ordered and price is stored. The common field among the two tables `orders` and `orders_details` to relate these two tables is order_no.

ORDERS TABLE

`Orders` table is the table where order number, order date, userid and shipping information are stored along with the mode of payment. Its structure is shown in Figure B.4.

```
mysql> describe orders;
+------------------+-------------+------+-----+---------+-------+
| Field            | Type        | Null | Key | Default | Extra |
+------------------+-------------+------+-----+---------+-------+
| order_no         | int<4>      | NO   | PRI | NULL    |       |
| order_date       | date        | YES  |     | NULL    |       |
| userid           | varchar<50> | YES  |     | NULL    |       |
| shipping_address | text        | YES  |     | NULL    |       |
| shipping_city    | varchar<50> | YES  |     | NULL    |       |
| shipping_state   | varchar<50> | YES  |     | NULL    |       |
| shipping_country | varchar<50> | YES  |     | NULL    |       |
| paymode          | varchar<50> | YES  |     | NULL    |       |
| shipping_zipcode | varchar<15> | YES  |     | NULL    |       |
+------------------+-------------+------+-----+---------+-------+
9 rows in set <0.06 sec>
```

Figure B.4 ***Structure of Orders Table***

Usage of the fields

Field	**Description**
order_no	It is the unique integer which is automatically incremented for every new order (beginning from 1) and can be used by the customer for future reference. To get the complete list of items purchased by the customer, this order number is referenced in the `order_details` table
order_date	Here the date on which order is placed is stored
userid	This field is for storing the userid of the customer placing the order

shipping_address	The address where the order has to be delivered is stored in this field
shipping_city	The name of the city to which order has to be delivered is stored here
shipping_state	The name of the state where to deliver the order is stored here
shipping_country	The name of the country where order has to delivered is stored here
paymode	The payment mode of the customer i.e. the details of the card by which payment will be done is stored here. The possible choices are: Master Card, Visa and ANZ Grindlays. Note: We can add more options like Paypal or cheque number etc.
shipping_zipcode	The zip code of the city where delivery of the order will be done is stored here

Orders_Details Table

`Order_Details` is the table where all the information of the items purchased by the customer is stored. All the items belonging to a particular customer bear the same order number. So, if we want to know all the items that are purchased by a particular customer, we first query the Orders table with the given userid and retrieve his order_no. Then, we query the `order_details` table with the given order_no and all the rows with the same order_no are displayed on the screen. That is, the information of all the items (item code, item name, quantity and price) that have the same order_no is displayed on the screen. The order_no is a field common to both tables: `orders` and `orders_details`. Its structure is shown in Figure B.5.

```
mysql> describe orders_details;
+----------------+---------------+------+-----+---------+-----------+
| Field          | Type          | Null | Key | Default | Extra     |
+----------------+---------------+------+-----+---------+-----------+
| order_no       | int<4>        | NO   |     |         |           |
| item_code      | int<4>        | NO   |     |         |           |
| item_name      | varchar<50>   | NO   |     |         |           |
| quantity       | int<4>        | NO   |     |         |           |
| price          | float         | YES  |     | NULL    |           |
+----------------+---------------+------+-----+---------+-----------+
5 rows in set <0.03 sec>
```

Figure B.5 ***Structure of Orders_Details Table***

Usage of the fields

Field	**Usage**
order_no	It is the unique integer which designates all the items purchased by a particular customer. (All items purchased by a particular customer have the same order number). The order_no from the `orders` table is automatically copied in this field
item_code	The item_code of the product selected by the visitor is copied in this field
item_name	The item name of the product purchased is stored in this field
quantity	The quantity of the purchased item is stored here
price	The selling price of the item purchased by the customer is stored in this field

LIST OF PROGRAMS USED IN THE SHOPPING CART PROJECT

The following is a list of PHP programs and their role in the project:

Program name	**Role**
index.php	Displays a welcome screen along with a header at the top and a menu on the left
header.php	Displays the title of our website: `"E-Shopping"` along with an icon of Showcart to display all the items selected in the Shopping Cart
menu.php	Displays a Category dropdown list control to display the different categories of products for sale on our website. It also contains three links: Login, Create Account and Contact Us that invokes login.php, create_account.php and contactus.php program respectively
showitems.php	Displays all the products of the selected category in a tabular format. It also displays a Details link with every product that invokes the program: `itemdetails.php` to display the details of the selected product
itemdetails.php	It displays the details of the product like item code, item name, description and price along with its image of the selected product. It also allows the user to specify the quantity of the selected product to be purchased and includes a button `Add to Cart` which when selected, adds the product into the Shopping Cart
cart.php	Displays the list of the product(s) selected in the cart along with a facility to update its contents. That is, we can change `quantity` of any product in the cart and can even `delete` any product form the cart. It also contains a button to `Empty the Cart` and a button to `Checkout` i.e. to place the order. All the changes made in the cart are reflected in the `cart table`. That is, if the user changes the quantity of any product, the updating will be done in the `cart` table to reflect the changes made. In other words, the contents of the `cart` table are manipulated according to the action taken by the user
showcart.php	It displays the contents of the shopping cart along with the facility to update its contents but the coding to manipulate the `cart` table is not written in this program; instead it invokes the cart.php file to reflect the changes in the `cart` table
checklogin.php	It checks if the user is logged in or not. If not, then he is diverted to either Login program (login.php) or Create an Account program (create_account.php) depending on whether he is already registered on our website or not. If the user is already logged in, he is asked to enter the Shipping Information
create_account.php	It asks the user to enter information like userid, password, name, address, city, state, country, zip code, email address, phone number etc. and passes that information to another PHP program: `adduser.php` for further action

adduser.php	It fetches the information of the user passed by `create_account.php` program and stores it in the `customers` table of `shopping` database. After successful insertion of the customer's information in the `customers` table, this program provides two options to the customer, either to continue shopping or to provide shipping information (if shopping is over)
login.php	It asks the visitor to enter userid and password. If the userid and password are entered correctly, the visitor is greeted with a Welcome message. Also, if his shopping cart is empty, he is given a message to do shopping by selecting items from the menu and if there are some items present in his shopping cart, he is provided with two options to select from: either to do more shopping or supply shipping information (if shopping is over)
shipping_info.php	It fetches the information of the visitor (who is already logged in) like userid, first name, last name, address, city, state, country, zip code, email id, phone number from the `customers` table and displays it on the screen and also asks the user to enter the shipping information i.e. the address, city, state, country, zip code of the location to deliver the order. Also the visitor is asked to enter the mode of payment
purchase.php	This program fetches the shipping information entered by the visitor in shipping_info.php program and stores the information into the orders table. Also the information in the cart table (having details of the individual products selected in the cart) is fetched and stored in `orders_details` table
contactus.php	This program displays the organisation's name, address, phone number and email address to the visitor for future contact

The main file by which the whole project is linked is index.php.

index.php

This program displays a welcome screen along with a header at the top and a menu on the left. It contains the following code:

```
<html>
   <head>
   </head>
   <body>
      <table width="100%" cellspacing="0" cellpadding="5">
         <tr>
            <td colspan=2 align="centre">
               <?php
                  include('header.php');
               ?>
            </td>
         </tr>
```

```
        <tr  align="top">
        <td width="20%">
              <?php
                 include('menu.php');
              ?>
           </td>
        <td width="80% align="centre">
              <h1> Welcome to our Shopping Mall </h1>
              <h2>We provide a wide range of items ranging from luxury
                 items to electronic items</h2>
              Select any item from the menu on left side and enjoy
              amazing Shopping experience
        </td>
        </tr>
     </table>
  </body>
</html>
```

EXPLANATION OF THE PROGRAM ABOVE

This program is for displaying the first page of the website. It consists of three parts: header at the top, menu on the left and a brief introduction to the website on the right.

`include()` statement is used for including and evaluating the specified file in the current page. When we want a particular header or footer or some content to be repeated in every page, we store that content in one file and include that file in every page. When a file is included, the code it contains inherits the variable scope of the line on which the include statement occurs. Any variables available at that line in the calling file will be available within the target file. However, all functions and classes defined in the included file have a global scope.

When a file is included, parsing drops out of PHP mode and into HTML mode at the beginning of the target file, and resumes at the end. So, if the target file contains some PHP code, it must be enclosed between a pair of <?php and ?> tags.

The benefit of using header, footer files for contents which are usually repeated in all pages is that, if we want to alter the contents of heading, we need to make changes in just one file: header file

Note: There is another function called **require()** function which does the same thing i.e. includes the specified file but it results in fatal error in case the specified file is not found. Server Side Includes

Example

<?php require('header.php'); ?>

include_once()

The `include_once()` statement also includes and evaluates the specified file at the place of the call. It is same as `include()` statement, with the difference that if the code from a file has already been included, it will not include it again (target file will be included just once). This statement is used to ensure that a file is included exactly once to avoid problems of function redefinitions, variable value reassignments, etc.

The output of this code is shown in Figure B.6.

Figure B.6 *Output of the Code Given Above*

header.php

This program displays the title of our website: “E-Shopping” along with an icon of “Show Cart” to display all the items selected in the Shopping Cart. Its code is as follows:

```
<html>
    <head>
    </head>
    <body>
        <table width=”100%” cellspacing=”0" cellpadding=”5">
            <tr>
            <td bgcolor=”cyan”><font size=”15" color=”Navy”>
                <b>E-Shopping</b></font>
            </td>
                <td>
                    <a href=”showcart_withmenu.php”><img width=”70"
                        height=”70" src=”images/showcart.jpg”></img></a>
                </td>
            </tr>
        </table>
    </body>
</html>
```

EXPLANATION OF THE PROGRAM ABOVE

The code above just displays the header of the website along with a picture of Show Cart on the right side which when clicked opens the file: showcart_withmenu.php. The output of this code is shown in Figure B.7.

Figure B.7 ***Output of the program header.php***

menu.php

This program displays a Category dropdown list control to display different categories of products available for sale on our website. Beside this, it also displays three links: Login, Create Account and Contact Us that invoke login.php, create_account.php and contactus.php programs respectively. The code of this program is as follows:

```
<html>
    <head>
    </head>
    <body>
        <form action="showitems.php" method="post">
            <table border="0" bgcolor="cyan" cellspacing="10"
                cellpadding="5" align="top">
                <tr>
                <td>Category</td>
                <td><select name="category">
                <option value="" selected>Select Products
                        Category</option>
                <option value="Camera">Camera</option>
                <option value="Mobile">Mobile</option>
                <option value="Book">Book</option>
                    </select>
                </td>
                </tr>
                <tr>
                <td colspan=2 align="center">
                    <input type="submit" name="Submit" value="Search">
                </td>
                </tr>
                <tr>
                <td colspan=2 align="left">
                    <a href="login.php">Login</a>
                </td>
                </tr>
```

```
            <tr>
            <td colspan=2 align="left">
               <a href="create_account.php">Create Account</a>
      </td>
            </tr>
            <tr>
            <td colspan=2 align="left">
               <a href="contact_us.php">Contact Us</a><br><br><br>
               </td>
            </tr>
         </table>
      </form>
   </body>
</html>
```

EXPLANATION OF THE PROGRAM ABOVE

This code displays a combo box and three hyperlinks leading to three different PHP scripts. The combo box is displayed with the help of html <select> tag. The select tag displays different categories of items available for sale on our website like: Camera, Mobile, Book. The category selected by the user is stored in variable: `category`. When the user selects a type of category and clicks the Search button, showitems.php script file is executed. Recall that the "action" points to php script file to be executed on clicking a submit type button and the method decides the array type in which the type of category selected is stored. This means the form will be submitted to "showitems.php" using the HTTP request-method POST.

The `$_POST` variable is an array which stores the variable names and values sent by the HTTP POST method. The `$_POST` variable is used to collect values from a form the information of which is passed with "post" method.

The output of this code is shown in Figure B.8.

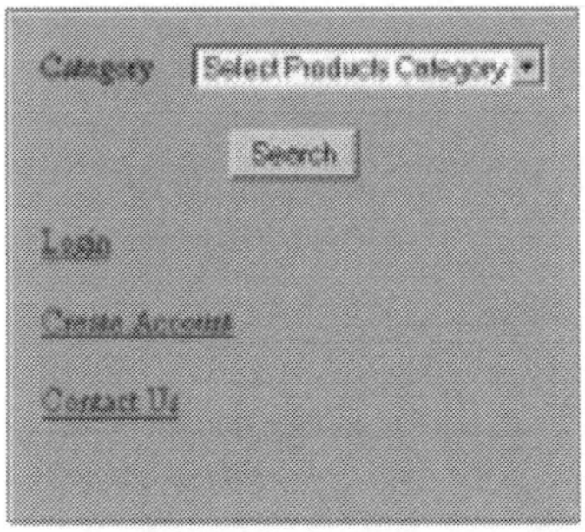

Figure B.8 ***Output of the Program Menu.php***

showitems.php

This program displays all the products of the selected category in a tabular format. It also displays a Details link with every product that invokes the program: itemdetails.php to display the details of the selected product. Its code is as follows:

```
<?php
   include('top.php');
   $connect = mysql_connect("localhost", "root", "mce")
      or die("Please, check your server connection.");
   mysql_select_db("shopping");
   $category=$_POST['category'];
   $query = "SELECT item_code, item_name, description, price " . "FROM
      products " . "where category like '$category' order by
      item_code";
   $results = mysql_query($query) or die(mysql_error());
   echo "<table border=\"1\">";
echo "<th>Item Code</th><th>Name of Item</th><th>Description</th>
   <th> Price</th><th>Details</th>";
   while ($row = mysql_fetch_array($results)) {
      extract($row);
      echo "<tr>";
   echo "<td>";
   echo $item_code;
   echo "</td>";
   echo "<td>";
   echo $item_name;
   echo "</td>";
   echo "<td>";
   echo $description;
   echo "</td>";
   echo "<td>";
   echo $price;
   echo "</td>";
      echo "<td>";
      echo "<a href=itemdetails.php?itmcode=$item_code>";
      echo "Detail";
      echo "</a>";
   echo "</td>";
      echo "</tr>";
   }
   echo "</table>\n";
   include('bottom.php');
?>
```

EXPLANATION OF THE PROGRAM ABOVE

This code first connects with the MySQL server as a user `root`. Then, the `shopping` database is selected and the category of item sent from the menu.php script is accessed from the `$_POST` array and is stored in a variable `$category`. Then an SQL statement is written to retrieve the records from the `products` table belonging to the supplied category. Then, that query is executed and the fetched items from the products table are stored in `$results` array. After that with the help of a `while` loop, one row at a time is fetched from `$results` array and is displayed on the screen in the form of a table. The last column of the table contains a hyperlink: Detail which when selected invokes the itemdetails.php script, and the item_code of the selected product stored in `itmcode` variable is sent along with it.

Note: `include('bottom.php')` and `include('top.php')` statements are used for including and hence displaying the header and menu on this web page.

mysql_connect()

This function is used for establishing a connection to the MySQL database. It returns `true` if the connection is established else `false` is returned. This function takes three parameters, first hostname then user-id and then password.

Syntax:

```
mysql_connect ("$servername","$dbuser","$dbpassword");
```

Example:

```
$connect = mysql_connect("localhost", "root", "mce");
if(!$connect) { die("Please, check your server connection."); }
```

`die` is the command to exit. If `mysql_connect()` returns false then we exit from the PHP scripts using a `die` command after displaying the message: "Please, check your server connection."

This example can also be written as:

```
$connect = mysql_connect("localhost", "root", "mce") or die("Please, check your server connection.");
```

When two statements are connected with the `or` operator, then the second statement is only executed if the first statement returns `false`.

mysql_select_db()

This function is used for selecting a MySQL database to be operated on.

Syntax:

bool mysql_select_db (string $database_name [, resource $link_identifier])

It selects the active database on the server with which connection is established by using a link identifier. If the link identifier is not specified, the last link opened by `mysql_connect()` is assumed. If no such link is found, it will create one by executing `mysql_connect()` with no arguments. An error is displayed if a connection is not established. It returns `true` if the database is found in the MySQL server else `false` is returned.

Examples:

- `mysql_select_db("shopping",$connect);`

- `mysql_select_db("shopping");`

$category=$_POST['category'];

We know that menu.php script has submitted the form using the HTTP request-method POST, so the category of item selected through <select> tag in menu.php script is stored in the variable: `category` and is stored in `$POST` array. That category selected is accessed in showitems.php file and is stored in a variable `$category`.

Note: The name of the form field becomes the ID key in the `$_POST` array.

`mysql_query()`

This function sends the query to the currently active database on the server and the records fetched are stored in an array.

Syntax:

resource mysql_query (string $query [, resource $link_identifier])

link_identifier identifies the connection established with MySQL. If the link identifier is not specified, the last link opened by `mysql_connect()` is assumed. If no such link is found, it tries to create one by executing `mysql_connect()` with no arguments. An error is displayed if a connection is not established.

The returned result resource may be passed to `mysql_fetch_array()`, to display fetched records one by one.

Example:

```
$results = mysql_query($query) or die(mysql_error());
```

`mysql_fetch_array()`

This function is used for fetching one record at a time from the array of records (produced as a result of a query). It gets one row from the recordset and returns `true`, and `false` when there are no more rows left in the recordset. It returns a row from a recordset as an associative array or a numeric array.

Syntax:

row=mysql_fetch_array(data,array_type)

The data pointer is the result from the `mysql_query()` function.

array_type Optional. Specifies what kind of array to return. Its value can be:

MYSQL_ASSOC-	Associative array
MYSQL_NUM-	Numeric array
MYSQL_BOTH-	Default. Both associative and numeric array

Note: After the data is retrieved, this function moves to the next row in the recordset. Each subsequent call to `mysql_fetch_array()` returns the next row in the recordset.

Example:

```
$row = mysql_fetch_array($results)
```

One record is extracted from the recordset `$results` and is stored in variable: `$row`.

extract()

This function is used for extracting all the variables stored in the specified array (or record).

Syntax:

extract(array name)

Example:

```
extract($row);
<a href=itemdetails.php?itmcode=$item_code>
```

This statement shows a hyperlink: "Detail" which when selected invokes itemdetails.php script and the item_code of the selected product stored in itmcode field is sent along with it. The item_code sent can be retrieved in itemdetails.php script using the `$_REQUEST` array.

The output of the code above is shown in Figure B.9. We select a `Category` type and click the **`Search`** button.

Figure B.9 ***Selection of product category***

The items of the selected category are retrieved from the `products` table of the `shopping` database and displayed in the form of a table (Figure B.10).

itemdetails.php

This program displays the details of the product (of which detail link is selected by the visitor) like item code, item name, description and price along with its image. It also allows the user to specify the quantity to be purchased of the selected product and also includes a button Add to Cart which when selected, adds the product into the Shopping Cart. The code of this program is:

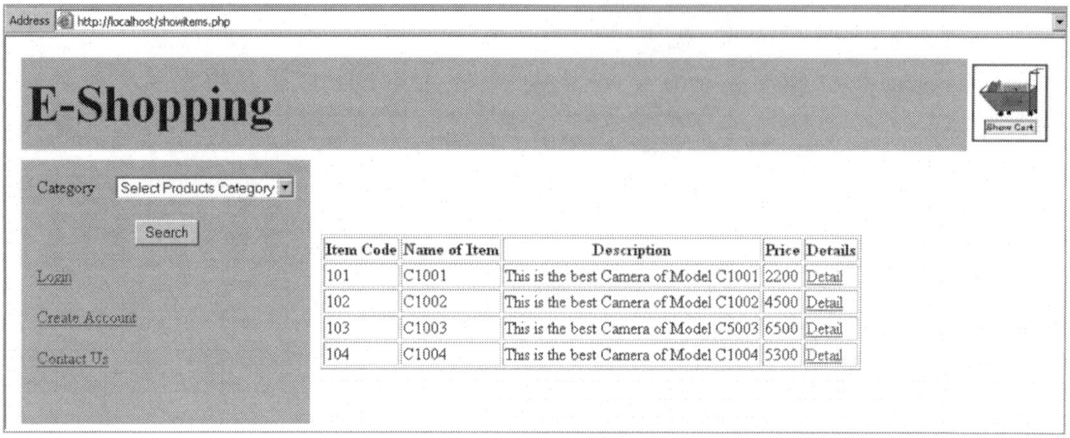

Figure B.10 ***Items are Displayed in the Form of a Table***

```
<?php
    include(‘top.php’);
    $connect = mysql_connect(“localhost”, “root”, “mce”) or die(“Please,
        check your server connection.”);
    mysql_select_db(“shopping”);
    $code=$_REQUEST[‘itmcode’];
    $query = “SELECT item_code, item_name, description, imagename,
        price” . “FROM products “ . “where item_code=$code”;
    $results = mysql_query($query) or die(mysql_error());
    echo “<table border=\”1\”>”;
echo “<th>Item Code</th><th>Name of Item</th><th>Description</th>
    <th>Price</th><th>Enter Quantity</th>”;
    $row = mysql_fetch_array($results);
    extract($row);
    echo “<tr>”;
    echo ‘<img width=”140" height=”170" src=’ . $imagename . ‘></img>’;
    echo “</tr>”;
    echo “<tr>”;
   echo “<td>”;
   echo $item_code;
   echo “</td>”;
    echo “<td>”;
   echo $item_name;
   echo “</td>”;
   echo “<td>”;
   echo $description;
   echo “</td>”;
   echo “<td>”;
```

```
  echo $price;
  echo "</td>";
?>
<form method="POST" action="cart.php?action=add&icode=<?php echo
   $item_code ?>&iname=<?php echo $item_name ?>&iprice=<?php echo
   $price?>">
   <td>
      <input type="text" name="qty" size="2">
   </td>
   </tr>
   </table>
   <input type="submit" name="Submit" value="Add to cart">
</form>
<?php
   include('bottom.php');
?>
```

EXPLANATION OF THE PROGRAM ABOVE

First we establish a connection to the MySQL server followed by selecting the `shopping` database. The itmcode field containing the item_code sent by showitems.php script (whose details are required) is retrieved using `$_REQUEST` array and is stored in `$code` variable. The details of the product of supplied itemcode consisting of item_code, item_name, description, imagename and price are retrieved from the `products` table and stored in `$row` array. The product fields are extracted from `$row` array and are displayed in the form of a table. In the last column of the table, a textbox is provided to enter the quantity to be purchased of the item selected. The quantity entered by user is stored in `qty` field and is sent to cart.php script along with item_code, item_name and price of the item when the user clicks the Add to cart button. Also, action field set to value "add" is sent to cart.php to add the item to the cart. The action may be set to "add", "change", "delete" or "empty" in order to add item to cart, modify quantity of an item in the cart, delete an item from the cart or to empty the cart.

Note: `include('bottom.php')` and `include('top.php')` statements are used for including and hence displaying the header and menu on this web page.

The output of this code is shown in Figure B.11.

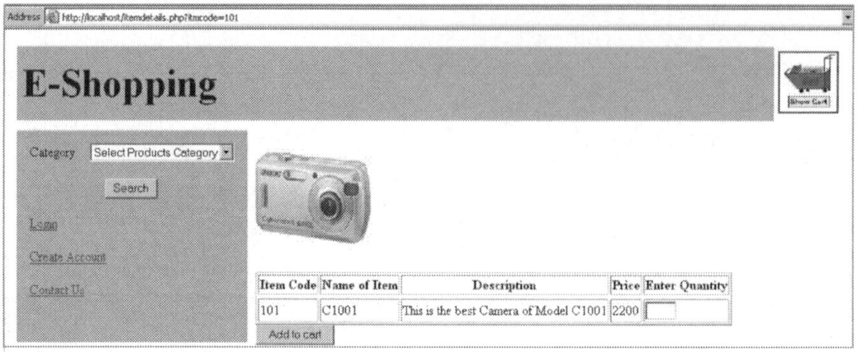

Figure B.11 *Output of Item_details.php*

The user can enter the quantity of the selected item to purchase and click **Add to cart** button (Figure B.12).

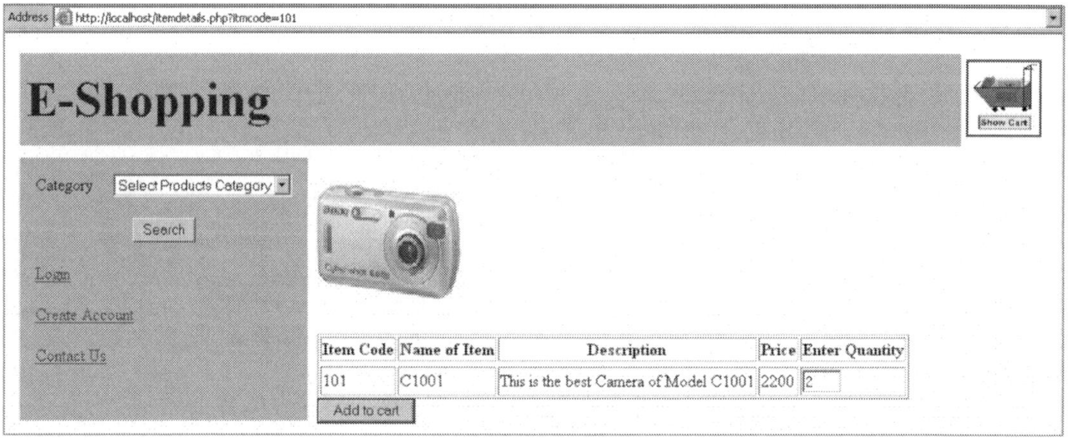

Figure B.12 *Enter the Quantity Required and Click on Add to Cart Button*

cart.php

This program displays the list of the product(s) selected in the shopping cart along with a facility to update its contents. That is, we can change the quantity of any product present in the cart and can even delete any product from the cart (if we change our minds). It also contains two more buttons: `Empty the Cart` and `Checkout` used for erasing all the products from the Shopping Cart and to place the order respectively. All the changes made in the cart are reflected in the `cart` table. That is, if the user changes the quantity of any product, the updating will be done in the `cart` table to reflect the changes made. In other words, the contents of the `cart` table are manipulated according to the action taken by the user. The code in this program is as follows:

```
<?php
   include('top.php');
```

```
session_start();
$connect = mysql_connect("localhost", "root", "mce") or die("Please, check
   the server connection.");
mysql_select_db("shopping");
$qty = trim($_POST['qty']);
if ($qty=='')
{
   $qty=1;
}
if($qty <=0)
{
   echo "Quantity value is invalid ";
   echo "Go Back and enter a valid value";
}
else
{
   if (isset($_REQUEST['icode'])) {
      $itmcode = $_REQUEST['icode'];
   }
   if (isset($_REQUEST['iname'])) {
      $item_name = $_REQUEST['iname'];
   }
   if (isset($_REQUEST['iprice'])) {
      $price = $_REQUEST['iprice'];
   }
   if (isset($_POST['modified_qty'])) {
      $modified_qty = $_POST['modified_qty'];
   }
   $sess = session_id();
   $action = $_REQUEST['action'];

   switch ($action) {
      case "add":
         $query="select * from cart where cart_sess = '$sess' and " .
            "cart_itmcode=$itmcode";
         $result = mysql_query($query) or die(mysql_error());
         if(mysql_num_rows($result)==1)
         {
            $row=mysql_fetch_array($result);
            $qt=$row['cart_qty'];
            $qt=$qt+$qty;
            $query="UPDATE cart set cart_qty=$qt where cart_sess = '$sess'
               " . "and cart_itmcode=$itmcode";
            $result = mysql_query($query)  or die(mysql_error());
         }
         else
```

```
        {
        $query = "INSERT INTO cart (cart_sess, cart_qty, cart_itmcode,
              cart_item_name, cart_price) VALUES ('$sess',$qty,$itmcode,
              '$item_name', $price)";
        $message = "<div align=\"center\"><strong>Item added.</strong>
              </div>";
        }
    break;

    case "change":
        if($modified_qty==0)
        {
        $query = "DELETE FROM cart WHERE cart_sess = '$sess' " . "and
              cart_itmcode=$itmcode";
        $message = "<div align='center'><strong>Item deleted.</strong>
              </div>";
        }
        else
        {
            if($modified_qty <0)
            {
                echo "Invalid quantity entered";
            }
            else
            {
            $query = "UPDATE cart SET cart_qty = '$modified_qty'  WHERE
                  cart_sess = '$sess' " . "and cart_itmcode=$itmcode";
            $message = "<div align='center'><strong>Quantity changed.
                  </strong> </div>";
            }
        }
    break;

    case "delete":
    $query = "DELETE FROM cart WHERE cart_sess = '$sess' " . "and
          cart_itmcode=$itmcode";
    $message = "<div align='center'><strong>Item deleted.</strong>
          </div>";
    break;

    case "empty":
    $query = "DELETE FROM cart WHERE cart_sess = '$sess'";
    $message = "<div align='center'><strong>Cart emptied.</strong>
          </div>";
break;
}
```

```
        $results = mysql_query($query) or die(mysql_error());
        echo $message;
        include("showcart.php");
    }
    include('bottom.php');
?>
```

EXPLANATION OF THE PROGRAM ABOVE

The program begins by starting the session as the session id will be used to remember the items selected in the cart of the particular user. Then, a connection with the MySQL server is established and the `shopping` database file is selected. The quantity of the item purchased (stored in `qty` field) is retrieved from `$_POST` array. If the user has not filled any quantity, default quantity set is 1. Also, it is confirmed that the quantity entered is a non-negative number. The item code, item name, and price (stored in fields: icode, iname and iprice) sent from the itemdetails.php script are retrieved using `$_REQUEST` array and stored in variables: `$itmcode`, `$item_name` and `$price`. A session is generated and stored in `$sess` variable. This session id is assigned to the cart as id to know the items selected by a particular user. The value of the action field is retrieved and checked to see what operation has to be carried on to the cart. If the action is "add" then we first check that whether the user has already selected that item or not. If that item is already added to the cart, then just its quantity is updated. If the item is fresh, then a new entry is made in the cart table.

session_start()

It initialises session data. It creates a session or resumes the current one based on the current session id that's being passed via a request, such as GET, POST, or a cookie.

Syntax:

bool session_start (void)

This function always returns TRUE. If we want to use a named session, we must call `session_name()` before calling `session_start()`.

A session is a combination of a server-side file containing all the data we wish to store, and a client-side cookie containing a reference to the server data. The file and the client-side cookie are created using the function `session_start()`. It has no parameters, but informs the server that sessions are going to be used.

When we call `session_start()`, PHP checks to see whether the visitor sent a session cookie - if yes, PHP loads the session data. Otherwise, PHP creates a new session file on the server, and sends an ID back to the visitor to associate the visitor with the new file. Because each visitor has their own data locked away in their unique session file, we need to call `session_start()` before we try to read session variables. As `session_start()` needs to send the reference cookie to the user's computer, we write this statement before the body of our web page - even before any spaces.

Since HTTP is a stateless protocol, the interaction between browsers and web servers is stateless. Each HTTP request a browser sends to a web server is independent of any other request. The stateless nature of HTTP allows users to browse the web by following hypertext links and visiting pages in any order. HTTP also allows applications to distribute or even replicate content across multiple servers to balance the load generated by a high number of requests. These features are possible because of the stateless nature of HTTP.

But sometimes, we need to remember certain data between web pages like what are the items added to his cart by a particular user, his areas of interest etc. That is, we need to remember all the items added in cart while requesting order page, for this purpose session management is preferred. In other words, stateful web database applications can be built using sessions.

session_id()

This function is used to get or set the session id for the current session.

Syntax:

string session_id ([string $id])

`session_id()` returns the session id for the current session or the empty string ("") if there is no current session (no current session id exists).

id

If id is specified, it will replace the current session id. `session_id()` needs to be called before `session_start()` for that purpose.

Note: When using session cookies, specifying an id for `session_id()` will always send a new cookie when `session_start()` is called, regardless of whether the current session id is identical to the one being set.

isset()

This function determines whether a variable is set.

Syntax:

bool isset (variable/variable list)

If a variable has been unset with `unset()` or is set to NULL, the function returns `false`.

If multiple parameters are supplied then `isset()` will return `true` only if all of the parameters are set. Evaluation goes from left to right and stops as soon as an unset variable is encountered.

`mysql_num_rows()`

This function is used to find out how many rows are returned in a recordset (on execution of a SELECT statement in a SQL query).

Syntax:

int mysql_num_rows (recordset)

recordset is nothing but the records retrieved as a result of the `mysql_query()` function. This function returns `false` on failure.

`mysql_affected_rows()`

This function is used to find out how many rows are affected by a DELETE, INSERT, REPLACE, or UPDATE statement executed in an SQL query.

The output of this code is shown in Figure B.13.

showcart.php

This program displays the contents of the shopping cart along with the facility to update its contents but this program does not manipulate the `cart` table; instead it invokes the cart.php file which in turn updates the contents of the cart table depending on the parameter passed by this program. The parameter passed by this program to cart.php depends on the action taken by the visitor. The code of this program is as follows:

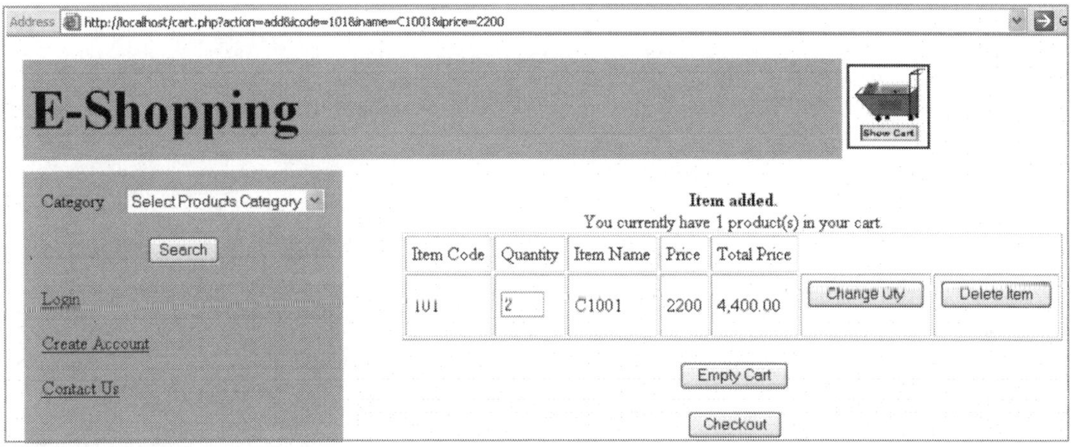

Figure B.13 ***Output of cart.php***

```
<?php
   if (!session_id()) {
      session_start();
   }
   $connect = mysql_connect("localhost", "root", "mce") or die ("Please, check
      your server connection.");
   mysql_select_db("shopping");
?>
<html>
   <head>
      <title>Shopping Cart</title>
   </head>
   <body>
      <div align="center">
```

```
<?php
   $sessid = session_id();
   $query = "SELECT * FROM cart WHERE cart_sess = '$sessid'";
   $results = mysql_query($query) or die (mysql_query());
   if(mysql_num_rows($results)==0)
   {
      echo "Your Cart is empty ";
   }
   else
   {
      echo "You currently have ";
      $rows = mysql_num_rows($results);
      echo $rows . " ";
      ?>
      product(s) in your cart.<br>
      <table border="1" align="center" cellpadding="5">
      <tr>
      <td> Item Code</td>
   <td>Quantity</td>
   <td>Item Name</td>
   <td>Price</td>
   <td>Total Price</td>
      <?php
         while ($row = mysql_fetch_array($results)) {
            extract($row);
            echo "<tr>";
            echo "<td>";
            echo $cart_itmcode;
            echo "</td>";
   echo "<td> <form method=\"POST\" action= \"cart.php?
      action=change &icode=$cart_itmcode\"> <input
      type=\"text\" name=\"modified_qty\" size=\"2\"
      value=\"$cart_qty\">";
            echo "</td>";
            echo "<td>";
            echo $cart_item_name;
            echo "</td>";
            echo "<td>";
            echo $cart_price;
            echo "</td>";
            echo "<td>";
            $totprice = number_format($cart_price * $cart_qty, 2);
            echo $totprice;
            echo "</td>";
            echo "<td>";
```

```
                    echo "<input type=\"submit\" name=\"Submit\" value=
                       \"Change Qty\"> </form></td>";
                    echo "<td>";
                    echo "<form method=\"POST\" action=\"cart.php?
                       action=delete&icode=$cart_itmcode\">";
                    echo "<input type=\"submit\" name=\"Submit\" value=
                       \"Delete Item\"> </form></td>";
                    echo "</tr>";
                 }
              ?>
              </table>
              <form method="POST" action="cart.php?action=empty">
                 <input type="submit" name="Submit" value="Empty Cart">
              </form>
              <form method="POST" action="checklogin.php">
                 <input type="submit" name="Submit" value="Checkout">
              </form>
        </body>
     </html>
  <?php
  }
  ?>
```

EXPLANATION OF THE PROGRAM ABOVE

The program checks whether session id is already set or not. If not, a new session is started. A connection to the MySQL server is established and the `shopping` database is selected. We execute an SQL query to check if there is already a cart with the given session id, if yes, then all the items stored in the cart along with the number of items in that cart are displayed and if not, the user is informed that he has 0 products selected in his cart.

The user can add more items to the cart by selecting a category of item from the menu on the left. He can also modify the quantity of any item, delete an item or empty the cart by selecting the buttons: Change Qty, Delete Item and Empty Cart respectively. The user can also Checkout if he has finished shopping.

The user can select more items to purchase by selecting the category of item from the menu on the left. On selecting the category Mobile, all the items under Mobile category are retrieved from the `products` table and displayed in the form of a table (Figure B.14).

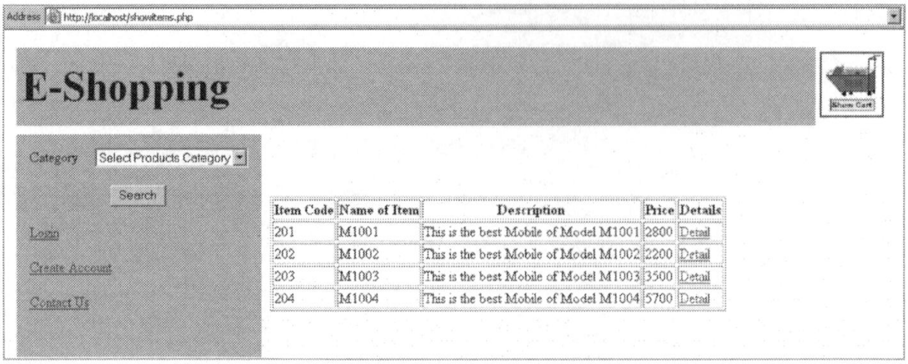

Figure B.14 ***Products List in Mobile Category***

On selecting Detail link of any item, the details of the item along with the image are displayed on the screen. We are prompted to enter the quantity of the item selected (Figure B.15).

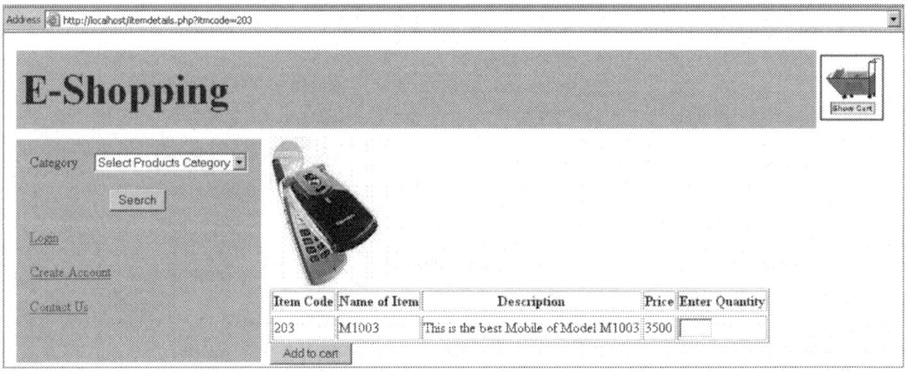

Figure B.15 ***Detailed Information of Any Particular Item***

We can enter any quantity of the item selected and select **Add to cart** button (Figure B.16).

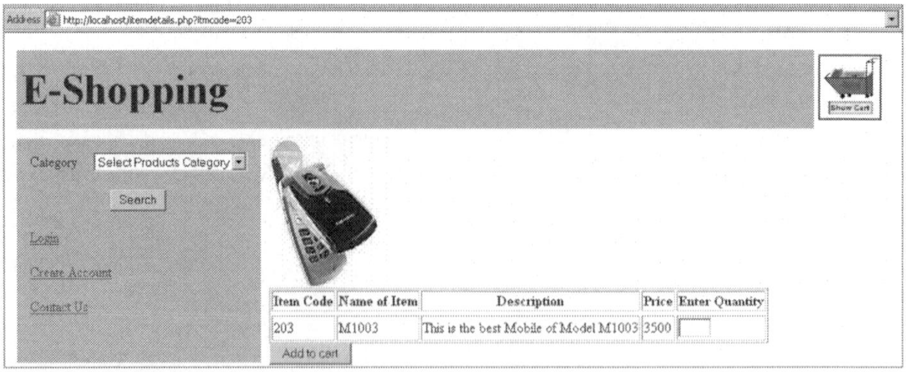

Figure B.16 ***Enter the Quantity and Click Add to Cart Button***

All the items added to the cart are displayed together (Figure B.17).

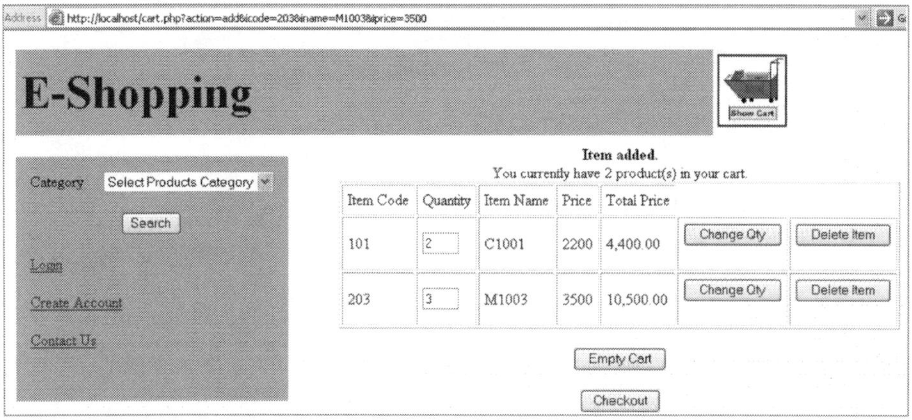

Figure B.17 ***Display of All the Items Selected***

If we want to change the quantity of the first item selected in the cart from 2 to 1, we can edit the value in the textbox and press `Change Qty` button (Figure B.18).

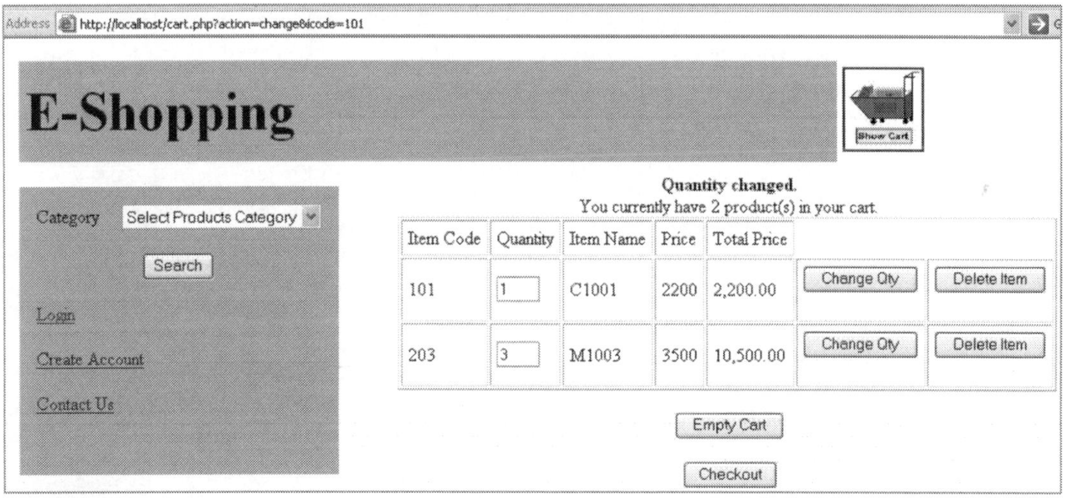

Figure B.18 ***Alteration in the Quantity and Clicking Change Qty Button***

We can also delete any item from the cart by just selecting **Delete Item** button of that respective item (Figure B.19).

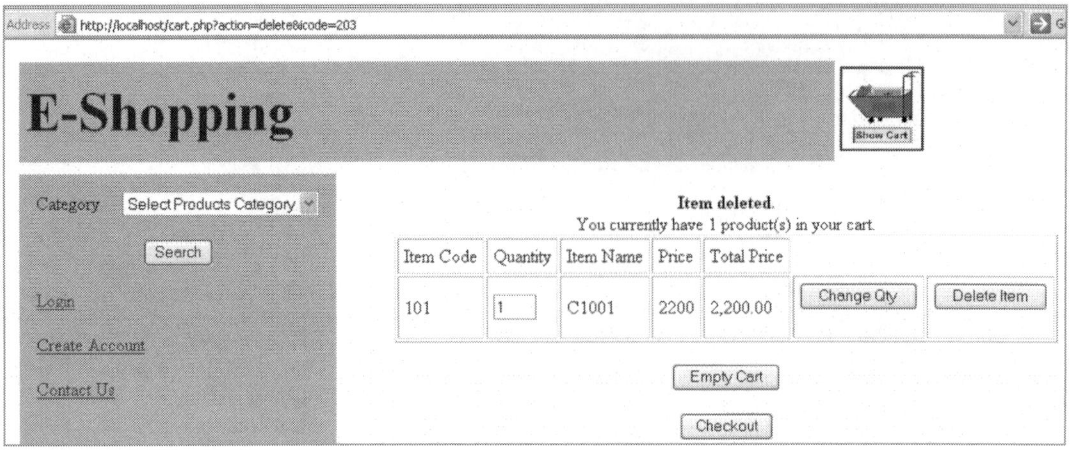

Figure B.19 ***Deletion of An Item***

checklogin.php

This program checks whether the user is logged in or not. If he is not yet logged in, then he is diverted to either Login program (login.php) - if he is already registered on our website or Create an Account program (create_account.php) – if he is not registered. If the user is already logged in, he is asked to enter the Shipping Information where the order has to be shipped. The code of this program is as follows:

```
<?php
   include('top.php');
   session_start();
   $connect = mysql_connect("localhost", "root", "mce")  or die("Please,
      check the server connection.");
   mysql_select_db("shopping");
   $uid=$_SESSION['userid'];
   $pwd=$_SESSION['password'];
   if ((isset($_SESSION['userid']) && $_SESSION['userid'] != "") ||
      (isset($_SESSION['password']) && $_SESSION['password'] != "")) {
      $sess = session_id();
      $query="select * from cart where cart_sess = '$sess'";
      $result = mysql_query($query) or die(mysql_error());
      if(mysql_num_rows($result)>=1)
      {
         echo "If you have finished Shopping ";
      echo "<a href=shipping_info.php>Click Here</a> to supply
            Shipping Information";
         echo "Or You can do more purchasing by selecting items from
            the menu ";
      }
```

```
        else
        {
            echo "You can do purchasing by selecting items from the menu
            on left side";
        }
    }
    else
    {
    ?>
        <html>
            <head>
            </head>
            <body>
                <h3>Not Logged in yet</h1>
                <p>
                You are currently not logged into our system.<br>
                You can do purchasing only if you are logged in.<br>
                If you have already registered,
                <a href="login.php">click here</a> to login,
                    or if would like to create an account,
                <a href="create_account.php">click here</a> to register.
                </p>
            </body>
        </html>
    <?php
    }
        include('bottom.php');
?>
```

EXPLANATION OF THE PROGRAM ABOVE

First the session is started. Recall that a session is a combination of a server-side file containing all the data we want to store about the visitor and a client-side cookie containing a reference to the server data. The file and the client-side cookie are created using the function `session_start()`. The function informs the server that sessions are used. When we call `session_start()`, PHP checks to see whether the user has sent a session cookie. If yes, PHP loads the session data. Otherwise, PHP creates a new session file on the server, and send an ID back to the user to associate him with the new file. As every user has their respective data stored in their unique session file, we should call `session_start()` before reading session variables. After that, a connection to the MySQL server is established and the `shopping` database is selected. The userid and password in the `$_SESSION` array are retrieved (if they are set by any web page earlier). The `$_SESSION` array elements can only be set in case the user is registered and has logged in otherwise its elements are not set. If the userid and password is set in `$_SESSION` array i.e. if the user is already logged in then he is provided with two options: first to provide Shipping Information if he has finished shopping and second to continue shopping by selecting the category of item from the menu on the left. But in case the userid and password are not set in $_SESSION array, then the user is asked either to log in or create an account if he is not registered. The output of above given code is shown in Figure B.20.

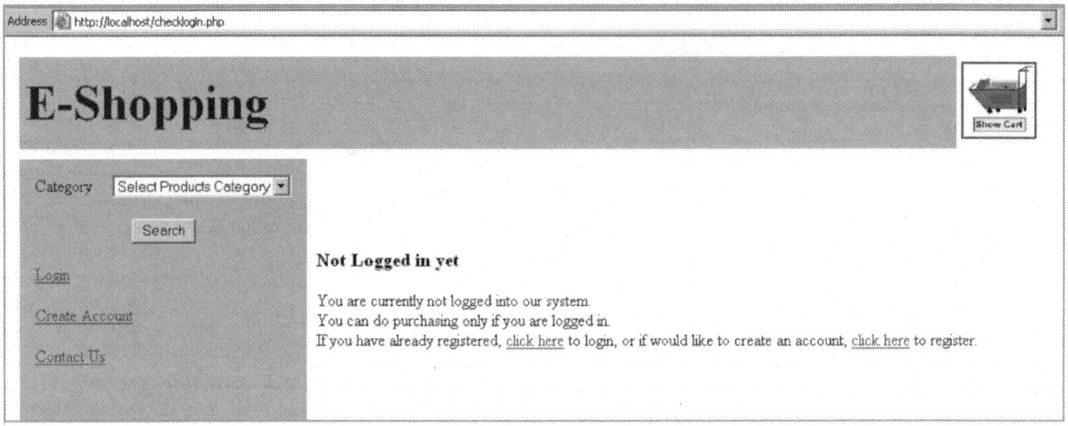

Figure B.20 *Output of the Program checklogin.php*

create_account.php

This program displays a series of textboxes and asks the user to enter information like userid, password, name, address, city, state, country, zip code, email address, phone number etc. and passes that information to another PHP program: adduser.php for further action. The code of this program is as shown:

```
<?php
   include('top.php');
   session_start();
   $conn = mysql_connect("localhost", "root", "mce") or die("Could not
      connect: " . mysql_error());
   mysql_select_db("shopping", $conn) or die (mysql_error());
?>
<html>
   <head>
   </head>
   <body>
      <form action="adduser.php" method="post">
         <table border="0" cellspacing="1" cellpadding="3">
            <tr><td>Userid: </td><td> <input size="20" type="text"
               name="userid"></td></tr>
            <tr><td>Password: </td><td>  <input size="20"
               type="password" name="password"></td></tr>
            <tr><td>ReType Password:  </td><td> <input size="20"
               type="password" name="repassword"></td></tr>
```

```
            <tr><td>First Name: </td><td> <input size="30" type="text"
               name="first_name"></td></tr>
            <tr><td>Last Name: </td><td> <input size="30" type="text"
               name="last_name"></td></tr>
            <tr><td>Address1: </td><td> <input size="80" type="text"
               name="add1"></td></tr>
            <tr><td>Address2: </td><td> <input size="80" type="text"
               name="add2"></td></tr>
            <tr><td>City: </td><td> <input size="30" type="text"
               name="city"></td></tr>
            <tr><td>State: </td><td> <input size="30" type="text"
               name="state"></td></tr>
            <tr><td>Country: </td><td> <input size="30" type="text"
               name="country"></td></tr>
            <tr><td>Zip Code: </td><td> <input size="20" type="text"
               name="zipcode"></td></tr>
            <tr><td>Email Id: </td><td> <input size="30" type="text"
               name="emailid"></td></tr>
            <tr><td>Phone No: </td><td> <input size="30" type="text"
               name="phone_no"></td></tr>
            <tr><td><input type="submit" name="submit" value="Submit">
               </td><td><input type="reset" value="Cancel"></td></tr>
         </table>
      </form>
   </body>
</html>
<?php
include('bottom.php');
?>
```

EXPLANATION OF THE PROGRAM ABOVE

First the session is started. After that, a connection to the MySQL server is established and the `shopping` database is selected. Several textboxes are displayed for the user to feed userid, password, first name, last name, address, city, state, country, zipcode, email id and phone number. The data entered by the user are stored in respective fields and are passed to the adduser.php script. The form in the above script is submitted to "adduser.php" using the HTTP request-method POST. Recall that `$_POST` is an array which stores the variable names and values sent by the HTTP POST method. In adduser.php script, the information is retrieved from `$_POST` array. The output of the code above is a blank form (Figure B.21).

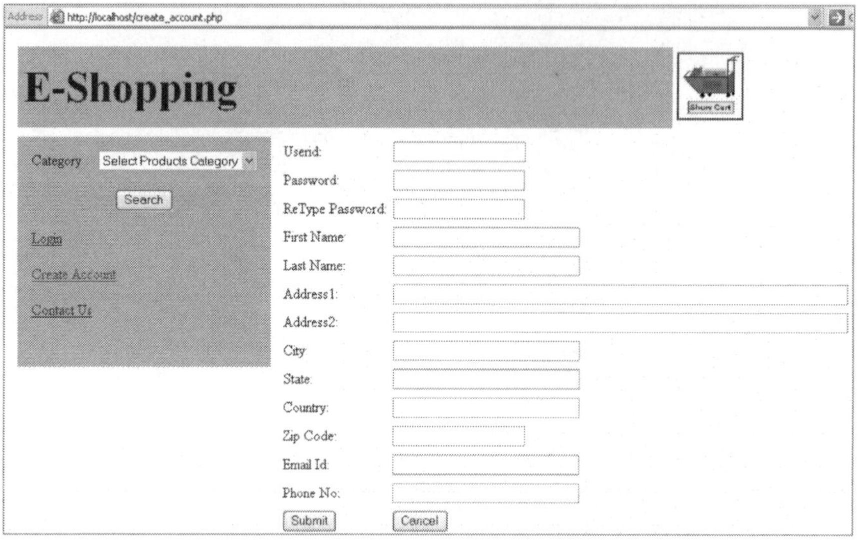

Figure B.21 *Output of the program Create_Account.php*

adduser.php

This program fetches the information of the user passed by create_account.php program and inserts it in the `customers` table of shopping database. After successful insertion of the customer's information in the `customers` table, this program provides two options to the customer, either to continue shopping or to provide shipping information (if shopping is over). The code of this program is as follows:

```
<?php
   include('top.php');
   session_start();
   connect = mysql_connect("localhost", "root", "mce") or die ("Please,
      check the server connection.");
   sql_select_db("shopping");
   userid = $_POST['userid'];
   password = $_POST['password'];
   repassword = $_POST['repassword'];
   first_name = $_POST['first_name'];
   last_name = $_POST['last_name'];
   add1 = $_POST['add1'];
   add2 = $_POST['add2'];
   city = $_POST['city'];
   state = $_POST['state'];
   country = $_POST['country'];
   zipcode = $_POST['zipcode'];
   emailid = $_POST['emailid'];
```

```
phone_no = $_POST['phone_no'];
if($password==$repassword)
{
   $sql = "INSERT INTO customers (userid, password, first_name,
      last_name, add1, add2, city, state, country, zipcode, emailid,
      phone_no) VALUES ('$userid',(PASSWORD('$password')),
      '$first_name','$last_name','$add1','$add2','$city', '$state',
      '$country','$zipcode','$emailid','$phone_no')";
   $result = mysql_query($sql) or die(mysql_error());
   $_SESSION['userid'] = $_POST['userid'];
$_SESSION['password'] = $_POST['password'];
   ?>
   <p>Dear, <?php echo $_POST['first_name'] . " " .
$_POST['last_name']; ?> your account is successfully created
<br>
   <?php
      $_SESSION['userid'] = $_POST['userid'];
   $_SESSION['password'] = $_POST['password'];
      $sess = session_id();
      $query="select * from cart where cart_sess = '$sess'";
      $result = mysql_query($query) or die(mysql_error());
      if(mysql_num_rows($result)==1)
      {
         echo "If you have finished Shopping ";
      echo "<a href=shipping_info.php>Click Here</a> to supply
            Shipping Information";
         echo "Or You can do more purchasing by selecting items from
            the menu ";
      }
      else
      {
         echo "You can do purchasing by selecting items from the
            menu on left side";
      }
   }
   else
   {
      echo "Your Passwords do not match, Try again";
   ?>
      <form action="adduser.php" method="post">
      <table border="0" cellspacing="1" cellpadding="3">
      <tr><td>Userid: </td><td> <input size="20" type="text"
         name="userid" value="<?php echo $userid ?>"></td></tr>
      <tr><td>Password: </td><td>  <input size="20" type="password"
         name="password"></td></tr>
      <tr><td>ReType Password:  </td><td> <input size="20"
```

```
            type="password" name="repassword"></td></tr>
        <tr><td>First Name:  </td><td> <input size="30" type="text"
            name="first_name"  value="<?php echo $first_name ?>"></td>
        </tr>
        <tr><td>Last Name:  </td><td> <input size="30" type="text"
            name="last_name"  value="<?php echo $last_name ?>"></td>
        </tr>
        <tr><td>Address1:  </td><td> <input size="80" type="text"
            name="add1"  value="<?php echo $add1 ?>"></td></tr>
        <tr><td>Address2:  </td><td> <input size="80" type="text"
            name="add2"  value="<?php echo $add2 ?>"></td></tr>
        <tr><td>City:  </td><td> <input size="30" type="text"
            name="city"  value="<?php echo $city ?>"></td></tr>
        <tr><td>State:  </td><td> <input size="30" type="text"
            name="state"  value="<?php echo $state ?>"></td></tr>
        <tr><td>Country:  </td><td> <input size="30" type="text"
            name="country"  value="<?php echo $country ?>"></td></tr>
        <tr><td>Zip Code:  </td><td> <input size="20" type="text"
            name="zipcode"  value="<?php echo $zipcode ?>"></td></tr>
        <tr><td>Email Id:  </td><td> <input size="30" type="text"
            name="emailid"  value="<?php echo $emailid ?>"></td></tr>
        <tr><td>Phone No:  </td><td> <input size="30" type="text"
            name="phone_no"  value="<?php echo $phone_no ?>"></td></tr>
    <tr><td> <input type="submit" name="submit" value="Submit">
    </td><td> <input type="reset" value="Cancel"></td></tr>
    </table>
</form>
<?php
}
    include('bottom.php');
?>
```

EXPLANATION OF THE PROGRAM ABOVE

The session is started and a connection to the MySQL server is established. The `shopping` database is selected. The information of the user sent by create_account.php script in the form of `$_POST` array is retrieved and stored in different variables. The data in password and ReType Password fields are compared. If they are not the same, the user is shown an error message: "Your Passwords do not match, Try again" and is asked to feed them again. If the Password and ReType Password are identical, then an SQL statement to insert a record in `customers` table is executed and the user is informed about his successful account creation and is offered two options: first to supply Shipping information if he has finished shopping and second to continue shopping by selecting the category of item from the menu on the left. The output of this code is a blank form (Figure B.22).

The user can feed his details. The only thing to remember is that the Password and ReType Password fields should both have the same contents.

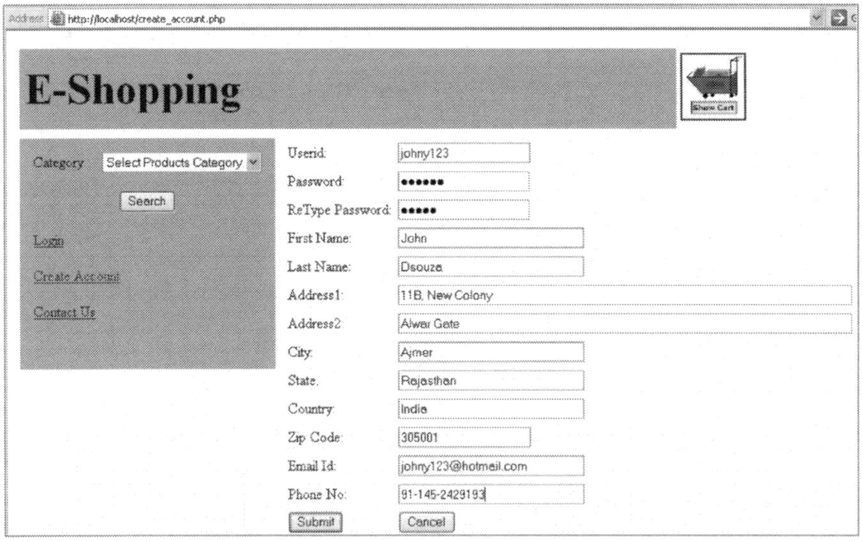

Figure B.22 ***Output of the program adduser.php. Password and ReType Password fields Should Have Identical Contents***

If the contents of Password and ReType Password fields do not match, we get an error message: `Your Passwords do not match. Try again` (Figure B.23) and the visitor is asked to fill them again.

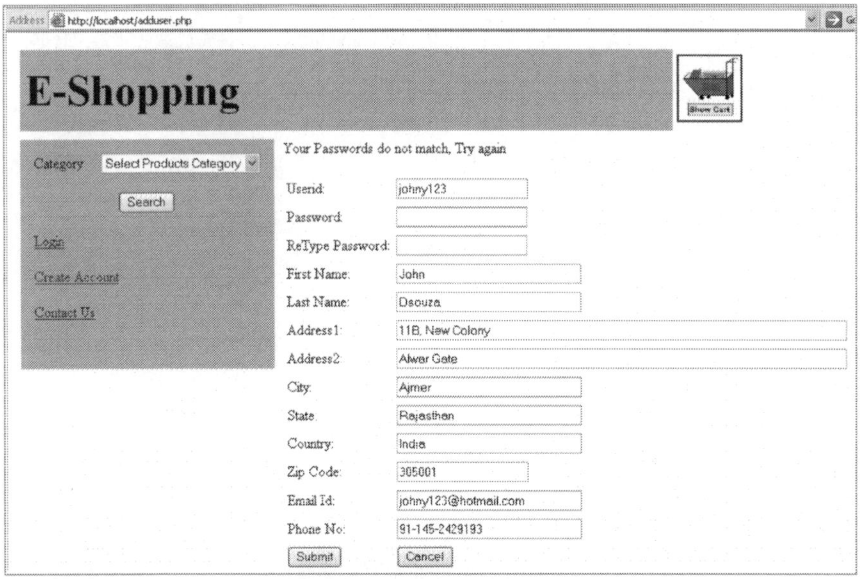

Figure B.23 ***Refilling Both the Fields as They Did not Match***

Let us enter the user information correctly and select `Submit` button (Figure B.24).

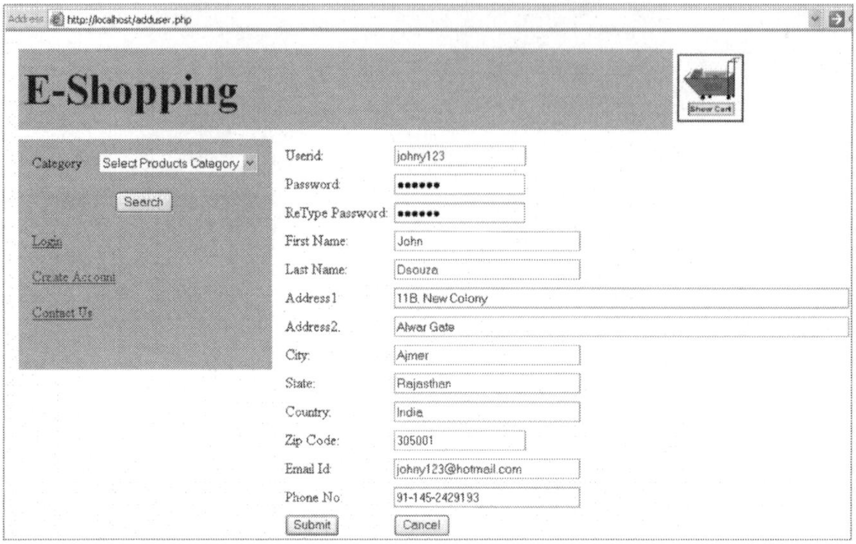

Figure B.24 *Selection of Submit Button*

If the information is properly filled and Password and ReType Password field contents are exactly the same, we get the message of successful account creation (Figure B.25).

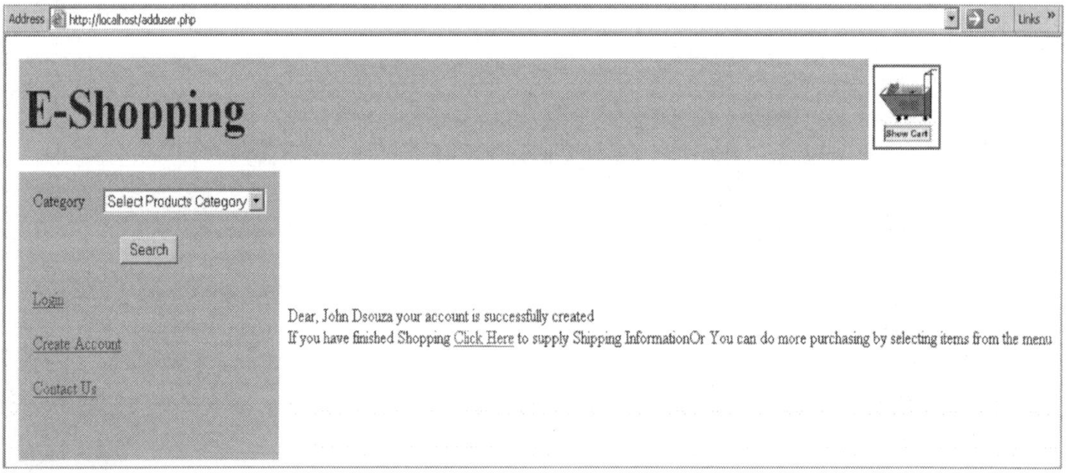

Figure B.25 *Successful Account Creation*

login.php

This program prompts the visitor to login by entering userid and password. If the userid and password are entered correctly, the visitor is greeted with a `Welcome` message else a message `"Invalid Username and/or Password"` is displayed and the visitor is asked to Create his account. If the login is successful and the shopping cart of the visitor is still empty, he is given a message to do shopping by selecting different categories of items from the menu. If the visitor has already selected some items in his shopping cart, he is provided with two options to select from: either to do more shopping or to supply shipping information (if shopping is over). The code of this program is as shown:

```
<?php
   include('top.php');
   session_start();
   $connect = mysql_connect("localhost", "root", "mce") or die("Please,
      check the server connection.");
   mysql_select_db("shopping");
   if (isset($_POST['submit'])) {
      $query = "SELECT userid, password FROM customers " . "WHERE
         userid like '" . $_POST['userid'] . "' " . "AND password like
         (PASSWORD('" . $_POST['password'] . "'))";
      $result = mysql_query($query) or die(mysql_error());
      if (mysql_num_rows($result) == 1) {
      $_SESSION['userid'] = $_POST['userid'];
      $_SESSION['password'] = $_POST['password'];
         echo "Welcome " . $_POST['userid'] . " to our Shopping Mall
            <br>";
         $sess = session_id();
         $query="select * from cart where cart_sess = '$sess'";
         $result = mysql_query($query) or die(mysql_error());
         if(mysql_num_rows($result)>=1)
         {
            echo "If you have finished Shopping ";
         echo "<a href=shipping_info.php>Click Here</a> to supply
               Shipping Information";
            echo "Or You can do more purchasing by selecting items from
               the menu ";
         }
         else
         {
            echo "You can do purchasing by selecting items from the
               menu on left side";
         }
      }
      else {
      ?>
         <html>
            <head>
            </head>
            <body>
               Invalid Username and/or Password<br>
               Not registered?
               <a href="create_account.php">Click here</a> to
                  register.<br> <br><br>
               Want to Try again<br>
```

```
            <a href="login.php">Click here</a> to try login
               again.<br>
         </body>
      </html>
   <?php
   }
}
else
{
?>
   <form action="login.php" method="post">
      <table border="0" cellspacing="1" cellpadding="3">
      <tr>
      <td>Userid:</td><td> <input type="text"
            name="userid"></td></tr>
      <tr>
         <td>Password:</td><td> <input type="password"
            name="password"></td></tr>
      <tr>
      <td colspan=2 align="center">
         <input type="submit" name="submit" value="Login">
      </td>
      </tr>
      </table>
   </form>
   <?php
}
include('bottom.php');
?>
```

EXPLANATION OF THE PROGRAM ABOVE

This script is executed when the user selects the login option (if he is already registered). A session is started. A connection to the MySQL server is established and the `shopping` database is selected. If a submit button is not set that is when this script is executed for the first time then two textboxes are provided to the user to feed in userid and password. After feeding the userid and password, the user is prompted to click a submit type button. On doing this, the same script i.e. login.php is executed. When login.php executes itself, this time submit button is set. If a submit button is set, an SQL query is executed to see whether any record exists in the customers table with the supplied userid and password. If yes, then the session variables are set. By using the statements: $_SESSION['userid'] = $_POST['userid']; and $_SESSION['password'] = $_POST ['password']; the array elements of `$_SESSION` array are set and the logged in userid and password values are stored in it. A Welcome message is displayed on the screen. The `cart` table is searched to find if there is any record with the given session id (i.e. whether the user has added something to his cart or not). If there is any record in the cart then the user is asked to either supply Shipping Information or to continue purchasing.

But if the user has not selected anything in the cart then he is advised to continue shopping by selecting the category of the item from the menu on the left.

If in the `customers` table we don't find any record with the supplied userid and password, then a message: "Invalid Username and/or Password" is displayed and the user can either select the option to try again or to create an account.

shipping_info.php

This program fetches the information of the visitor (who is already logged in) like his userid, first name, last name, address, city, state, country, zip code, email id and phone number from the `customers` table and displays it on the screen and also asks the user to enter the shipping information i.e. the address, city, state, country, zip code of the location where the order has to be delivered. The visitor is also asked to specify the mode of payment. The code of this program is as shown:

```
<?php
    include('top.php');
    session_start();
    $connect = mysql_connect("localhost", "root", "mce") or die("Please,
        check your server connection.");
    mysql_select_db("shopping");
    $uid=$_SESSION['userid'];
    $pwd=$_SESSION['password'];
    if ((isset($_SESSION['userid']) && $_SESSION['userid'] != "") ||
    (isset($_SESSION['password']) && $_SESSION['password'] != "")) {
        $query = "SELECT * FROM customers " . " where userid like '$uid'
            and " . "password like (PASSWORD('$pwd'))";
        $results = mysql_query($query) or die(mysql_error());
        $row = mysql_fetch_array($results);
        extract($row);
        ?>
        <form action="purchase.php" method="post">
            <table border="0" cellspacing="1" cellpadding="3">
                <tr><td>Userid:</td><td> <input size="20" type="text"
                    name="userid" value="<?php echo $userid; ?>"></td></tr>
                <tr><td>First Name: </td><td> <input size="30" type="text"
                    name="first_name" value="<?php echo $first_name;?>">
                </td></tr>
                <tr><td>Last Name: </td><td> <input size="30" type="text"
                    name="last_name" value="<?php echo $last_name; ?>">
                </td></tr>
                <tr><td>Address1:  </td><td> <input size="80" type="text"
                    name="add1" value="<?php echo $add1; ?>"></td></tr>
                <tr><td>Address2:  </td><td> <input size="80" type="text"
                    name="add2" value="<?php echo $add2; ?>"></td></tr>
                <tr><td>City:  </td><td> <input size="30" type="text"
                    name="city" value="<?php echo $city; ?>"></td></tr>
                <tr><td>State:  </td><td> <input size="30" type="text"
```

```
            name="state" value="<?php echo $state; ?>"></td></tr>
         <tr><td>Country: </td><td> <input size="30" type="text"
            name="country" value="<?php echo $country; ?>">
         </td></tr>
         <tr><td>Zip Code: </td><td> <input size="20" type="text"
            name="zipcode" value="<?php echo $zipcode; ?>">
         </td></tr>
         <tr><td>Email Id: </td><td> <input size="30" type="text"
            name="emailid" value="<?php echo $emailid;?>"></td></tr>
         <tr><td>Phone No: </td><td> <input size="30" type="text"
            name="phone_no" value="<?php echo $phone_no;?>">
         </td></tr>
         <tr><td colspan=2 align="center">Shipping Information
         </td> </tr>
         <tr><td>Address to deliver at:</td><td> <input type="text"
            size="80" name="ship_add"></td></tr>
         <tr><td>City: </td><td> <input size="30" type="text"
            name="ship_city"></td></tr>
         <tr><td>State: </td><td> <input size="30" type="text"
            name="ship_state"></td></tr>
         <tr><td>Country: </td><td> <input size="30" type="text"
            name="ship_country"></td></tr>
         <tr><td> Zip Code: </td><td> <input type="text" size="20"
            name="ship_zipcode"></td></tr>
         <tr><td>Payment Mode:</td><td><input type="radio" name=
            "paymode" value="Credit Card" checked> Credit Card<br>
         <input type="radio" name="paymode" value="Cheque">
            Cheque</td></tr>
         <tr><td><input type="submit" name="submit" value="Submit">
         </td><td> <input type="reset" value="Cancel"></td></tr>
      </table>
   </form>
   <?php
   }
 include('bottom.php');
?>
```

EXPLANATION OF THE PROGRAM ABOVE

A session is started. A connection is established with the MySQL server and the `shopping` database is selected. The userid and password which were entered during the log in operation (which were stored in `$_SESSION` array) are retrieved and stored in `$uid` and `$pwd` variables. An SQL statement is executed to retrieve all the details of the customer like first_name, last_name, address1, address2, city, state, country, zipcode, emailid, phone_no from the `customers` table and are displayed on the screen. After that the user is asked to supply Shipping Information i.e. where the product has to be delivered. The user has to fill in address, city, state, country, zipcode of the place where items have to be delivered and also the payment mode i.e. whether he will pay through credit card or by cheque. When the user clicks the submit button, all the information is passed to purchase.php script for further processing. The output of this code is shown in Figure B.26.

purchase.php

This program fetches the shipping information entered by the visitor in shipping_info.php program and stores the information in the **orders** table. Also the information in the **cart** table (details of the individual products selected in the cart) is fetched and stored in **orders_details** table. The code for this program is shown below:

```
<?php
    include(‘top.php’);
    session_start();
    $connect = mysql_connect(“localhost”, “root”, “mce”) or die (“Please,
        check the server connection.”);
    mysql_select_db(“shopping”);
    $ship_add = $_POST[‘ship_add’];
    $ship_city = $_POST[‘ship_city’];
    $ship_state = $_POST[‘ship_state’];
    $ship_country = $_POST[‘ship_country’];
    $ship_zipcode = $_POST[‘ship_zipcode’];
    $paymode = $_POST[‘paymode’];
```

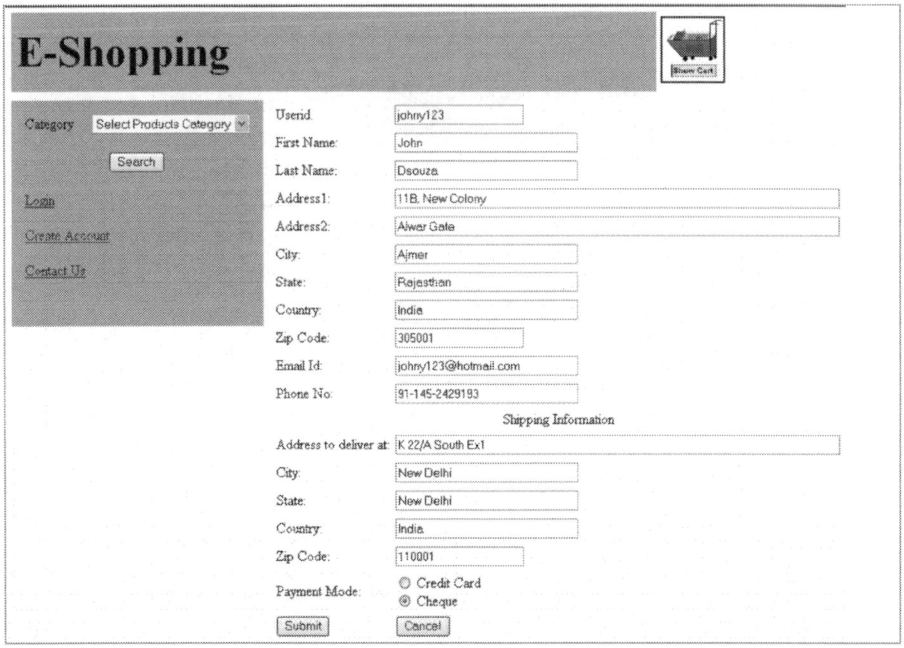

Figure B.26 ***Output of the Program shippinginfo.php***

```
    $userid= $_SESSION['userid'] ;
    $today = date("Y-m-d");
    $sessid = session_id();
    $sql = "INSERT INTO orders (
       order_date, userid, shipping_address, shipping_city,
       shipping_state, shipping_country, shipping_zipcode, paymode)
       VALUES ('$today','$userid','$ship_add','$ship_city',
       '$ship_state', '$ship_country','$ship_zipcode','$paymode')";
    $result = mysql_query($sql)  or die (mysql_error());
    $orderid = mysql_insert_id();
    $query = "SELECT * FROM cart WHERE cart_sess='$sessid'";
    $results = mysql_query($query)  or (mysql_error());
    while ($row = mysql_fetch_array($results)) {
       extract($row);
       $sql2 = "INSERT INTO orders_details ( order_no, item_code,
          item_name, quantity, price) VALUES ($orderid,$cart_itmcode,
          '$cart_item_name', $cart_qty,$cart_price)";
       $insert = mysql_query($sql2) or die (mysql_error());
    }
    $query = "DELETE FROM cart WHERE cart_sess='$sessid'";
    $delete = mysql_query($query);
    echo "Your order is accepted and we will deliver it soon<br>";
    echo "Please, remember your Order number is $orderid<br>";
    session_destroy();
    include('bottom.php');
?>
```

EXPLANATION OF THE PROGRAM ABOVE

A session is started. A connection to the MySQL server is established and the `shopping` database is selected. The shipping information like shipping address, city, state, country, zip code and payment mode entered by the user in shipping_info.php script is retrieved from `$_POST` array and an SQL statement is executed to store that information in the `orders` table along with the system date (the date shopping was done). In the `orders` table a primary key field is made, order_no, which is of integer type and which is set to auto_increment mode (its value is automatically incremented by 1 on insertion of every record) with the help of the following statement:

```
$orderid = mysql_insert_id();
```

The id i.e. order_no of the inserted record in the `orders` table is retrieved and is stored in `$orderid` variable. (This order number is added to each item in the `orders_details` table in order to know all the items that have been purchased with a particular order number).

All the records in the `cart` table with the given session id (of the same user) are extracted one by one and stored in the `orders_details` table. After that all the items from the `cart` table with the given session id are deleted. The user is given a message of "Order Acceptance" and the order id is displayed for future communication. At the end the session is destroyed. The output of this code is shown in Figure B.27.

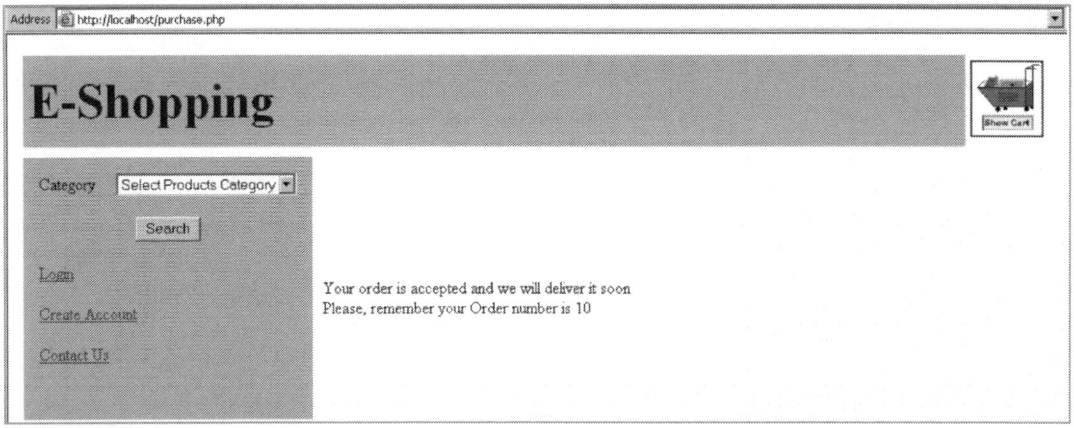

Figure B.27 *Output of the Program purchase.php*

contact_us.php

This program displays the website organisation's name, address, phone number and email address on the screen so that the visitor can contact the organisation in future. The code in this program is as shown below:

```
<?php
   include('top.php');
?>
<html>
   <head>
   </head>
   <body>
      <h2> For amazing Shopping Experience </h2>
      You can contact us at following address: <br><br>
      <b>PHP Shopping Cart Site<br>
      Microchip Computer Education (MCE)<br>
      Sri Nagar Road, Ajmer <br>
      (Rajasthan) India <br>
      Phone: 91-0145-2429193, 2627312 <br><br>
      Email:
         <a href="mailto:bmharwani@yahoo.com">bmharwani@yahoo.com</a>
   </body>
</html>
<?php
   include('bottom.php');
?>
```

showcart_withmenu.php

This program is executed when the "Show Cart" icon in the header of the web site is selected. This program in turn invokes the showcart.php along with top.php and bottom.php programs as shown below:

showcart_withmenu.php

```
<?php
include('top.php');
include('showcart.php');
include('bottom.php');
?>
```

The working of showcart.php program, we have just seen. The top.php is a program that includes the header.php and the menu.php programs to display the header of our web site and the menu on the left side. Since the header and menu are required in every web page, the top.php program is included in almost all the PHP programs of our web site. The code in top.php is as shown below:

```
top.php
<html>
<head>
    </head>
    <body>
        <table width="100%" cellspacing="0" cellpadding="5">
        <tr>
            <td colspan=2 align="centre">
                <?php
                    include('header.php');
                ?>
            </td>
        </tr>
        <tr>
        <td valign="top" width="20%">
                <?php
                    include('menu.php');
                ?>
        </td>
    <td width="80%">
```

We can see that top.php includes the header.php and menu.php nested inside the table i.e. it makes use of <table>, <tr> and <td> elements to display the header at the top and the menu on left side. The bottom.php is meant for closing all the tags that were opened by top.php like: <table>, <tr> and <td> tags. The code in bottom.php is as shown below:

bottom.php

```
</td>
</tr>
</table>
</body>
</html>
```

Appendix C

Shopping Cart Project in AJAX

With AJAX (Asynchronous JavaScript and XML) technology, as we know, we can request and receive data from the server in the background and can display the response on the page without a reload, making the web application highly responsive. In AJAX, JavaScript communicates directly with the server with the help of the JavaScript XMLHttpRequest object (XML over HTTP). Using an XMLHttpRequest object, a web page can make a request to, and get a response from a web server without reloading the page.

The first screen on execution of our Shopping Cart site (AJAX based) that we get is shown in Figure C.1.

Figure C.1 *First Screen on Execution of Shopping Cart site*

We can see in the initial screen of the website that at the top is a header which contains the title of our website: E-Shopping and a `Show cart` icon at the top right corner (handy tool for the user to know what has been selected in the cart up till now). On the left is a menu that displays the category of items available for sale on our website. We can choose any Category from the dropdown list to get the list of products under that category. Beside that, there are links provided for the user to `create an account`, `login` to the website and a link "`Contact Us`" to supply email id and address of the organisation to the user (to be used for future communication).

If we select a category say "`Camera`" to see all the products falling in the Camera category, we get the output as shown in Figure C.2. This time after selecting the Category of product from the dropdown list, we don't have to select `Search` button as we used to do in the simple Shopping Cart we saw earlier. Instead, we get the list of products of the selected category immediately on selecting a category from the Category dropdown list.

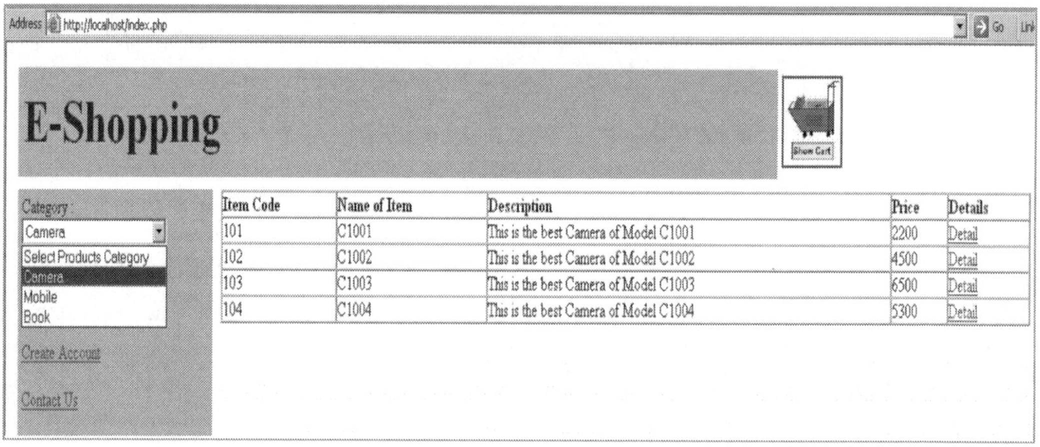

Figure C.2 ***Selection of Camera Category***

We can see in the list of products that on every row (product), there is a link: "`Detail`". The `Detail` link on the right of each product is meant for displaying more information on the selected product. If we select the `Detail` link of the product say with item code=101, we may get the output as shown in Figure C.3. We can see that the complete information of the selected product along with its image is displayed on the screen.

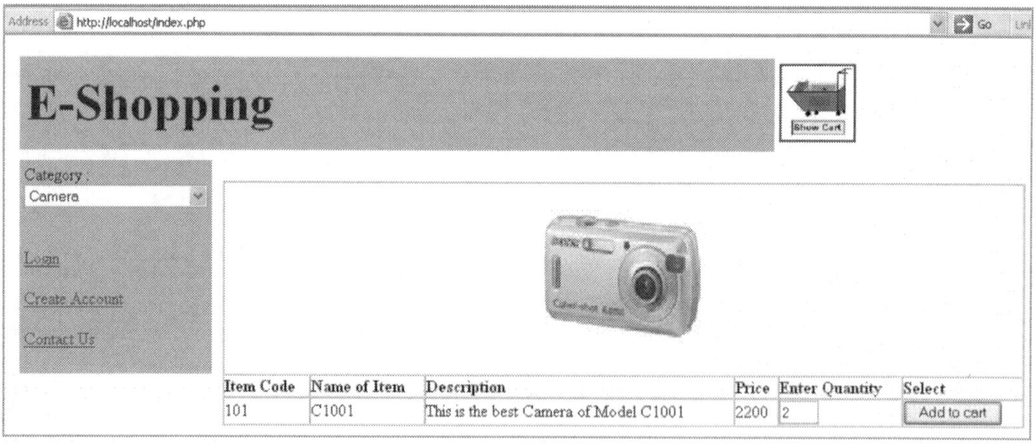

Figure C.3 ***Detailed Information About a Selected item***

The textbox under the heading "Enter Quantity" is to enter what quantity of the selected product we want to purchase. If we leave it blank and click the Add to cart button, the default quantity of the selected product (assumed to be purchased) is 1. Suppose we want to purchase 2 pieces of product 101, we enter value 2 in the textbox and then click the Add to cart button. The selected item along with the entered quantity is added to the cart.

Suppose we want to purchase more. Let us see all the items under the Book category (i.e. all the books that are available for sale on our website). On selecting the Book category from the dropdown list, we get the list of all the books (Figure C.4).

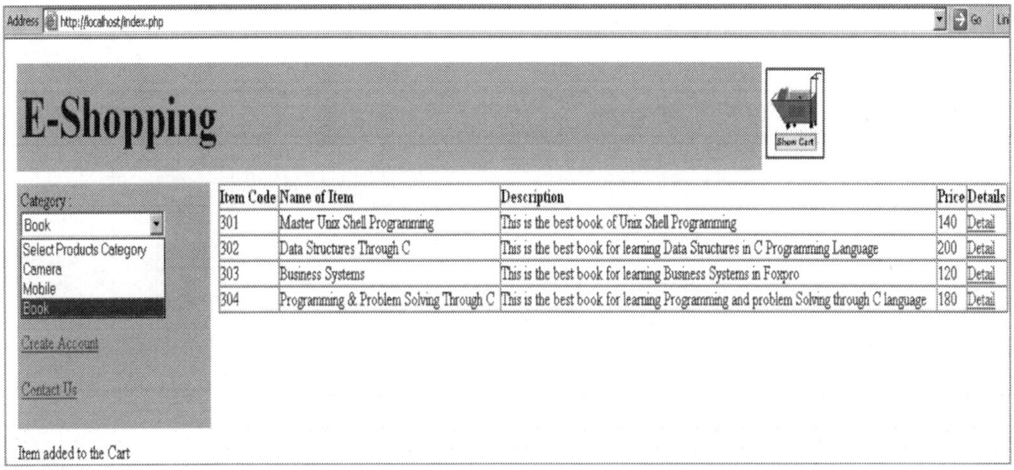

Figure C.4 ***List of all the Books on Sale***

We can see the details of any item by selecting the Detail link on its right. Suppose we want to see the complete information of the book with code 301, we select its "Detail" link and get the details of the selected book along with its image (Figure C.5).

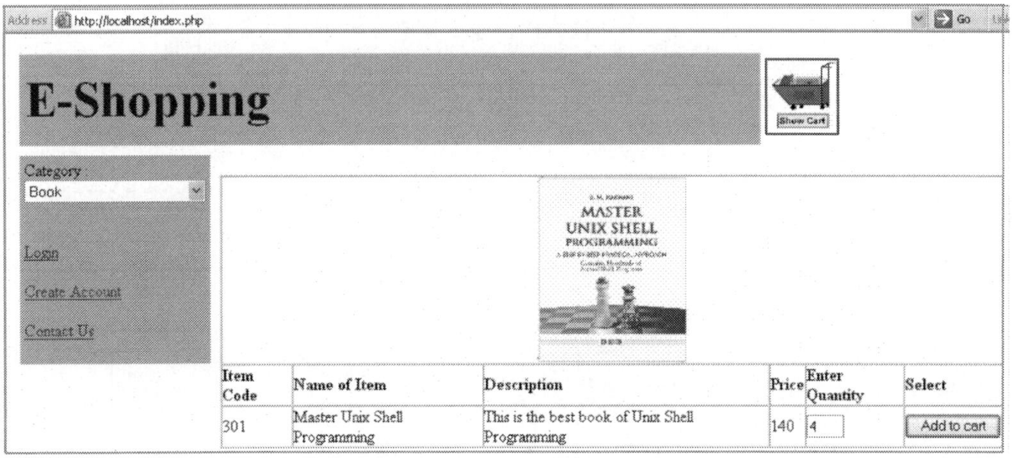

Figure C.5 ***Description of the Book Selected***

Again the textbox under the heading "`Enter Quantity`" is for specifying the quantity of the selected product we want to purchase (default value is `1`). Let us specify the quantity for this product as `4` and click the `Add to cart` button. The selected item will be added to the cart.

To see how many items have been added to our Shopping Cart so far, we select the "`Show Cart`" icon at the top and get all the items currently present in the shopping cart (Figure C.6). We can see in the figure that to every product (row) in the Shopping cart, attached is a `Quantity` textbox and two buttons: `Delete Cart` and `Update Cart`. Clicking the `Delete Cart` button of any product (row) will erase that product from the Shopping Cart. To update the quantity of any product, we need to insert the desired quantity in its `Quantity` textbox and click the `Update Cart` button.

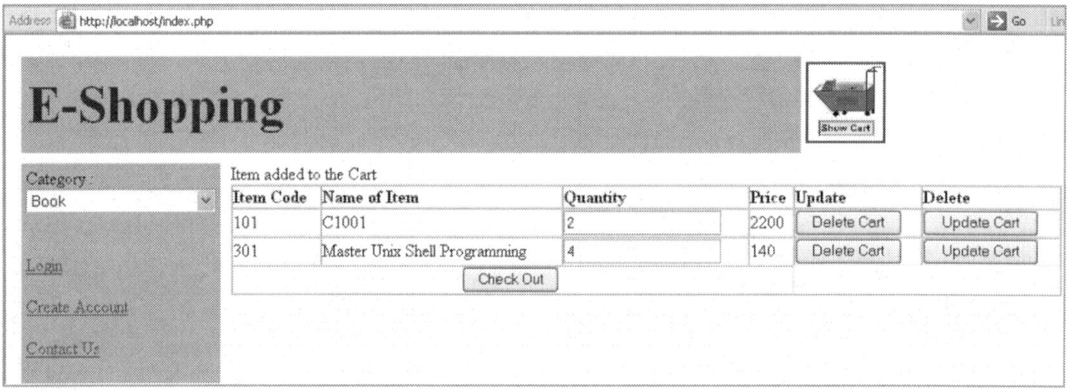

Figure C.6 ***List Displayed of all Selected Items as Add to Cart Icon is Clicked***

Let us try deleting the product with item name: "`C1001`" from the Shopping Cart. On clicking the `Delete Cart` button of the row with Name of Item=C1001, the product will be removed from the Shopping Cart and the updated Shopping Cart will be displayed (Figure C.7).

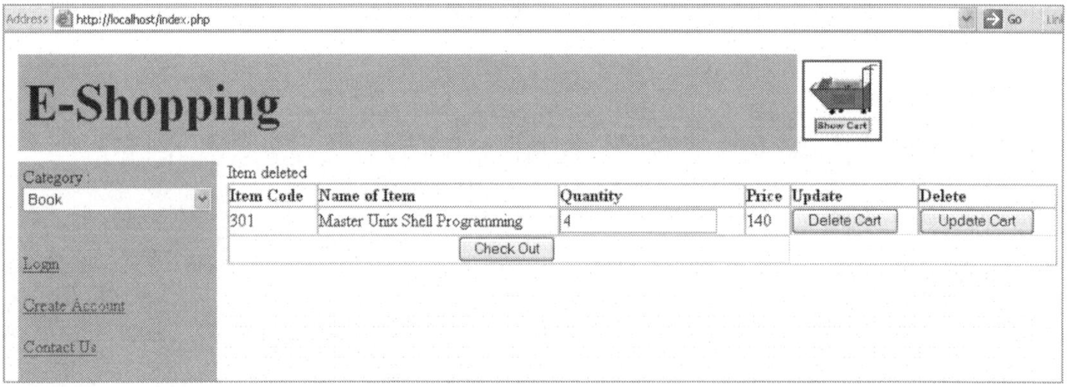

Figure C.7 ***Deletion of an Item Name***

We are left with only one product in the Shopping Cart with item code: 301. The `quantity` of this product at present is `4` (i.e. we are interested in purchasing 4 pieces of this product). Let us update the quantity of this product from 4 to 2. We need to change the value from 4 to 2 in the `Quantity` textbox of this product followed by clicking the "`Update Cart`" button. Our shopping cart will be updated and may appear as shown in Figure C.8.

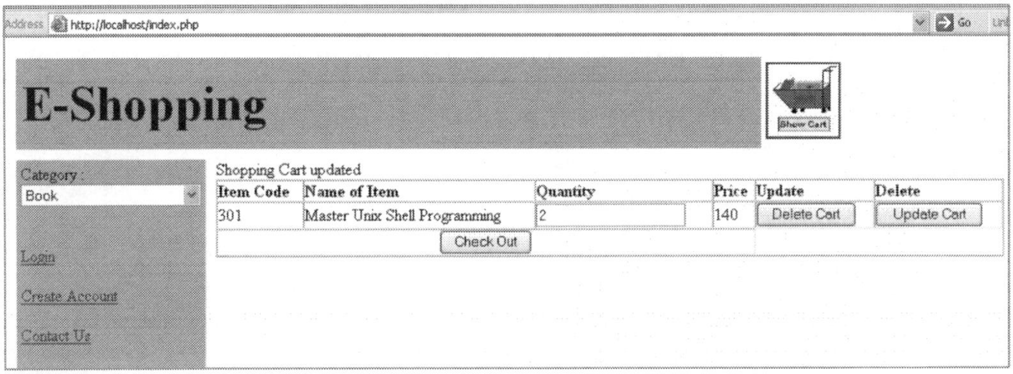

Figure C.8 ***Updating of the Quantity of the Product***

If we have finished choosing items, we can click the `Check Out` button. The most important thing that we need to remember while visiting this website is our login status i.e. whether we are logged in before beginning choosing items on the website or not. If we have created our account on the website earlier (by using the `Create Account` link from the menu) and are currently logged in, then by clicking the `Check Out` button, user information like name, address, contact number etc. will be automatically fetched and displayed and we need to just supply shipping information (location where order has to be delivered). But if we are not logged in yet, we will get the following message on the screen (Figure C.9). The message is:

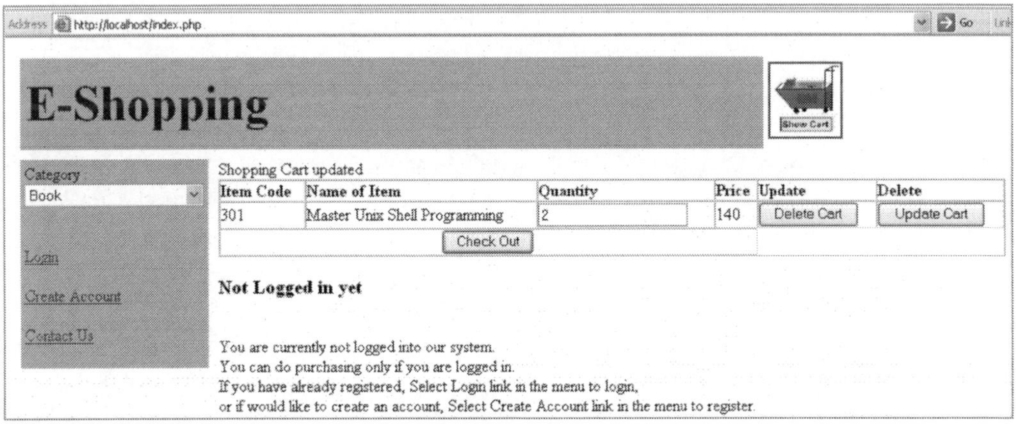

Figure C.9 ***Screen if User is Not Logged in Yet***

Not Logged in yet

You are currently not logged into our system.

You can do purchasing only if you are logged in.

If you have already registered, Select Login link in the menu to login, or if would like to create an account, Select Create Account link in the menu to register

If the user has not created an account earlier, he is prompted to do that first. And if he has already created an account before, he will be prompted to login. If we select the `create account` link, we get a screen to fill in user details (Figure C.10). The screen consists of several textboxes where the user has to specify information like userid (used for login), Password, Re-Type password, first name, last name, address1, address2 (in case address is large), city, state, country, zip code, email id and phone number.

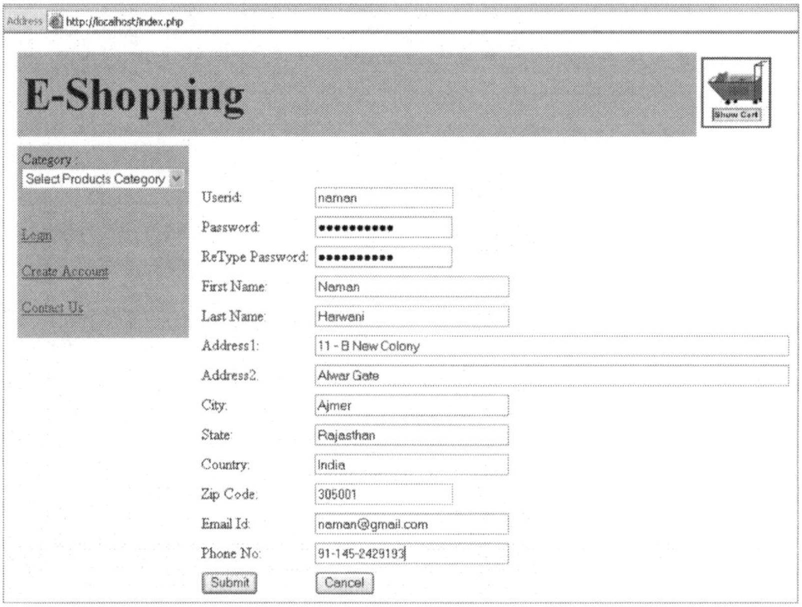

Figure C.10 ***Screen for Create-Account Link***

While filling in the form, proper care has to be taken while filling the two fields: `Password` and `ReType Password`. They must be identical. If the contents of both the fields don't match, the user is displayed an error message (Figure C.11).

Figure C.11 ***Error Message When Password and ReType Password don't Match***

Let us enter the desired information in the textboxes and exactly the same password in both the fields and select `Submit` button. We get a message that the `Account is Created` and the visitor can now login to our website (Figure C.12).

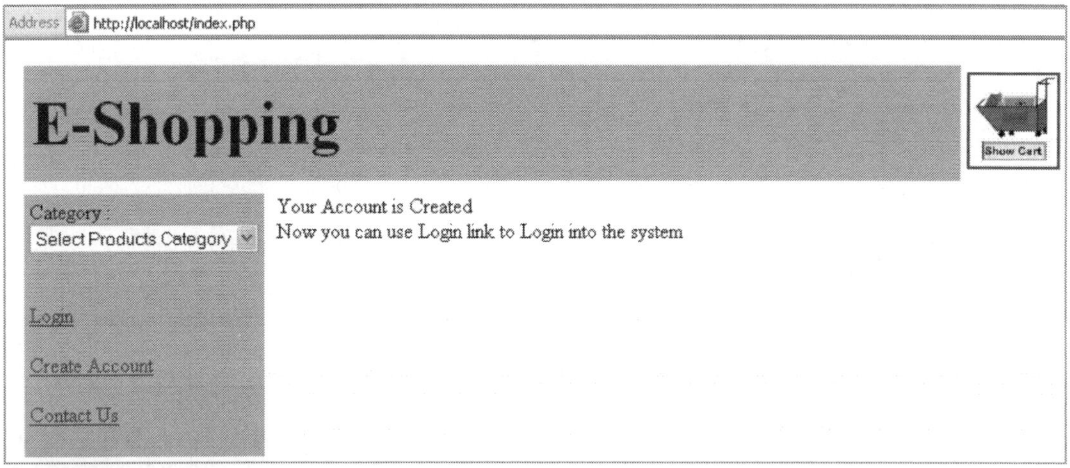

Figure C.12 *Message on Successful Creation of Account*

On selecting the `Login` link from the menu on the left, we are prompted to provide Userid and Password (Figure C.13).

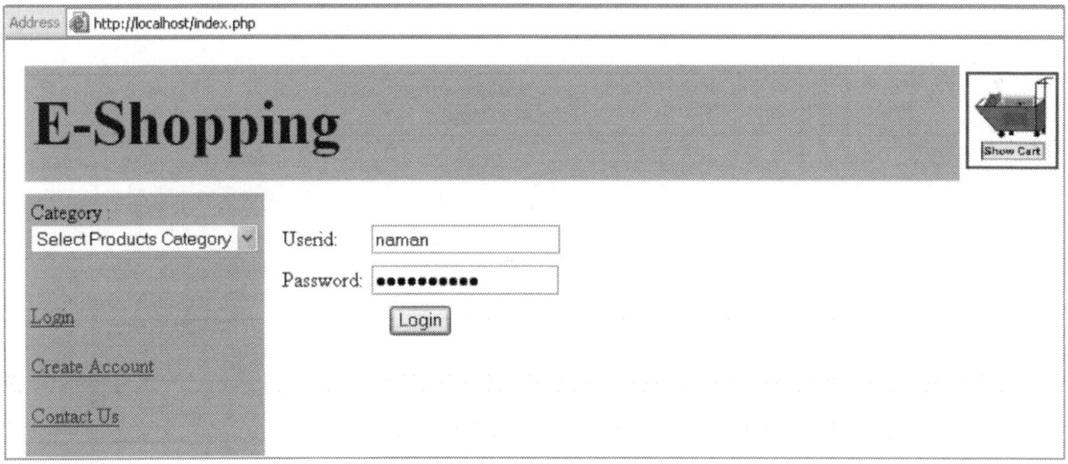

Figure C.13 *Screen for Entering Userid and Password*

If correct Userid and Password are specified, the visitor will be logged in to our website and is given two options: Either to continue Shopping or to Checkout (Figure C.14)

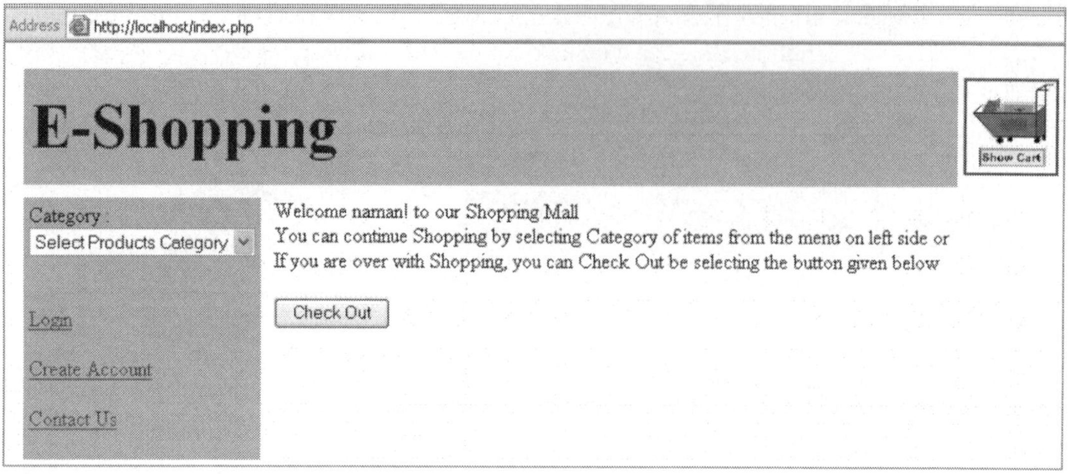

Figure C.14 ***Screen on Logging into the Website***

On selecting the Check Out button, the complete information of the visitor (that was entered while creating the account) is fetched from the tables and is displayed on the screen. Beside this, the visitor is asked to enter Shipping Information where the order has to be delivered (Figure C.15). The visitor is supposed to specify address, city, state, country and zip code of the place of delivery and also the mode of payment i.e. whether he want to pay by cheque or credit card.

Figure C.15 ***Screen for Entering Shipping Information***

After supplying the shipping information, if we click the `Submit` button, we get a message that our Order has been accepted and the Order Number is displayed for future correspondence (Figure C.16).

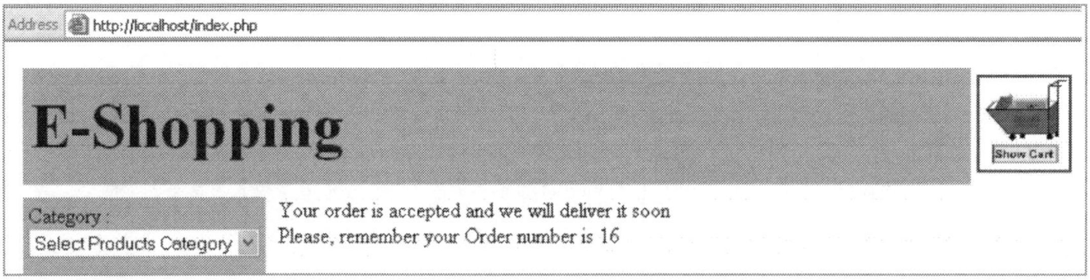

Figure C.16 ***Order Number is Displayed for Future Correspondence***

If we select the `Contact Us` link from the menu on the left, the address and email id of the organisation is displayed to the visitor (Figure C.17) for future contact.

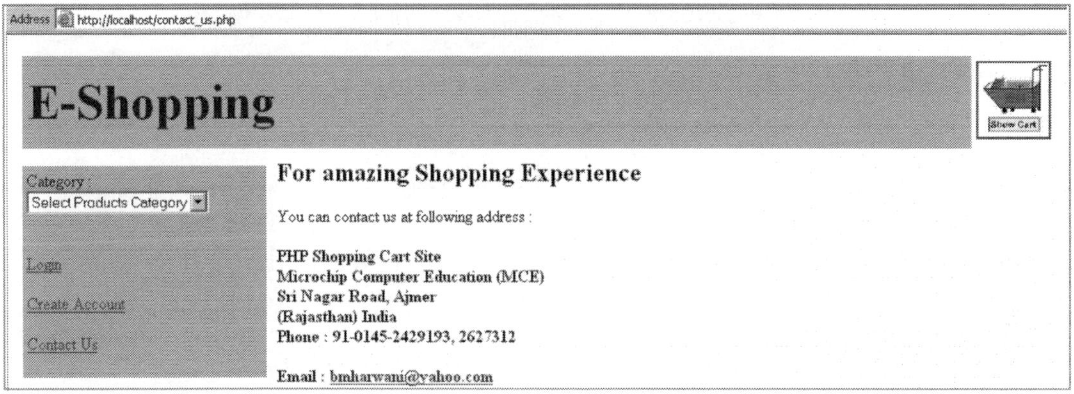

Figure C.17 ***Complete Address and email id of the Organisation***

Appendix D

Source Code of the AJAX based Shopping Cart

The source code of the AJAX based Shopping Cart consists of seventeen program files. The names and the roles these programs play in the website are as follows:

Program name	Role
1. index.php	Displays a welcome screen along with a header at the top and a menu on the left
2. header.php	Displays the title of our website: **"E-Shopping"** along with an icon of **Show Cart** to display all the items selected in the Shopping Cart
3. menu.php	Displays a Category dropdown list control to display the different categories of products available for sale on our website. It also contains three links: **Login, Create Account** and **Contact Us** that invoke loginajax.php, create_account.php and contact_us.php programs respectively
4. ajaxfun.js	This program is the heart of the website, it is a JavaScript program that contains several functions to serve the purpose of different modules of the website. The list of functions in this program and their purpose is as follows:

Functions	Purpose
createRequestObject()	This function is used for creating an XMLHttpRequest object (which is the core behind implementing AJAX)
itemdisplay(cat)	This function is used to search for items from the supplied category – `cat` from the `products` table and display their details including item_code, item_name, description and price on the screen
showdetails(cod)	This function is for displaying the details of the desired product (whose item code – `cod` is supplied) along with its image

addtocart(cod)	This function adds the item with the given item code - `cod` to the shopping cart
updatecart(cod,itm)	This function is to update contents of the cart item (changing quantity of the product whose item code – `cod` is supplied)
deletecart(cod)	This function is for deleting an item from the shopping cart whose item code -`cod` is supplied
showcart()	This function is for showing the contents of the cart
createaccount	This function asks the user to enter information like userid, password, name, address, city, state, country, zip code, email address, phone number etc. and passes that information to insertrec() function for inserting it into the table
insertrec()	This function is for accessing the visitors information and passing them to `insertuserrec.php` for creating a new user account
checkpasswd()	This function is for displaying an error message to the visitor if the Password and Re Type Password do not match.
login()	This function asks the visitor to enter Userid and Password and passes the information to `checklogin()` function for validation
checklogin()	This function is meant to check whether the login information i.e. userid and password entered by the user are valid or not
checkout()	This function is used to place the order and direct the user to `checklogin.php` program to check whether the user placing the order is logged in or not
purchase()	This function is meant for accessing the form elements (contents in different boxes) and passing them to `saveorder.php` for saving the order
contactus()	This function displays the organisation's name, address, phone number and email address to the visitor for future contact

5. dofind.php — It retrieves the products of the desired category from the `products` table.
6. doitem.php — It retrieves the information of the product along with its image whose `item_code` is supplied from the `products` table
7. docart.php — It updates the contents of the Shopping cart depending on the value of the parameter: `action` supplied. That is, if the value of the action parameter is "`add`", the item is added to the cart, if its value is "`update`", the quantity of the selected product in the shopping cart is updated and if the value of action

		parameter is `"delete"`, the product with the specified item code is erased from the Shopping Cart
8.	cartitems.php	This program displays all the products that are currently present in the shopping cart
9.	checklogin.php	This program checks whether the supplied userid and password are valid or not. That is, whether the userid and password entered by the user exist in the `customers` table or not. If the userid and password are found valid, the information of that user comprising userid, first name, last name, address1, address2 (in case of large addresses), city, state, country, zip code, email id, phone number is fetched from the `customers` table and displayed on the screen. The program also asks the user to enter shipping information. If the user is not logged in, he is asked to first login to the website or create an account if not registered earlier.
10.	checkuser.php	It checks whether the userid and password entered by the user are correct and exist in the `customers` table. If not, it displays a message: `"Invalid Username and/or Password"`. If the userid and password are found valid, the information of the customer is retrieved from the `customers` table and displayed on the screen and the user is finally asked to enter shipping information
11.	saveorder.php	This program receives the shipping information and stores it in the `orders` table. Also, all the products found in the `cart` table (of the logged in user) i.e. all the products selected in the shopping cart are retrieved and inserted in the `orders_details` table. The products that are moved to the `orders_detail` table are then deleted from the `cart` table to avoid any duplication
12.	insertuserrec.php	It receives the information of the user like userid, password, first name, last name, address, city etc. and stores it in the `customers` table of the `shopping` database. After successful insertion of the customer's information in the `customers` table, this program provides a link to the visitor to login to the website
13.	top.php	This program displays the combination of `header.php` and `menu.php` i.e. it displays the title of our Shopping Cart website as well as a menu on the left that contains links to access different modules of the website.
14.	bottom.php	It contains the div id `"itemdetails"` to display different information

The source of each file is as follows:

index.php

This program displays a welcome screen along with a header at the top and a menu on the left. Its code is as follows:

```
<html>
<head>
```

```
</head>
<body>
   <table width="100%" cellspacing="0" cellpadding="5">
   <tr>
      <td colspan=2 align="centre">
      <?php
         include('header.php');
      ?>
      </td>
   </tr>
   <tr  align="top">
   <td width="20%" valign="top">
      <?php
         include('menu.php');
      ?>
      </td>
      <TD VALIGN="TOP" width="80%" bgcolor="white">
         <div id="cartmessage"></div>
         <DIV ID="itempanel">
            <h1> Welcome to our Shopping Mall </h1>
            <h2>We provide a wide range of items ranging from luxury items to
               electronic items</h2>
            Select any item from the menu on left side and enjoy amazing
               Shopping experience
         </DIV>
         <DIV ID="itemdetails">
         </DIV>
      </TD>
   </tr>
   <tr>
      <td colspan=2 align="centre" bgcolor="white">
      </TD>
   </tr>
</table>
</body>
</html>
```

header.php

This program displays the title of our website: "E-Shopping" along with an icon of Show Cart to display all the items selected in the Shopping Cart. Its code is as follows:

```
<html>
<head>
<SCRIPT SRC="ajaxfun.js"> </SCRIPT>
</head>
<body>
<table width="100%" cellspacing="0" cellpadding="5">
```

```
<tr>
   <td bgcolor="cyan"><font size="15" color="Navy">
   <b>E-Shopping</b></font>
   </td>
   <td>
      <a href="javascript:showcart()"><img width="70" height="70"
         src="images/showcart.jpg"></img></a>
   </td>
</tr>
</table>
</body>
</html>
```

menu.php

This program displays a Category dropdown list control to display the different categories of products available for sale on our website. It also contains three links: Login, Create Account and Contact Us that invoke loginajax.php, create_account.php and contact_us.php programs respectively. Its code is as follows:

```
<html>
<head>
<SCRIPT SRC="ajaxfun.js"> </SCRIPT>
</head>
<body>
<table border="0" bgcolor="cyan" cellspacing="2" cellpadding="2" align="top">
  <tr>
    <td valign="top" width="20%">Category :
    <select name="Category" onChange='itemdisplay(this.value)' >
       <option value="" selected>Select Products Category</option>
       <option value="Camera">Camera</option>
       <option value="Mobile">Mobile</option>
       <option value="Book">Book</option>
    </select><br><br><br>
<a href="javascript:login()">Login</a><br><br>
    <a href="javascript:createaccount()">Create Account</a>  <br><br>
    <a href="javascript:contactus()">Contact Us</a> <br><br>
  </tr>
</table>
</body>
</html>
```

ajaxfun.js

This program is the heart of the website, it is a JavaScript program that contains several functions to serve the purpose of different modules of the website. The list of functions in this program and their purpose is as follows:

Functions	**Purpose**
createRequestObject()	This function is used for creating an XMLHttpRequest object (which is the core behind implementing AJAX)
itemdisplay(cat)	This function is used to search for items from the supplied category – cat from the products table and display their details including item_code, item_name, description and price on the screen
showdetails(cod)	This function is for displaying the details of the desired product (whose item code – cod is supplied) along with its image
addtocart(cod)	This function adds the item with the given item code – cod to the shopping cart
updatecart(cod,itm)	This function is to update contents of the cart item (changing quantity of the product whose item code – cod is supplied)
deletecart(cod)	This function is for deleting an item from the shopping cart whose item code – cod is supplied
showcart()	This function is for showing the contents of the cart
createaccount	This function asks the user to enter information like userid, password, name, address, city, state, country, zip code, email address, phone number etc. and passes that information to insertrec() function for inserting it into the table
insertrec()	This function is for accessing the visitors information and passing them to insertuserrec.php for creating a new user account
checkpasswd()	This function is for displaying an error message to the visitor if the Password and Re Type Password do not match.
login()	This function asks the visitor to enter Userid and Password and passes the information to checklogin() function for validation
checklogin()	This function is meant to check whether the login information i.e. userid and password entered by the user are valid or not
checkout()	This function is used to place the order and direct the user to checklogin.php program to check whether the user placing the order is logged in or not
purchase()	This function is meant for accessing the form elements (contents in different boxes) and passing them to saveorder.php for saving the order
contactus()	This function displays the organisation's name, address, phone number and email address to the visitor for future contact

The code in this program is as follows:

```
function createRequestObject()
{
   var xmlhttp=false;
```

```
    try
    {
        xmlhttp = new ActiveXObject("Msxml2.XMLHTTP");
    }
    catch (e)
    {
        try
        {
            xmlhttp = new ActiveXObject("Microsoft.XMLHTTP");
        }
        catch (E)
        {
            xmlhttp = false;
        }
    }
    if (!xmlhttp && typeof XMLHttpRequest!='undefined')
    {
        xmlhttp = new XMLHttpRequest();
    }
    return xmlhttp;
}

function itemdisplay(cat)
{
    document.getElementById('cartmessage').innerHTML ="";
    var request = createRequestObject();
    request.open('GET', 'dofind.php?&Category='+cat, true);
    request.onreadystatechange = function()
    {
        if(request.readyState == 4)
        {
            if(request.status == 200)
            {
                eval("var response = (" + request.responseText + ")");
                var msg = '<TABLE BORDER="1" CELLSPACING="0" CELLPADDING="0"
                    WIDTH="100%">';
                msg += '<TR>';
                msg += '<TH align="left">Item Code</TH>';
                msg += '<TH align="left">Name of Item</TH>';
                msg += '<TH align="left">Description</TH>';
                msg += '<TH align="left">Price</TH>';
                msg += '<TH align="left">Details</TH>';
                msg += '</TR>';
                for(var i in response)
                {
                    msg += '<TR>';
```

```
                msg += '<TD>' + response[i].item_code + '</TD>';
                msg += '<TD>' + response[i].item_name + '</TD>';
                msg += '<TD>' + response[i].description + '</TD>';
                msg += '<TD>' + response[i].price + '</TD>';
                msg += '<TD><a href="javascript:showdetails(' +
                   response[i].item_code + ')">Detail</a></TD>';
                msg += '</TR>';
             }
             msg += '</TABLE>';
             document.getElementById('itempanel').innerHTML = msg;
             document.getElementById('itemdetails').innerHTML = "";
          }
       }
    }
    request.send(null);
}


function showdetails(cod)
{
    var request = createRequestObject();
    request.open('GET', 'doitem.php?&Code='+cod, true);
    request.onreadystatechange = function()
    {
       if(request.readyState == 4)
       {
          if(request.status == 200)
          {
             eval("var response = (" + request.responseText + ")");
             var msg = '<TABLE BORDER="1" CELLSPACING="0" CELLPADDING="0"
                WIDTH="100%">';
             msg += '<TR>';
             msg += '<TD ALIGN="center" COLSPAN="6"><IMG BORDER="0"
                HEIGHT="180" WIDTH="150" SRC="' + response.imagename +'">
                </IMG></TD>';
             msg += '</TR>';
             msg += '<TR>';
             msg += '<TH align="left">Item Code</TH>';
             msg += '<TH align="left">Name of Item</TH>';
             msg += '<TH align="left">Description</TH>';
             msg += '<TH align="left">Price</TH>';
             msg += '<TH align="left">Enter Quantity</TH>';
             msg += '<TH align="left">Select</TH>';
             msg += '</TR>';
             msg += '<TR>';
             msg += '<TD>' + response.item_code + '</TD>';
```

```
            msg += '<TD>' + response.item_name + '</TD>';
            msg += '<TD>' + response.description + '</TD>';
            msg += '<TD>' + response.price + '</TD>';
            msg += '<TD>  <input type="text" name="qty" size="2"></TD>';
            msg += '<TD><input type="submit" name="submit" value="Add to cart"
               onclick="addtocart(' + response.item_code +')"></TD>';
            msg += '</TR>';
            msg += '</TABLE>';
            document.getElementById('itempanel').innerHTML = msg;
         }
      }
   }
   request.send(null);
}

function addtocart(cod)
{
   qnty=document.getElementById('qty').value;
   var request = createRequestObject();
   request.open('GET', 'docart.php?&code='+cod+'&qty='+qnty+'&action=add',
      true);
   request.onreadystatechange=function() {
      if (request.readyState==4 && request.status == 200) {
         var content = request.responseText;
         if( content ){
            document.getElementById('cartmessage').innerHTML = content;
         }
      }
   }
   request.send(null);
   showcart();
}

function updatecart(cod,itm)
{
   var request = createRequestObject();
   request.open('GET', 'docart.php?&code='+cod+'&qty='+itm.value+ '&action=
      update', true);
   request.onreadystatechange=function() {
      if (request.readyState==4 && request.status == 200) {
         var content = request.responseText;
         if( content ){
            document.getElementById('cartmessage').innerHTML = content;
         }
      }
   }
```

```
    request.send(null);
    showcart();
}
function deletecart(cod)
{
    var request = createRequestObject();
    request.open('GET', 'docart.php?&code='+cod+'&action=delete', true);
    request.onreadystatechange=function() {
        if (request.readyState==4 && request.status == 200) {
            var content = request.responseText;
            if( content ){
                document.getElementById('cartmessage').innerHTML = content;
            }
        }
    }
    request.send(null);
    javascript:showcart();
}

function showcart()
{
    var request = createRequestObject();
    request.open('GET', 'cartitems.php', true);
    request.onreadystatechange = function()
    {
        if(request.readyState == 4)
        {
            if(request.status == 200)
            {
                eval("var response = (" + request.responseText + ")");
                var msg = '<TABLE BORDER="1" CELLSPACING="0" CELLPADDING="0"
                    WIDTH="100%">';
                msg += '<TR>';
                msg += '<TH align="left">Item Code</TH>';
                msg += '<TH align="left">Name of Item</TH>';
                msg += '<TH align="left">Quantity</TH>';
                msg += '<TH align="left">Price</TH>';
                msg += '<TH align="left">Update</TH>';
                msg += '<TH align="left">Delete</TH>';
                msg += '</TR>';
                for(var i in response)
                {
                    msg += '<TR>';
                    msg += '<TD>' + response[i].cart_itmcode + '</TD>';
                    msg += '<TD>' + response[i].cart_item_name + '</TD>';
            msg += '<TD><input type="text" name="newqty'+i+'" value=' +
```

```
            response[i].cart_qty + '></TD>';
               msg += '<TD>' + response[i].cart_price + '</TD>';
               msg += '<TD><input type="submit" name="submit" value="Delete
                  Cart" onclick="deletecart(' + response[i].cart_itmcode
                  +')"></TD>';
               msg += '<TD><input type="submit" name="submit" value="Update
                  Cart" onclick="updatecart(' + response[i].cart_itmcode +',
                  newqty'+i+')"></TD>';
               msg += '</TR>';
            }
            msg+='<TR><TD COLSPAN="4" align="center"><input type="submit"
               name="submit" value="Check Out" onclick="checkout()">
               </TD></TR>';
            msg += '</TABLE>';
            document.getElementById('itempanel').innerHTML = msg;
            document.getElementById('itemdetails').innerHTML = "";
         }
      }
   }
   request.send(null);
}

function createaccount()
{
   document.getElementById('cartmessage').innerHTML = "";
   var msg = '<form method="post" onsubmit="insertrec(); return false">';
   msg += '<table border="0" cellspacing="1" cellpadding="3">';
   msg += '<tr><td>Userid: </td><td> <input size="20" type="text"
      name="userid"></td></tr>';
   msg += '<tr><td> Password: </td><td>  <input size="20" type="password"
      name="password"></td></tr>';
   msg += ' <tr><td> ReType Password:  </td><td> <input size="20"
      type="password" name="repassword" onblur="checkpasswd()"></td></tr>';
   msg += '<tr><td> First Name:  </td><td> <input size="30" type="text"
      name="first_name"></td></tr>';
   msg += '<tr><td>   Last Name:  </td><td> <input size="30" type="text"
      name="last_name"></td></tr>';
   msg += '<tr><td> Address1:  </td><td> <input size="80" type="text"
      name="add1"></td></tr>';
   msg += '<tr><td>Address2:  </td><td> <input size="80" type="text"
      name="add2"></td></tr>';
   msg+='<tr><td> City:  </td><td> <input size="30" type="text"
      name="city"></td></tr>';
   msg+=' <tr><td>State:  </td><td> <input size="30" type="text"
      name="state"></td></tr>';
   msg+=' <tr><td>Country:  </td><td> <input size="30" type="text"
```

```
        name="country"></td></tr>';
    msg+=' <tr><td>Zip Code:  </td><td> <input size="20" type="text"
        name="zipcode"></td></tr>';
    msg+='<tr><td>Email Id:  </td><td> <input size="30" type="text"
        name="emailid"></td></tr>';
    msg+='<tr><td>Phone No:  </td><td> <input size="30" type="text"
        name="phone_no"></td></tr>';
    msg+=' <tr><td> <input type="submit" name="submit" value="Submit" >
        </td><td> ';
    msg+='  <input type="reset" value="Cancel"></td></tr>';
    msg+='</table></form>';
    document.getElementById('itempanel').innerHTML = msg;
    document.getElementById('itemdetails').innerHTML = "";
}

function insertrec()
{
    pswd=document.getElementById('password').value;
    repswd=document.getElementById('repassword').value;
    if(pswd!=repswd)
    {
        alert("Password and Re Type Password do not match. Try Again");
    }
    else
    {
        var xmlhttp=createRequestObject();
        queryString="";
        var frm = document.forms[0];
        var numberElements =  frm.elements.length;
        for(var i = 0; i < numberElements; i++)  {
            if(i < numberElements-1)  {
                queryString += frm.elements[i].name+"="+
                encodeURIComponent(frm.elements[i].value)+"&";
            } else {
                queryString += frm.elements[i].name+"="+
                encodeURIComponent(frm.elements[i].value);
            }
        }
        xmlhttp.open('POST', 'insertuserrec.php', true);
        xmlhttp.setRequestHeader("Content-Type","application/x-www-form-
            urlencoded; charset=UTF-8");
        xmlhttp.onreadystatechange=function() {
            if (xmlhttp.readyState==4 && xmlhttp.status == 200) {
                var content = xmlhttp.responseText;
                if( content ){
                    document.getElementById('itempanel').innerHTML = "";
```

```
                    document.getElementById('cartmessage').innerHTML = content;
                }
            }
        }
        xmlhttp.send(queryString)
    }
}

function checkpasswd()
{
    pswd=document.getElementById('password').value;
    repswd=document.getElementById('repassword').value;
    if(pswd!=repswd)
    {
        alert("Password and Re Type Password do not match. Try Again");
    }
}

function login()
{
    document.getElementById('cartmessage').innerHTML = "";
    document.getElementById('itemdetails').innerHTML = "";
    var msg = '<table border="0" cellspacing="1" cellpadding="3">';
    msg += '<tr><td>Userid:</td><td> <input type="text" name="userid">
        </td></tr>';
    msg += '<tr><td>Password:</td><td> <input type="password" name="password">
        </td></tr>';
    msg += ' <tr><td colspan=2 align="center"> <input type="submit"
        name="submit" value="Login" onclick="checklogin()"></td> </tr>';
    msg += '</table>';
    document.getElementById('itempanel').innerHTML = msg;
}

function checklogin()
{
    var xmlhttp=createRequestObject();
    user=document.getElementById('userid').value;
    pswd=document.getElementById('password').value;
    var div=document.getElementById("cartmessage");
    xmlhttp.open('GET', 'checkuser.php?userid='+user+'& password='+pswd, true);
    xmlhttp.onreadystatechange=function() {
        if (xmlhttp.readyState==4 && xmlhttp.status == 200) {
            var content = xmlhttp.responseText;
            if( content ){
                document.getElementById('itempanel').innerHTML = "";
                div.innerHTML = content;
```

```
            }
        }
    }
    xmlhttp.send(null);
}

function checkout()
{
    var request = createRequestObject();
    request.open('GET', 'checklogin.php', true);
    request.onreadystatechange=function() {
        if (request.readyState==4 && request.status == 200) {
            var content = request.responseText;
            if( content ){
                document.getElementById('itemdetails').innerHTML = content;
            }
        }
    }
    request.send(null);
}

function purchase()
{
    var xmlhttp=createRequestObject();
    queryString="";
    var frm = document.forms[0];
    var numberElements =  frm.elements.length;
    for(var i = 0; i < numberElements; i++)  {
        if(i < numberElements-1)  {
    queryString += frm.elements[i].name+"="+encodeURIComponent
    (frm.elements[i].value)+"&";
        }
        else {
            queryString += frm.elements[i].name+"="+encodeURIComponent
            (frm.elements[i].value);
        }
    }
    xmlhttp.open('POST', 'saveorder.php', true);
    xmlhttp.setRequestHeader("Content-Type","application/x-www-form-urlencoded;
        charset=UTF-8");
    xmlhttp.onreadystatechange=function() {
        if (xmlhttp.readyState==4 && xmlhttp.status == 200) {
            var content = xmlhttp.responseText;
            if( content ){
                document.getElementById('cartmessage').innerHTML = content;
                document.getElementById('itempanel').innerHTML = "";
```

```
                document.getElementById('itemdetails').innerHTML = "";
            }
        }
    }
    xmlhttp.send(queryString)
}

function contactus()
{
    var msg = '<h2> For amazing Shopping Experience </h2>';
    msg += 'You can contact us at following address :<br><br>';
    msg += '<b>PHP Shopping Cart Site<br>';
    msg += 'Microchip Computer Education (MCE)<br>';
    msg += 'Sri Nagar Road, Ajmer <br>';
    msg += '(Rajasthan) India <br>';
    msg += 'Phone : 91-0145-2429193 <br><br>';
    msg += 'Email :<a href="mailto:bmharwani@yahoo.com">bmharwani@yahoo.com</
a>';
    document.getElementById('itempanel').innerHTML = msg;
    document.getElementById('cartmessage').innerHTML = "";
}
```

dofind.php

This program retrieves the products of the desired category from the `products` table. Its code is as follows:

```
<?php
    require_once "JSON.php";
    $conn = mysql_connect("localhost", "root", "mce")
        or die("Could not connect: " . mysql_error());
    mysql_select_db("shopping", $conn) or die (mysql_error());

    /* Storing the query in a variable */
    $arr=array();
    $query = "SELECT item_code, item_name, price, description FROM products WHERE
        category like '" . $_GET['Category'] . "' order by item_code";
    $resultSet = mysql_query($query);
    while($obj = mysql_fetch_object($resultSet)) { $arr[] = $obj; }
    $json = new Services_JSON();
    echo( $json->encode( $arr ) );
?>
```

doitem.php

This program retrieves the information of the product whose item_code is supplied along with its image from the `products` table. Its code is as follows:

```
<?php
   require_once "JSON.php";
   $conn = mysql_connect("localhost", "root", "mce")
      or die("Could not connect: " . mysql_error());
   mysql_select_db("shopping", $conn) or die (mysql_error());

   /* Storing the query in a variable */
   $query = "SELECT item_code, item_name, price, description, imagename FROM
      products WHERE item_code=" . $_GET['Code'] ;
   $resultSet = mysql_query($query);
   $obj = mysql_fetch_object($resultSet);
   $json = new Services_JSON();
   echo( $json->encode( $obj ) );
?>
```

docart.php

This program updates the contents of the Shopping Cart depending on the value of the parameter: action supplied. That is, if the value of the action parameter is "add", the item is added to the cart, if its value is "update", the quantity of the selected product in the Shopping Cart is updated and if the value of action parameter is "delete", the product with the specified item code is erased from the Shopping Cart. Its code is as follows:

```
<?php
   require_once "JSON.php";
   $conn = mysql_connect("localhost", "root", "mce")
      or die("Could not connect: " . mysql_error());
   mysql_select_db("shopping", $conn) or die (mysql_error());
   $code = trim($_GET['code']);
   $action=trim($_GET['action']);
   switch($action)
   {
      case "add":
         $qty = trim($_GET['qty']);
         if ($qty=='')
         {
            $qty=1;
         }
         if($qty <=0)
         {
            echo "Quantity value is invalid ";
            echo "Go Back and enter a valid value";
```

```
        }
        else
        {
            if (!session_id()) {
                session_start();
            }
            $sess = session_id();
            $query="select * from cart where cart_sess = '$sess' and " .
                "cart_itmcode=$code";
            $result = mysql_query($query) or die(mysql_error());
            if(mysql_num_rows($result)==1)
            {
                $row=mysql_fetch_array($result);
                $qt=$row['cart_qty'];
                $qt=$qt+$qty;
                $query="UPDATE cart set cart_qty=$qt where cart_sess = '$sess'
                    " . "and cart_itmcode=$code";
                $result = mysql_query($query)  or die(mysql_error());
                echo "Shopping Cart updated";
            }
            else
            {
                $query="select * from products where item_code  =$code";
                $result = mysql_query($query) or die(mysql_error());
                $row=mysql_fetch_array($result);
                $itmname=$row['item_name'];
                $price=$row['price'];
            $query = "INSERT INTO cart (cart_sess, cart_qty, cart_itmcode,
                    cart_item_name, cart_price) VALUES ('$sess',$qty,$code,
                    '$itmname', $price)";
                $result = mysql_query($query) or die(mysql_error());
                echo "Item added to the Cart";
            }
        }
        break;

    case "update":
        $qty = trim($_GET['qty']);
        if ($qty=='')
        {
            $qty=1;
        }
        if($qty <0)
        {
            echo "Quantity value is invalid ";
            echo "Go Back and enter a valid value";
```

```
        }
        else
        {
            if (!session_id()) {
                session_start();
            }
            $sess = session_id();
            $query="UPDATE cart set cart_qty=$qty where cart_sess = '$sess' "
            . "and cart_itmcode=$code";
            $result = mysql_query($query)  or die(mysql_error());
            echo "Shopping Cart updated";
        }
        break;

    case "delete":
        if (!session_id()) {
            session_start();
        }
        $sess = session_id();
        $query="delete from cart where cart_sess = '$sess' " .
            "and cart_itmcode=$code";
        $result = mysql_query($query)  or die(mysql_error());
        echo "Item deleted";
        break;

    }
?>
```

cartitems.php

This program displays all the products that are currently present in the Shopping Cart. Its code is as follows:

```
<?php
    require_once "JSON.php";
    $conn = mysql_connect("localhost", "root", "mce")
        or die("Could not connect: " . mysql_error());
    mysql_select_db("shopping", $conn) or die (mysql_error());
    if (!session_id()) {
        session_start();
    }
    $sessid = session_id();
    $query = "SELECT * FROM cart WHERE cart_sess = '$sessid'";
    $results = mysql_query($query) or die (mysql_query());
    $arr=array();
    while($obj = mysql_fetch_object($results)) { $arr[] = $obj; }
```

```
    $json = new Services_JSON();
    echo( $json->encode( $arr ) );
?>
```

checklogin.php

This program checks whether the supplied userid and password are valid or not. That is, whether the userid and password entered by the user exist in the `customers` table or not. If the userid and password are found valid, the information of that user comprising userid, first name, last name, address1, address2 (in case of large addresses), city, state, country, zip code, email id, phone number is fetched from the `customers` table and displayed on the screen. The program also asks the user to enter shipping information. If the user is not logged in, he is asked to first login to the website or create an account if not registered earlier. Its code is as follows:

```
<?php
    require_once "JSON.php";
    if (!session_id()) {
        session_start();
    }
    $connect = mysql_connect("localhost", "root", "mce")
        or die("Please, check the server connection.");
    mysql_select_db("shopping");
    $uid=$_SESSION['userid'];
    $pwd=$_SESSION['password'];
    if ((isset($_SESSION['userid']) && $_SESSION['userid'] != "") ||
        (isset($_SESSION['password']) && $_SESSION['password'] != ""))
    {
        $sess = session_id();
        $query="select * from cart where cart_sess = '$sess'";
        $result = mysql_query($query) or die(mysql_error());
        if(mysql_num_rows($result)>=1)
        {
            $query = "SELECT * FROM customers " . " where userid like '$uid' and "
                . "password like '$pwd'";
            $results = mysql_query($query) or die(mysql_error());
            $row = mysql_fetch_array($results);
            extract($row);
            ?>
            <p align=center>Please enter Shipping Information  </p>
            <table border="0" cellspacing="1" cellpadding="3">
            <tr><td>Userid:</td><td> <input size="20" type="text" name="userid"
                value="<?php echo $userid; ?>"></td></tr>
            <tr><td>First Name: </td><td> <input size="30" type="text"
                name="first_name" value="<?php echo $first_name; ?>"></td></tr>
            <tr><td>Last Name: </td><td> <input size="30" type="text"
                name="last_name" value="<?php echo $last_name; ?>"></td></tr>
```

```
        <tr><td>Address1: </td><td> <input size="80" type="text" name="add1"
           value="<?php echo $add1; ?>"></td></tr>
        <tr><td>Address2: </td><td> <input size="80" type="text" name="add2"
           value="<?php echo $add2; ?>"></td></tr>
        <tr><td>City: </td><td> <input size="30" type="text" name="city"
           value="<?php echo $city; ?>"></td></tr>
        <tr><td>State: </td><td> <input size="30" type="text" name="state"
           value="<?php echo $state; ?>"></td></tr>
        <tr><td>Country: </td><td> <input size="30" type="text"
name="country"
           value="<?php echo $country; ?>"></td></tr>
        <tr><td>Zip Code: </td><td> <input size="20" type="text"
           name="zipcode" value="<?php echo $zipcode; ?>"></td></tr>
        <tr><td>Email Id: </td><td> <input size="30" type="text"
           name="emailid" value="<?php echo $emailid; ?>"></td></tr>
        <tr><td>Phone No: </td><td> <input size="30" type="text"
           name="phone_no" value="<?php echo $phone_no; ?>"></td></tr>
        <tr><td colspan=2 align="center">Shipping Information</td></tr>
        <form method="post" onsubmit="purchase(); return false">
        <tr><td>Address to deliver at: </td><td> <input type="text" size="80"
           name="ship_add"></td></tr>
        <tr><td>City: </td><td> <input size="30" type="text" name="ship_city">
           </td></tr>
        <tr><td>State: </td><td> <input size="30" type="text"
           name="ship_state"> </td></tr>
        <tr><td>Country: </td><td> <input size="30" type="text"
           name="ship_country"> </td></tr>
        <tr><td>Zip Code: </td><td> <input type="text" size="20"
           name="ship_zipcode"></td></tr>
        <tr><td>Payment Mode: </td><td> <input type="radio" name="paymode"
           value="Credit Card" checked>Credit Card<br>
     <input type="radio" name="paymode" value="Cheque"> Cheque</td></tr>
        <tr><td> <input type="submit" name="submit" value="Submit"> </
td><td>
     <input type="reset" value="Cancel"></td></tr>
        </table>
        <?php
     }
     else
     {
        echo "Your Shopping Cart is empty <br>";
        echo "You can do purchasing by selecting items from the menu on left
           side";
     }
  }
  else
```

```
    {
        echo "<h3>Not Logged in yet</h1><br>";
        echo "  You are currently not logged into our system.<br>";
        echo "  You can do purchasing only if you are logged in.<br>";
        echo "  If you have already registered, ";
        echo "  Select Login link in the menu to login, <br>";
        echo "  or if would like to create an account, ";
        echo "  Select Create Account link in the menu to register.";
    }
?>
```

checkuser.php

This program checks whether the userid and password entered by the user are correct and exist in the `customers` table. If not, it displays a message: "Invalid Username and/or Password". If the userid and password are found valid, the information of the customer is retrieved from the `customers` table and displayed on the screen and the user is finally asked to enter shipping information. Its code is as follows:

```
<?php
    require_once "JSON.php";
    $uid = $_GET["userid"];
    $pwd = $_GET["password"];
    mysql_connect("localhost", "root", "mce");
    mysql_select_db("shopping");
    if (!session_id()) {
        session_start();
    }
    $sql = "SELECT * FROM customers WHERE userid like '" . $uid . "' and
        password like '" . $pwd . "'";
    $result = mysql_query($sql) or die(mysql_error());
    if (mysql_num_rows($result) == 1) {
        $_SESSION['userid'] = $uid;
    $_SESSION['password'] = $pwd;
        echo "Welcome " . $uid . "! to our Shopping Mall <br>";
        $sess = session_id();
        $query="select * from cart where cart_sess = '$sess'";
        $result = mysql_query($query) or die(mysql_error());
        if(mysql_num_rows($result)>=1)
        {
            echo "You can continue Shopping by selecting Category of items from
                the menu on left side or <br>";
            echo "If you are over with Shopping, you can Check Out be selecting
                the button given below <br><br>";
            echo '<input type="submit" name="submit" value="Check Out"
                onclick="checkout()">';
```

```
        }
        else
        {
            echo "Your Shopping Cart is Empty <br>";
            echo "You can do purchasing by selecting items from the menu on left
                side";
        }
    }
    else {
        echo "Invalid Username and/or Password. <br>";
        echo "You need to create an Account";
    }
?>
```

saveorder.php

This program receives the shipping information and stores it in the `orders` table. Also, all the products that are found in the `cart` table (of the logged in user) i.e. all the products selected in the shopping cart are retrieved and inserted in the `orders_details` table. The products that are moved to the `orders_detail` table are then deleted from the `cart` table to avoid any duplication. Its code is as follows:

```
<?php
    require_once "JSON.php";
    mysql_connect("localhost", "root", "mce");
    mysql_select_db("shopping");
    $ship_add = $_POST['ship_add'];
    $ship_city = $_POST['ship_city'];
    $ship_state = $_POST['ship_state'];
    $ship_country = $_POST['ship_country'];
    $ship_zipcode = $_POST['ship_zipcode'];
    $paymode = $_POST['paymode'];
    $userid= $_SESSION['userid'] ;
    $today = date("Y-m-d");
    $sessid = session_id();

    $sql = "INSERT INTO orders ( order_date, userid, shipping_address,
    shipping_city, shipping_state, shipping_country, shipping_zipcode,
        paymode)                                                    VALUES
 ('$today','$userid','$ship_add','$ship_city','$ship_state'
        , '$ship_country','$ship_zipcode','$paymode')";
    $result = mysql_query($sql)  or die (mysql_error());
    $orderid = mysql_insert_id();
    $query = "SELECT * FROM cart WHERE cart_sess='$sessid'";
    $results = mysql_query($query)  or (mysql_error());
    while ($row = mysql_fetch_array($results)) {
```

```
        extract($row);
      $sql2 = "INSERT INTO orders_details ( order_no, item_code, item_name,
          quantity, price) VALUES ($orderid,$cart_itmcode,'$cart_item_name',
        $cart_qty,$cart_price)";
        $insert = mysql_query($sql2) or die (mysql_error());
    }
    $query = "DELETE FROM cart WHERE cart_sess='$sessid'";
    $delete = mysql_query($query);
    echo "Your order is accepted and we will deliver it soon<br>";
    echo "Please, remember your Order number is $orderid<br>";
?>
```

insertuserrec.php

This program receives the information of the user like userid, password, first name, last name, address, city etc. and stores it in the `customers` table of the `shopping` database. After successful insertion of the customer's information in the `customers` table, this program provides a link to the visitor to login to the website. Its code is as follows:

```
<?php
    mysql_connect("localhost", "root", "mce");
    mysql_select_db("shopping");
    $uid = $_POST["userid"];
    $pwd = $_POST["password"];
    $fname = $_POST["first_name"];
    $lname = $_POST["last_name"];
    $add1 = $_POST["add1"];
    $add2 = $_POST["add2"];
    $city = $_POST["city"];
    $state = $_POST["state"];
    $country = $_POST["country"];
    $zipcode = $_POST["zipcode"];
    $emailid = $_POST["emailid"];
    $phoneno = $_POST["phone_no"];
    $sql = "insert into customers(userid, first_name, last_name, add1, add2,
       city, state, zipcode, emailid, password, phone_no, country) values('" .
       $uid . "', '" . $fname . "', '" . $lname . "','" . $add1 . "','" . $add2
.
       "', '" . $city . "','" . $state . "','" . $zipcode . "','" . $emailid .
       "','" . $pwd . "','" . $phoneno . "','" . $country . "')";
    $query = mysql_query($sql) or die(mysql_error());
    echo 'Your Account is Created <br>';
    echo 'Now you can use Login link to Login into the system';
?>
```

top.php

This program displays the combination of header.php and menu.php i.e. it displays the title of our Shopping Cart website as well as a menu on the left that contains links to access different modules of the website. Its code is as follows:

```
<html>
<head>
</head>
<body>
   <table width="100%" cellspacing="0" cellpadding="5">
   <tr>
      <td colspan=2 align="centre">
         <?php
            include('header.php');
         ?>
      </td>
   </tr>
   <tr  align="top">
   <td width="20%" align="top" >
         <?php
            include('menu.php');
         ?>
      </td>
      <TD VALIGN="TOP" width="80%" bgcolor="white">
         <DIV ID="itempanel">
```

bottom.php

This program contains the div id "itemdetails" to display different information. Its code is as follows:

```
</td>
</tr>
<tr>
   <td colspan=2 align="centre" bgcolor="white">
      <DIV ID="itemdetails">
      </DIV>
   </td>
</tr>
</table>
</body>
</html>
```

Index

Symbols

A

B

C

D

U

V

W

X

Author's Profile

B.M. Harwani is Managing Director of Microchip Computer Education (MCE), Ajmer, India. He holds a BE degree in computer engineering from the University of Pune, and a 'C' Level Master's Diploma in computer technology from DOEACC, Government of India. Being involved in teaching field for over 15 years, he has developed the art of explaining even the most complicated topics in a manner that everybody can easily understand. He has written several popular books, including *Programming & Problem Solving through C* (BPB, 2004), *Learn Tally in Just Three Weeks* (Pragya, 2005), *Data Structures and Algorithms through C* (CBC, 2006), *Master Unix Shell Programming* (CBC, 2006), *Business Systems* (CBC, 2006), *Practical Java Project* (Shroff, 2007), *Practical Web Services* (Shroff, 2007), *Java for Professionals* (Shroff, 2008), *C++ for Beginners* (Shroff, 2009), *Practical ASP.NET 3.5 Projects* (Shroff, 2009), *Java Server Faces—A Practical Approach for Beginners* (PHI Learning, 2009), *Practical JSF Project using NetBeans* (PHI Learning, 2009), *Foundation Joomla* (Friends of ED, 2009), and *Practical EJB Project* (Shroff, 2009). He has also written Web articles on Computing. To know more about Harwani, visit bmharwani.com

Made in United States
Orlando, FL
04 November 2026

90201134R00238